In Memory of

Ruth Garrison Scurlock

Mary and John Gray Library
Lamar University

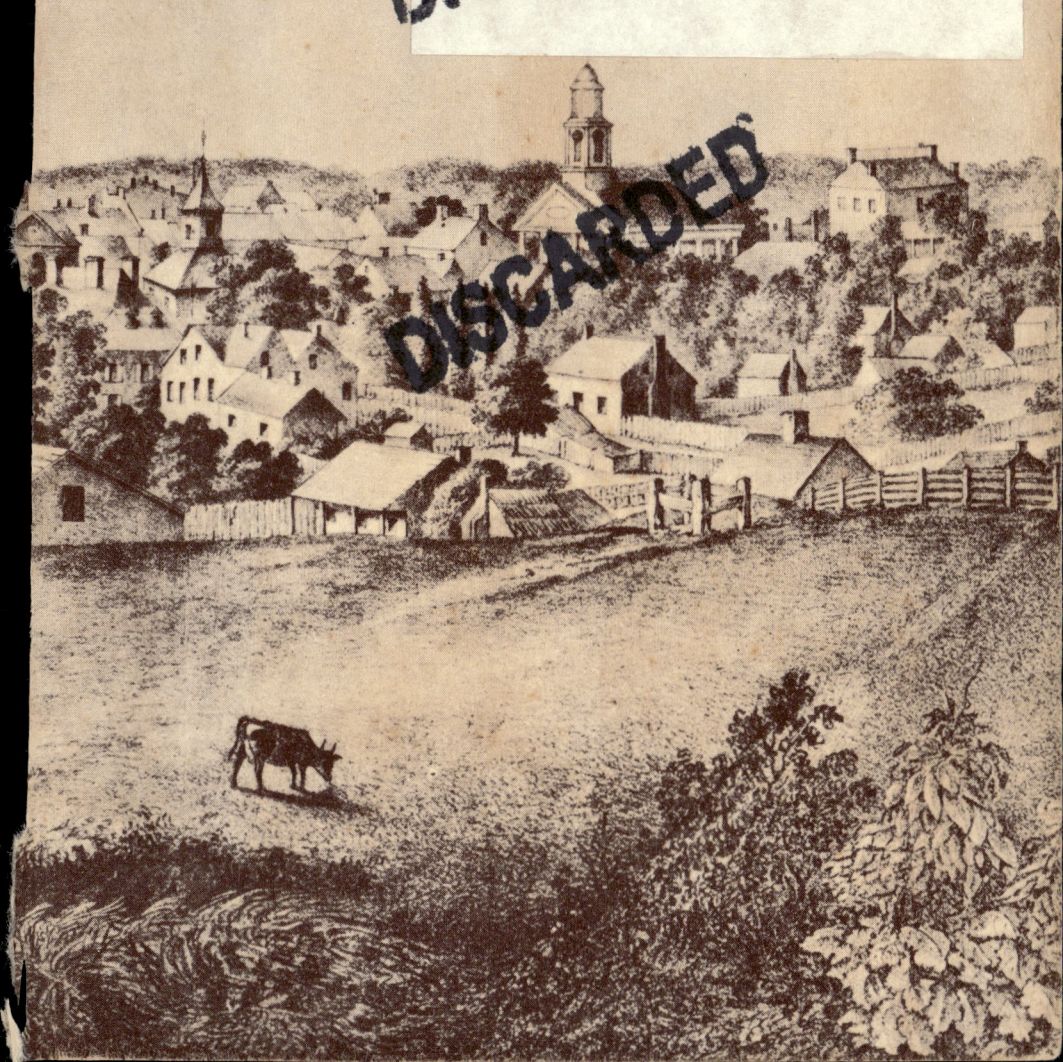

↑ 673433

**MARY AND JOHN GRAY
LIBRARY
LAMAR UNIVERSITY
BEAUMONT, TEXAS**

For Ruth & Bill Scurlock —

who held my hand — & steered me skillfully — on a crowded night & day

NATCHEZ
ON THE MISSISSIPPI

In appreciation of their generous interest —

Harnett T. Kane —

BOOKS BY HARNETT T. KANE

LOUISIANA HAYRIDE:
The American Rehearsal for Dictatorship

THE BAYOUS OF LOUISIANA

DEEP DELTA COUNTRY
(In the American Folkways Series)

PLANTATION PARADE:
The Grand Manner in Louisiana

NEW ORLEANS WOMAN:
A Biographical Novel of Myra Clark Gaines

NATCHEZ ON THE MISSISSIPPI

NATCHEZ

on the Mississippi

by HARNETT T. KANE

WILLIAM MORROW & COMPANY, NEW YORK, 1947

Copyright, 1947, by Harnett T. Kane. All rights reserved. This book, or parts thereof, must not be reproduced in any form without permission of the publisher. Published simultaneously in the Dominion of Canada by McClelland & Stewart Limited, Toronto. Printed in the United States of America

fjl

CONTENTS

	INTRODUCTION: RIVER COUNTRY	1
I	THE HEROES, AND "THE GIRLS"	22
II	THE WILLIAM WHO WASN'T A SIR	43
III	BLOOD ON THE NATCHEZ TRACE	61
IV	MR. AMIABLE AND MR. BLUNT	79
V	A MAN WITHOUT A COUNTRY?	97
VI	PURITAN IN THE SINFUL SOUTH	112
VII	HELL UNDER THE HILL	125
VIII	THE GOLDEN SURGETS	144
IX	ALWAYS INVITE THE RIGHT PEOPLE	159
X	KING DAVID AND HIS DAUGHTERS	174
XI	THREE IN ONE	190
XII	THE APPLECART THAT OVERTURNED	204
XIII	*VIVA LA REVOLUCION!*	220
XIV	VARINA OF THE CAMELLIAS	236
XV	THE LOVES OF THREE LADIES	251
XVI	ELIZA, THE EARLY BRIDE	264
XVII	"I DREAMT I DWELT IN MARBLE HALLS..."	278

XVIII	THE *NATCHEZ* AND THE *ROBERT E. LEE*	295
XIX	GOAT CASTLE	312
XX	PAGEANT OF THE HOOPSKIRTS	334
	ALONG THE WAY	351
	ACKNOWLEDGMENTS	357
	BIBLIOGRAPHY	361
	INDEX	367

ILLUSTRATIONS

Natchez, The River's Sweep	FACING PAGE 6
Elmscourt	7
Hope Farm	7
Windy Hill	22
Elgin	23
Springfield	23
King's Tavern	54
Aaron Burr Oaks	55
Natchez Trace	55
Connelly's Tavern	86
Concord	87
Concord Today	87
Gloucester	118
Magnolia Vale	119
Linden	150
Doorway and Punkah	151
Arlington	166
Doorways	167

	ILLUSTRATIONS
Lansdowne	FACING PAGE 182
Homewood	183
D'Evereux	198
Ironwork and Balcony	199
Auburn	214
Doorway and Staircase	215
Monmouth	230
Cherokee	231
The Briers	246
Richmond	247
Green Leaves	262
Dunleith	262
Stanton Hall	263
Melrose	278
Doorway and Parlor	279
Longwood	310
Steamboat Glory	311
Goat Castle	326
Rosalie	327

The front endpaper is *Natchez on the Hill, from the old Fort*, sketched by James Tooley, 1833-35, photographed by Dan Leyrer. Courtesy Albert Lietaud. The back endpaper is *View of the Fort of Natchez*, Collot's Atlas, 1795. Courtesy of Stanley C. Arthur, Director of Louisiana State Museum. The drawings in the text are by Tilden Landry.

NATCHEZ
ON THE MISSISSIPPI

RIVER COUNTRY

In its surging passage below Memphis toward the Gulf of Mexico, the Mississippi, greatest of American rivers, comes to a high, sun-splashed hill. To the West, the green, alluvial lowlands of Louisiana stretch mistily toward the horizon. To the East, bordering the state of Mississippi, rise two hundred feet of red-brown bluff, crowned by vines of wild grape, magnificent magnolias and the sweep of oak. The river itself seems to change here. As if reluctant to leave, it makes a wide crescent of lake-like tranquillity; then it turns again to glide, silver and yellow, into the distance.

The tops of a few gleaming white columns, the mighty among myriad smaller buildings, all flanked by clusters of verdant growth, are just barely in sight above the hill. At the base of the bluff, a huddle of weather-worn huts leads to a road that climbs with occasionally sharp steepness to the old town of Natchez. From the ancient plaza, dating from the days of the Spaniards, tree-bordered streets fan out in several directions over the slow lift and fall of the land. These thoroughfares rapidly peter out into side-roads and trails leading to the half-concealed houses of the planter families.

To reach the early homes, the heart of the region, means traveling over a pastoral terrain without parallel in the nation. This bluff soil is composed of loess, a thin, chalk-like deposit borne by the winds and deposited for only a few miles' width along the Mississippi's course. On the flat Western side of the river, the passage of the silt-laden waters built up the rich, dark ground. Natchez' bluff, however, grew through the centuries by infinitesimal degrees, under the endless rush of air. In only a few places is such soil found; China is one of them.

This soft earth wears rapidly, and under the constant movement of man and vehicle through the years the roads have been ground lower and lower. Almost perpendicular walls of earth, sometimes twenty-five feet high or higher, rise from the sides of the sunken trails. A ride along one of them is like a journey through a three-sided tunnel, into which crawl, far above, the roots of trees and shrubs, as if reaching for those who pass. Still farther up, the tops golden in the sun, thick vegetation climbs toward the sky. Along these routes is a cool gloom, damp and rustling with fallen leaves, fragrant with pine and crushed flowers and the elemental smell of the wet soil. Then comes a turn and in the distance, crowning a slope, stands the plantation house in the clear white light.

Natchez . . . The town and the country about it had a long appointment with American destiny, a history alternately turbulent and placid. Through the centuries, men of many nations halted here, stirred by the soaring beauty of the point and its promise of advantage. The name came from a nation of Indians, advanced, haughty, apparently an offshoot of the Aztecs to the South. In 1682 La Salle and his followers floated past in their search for the river's mouth, and first told the world of the high bluff. Then for nearly forty years, only the ceremonial drums of the Indians and the darkening flights of wild birds disturbed the silences of the Mississippi.

In 1700, the French founders of Louisiana chose the spot as the river's finest for a permanent settlement—healthful, wind-swept, well above the murky swamps of its vicinity. It became a military post, and almost found itself the political capital of all the lower valley. The designation lay between it and a marshy flat closer to the Gulf, La Nouvelle Orléans. By a small margin, the latter won; nevertheless a corner of France grew up at Natchez.

Within a few more years the French saw tragedy. They placed a petty dictator in charge, who unceremoniously took a sacred Natchez village for his own. Skilfully, slyly, the Indians staged a massacre, one of the bloodiest episodes of the era. The French marched upon them for ruthless revenge, wiping out most of the nation, sentencing the rest to body-breaking slavery in the islands. The name of Natchez turned into a synonym for horror. A scattering of men stayed, but most settlers avoided the lovely, empty place as they would a curse, and from the fecund soil, vines and creepers reached up to encircle the ruins of their cabins. Yet, conversely, the incident helped make the spot a romantic dream for thousands who never saw it; the French novelist Chateaubriand used it as the material for his imaginative treatment of the noble savage, "Les Natchez."

Then all at once Natchez had an owner who prized it. With the end of the French and Indian War, England received this East bank of the Mississippi, and set out quickly to create a bastion of power along the river. Letters filled with warm descriptions of this richest part of West Florida, so named to distinguish it from the Spanish colony toward the Atlantic. Land grants went freely to retired soldiers and favored civilians—twenty-five hundred acres, five thousand. Officialdom established a pattern of big holdings, of privilege for the well-to-do.

In this small version of Tory England, the "fourteenth colony," a grand style started early—powdered wigs, soft linen, family portraits brought on the first trip to the wilderness, or the second. At its core Natchez was English, in contrast with the nearest river town, Gallic New Orleans, three hundred miles below. Orleanians loved the chanson; Natchezians preferred the reel and the cotillion. Neither was Puritan; both enjoyed the drinking song, over warm rum or a glass of Madeira. Luxury was not long in coming for those of the privileged element; bills of lading attest to their desire for such items as "faint blue" stationery, white silk stockings for men, "Spanish segars" and the best quality of London porter.

When the Atlantic coast colonials lifted the banner of liberty, Natchez did not follow. Isolated, set in their own ways, the Natchezians saw no cause for defection from their good King. From the Carolinas and Georgia moved other loyalists, glad of a refuge in a sympathetic territory, and others who termed themselves neutral and wanted to keep out of the fight. Natchez' conservatism grew. But however they felt about George the Third, the Natchezians lost the right to call him theirs. Sixteen years after Britain went to Natchez, Spain sped up the Mississippi and took the region from her. As the native Joseph D. Shields put it, Natchez was "like a gay widow who often changed her name."

Spain came, but sent very few Spaniards. The population, its language and philosophy remained Anglo-Saxon, and the dons wisely tried to do little to change any of it. (A few Irish priests were sent to convert the infidel Protestants to the mother church; these got along as well as do most Irishmen and Englishmen, though no blood was shed.) The Spaniards gave an impetus to large-scale planting, a new punctilio in their ceremonial social life with its balls and parades and, architecturally, a touch of stuccoed grace, an addition of iron ornamentation under a sloping roof.

Yet once more a change. At this strategic locale, a place of growing prosperity, several nations were preparing grabs. Reluctantly Spain gave up the prize to the Americans, and the fledgling nation took its first great Westward step. Another Southern frontier was opened, a new movement got under way. Down the river, Louisiana also passed to the Americans; on to Natchez swept one of the great surges of continental movement.

Wide, fat land lay ready for the taking. Cotton was revolutionizing North American agriculture. Whitney's gin had been perfected, and the fields about Natchez were whitening with the soft, lightly-packed bolls. Here, on the Mississippi side and also in Louisiana lay soil that was as fine for the crop as any in the world, with a return as quick as any that could be imagined. Let a man get hold of a parcel of slaves and, barring accidents, they might earn back their cost in a year. Before long, if he held to his luck, the master would be gaining a dazzling increase of twenty percent a year. Make way for one of the great American booms!

Almost overnight Natchez found itself the capital of a cotton empire, an El Dorado of the nineteenth century. All over the country men talked of it, as a key to riches. When they heard the name they grinned, or swore in envy, or fell to calculating how they could get down there. Damn it, it made a fellow feel like Midas, didn't it? The course of national fortune was altering. The older states on the Atlantic had passed their peak; Virginia and Carolina agriculture slowly grew less productive. Men were selling out or saving up, and moving Southwest. Hurriedly-gathered crews of blacks were taken to the forests, to transform them into fields of delicate color; and soon afterward came the houses—not so big at first, enlarging gradually into the splendor of mansions on the Mississippi.

Yet, even to get to Natchez was not easy. For years it remained isolated from the rest of America at the end of the Natchez Trace, the dangerous pioneer trail that was its only land link to the East. For hundreds of miles, men and women crept through forest and valley and bog, praying to God that they might survive the risks of the trail.

The route preceded history. Herds of buffalo first established it, picking the easiest passages along the ridges that led to the South. The Indians, discovering they could make little improvement in the course, whacked narrow trails through the undergrowth, marked trees and cut the twisting lines ever deeper. White men used it with only slight changes. Spaniard, Frenchman, Englishman, each trod or rode it for his purposes. For years there was not even a wagon road; those who went to the new country had to travel on foot or by horse, bringing whatever meager supplies they could expect their beasts to bear.

Over the Natchez Trace traveled most of the Americans who had to get to the Southwest. The sweeping branches of its overhanging trees shaded planters and slave traders, flatboatmen on their way back home, grand ladies and farmers' wives, peddlers, preachers, schemers, men good and evil and in between. To the Trace came Andrew Jackson, heading toward marriage and a honeymoon in the Natchez country. Down it moved Aaron Burr on several canvasses, sounding out men with his schemes of Empire; and the naturalist Audubon, seeking birds, and a bare living for his family, in the perfumed woods about the bluff. It was over the Trace in 1814 that the Westerners tramped on their way to the Battle of New Orleans and glory behind the Louisiana levee.

For days the traveler might have to advance alone over the curving trail. When he met an occasional stranger, he looked warily at him, and his fingers sought his gun. For everybody knew the pickings were good on this great route. Settlers carried everything they owned in their saddle bags and purses. Men returning East brought the profits of their sales of slaves or cotton, grain or hides. Merchants who had transacted family business in Natchez or New Orleans tied the proceeds in their belt. When travelers could manage it—or when they trusted those in whose company they found themselves—they banded together in caravans. But this might be difficult to arrange; it slowed up the tedious progress along the rutty road; and always there were the innocent or the careless who ventured forth singly. Under such conditions developed a saga of bloody banditry, the story of murder and ambush on the road to Natchez.

Natchez was the focus of another kind of violence. For hundreds of miles it was the only settlement of any size, a

NATCHEZ:
The River's Sweep, and the Gold-Green of Louisiana Below . . .

EARL M. NORMAN

ELMSCOURT
Behind the Ironwork, "Ball of a Thousand Candles"

EARL M. NORMAN

HOPE FARM
The Spanish Governor Had a Creole Retreat

EARL M. NORMAN

brightly-lighted crossroads point in the drabness of a thinly settled terrain. Down past Natchez swung the traffic of the great river-barge, flatboat, keel, eventually steamboat, bearing the migrating planter, trapper, fat merchant, river rat. It had become a major way-point on the path of American movement. Kentuckians and Tennesseeans brought grain and furs, pigs and smoked goods; to the river's edge rolled the wagons with their cotton, to be sent forth to the world. On the bluff and beyond, the cotton planters enjoyed a calm, secure existence, the high style at the edge of the wilderness. At the same time Natchez was part of the frontier, and also a port; and both connections gave it a roaring zest that became proverbial in America.

Below the bluff, the river left a narrow table of muddy ground—Natchez under the Hill, a hell-raising, rampaging sin-spot, mecca of men who wanted liquor, song and women, all raw. It was the turbulent meeting-place of a willful crew of hard-faced humanity. For decades Americans talked, with fuming rage or, perhaps merely a hot-eyed interest, of "Natchez Under"—a place where anybody could get away with anything he wished if he had big enough fists, or a trigger finger to support him.

Under the Hill clustered the warm-tempered Mississippi boatmen, for a fling before the last easy stages of the trip to New Orleans. Not far off sauntered some of the plantation men with lace cuffs and ruffled shirts, out for an evening "down the line." All prices, all scales—something for every mood, the boys said. Under the Hill, too, gathered cheats and card sharks who saw prey in the gullible river travelers; after them slipped hangers-on, crude and clumsy fingered, ready to do the lesser work. Thieves, murderers, habitual brawlers, fugitives from assorted brands of justice—for them all the place offered a haven.

Riots broke out by the hour. Gambling dens, dance halls, bar-rooms, rooming houses, race tracks, houses of harlots, peep shows—it was everything and anything, crowded close together. Here thrived a combination of Western boom town, red-light heaven and European-style gaming hell, with an international flavor, from Spaniard to Scotsman, Italian to Greek to Louisiana Cajun.

Such was Natchez, a town with a split personality. Up there were the clear and sunny esplanade, the tranquil streets —the elegance of the wind-swept heights. Below squatted the rowdy and the loud, with smelly flares, the beating of heavy drums, the whine of red-cheeked women—squalor on the steaming mud flats. As many observed, Natchez could truly be called a town with feet of clay.

Yet the day itself was a hard-living, rambunctious one. Even on the serene acres outside the town, the men often drank hard, played hard, lived hard. Natchez remained closer to the frontier than some cared to admit. Often on the plantations themselves there were sharp variations—the splendor of an imported carpet over a rough-planked floor, a delicate set of carved furniture beneath the coarse beaming of a ceiling. This was the "new" South as well as part of an older one, and many called it "the West," a jumping-off place. At Natchez were crystallized the hopes and plans of countless parties that went forth to Texas and Mexico for stealthy gain or conquest. Spain held thousands of miles in the distance; hordes of Americans wanted part or all of it.

For those who stayed here and tied themselves to the plantation system, the years had their rewards. Everything seemed to come bigger in Natchez—the houses, the acreage, alligators, mosquitoes and ambitions. Men's fortunes multiplied, or they failed with a resounding crash. All, of course, was not as casual a multiplication of wealth as it looked. Cotton could be precarious; a sag in the market, an epidemic that decimated the slaves, a flood over the Louisiana holdings, and a grower had to give up with a groan, or a bullet in his head. Someone else took over, with fresh capital and fresh luck.

In 1818 James Steer wrote Estevan Minor: "After reflecting, I feel disposed to decline taking any bank stock. For a young man just commencing in life, the best stock in which he can invest is, I think, negro stock. When cotton can command twenty to thirty cents per pound, negroes will yield a much larger income than any bank dividend." By the 1830s speculation was growing ever more frenzied; masses of paper churned about in the factor's offices. Nothing could stop this Natchez! About this time, it has been estimated, the town had more millionaires than any American settlement except New York and two or three others. The smell and feel of cotton were all over the place. Though more than four hundred miles upriver, Natchez became a full-fledged seaport, receiving goods directly from Europe, selling part of its cotton to Liverpool, Paris and London.

The town's population changed almost as fast as New Orleans'. A visitor (a woman) commented on the "peculiar bachelor caste" of the place; of any thirteen men, only three were married. The unattached males strolled about the hotels, lolled at the bars, and surveyed the world through the aromatic smoke of their cigars. At a fairly early date Natchez enjoyed a certain renown as a paradise for professional wife hunters. So many eligible planters' daughters, with assured incomes for years ahead . . . Calculating males refurbished wardrobes, gathered letters of introduction, slicked down their hair and went forth. A contemporary described an individual, supposedly typical, who "pretended to practice law, but his real business was marrying for money." When he took a bride, the comment was: "He would have married her in her winding sheet if she had been as ugly as original sin, and only had enough breath in her to say yes to the preacher."

Though the vicinity of the town retained the greatest concentration, settlers spread up and down the river. About forty miles to the South began the state line, bordering the Feliciana land of Louisiana, geographically and culturally similar to the Natchez territory, but separated by political circumstance. About eighty miles up from the town sat Vicksburg, the old Walnut Hills, upper limit of the Natchez country or "the

Natchez," as it was often called. All along the Mississippi settlements were strung like small beads on a twisted string: Second Creek, Bayou Pierre, Rodney's Landing.

The cosmopolitan tone increased. Pennsylvania, New Jersey, New York, New England gave Natchez as many planters as did Virginia, the Carolinas or Georgia. Some came as doctors, others as lawyers; but they all wanted to become successful cotton planters—and quickly. Such was the infectiousness of the scene that the firmest Northerners turned into fierce Natchezians, belligerent Southerners, ready to run through any former friend who cast aspersions on the wonder spot. S. S. Prentiss, Mississippi's golden orator (from Maine) fell victim to the contagion. He wrote home that the Natchezians "lived rather more *freely* than we of the North, and are what perhaps we should call a little dissipated." On the whole, however, he found Natchez society "more correct and the people more moral than they are usually considered." As an indication of that "usual consideration," a preacher wrote another newcomer: "Rumor has it that ministers rarely fail to marry rich wives in that country, that they fall off gradually in their devotions, and become the most rigorous task-masters and cotton-makers. . . ." Going native with a vengeance! A more earthy friend asked the same man, rather eagerly: "Does every master keep his mulatto concubine, and his harem of darkies? Do men from the land of steady habits fall into these practices?" Truly America was convinced that in Natchez "they lived freely."

Nobody ever called it a blue-nose's paradise. It was many things in one: elegance and the raucous brawl, white-stocked cotton grower and belching keel-boatman, graceful cotillions in the high-ceilinged drawing room and pistol shots or murderous Bowie knives on the streets. Some claim that the last-named implement is a Natchez product; certainly it was used here with frequency and precision. Under the fervent Mississippi sun, tempers broke easily. In 1819 a stranger observed casually to a young native that the town was sickly. The

Natchezian darted at him, face livid; he could not endure so foul a reflection on his native town, sir. The caller explained that he meant nothing personal, but pointed to the churchyard, where about five hundred people had been buried during a short epidemic. That, cried the Natchezian, was no justification. Men didn't live forever, even in New England! He would have to call the insulter out, and he did. Regularly challenges were snarled, and little bands met at dawn on the sandbar of Vidalia, the Louisiana town on the opposite bank, for the formalized murder of the gun duel. "Knives are oftener drawn in anger on the Mississippi than they are in Italy or Spain," snapped another visitor.

Meanwhile Natchez had seen an intensification of plantation-house building. Within a radius of a few miles there rose at least a hundred houses of masterly design. Such concentration —probably greater than in any comparable area of the Deep South—was due to two facts. The town and its vicinity were on the highest ground for miles, freer of danger from yellow fever and other ailments than, for instance, the low fields of Louisiana. Many received their major wealth from the cross-river flats, but settled their families in the Natchez upland. Others had great plantings on the Mississippi side, yet preferred to live in or close to the main settlement. A few put up what frankly were town houses, but most grew crops about their residences. This closeness of many homes and families in turn meant an intensification of the social life, a further heightening of what the rest of Mississippi termed "the Natchez spirit."

The growers had rich materials from which to pick. The forests and swamps held giant trees, ready to be ringed and seasoned. Brick could be baked on the grounds, of clay taken from the river bank or the rolling hills. In the slave quarters lived artisans, cabinet makers, carpenters, draftsmen who did most or all of the construction, though frequently other artists were imported. Using their seaport facilities, the Natchezians could draw on the world.

Not one, but several influences determined the kind of house that grew up here. The earliest residences were in the pattern inherited from France and Spain and modified in the New World. Now and then visitors saw similarities to West Indian towns in the many balconies and piazzas and the flavor of half-tropical living. The Creoles* of Natchez' early days taught the value of the raised house with its upper floor, the main one, set high to catch the air and escape the dampness, and broad porches beneath deep roofs for the hot afternoons. Usually brick below and wood above, with slender posts, low ceilings and exposed beams, most of these houses disappeared with time and changing tastes; yet a fair number remain, as memorials to grace and appropriateness.

From the rest of America came the flood of Anglo-Saxon settlers, bringing with them their own kind of architecture, derived largely from England, with touches of the delicate early Georgian. The Creole pattern was modified to a single-storied gallery, a sprawling, easy-going home sometimes called "Southern Planter." This again changed as the Greek Revival swept America and the growers found it admirably suited to their enlarged ambition, increasingly heavy pocketbooks, and hot climate. Thick columns rose at front and back, with pediments in the manner of the Greek Temple, and a hipped roof crowned by a balustraded captain's walk, to permit final inspection of their acres. Everything enlarged, including the height of the rooms and width of hallways. Curved stairways twisted up in magnificent swirls; fanlighted doorways grew taller, wider, proper frames for the expansive life that would be lived behind them.

In most Natchez examples this neo-classic mode was kept in restraint, the columns of the simple Doric order, ornamentation subordinated. Later, in the last years before the Civil war,

* Creole, as generally used in this region, means white, not Negro.

columns became yet more lofty, and there appeared elaboration for elaboration's sake. The "Golden Age" approached the rococo; the gold showed a hint of tinsel. In most cases, however, these homes have simplicity with their spaciousness; they fit their scene.

The main house formed only part of the plantation design. To the side were the auxiliaries, often galleried lesser versions —the kitchen of brick or wood, dairy, office, school rooms, billiard hall. Far to the back stood a small village of hut-like buildings in long rows, the "quarters" of the blacks whose backs supported the whole system. Only one more ingredient remained to be added, the plantings—rows of trees for approaches and borders, precise green hedges, thickening bushes of azaleas and camellias, roses and wisterias that twined about the tallest branches, growing high in the air until the vines seemed to have turned to trees, thrusting pale lavendar blossoms against the skies.

Sometimes series of terraces dropped gradually to low-lying gardens, with contrasting designs at each level. Latticed summer houses and pavilions sat a distance away, half-swallowed among vines and flowers; in the background, thick borders of trees and wild plants marked a dry bayou, cutting deep within the thin soil. Over all the scene was a stillness, broken only by the murmurs of children in the shadows of the galleries, and the drone of bees as the heat shimmered over the lawn.

To the back began the cotton fields, bursting into spring blossom with their pink and white flowers, and their cups of snowy stuff that would soon extend for miles. In picking time, gangs of slaves, men and women, moved across the land in vari-colored files, reds and faded brown, with handkerchiefs and bandannas on their heads. Behind them they dragged long bags into which they stuffed the cotton. Mule-drawn wagons stood ready to take it to the gins; and when cotton prices rose, the owner's nerves strained as he saw all that money spread out in the fields. Season's end meant, for those who had done the work, a brief frolic, skylarking and gifts; for the owner, a call on his factor to settle accounts. The goose hung high; all looked right with the world, for another twelve months anyway.

It was a civilization that had style and leisure, a native culture flowering from a base of controlled abundance. The planters sent to France for their home furnishings, Italy for marbles and oils, England for glassware; they acquired libraries and kept them stocked. At their own track they raced the blooded horses that they had also imported. They called in continental landscape artists to refashion their plantings, they had traveling artists do their portraits, they acquired successions of governesses and fencing masters for their children. And regularly they went in little caravans to the watering springs of the East, or Europe. Even to modern observers, the plantation Natchezians seemed to be ever traveling.

The hospitality, for those within the circle, had an authentically fabulous quality. Distant relatives or merely friends, as the stories go, dropped in for a weekend and stayed a year. In one instance an acquaintance, met on a continental trip, got off a steamboat to stop for a day. He remained for more than twenty years. He talked intermittently of going home but none, including himself, took it seriously. He received a manservant of his own; the family made slight modifications in its cuisine to fit his tastes. Erecting a new house miles away, they took him with them and gave him a separate wing. When the master died, the friend was remembered in the estate; when he himself breathed his last, he was buried in the plantation cemetery. They'd forgotten where his family lived!

Sometimes, to be sure, there was sham and pretension. The actor Tyrone Power—great-grandfather of the current movie actor—called at Natchez in 1836 and found an exhibition of "master" paintings from England. Practically all, he thought, were "worse pictures than are offered to connoisseurs at a pawnbroker's sale in London." He noted that "the quantity of raw material used in a work" seemed to be "a great consideration with the lovers of art here."

The realistic observer, Frederick Olmsted, described how one family rose so high it replaced the Negro mammy by a French nurse and went riding about as if on parade. And he quoted a possibly envious neighbor who had only scorn for the planters' sons: "You can tell their children as far off as you can see them. They sort o' throw out their legs as if they hadn't got strength to lift 'em and put 'em down in any particular place. They do want so bad to look as if they weren't made of the same clay as the rest o' God's creatures."

Other descriptions read more pleasantly. A stranger was frequently surprised to find that nearly everyone he met rode a horse, usually a quick, high-bred animal with an ornamental saddle. It was the simplest way to get about this region of long, winding roadways. On their mounts the planters carried themselves with a quiet competence. When their wives came in carriages, the men rode along *à cheval*. The women dressed with care, in tight-waisted costumes with expansive skirts. The men were garbed more casually, with wide hats of straw or felt, broadcloth suits and always their whips in their hands, as a symbol of authority.

It was an American town, with subtle differences, that the Natchezians knew. Along the old, jessamine-lined streets, first laid out by the Spaniards, they passed houses and stores, iron-balconied and stuccoed in the manner of the dons. They jogged along a wide esplanade and surveyed the tawny river from the rim of the green-hung plaza. The atmosphere was easy; stores stayed open on Sunday as on any other day. Business teemed, but all was careless and unhurried. Slaves with passes from their masters ambled along, packages balanced on their heads. Bazaar keepers continued the Creole custom of bringing their goods, fruits and vegetables and woven stuff, out into the sunlight, stacking it up for the inspection of all who sauntered by. In leisurely style the "quality" rode to the theater, an ample building on the outskirts, to see the latest entertainment that had come by steamboat from New Orleans.

As great a symbol of the region as the cotton boll were the steamboats—a prideful procession with their long white lines, flimsy gingerbread ornamentation and towering smokestacks. In the night, waiting on the bluff, men and women spied them out as one, then another, appeared in the distance, first a speck like a star, off in the immensity of the velvet-black evening, slowly enlarging in all its shining detail. They slid slowly closer, so close that in their lights the onlookers made out the people promenading the upper decks, and the roustabouts sprawled on the floor. Horns blew below; cannons boomed welcome. Steamboat comin' in . . . Nothing was ever like it, said the informed, on land or water. And they all stopped at Natchez.

Behind the columns rare human growths also sometimes developed. There was the planter, Henry Chotard, who decided he must give Natchez the world's grandest stables. He ordered stalls of mahogany, hand-panelled, hand-carved. He acquired troughs of choice marble. For each horse he fashioned a silver name-plate, the animal's title lettered in Gothic; before each stall must be silver posts and silver chains. A last touch called for a great mirror in each stall, gold-bordered like any in his parlors. "Nothing is too good for my animals," Henry Chotard boasted. He wanted his fillies to be able to toss their manes and admire themselves; and, as the story insists, they did.

Another planter, hearing his wife say she would like a new set of china, announced that he would get it for her in Paris. The next week they started out, their five children, and an aunt and uncle included. They had so good a time on the continent that they forgot the china—and went back again for it the following year. A third one, gourmet, patriarch and paternalist, would accept no invitation to dinner unless allowed to provide and prepare the meal with his own servants; accordingly he traveled about with an entourage in wagons and carriages. Another particularly lordly individual always saw that with their final coffee, his guests received saucers of sugared pecans. One by one he dropped his into the beverage; he had seen someone do it in Austria, and he liked the custom. He would survey the table: "I suggest that all of you do the same." All complied. A woman recalls: "Once I didn't, and he fixed me with his eye till I did." Such was the life that others, smiling or shaking their heads, called "the Natchez way."

So the high days of pride for Natchez; now, slowly, the lesser ones ... Apart from the world, apart even from the rest of the state, remained the cotton masters. This was the heart of the Mississippi territory, the center of its first history. Yet Natchez suffered early from hostile factors, which gradually intensified against her. She had been a Tory center, then a Whig stronghold, always a place of those who believed in rule from above; and she paid for her arrogance. By 1802 a new American territorial governor, William C. C. Claiborne, arrived in Mississippi. As a follower of Thomas Jefferson, a radical in Natchez' eyes, he was a man who spoke freely of the dangers of concentration of power in slaveholders' hands. The small farmers, receiving their first responsibility in government, complained that the cotton lords were joking about them, their manners and costumes, when they attended legislative sessions. Promptly the capital was shifted to tiny Washington, six miles east, whose main virtue lay in the fact that it was *not* Natchez.

The river edge was settled first; now the course of settlement moved away from it, toward the hills and central flatlands. The newer sections of the state, more populous, modified the constitution several times to take away more and more of Natchez' old powers; the rank of capital never returned. Some river country people talked excitedly of seceding from the rudely democratic majority and forming another state; nothing happened. Yet for decades the region maintained its wealth; none could take from it its twin sources of well-being, cotton and the river. Natchez supported the "aristocracy" of Mississippi; their homes were the showplaces of the river, their opulence the envy of others. The Natchezians could afford to feel superior for records showed that in the 1830s her town lots alone were worth more than those of all the rest of the state. Yet even that early the old town was feeling further losses. The depression of 1837 and the years that followed dug deep. Only three years later the worst tornado in her history damaged the town so badly that reports said it would be abandoned. Natchez rose again, but never quite so high.

In the background, less spectacular forces were at work. The upland soil wore badly under the wasteful plantation cultivation, a rape of the earth. The ground washed with every rain, and gullies grew with the season. Over in Louisiana the fresher soil maintained itself; in "the Natchez," the earth became slowly less fertile. Shortly before the Civil War, plantations were being abandoned, stables and Negro quarters left empty as growers moved on to Texas. Yet for those who stayed, so good was the market that planting seemed only slightly less glorious a thing than before.

The war came and Natchez was injured physically no more, in fact rather less, than most Southern towns. At hostilities' end it could lift its head; it still had its place on the river, didn't it? The first post-war years, when the packets found their markets still open, did not appear altogether gloomy. But then Natchez lost her last advantage; the railroads tapped the vast flow of goods on the river, lightly at first, then more and more steadily.

Bad times tightened in the '80s; everything shrank: bank

deposits, lands, the range of life. Outlying properties went, then all but a few acres; servants had to be dismissed, and the plantation family, or only part of it, stayed on. Yet here the ancient Natchez pride had its role. What was theirs, they would keep. In the twilight of the pillared houses, a will to retain grew at least as strongly as the weeds in the neglected gardens. Somehow they would hold on, borrow, mortgage, live on less; the house and its contents would remain. Rooms in which thousands had been entertained saw no visitors for a decade. In the finely-carved sideboards rare sets of china gathered dust; the family had little to put on them, but they would never give them up.

The town sat stranded in its trappings of ancient splendor. The streets sounded no more to the movement of polished victorias and gigs. The river, once filled with the lines of flatboats and the white-and-gold majesty of the packets, swept by, empty, and the shanty-dwellers dozed among their willows. Up and down the river country, from the Louisiana state line at the South, to Vicksburg and beyond, the regime dried up. The string of small settlements on the river "coast" died slowly on the vine, losing trade and population by the year. The Mississippi often played tricks, shifting its course a few miles to leave one stranded, cutting in to tear off another whole site. For mile after mile "the Natchez" became a land of silent ghost towns, decaying remnants of villages, hung with a glory of vine and flowered leaf.

But the big houses, in the silences of their sun-dappled surroundings, stayed on. Ironically, the region's ill luck saved it as a plantation museum unparalleled in the South. Slow poverty proved an agent of conservation, like the amber into which insects of another era have been saved for the study of succeeding peoples. In other parts of the South men and women were changing their places for the worse—modernizing, "improving," adding brackets and filigrees, the fashionable jigsaws to which all of America fell victim. Natchez, fortunately for itself, could not afford to put up the fake "medieval" towers, Swiss chalets and the rest. Now and then a home burned, or fell away. But the majority have remained more or less intact.

The situation bred idiosyncrasies—the dreamers out of touch with any reality. Years earlier, newcomers noticed that the Natchez plantation people were a small, tight group which grew smaller, tighter with the generations. Fifteen or twenty names, and the circle was complete. Intermarriage had begun early; the same names still merged. Now oddities developed.

A grande dame dressed in her best black and, accompanied by her last servant, the chauffeur, delivered milk. Another couple lived together forty years without exchanging a word, sending messages to each other through their cousins. A peculiar lady's fame was that she ventured forth once a day, and never came back without having "insulted somebody." An elderly woman, so used to holding on to things, never threw a newspaper away, collecting them for three decades until she had only a few feet of space left in which to move about her home. Another came back to town regularly from a trip, carrying two great valises in her hands. She would walk to the middle of the street and halt the first machine she saw: "I'm Miss ———. I live seven blocks left, four to the right, the second house. You will take me there." The driver, whoever he was, always did. Again, as we shall find, there were less happy incidents and individuals, more morbid hates, and spectacular tragedy in the shadow of the high-arched doorways.

Eccentricities can be milder, approaching the delightful. "Cudd'n Jane, she talks all the time," smiles Cousin Marie, who talks even more than Cudd'n Jane. Their next-door neighbors are maiden ladies, about sixty-five, who always go out together. One never finishes her sentences; the other does it for her. They and the rest speak of the three girls of sixty who set a clock between them when a guest came. Each would have fifteen minutes to say what she wanted, and the others agreed not to interrupt as they waited their turn.

Many, even in their worst days, did not forget that Natchez

had always been a by-word for happy entertaining. A friend of mine recalls a party some years ago. Everybody brought his own liquor to the dusty, dim old place. They danced by candlelight; no electricity had been installed, and that added to the effect. Two open fireplaces threw a brisk heat; no gas was available. The couples moved beneath chandeliers washed and cleaned that week for the first time in years, before oil paintings to which a bit of cobweb still clung. The middle-aged host and hostess had had to do all the cleaning themselves. Across two corners of the big drawing room, my friend noticed, rosewood sofas and chairs had been lined up like barriers. Staring discreetly, she found out why; the floors had broken through. But the owners had decided they needed a party, and their guests understood. They did the same things themselves! That, too, was the "Natchez spirit."

Now, as in its earlier years, Natchez has become a center of national interest. After decades of slow corrosion and decline, she blossoms as a plantation museum without parallel in the South. Again Americans hear of the place that their grandfathers gossiped over; again they talk of it and come to visit it, in greater numbers than their ancestors ever did. That, however, is the postscript to history. First, the rest of the story.

I

THE HEROES, AND "THE GIRLS"

A GAUNT young frontiersman, his light eyes searching for bargains, came to the Natchez country late in 1789, and never forgot it and what it meant in his stormy career. In the years that followed, Andrew Jackson was to win cheers as a hater of the Spaniards; but now Spain was offering land on the Mississippi to the Westerners, and Andy saw no reason why he shouldn't take a sample. Already he had become district prosecutor in Tennessee; but this Natchez also sounded good for a man on the rise.

At this stage Andy was far from being a mansionmaster; later he would have his own big place, but now he had to step lively. He inspected the first of the high-roofed houses that marked the rises in the land. The growers, he knew, would need supplies, plenty of them; and he set out to fit himself into the picture. About twenty five miles above the town, an embryo settlement clustered about the meeting place of tranquil Bayou Pierre and the river. On a hill overlooking the brown flood, Jackson threw together a cabin, ordered wines and "sundries" and solicited trade, scratching about, buying, selling in a way that might have repelled many of the emerging gentry. Up in Nashville an associate sent down Negroes. Though fist-pounding partisans tried to deny it in after years, the future President was a small-scale dealer in blacks. He

WINDY HILL
For Once, a Lady Said "No" to Aaron Burr

EARL M. NORMAN

ELGIN
For John Jenkins, a Great Debt, a Great Love
EARL M. NORMAN

SPRINGFIELD
For Andy Jackson . . . Joy and Then Tragedy
EARL M. NORMAN

also laid out a quarter race-track, and bet and joshed with the crowd.

Andy seldom found himself alone. At once he made friends with the Greens, his good-humored, prosperous neighbors. Becoming a business partner of the son, Thomas Marston Green, he visited him at his new house, Springfield. Striding in and out of the fine brick establishment, Andy did not conceal his liking for it. Nothing for miles around approached the scale of the powerful structure. Six tall pillars extended across the front, sheltering shaded galleries above and below, places of vine-hung coolness through most of the year. Each column stood upon a firm rectangular base; a simple wooden railing ornamented the upper gallery. Springfield had much to indicate its comparatively early construction—long, narrow windows, thick beams, the plain though paneled and side-lighted central doorway. Inside Andy gave his approval to touches of added elegance—carvings along the cornices, the careful hand-trimming of the mantels. A line of patriarchal oaks trailed gray moss over his shoulders as he cantered to and from the tree-framed beauty of Springfield.

Here the sandy-haired Jackson conferred on business during the day and danced after dark. For, loud though he might be in commercial dealings, he knew how and when to be deft-mannered. His connection grew with the Greens of Springfield. As the leading family of the vicinity, they helped Andy in several ways that he would always remember—one in particular. The development of that incident took him back to Tennessee, where his duties still lay from time to time. There, a little earlier, he had met the middle-aged Widow Donelson, head of a large household. Well-placed in the recent frontier of Nashville, the Donelsons were nevertheless glad to have a man boarder as a protection. Returning one day, Andy encountered Rachel Donelson Robards, only twenty, who was to be the single love of his life.

Fate had dealt badly with the red-lipped, olive-skinned Rachel, whose ample loveliness had made more than one man want her. At sixteen the cheerful girl had accepted a high-ranking suitor from Kentucky, and regretted it almost at once. A moody man, Captain Robards displayed a hot jealousy, storming at his young wife with vague accusations. His mother took Rachel's part, but at his insistence the girl had left him. Her pain showing in her eyes, Rachel went back to her family. Taking up his quarters in a side building on the family property, Andrew Jackson caught sight of her, and now asked to be presented.

Whether the pensive Rachel realized it or not, Andy grew quickly infatuated. Unexpectedly Captain Robards rode over from Kentucky to plead with Rachel: Wouldn't she accept him again? He was sorry, truly sorry. . . . Though reconciled, Robards began to mutter about the angular young boarder. The Donelsons felt an increasing tension; on one highly-charged morning, the men exchanged words—according to another source, a few shots as well. After the incident, Jackson moved away, while Rachel and Robards rode off to Kentucky. Dark months followed for Jackson. Hopelessly taken with the alluring Rachel, he could only wait.

As he probably expected, Rachel found again, and for the last time, that she could not stay with her hot-tempered husband. Miserably she sent a message to her family; the widow Donelson, her face fixed in new lines of worry, asked the family friend, Jackson, if he would not bring her Rachel home. Andy was delighted to oblige. Yet even now Robards came clattering back, to argue and appeal to Rachel. When he understood that she had closed the door forever against him, Robards made a few sneering remarks on the street. As in all small communities, the news flew, and Andrew Jackson's temper cracked.

Walking up to the man, he made a quiet threat: Any more of that kind of thing, and he'd cut off the fellow's ears. This appears to have quieted Robards, at least for the moment; but Rachel received word that Robards, ever more sullen, would "force" her to come back. The girl grew agitated. What would Robards try the next time? She was afraid to stay in Nashville. Learning that a group of men, known to the family, were about to leave for far-away Natchez, she begged that they let her accompany them. She could stay there with people she knew; she'd be no trouble.

The head of the party frowned as he pointed out the hazards—swamps, badly-marked trails, bandits. A woman along, Ma'am, would sure complicate things. . . . From the family, Jackson learned about the problem. He had his business dealings down in the Natchez; he'd go along to provide extra protection. And thus, with those others that the Widow Donelson trusted, they made the journey. At this point the estranged husband took a new course. To the Virginia general assembly (Kentucky was still under its authority) he offered a petition for a divorce. A committee refused to grant it, but a bill was passed to allow him to present a case in court. Thus a web of misunderstanding was woven. Tidings circulated that Robards actually received a divorce; Robards, says Marquis James, not only countenanced the report, but sent messages to the Donelsons: He bore no grudges, he wanted the past to lie dead.

And now Andy had taken Rachel to his good friends, the Greens of Springfield. There, in the fine red house at the end of the line of oaks, Rachel could rest and see what developed. Rejoining the Donelsons in Tennessee, Jackson was startled when told that Robards, when he obtained his divorce a little earlier, had charged Rachel with "eloping" from her husband's house with another man. Robards had lied, Andy cried. There had been nothing like that, and he'd be willing to swear it to the world. But what should he do next? He had to break this news to Rachel. This hard task—and also a new hope—spurred him as he raced through the wilderness on horseback to the Natchez territory.

When he had finished his awkward telling of the story, Rachel sat stunned. To have made a false claim like that, and to get a ruling against her without giving her a chance to reply! "I expected him to kill me, but this is worse! . . ." For the first time Rachel sensed that, however guiltless, she had shown little discretion in the matter. Until the hour of her death, there seemed to be an intermittent shadow of fear over her face.

However, she was now free, at least, and they were away from Nashville and all that reminded them of their difficulties. Andy, his composure recovered, pursued his wooing with determination. The life along Bayou Pierre was gay. At Springfield and the nearby plantations, Rachel attended the balls and cotillions. In little parties, the Greens and their guests rode down the sloping hills; often the couple halted with the others on the ledges of earth to watch the Mississippi in its yellow coilings toward the Gulf. For a while Rachel and Andrew could enjoy their easy hours.

One day, her strong face flushed with a happiness that recalled the earlier girl, Rachel annnounced that she had agreed to marry Andy.*

And so, late in the summer of 1791, as Springfield's narrow windows shone behind the long line of oaks, Andrew and Rachel stood before Magistrate Thomas Marston Green and became husband and wife. On the second floor, a flowered bridal chamber was set up. After a week or so they left, to spend the rest of their honeymoon in Andy's quiet cabin on the bluff that marked the meeting of the Mississippi and Bayou Pierre. In the mornings the sun's red rays stained a pathway over the waters about them; they stared upward at the lines of wild birds in shifting streams of flight. For too short a time,

---

* For years a family story told how, as a safeguard, Rachel obtained a Spanish divorce from Robards, in the Natchez country. Many official Spanish papers were lost, and so there can be no certainty on the point. W. H. Sparks, a connection of the Greens, declared flatly that such a decree was granted; and he insisted that nothing disreputable could have been attached to Rachel's name. She spent fifteen months with the Greens, people of "pride and fastidiousness," who would have countenanced no person of "equivocal character."

they were alone in the Natchez country; and then, because Andy was a man with a way to make, they had to go.

Back home nothing more was heard of Robards until more than a year later. By accident, riffling through official documents, Andy came upon a paper with familiar names. Only a few months before this, Robards had been granted a divorce —on the claim that Rachel had deserted him for an adulterous affair! Jackson's lean face tightened. Then there had been no divorce up here at the time he and Rachel married . . . Why had Robards allowed the other story to spread; and why had he waited so long before bringing suit? It would be difficult to tell this to Rachel. The scene was worse than he had anticipated. Something collapsed within her when, at her friends' urging, she agreed to a second ceremony with Andrew.

The couple knew long, rewarding years together. Through several decades the ebullient soldier-Indian fighter-politician ranged the country, speaking firmly for the average man of his day—a hero or a contemptible radical, according to one's caste. For Rachel he showed a ripening affection, an unending consideration; and they eventually had their own great house, bigger than Springfield. Many times they talked of those dreamy hours in the Natchez region—the happiest, perhaps, that they ever spent. But many times both of them must have wondered if, at some point, they might have managed the matter differently. Andrew Jackson threatened several enemies over the matter; he shot one to death in a duel.

Yet for Rachel, the test came harder. With each of her husband's advancements, her fears grew. Tavern louts were making jokes, political schemers debating how best to drop an insinuation. . . . Andy, trying to soothe Rachel as she struggled with herself, reasoned anxiously. She must stop worrying. It would be all right; she'd see.

The Presidency loomed, but Rachel Jackson never knew the White House life which her husband planned for her. Preparations sped for Andy's inauguration, while Rachel looked on nervously. Suddenly she came upon papers that he had concealed, disclosing how far the stories had spread. Rachel's tenuous resolve broke and she sank to her bed. She seemed to improve; when Andy came to her she smiled. Then one evening she fell in a faint; rushing to her side, her husband watched her slowly die.

"May God Almighty forgive her murderers as I know she forgave them," he cried out. "I never can." Seven years later W. H. Sparks called upon the tired lion in the White House, bringing with him Mrs. Sparks, youngest daughter of the Greens of Springfield plantation. Holding the girl's hand, Jackson looked intently into her face. She was, he murmured, so like her mother, "the friend of my poor Rachel, when she so much needed a friend." Until he died there was a rock in Andrew Jackson's heart whenever he thought of his wife and her detractors. Yet Rachel had been a good woman, an admirable one. Today, under similar circumstances, few would point a hostile finger.

Their friends, the Greens, also went from the Natchez vicinity, leaving their Springfield, a mellowed place of thick red walls and white columns. Toward the bases of the shafts the colors fade; there is a hint of red through the white, and the rich mold-green that only the years can bring are marks of honorable age. But the crowded life of the Greens has no modern counterpart. The house stands in a district of deserted sites that time has left behind. The file of trees has vanished; the sunlight beats more harshly against the galleries. But it is possible to see the rooms that Andrew and Rachel Jackson knew during those days that brought them their greatest happiness. The darkening lines of wild birds that moved above them—these, too, will be heard no more. There remains the plantation house and, silent and gleaming in the distance, ever the river.

By chance, the same vicinity a few years later beheld the climax of the mysterious plottings of the enigmatic Aaron

Burr. It was at Bayou Pierre and among the nearby plantation owners that the debonair schemer came suddenly to realize that he had failed in his aim of establishing a new empire in the Southwest. And for another reason Burr probably never forgot the Natchez country; here, always a devotee of the feminine, he too found a love, but under circumstances different from Andrew Jackson's.

In January of 1806 the short and wiry Burr was desperate. From a place of greatness he had dropped almost into disgrace. He had been Vice-President; by one vote he had lost the Presidency to Jefferson. Afterward came the hapless duel in which he killed Alexander Hamilton. He must score a comeback, or sink into obscurity; and if Aaron Burr hated one thing above all others, it was obscurity. Natchez became his goal, with the mixed forces he had gathered. For months America had stirred with rumors about him; just what he wanted is still a mystery. He seldom offered two men the same story; speaking in eloquent tones, his bright eyes shining, he hinted and paused significantly, and his listeners drew their own conclusions.

Whatever the plot, Natchez was to be one of its places of fruition. Once it seemed to be a grand filibustering expedition against Mexico, to pull the prize from Spain's clutch. The next moment Burr, sneering at the American government, appeared to plan a new nation of his own, splitting off the Southwest and joining it to Mexico. (He might well find support for such visions; many Westerners fumed against the Atlantic seaboard, thinking of Europe and trade and ready to forget all about the country beyond the mountains.) Yet on other occasions Burr looked much more innocent. He had purchased a far-flung land grant in Louisiana. He appeared to be only a good citizen, hoping to colonize it with the families he brought along. His devices had many facets; men grew dazzled as the magnetic one gestured, and Burr had no trouble in convincing himself that they were his. General Wilkinson of the American Army would be at his side, he felt sure; even

Andy Jackson, he believed, favored certain of his designs. Ready to work with anybody, Burr offered to sell his country to the British, French or Spaniards; he found no takers, if only because these powers doubted his stories.

The time shortened; officials were sniffing suspiciously as Burr intrigued; warnings were beginning to ring against him. At last he had to set out down-river. If all turned out well, he would land in Natchez, throw open his arms—and the Southwest would leap behind him to a man. But Burr, whether fool or villain, showed himself to be a clumsy juggler. He never raised a fraction of the vast sums of money he had visioned; less than a hundred made up his party, including women and children. General alarm, too, was taking the place of the expected enthusiasm. In New Orleans General Wilkinson turned against him, denouncing him as a traitor, clapping Burr's friends into jail, ordering Burr's arrest. In the Mississippi Territory, now American, Acting Governor Mead fell into a hysterical fit. Mustering out the soldiers, buzzing about like a wild saw, he announced that the country's fate might depend on him, Mr. Mead. Good people quivered in their beds.

On a chill January day a band of nine unmartial-looking vessels pulled in near Bayou Pierre. Burr sipped his drink, stared and realized he would be lucky if he escaped with his life. Wilkinson would hang him in a moment. But if he fell into civilian hands, he would have the safeguards of civil law. With his usual urbanity, he let the agitated Mr. Mead know he was ready to face trial like any proper citizen. Arraigned, he was released on bond.

And now was Burr the object of fear and scorn among the Natchezians? On the contrary, planters competed with graceful compliments, receptions and dinners. Colonel Benijah Osmun, friend of Revolutionary days, took Aaron to his plantation at Halfway Hill. The wooden house topped a slow rise, surrounded by widening ravines, gashed into the red earth, that gave a look of wildness to the locale. A double line of cedars, following the slope, provided an approach with a sweeping vista. It took hours over winding, climbing roads to reach the Osmun place; and this suited Aaron Burr. Here he worked to extricate himself from his problem, dispatching notes in cipher, receiving many and mysterious guests.

Yet he had moments of leisure at Halfway Hill; and where Burr went, ladies were seldom far behind. Though he had reached fifty, it would be some years before women failed to find the dark, well-knit man anything but prepossessing. His sensitive nostrils quivered; the eyes changed, and the ladies caught their breath. This time he chose none of the Natchez widows or the debutantes who fluttered at his brisk footstep; Aaron discovered what he wanted close at hand.

Strolling along the paths of Halfway Hill, he passed an aproned girl. Barely twenty, Madeline Price had a virginal beauty, a head of brown curls, features so impressive that men later turned to stare at her on the streets of great cities. At this time, however, Madeline had a handicap; she was poor, very poor. On a nearby elevation sat a cottage in which she lived with her mother. Earlier they had come from Virginia with Madeline's father. In his purse he carried all of their means; on the way a highwayman leaped from the brush and shot him dead before them, then escaped with their money. Dragging themselves to the town's outskirts, widow and daughter held on as best they could.

If Aaron knew anything, it was women. He stood silent, deeply respectful at their first, accidental meeting. Madeline, coloring, went by. Quickly Aaron arranged with Colonel Osmun to meet these neighbors. He invited the widow and daughter to dinner; he accepted their invitation to tea. As she listened to the flow of his words, Madeline interrupted occasionally to ask about the crowded world she had never seen. Aaron found that Madeline had never had a beau among the plantation boys. They had asked permission to call, and Madeline had declined. Later, perhaps. . . . She had been very right, the expert Burr assured her.

Suddenly it became evident that Madeline had been awakened for the first time. Over her soft face there came a glow that none had ever seen; her shy gray eyes, following Aaron's, had lost their calmness. Suddenly there were many to see and talk about it. Bad roads or no bad roads, tidings traveled like the movements of the red-birds. Friends whom the Prices had not met in months called at Halfway Hill with jellies and grinning good wishes. On the road, noses pressed against carriage glasses to spy out the pair as they walked beneath the tips of the hanging moss, along the sun-spotted passages around the hill.

For once Aaron did not have his complete way. Madeline smiled at his compliments, then moved ahead along Colonel Osmun's terraced garden. That was all; her innocence proved a defense that even the resourceful Burr could not penetrate. Halfway Hill—did he swear to himself that the name was an apt one? The chase took on new interest; as the story goes, Aaron the boudoir dilettante, found that for the first time he had fallen in love. Nervous as a college boy, he asked her to marry him. Flushing, Madeline thanked him. Yes, she loved him, she admitted; she was more flattered than he realized. But wouldn't it be better, first, to see what happened to Aaron? He'd just told her he would appear in the case in a few days. . . . To every argument she shook her brown curls. Finally Aaron knew that for once a woman meant it when she said they'd wait.

The trial started in the town of Washington. A good show, it became so crowded that they all moved outside beneath the oaks. The Attorney-General shocked the apprehensive ones by recommending that the grand jury be sent home; Burr had violated no law. His colleagues cried protest; they had a big fish in their little net and they wanted him to stay there. The grand jury agreed with the Attorney-General, and castigated not Burr, but the officials themselves, for all their fuss and feathers. The hearing went into a hubbub, nobody knowing what to do with the polished rascal. At last the judge ordered Aaron to remain within reach, indefinitely.

Aaron grew disturbed. They were trying to hook him on another line, were they? He hesitated, while his advisors gave anxious counsel: He had best get out of here, quickly. After some days he agreed. With dusk he went up the hill to Madeline. If she loved him, she would ride away with him tonight. They could be married at the first opportunity, and she would see the world at his side.

Still, with her mother listening in the next room, Madeline demurred. When the matter ended, she told him, then he could come for her. (Did she fear her gallant would not make her his wife; or was Madeline simply a shrewd young lady, who knew precisely how she wanted things to be?) Burr kept up his ardent pleas, importunate one moment, with an air of hurt pride the next, while his friend Colonel Osmun nervously waited outside. Dawn came and, shaking his head, Aaron left. Waving from her window, Madeline called out: She'd be there when he came back. Silently, Aaron rode off.

Many miles away, he was captured; again the case collapsed. But now Burr was a ruined man, who must slip away in the dark. Fleeing to Europe, he realized that his career had forever ended. For several seasons Madeline walked alone along their favorite paths. Late one evening, a message arrived. Ripping it apart, she read the lines. She must forget him, he said; he might have to stay forever overseas. Like another individual of twisted plans, Aaron gave her advice: She should enter a convent.

This Ophelia got herself to no nunnery. She cried at first, of course; then, walking beneath the mossy trees, she decided that her life was not over. She kept thinking of that delightful world Aaron had outlined to her. Her mother died; and when a woman friend offered to take Madeline on a trip to Havana, she accepted at once. There she met numerous gallants. One, the British owner of the biggest business on the island, followed her back, and this time Madeline said yes.

Her old cottage cracked away in a storm. Colonel Osmun's bigger place passed into the hands of two families, the Brandons and Stantons. Ultimately General Robert Stanton married the energetic Jane Chapline, and they filled the house with their five children. One summer, when the husband was traveling in the North, yellow fever struck Natchez; the wife wrote the General to stay there. Replying that his place was with them, the General hurried back. As a result he and his three sons died; the wife and two daughters survived. The widow married the dead man's brother, the pink-faced Dr. Frederick Stanton, and this couple had another five children. (This recalls the Louisiana matron who, marrying twice, had the same number of offspring by each man. She couldn't be unfair to either, she observed.)

Now the stage was set for a metamorphosis of the house where Burr had plotted. For the crowded family, new rooms were added; a wide gallery received four columns, rather bigger and thicker than might have been expected, with a Greek pediment above. To left and right was attached a smaller replica of the main building, with peaked roof to match—a precise pattern reflecting bolder designs in other places. A wide fan-lighted doorway had carving of a concentrated richness and inside a spiral stairway lifted proudly to the second floor in an unsupported loop. About it all was a gay quality, a certain liveliness like that of a bright-mannered woman who made the most of her charms. The estate took a new name—Windy Hill Manor.

Along the slope that led to the house the Stantons lengthened Colonel Osmun's double line of cedars; and there stood the pillared house in the sunny clearing, its smaller companions to each side. They extended the wide garden at the side, with terracing and summer house, and carefully they embellished the path over which Burr and his Madeline had strolled. It became the more or less official Lover's Walk of the vicinity. Living, poor Aaron had failed to achieve his goal; in death he fostered a tradition of success in romance.

The Stanton cotton fields spread in the distance. The big family stayed isolated from town and not dissatisfied with their situation. They entertained frequently, but always a limited group. In these days, the 1840s and '50s, the girls went to boarding schools, the boys to military academies, the whole family in carriages to resort places for "the beneficial waters." Dr. Stanton—six feet two and weighing two hundred and twenty pounds—was a pater-familias of moon-like, ruddy face and thick sideburns that curled in the breeze. At Windy Hill Manor he functioned as a beaming host; among those not of the Stanton circle, he gave the impression of remoteness. In the evenings the doctor gathered his "two families," five of his own, two of his brother's, and they had their own orchestra, including piano, violin, harp, voice.

The Stantons loved acting—little dramas, curtsying recitations, maidens moaning their fate in rhymed couplets. Life meant nothing if it lacked the graces; there was a "way" of doing things, the only way. Cotton, big cotton, gave the security that made that way possible. The conversation, however, never touched on such earthy subjects; it dealt with the classics, art and ancestors; the household god—need it be added?—was Sir Walter Scott. The narrow family circle grew narrower yet. The more they saw of things outside Natchez, the more the Stantons valued what they had at Windy Hill.

Only a few were regarded as proper Stanton matrimonial material. A successful overseer's son asked permission to call, only to receive a reproof. A Stanton of Windy Hill did not accept a "person of lesser rank." When those of appropriate status did visit, they found the girls ladies from the behavior books—winsome and arch by turn, full of gestures. Somehow it did not seem to go with the boys. Nothing happened, but the Stanton misses went on being romantic in their own way. Also they collected; the house filled with trinkets, ornaments, pictures, strings of paper flowers, whatever the girls remembered with sentimental interest. Too, they went in for "the effect." With them nothing was plain or prosaic. If a dress,

Natchez had never seen finer; an evening party, truly the most enjoyable they remembered, truly. Friends said the Stantons had a special quality—What they wished to think, they thought; what they chose to ignore, no longer existed.

The girls passed their twenties, their thirties; they grew only more girlish, more ruffled. One married; eventually there remained three, "Sis Elizabeth," oldest and most positive; "Sis Bea," delicate and blonde; "Sis Maude," the most even-tempered, in some ways the most practical. Elizabeth developed gradually into the dominant sister. A tall, stately brunette of handsome appearance, she took on almost a regal quality with the years.

When visitors arrived, the younger ones chatted politely about pleasant, harmless subjects; they had the graces of their day, the ability to say nothing with good manners. Soon it was evident, however, that "Sis Bea" and "Sis Maude" were only preparing for the main event. The guests heard a clearing of a throat; the two sisters looked up. There, at the top of the stair, waited Miss Elizabeth. Now, head high, great fan waving, she advanced downward, always in a flowing costume of deep coloring and rich trimming. At the lowest step "Sis Elizabeth" bowed slowly from the waist. "It was the arrival of the queen," a caller said. The other sisters were the ladies-in-waiting.

Then bad luck fell. Taken ill, Dr. Stanton lay helpless. During a gloomy Christmas season, the mother died; ten months later the father followed. The girls had to take up the job of running the estate. It was, of course, the tall Elizabeth who stepped forward. Getting up at dawn, she rode about the fields (side saddle, to be sure), took charge of tenants' supplies, superintended the plantation store and the cotton gin, took over timber operations and also ran the house.

For a while things held up at Windy Hill Manor, but change could not be forever halted. Through long use their land became less productive, the acres making a fraction of their former yield. Perhaps they should sell? Those who made such proposals received a look that was a reprimand. Hunching their shoulders, the sisters went back to their new tasks. Most of the tenants drifted away; the house servants disappeared, all but one or two who had nowhere else to go. Vegetable gardens, once tended by many, must now be watched by the sisters themselves; pecan groves had to be picked by Stanton hands or not at all.

So it came about that the Stanton girls took on some of the behavior of their story-book heroes. Come hell, come high water, they would stay. Rigorously they set themselves to live within the limit of their shrunken means. No new clothes, no unnecessary foods, no fripperies. The terraced gardens went untended; there could be no experts to care for that fine double line of cedars over the slope that led to Windy Hill. The house stood unpainted, unrepaired, except where the sisters could make little changes. Their fingers, long ago taught to do the artistic—picture frames and "scenes"—grew skilled at more mundane tasks.

They let it be known that Thursday was their receiving day. Those who went at other times were met by the servant, with regrets. The Stanton sisters had more serious tasks to occupy them. On Thursday, however, matters would take their old manner: "Sis Elizabeth's" grand entrance down the curving stairs, polite conversation, songs at the piano. Miss Elizabeth had a favorite, about a soldier and a girl, and she sang it with feeling, lifted eyes and tremolo. At some point during the visit a "collation" appeared—little cakes or candies, lemonade, and "Sis Bea's" famous plum-dumb. Miss Bea would smile: "You must be careful. It has a *great* effect; too much and it strikes you dumb." No records have come down that anyone passed out on the Stanton floor; it was a notoriously mild cordial.

With all her other duties, Miss Elizabeth turned out a series of books and pamphlets, romances in high style, full of intrigues and waving plumes. One, written at Windy Hill, dealt appropriately with Burr and his high doings with the virgin

Madeline. Nor did Miss Elizabeth altogether neglect her artistic bent. In the ravines about the house she found clay deposits in several shades. Breaking off sections, she spied what resembled a face, a lily, a hill-top; she went to work with file and scissors to fashion them into closer likenesses. She filled a parlor, then another with bulky works in this medium. The sisters helped, heaping shelves and mantels and floors with the curious displays. The Stantons were always filling their own world in their own way.

But things grew still worse. From time to time another room had to be boarded up; the sisters made a further curtailment. A back wing developed a leaky roof and broken wall; they shut it off and stacked up pine trees as screens. When friends glanced over there, the sisters waved casually: That part of the house was "under construction." It remained "under construction" for years, until it dropped away. In this and other instances the sisters carried things off with dignity, a certain aplomb. They were making good use of that trait a friend had observed, their ability to ignore whatever they wished.

Frequently Miss Maude, the most matter-of-fact of the three, came into town with eggs and other supplies. She fixed little bouquets and cakes and her old-time "'mice candy," sweetmeats complete to tail and tiny whiskers. Candy and flowers and eggs, all helped. But an acquaintance was at Windy Hill when an antique dealer tried to buy several pieces of furniture. "Absurd," Miss Elizabeth pronounced in bell-like tones, "I never part with my possessions." Such a sale might have solved the problem of a tax-bill, the fear of a foreclosure, but they would not consider it.

A group of former friends, visiting Natchez, once invited the sisters into town for "dinner" at a hotel. No hour was mentioned; neither side thought it necessary. The friends gathered about 12:30. By 1 p. m. the sisters had not arrived. By 1:30 the visitors had their meal, then went upstairs. A little after 3 the Stantons arrived; they gave no excuse for the delay.

The friends, deciding that the sisters had forgotten being asked for the meal, said nothing but entertained them in the room. All parted with smiles and disguised puzzlement. Only later did the friends realize that the Stantons still had their meal at the traditional plantation hour of the last century, three o'clock; they had assumed everyone else did. And they had looked forward for a long time to a great event, their first hotel dinner in years . . .

Several decades passed. With infrequent paint, and attention to the square spindle rails, the sisters managed to keep the front of Windy Hill Manor in trim. At the back, of necessity, was wear and creeping decay. Walls sagged, servant quarters fell to pieces. Lapsing momentarily from her regal attitude, Miss Elizabeth spoke of the day when "my ship comes in." "I'll make several changes," she said, her hand sweeping in a vague circle; she would also make a world trip, "seeing my various friends."

With the years "Sis Elizabeth" acquired a poise that could be terrifying. "She'd classify you with a glance," a man said. More and more she talked genealogy; for her a family tree was light reading. Almost imperiously, she asked newcomers their names; at a word she would discourse on their ancestors. Or, more terrifyingly, she would fix them with a stare. She did not know that family. . . . As her voice faded, the stranger could almost hear the iron gates slam. She traced the Stantons to the last duke, the ultimate noble. Once, pointing her fan at a Yankee guest, she informed him: "Sir, our family antedates the Christian era!"

More and more Miss Elizabeth stressed her connection with royalty. On the mantel sat a photograph of Queen Victoria. Casually Elizabeth referred to it: "My close associate, the Queen." For a time she chose not to play the piano: "Oh, I haven't touched it since the Prince was last here." (This was enigmatic. Her hearers did not know if it meant she could not play for less blue-blooded an audience; and they dared not ask which Prince.)

Princes did come. A friend brought a young Englishman, soon to inherit a title. He met Miss Bea in a garden. Catching the name, Miss Bea flushed, her pretty eyes widened, and she sank to the ground in the lowest of bows, so low she couldn't get up again. The startled Britisher leaned over, kissed her hand and simultaneously, with a determined pull, drew her to her feet. Later he said nothing had ever made him feel so important. Miss Bea is remembered for another incident showing that romance never died for these Stantons. A doctor, finding her ill, lectured mildly: "You have to take this pill, you understand?" Miss Bea, in her seventies, gave a luxurious sigh: "Oh, I so appreciate a masterful man!"

Through the years the sisters hardly changed their costume. Theirs were the old styles, puffed sleeves, wide skirts, high necks, and also earrings, feathers, flowers, the touch of powder, the hint of pomade. Even in sickness Miss Elizabeth maintained the gala touch in her attire. Too ill to get up, she once agreed to receive a guest in her room. He found her sitting up in elaborate summer dress, her medals pinned firmly, her arms dangling bracelets. She held a red feathered fan; she wore a flowered picture hat, a yard or so wide, and she extended her hand as if it were indeed a party on the lawn. It was on another day, however, that she managed her most notable exploit. A minor item of nobility was brought to her. She rose to her full height and, hand firmly against her stomach, murmured: "Ah, your Highness. Royalty meets royalty." And she explained by going back six hundred years with her charts.

Despite all their originalities, the Stanton girls remained kind people; if they thought themselves favored, they never forgot. In time of trouble they dropped their own many concerns to help others. Yet always they must act within the mold of proper Stanton behavior. It was that way in Papa's and Mama's day; it would be that way for them. An Atlantan returned home, stuttering his admiration: "I went to a house where Aaron Burr stayed—the same house, the same carriage he rode in—and the same three old ladies that hid him!"

The sisters grew older, more angular, but their spirit stayed unchanged. In recent years things improved for the estate. Oil was located near their property. Yet better times came too late; Miss Elizabeth died in 1942, at the approximate age of ninety-one. Miss Bea went at eighty-one. On one of my last visits I spent several hours with that last sister, Miss Maude. It was clear she missed her lifelong companions. Walking about the silent rooms, in the light of the kerosene lamp, we saw that steeply curved stairway, we fingered the clay sculpture over which Miss Elizabeth had worked; we touched the Pleyel piano about which the family gathered, so long ago, to sing the old songs that the world sings no longer.

Outside, in the slowly-falling dusk, Windy Hill Manor stood among the dark, shifting shadows of its trees. One of the small temple-like side wings was gone; its counterpart, with its peaked roof, huddled at the opposite end, under the protection of the porticoed main building. At the back two or three brick chimneys raised themselves forlornly out of the grass; the rooms that they had served had long since fallen. Vines clogged the old plantings, and weeds grew out of the brickwork and the clotted drains. Miss Elizabeth's boat had not come in soon enough.

Under a lean-to waited the remains of the carriage in which the sisters once drove to town. Its shaft had broken, and tendrils of green had laced themselves about the unused wheels. Down the forgotten "lover's walk" of Aaron Burr and Madeline Price we could make out the passageway near the broken terrace where the Stanton children had once played.

In the final moments of our visit Miss Maude talked in a tired voice of the family, of old ways and new ones. "It's so different now—everything." Her voice trailed off. Because there seemed little else to say, I told her: "But you've done what you wanted, Miss Maude . . ." Her eyes lifted, and she gave a hint of a smile in the lamplight: "Have I?" Miss Maude,

I remembered, had always been the "practical one," who went into the town and saw more of affairs than the other two. In other parts of the Natchez country there were many Miss Maudes, who had watched life from a distance. Miss Maude waved goodbye at the big fan-lighted door, as she and her sisters had always waved goodbye to the rest of the world.

MONTEIGNE

{II}

THE WILLIAM WHO WASN'T A SIR

Had you scoured Scotland in the 1770s, you would have had a difficult time finding a less likely subject for colonization in dangerous America than youthful William Dunbar of Thunderton House, Morayshire. On a slate-gray winter day, in a room of the towered mansion house, this frail and nervous student sat in gloomy wonder about his future.

His young contemporaries regarded William as hardly an ornament to the family name. He was the son of Sir Archibald's second marriage; the title would have to change hands more than once if it were ever to reach him. Furthermore, William had little taste for the customary family life. He passed over the constant talk of earlier Dunbars: Sir James, hereditary sheriff; Gavin, Archbishop of Glasgow, Preceptor to James V. . . . He mused, instead, over mathematics and astronomy. His scholarly conversation made those of his age titter at him. William had gone to London for advanced study, to spend a happy time investigating ochres, "sea-feathers" and other curiosities, until overwork made him ill. Now, at twenty-two, he was trying to recuperate. Even here he found only unease. The family had suffered reverses, and old letters hint of frictions.

On this particular day, William Dunbar came to a decision. For him it would be the lands across the Atlantic. When he broke the news downstairs at tea, only two at the crowded table showed an alarm that reflected their love—his mother and his favorite younger sister, the gentle Peggy. No, he assured them, he wouldn't get killed; he'd watch out. He'd already decided what he'd do; he'd trade with the Indians. Since neither he nor the rest had ever seen an Indian, this brought new argument. Whatever his mother and Peggy said, that day and afterward, William's solemn blue eyes did not change; once he had made up his mind about anything, he carried on without let-up.

At London, methodical as in all things, he used up most of his money on supplies for Indian trading. On colonial soil, he went westward to Fort Pitt, to look up John Ross, a well-placed fellow-countryman and merchant. What would Mr. Ross advise him to do with his pack of Indian supplies? Mr. Ross, hardly impressed, jerked a thumb toward the woods: Get rid of it out there as fast as he could.

For months William was gone, and then one day he turned up again at Mr. Ross' office. The merchant stared at the fine pelts; the shrewdest Indian trader he knew couldn't have done better. Thereafter William was greeted more cordially; his credit grew steadily. The Indians respected him and after some hesitation the buck-skinned woodsmen did, too. He had a way, they said, once you got him right. And William liked them, and also his surroundings. Trudging for hours, sleeping under the skies, the youth found his skinny frame filling out; in the forest stillnesses, beneath the low-hanging stars, his nerves relaxed. As he lay on his back he gazed occasionally at the constellations and remembered his former calculations.

Late one evening William went to Mr. Ross, excitement barely contained within him. He had been hearing of His Majesty's acquisition of territory on the Mississippi, and he wanted to look over the place. Mr. Ross backed him, and he started at once on the long overland journey, by land and then by flatboat. Travel-weary, sweat-marked, he halted near Baton Rouge in Louisiana, below Natchez, and sighted a prepossessing spot. He followed the Governor to Pensacola for his title to the land, and then found yet another task before him—a journey to Jamaica for slaves.

Back on his lands, everything wrong seemed to happen to Planter Dunbar, and in steady sequence. For a brief time, soberly, economically, he cleared his land, tried the early crop of indigo, which provided a dye; rice, vegetables, stave-making. Then a delegation of anxious-faced neighbors called to report a conspiracy for freedom among the blacks, with Dunbar's quarters as the center. "Judge my surprise!" he wrote in his journal. "Of what avail is kindness and good usage when rewarded by such ingratitude?" A leader, arms tied while being taken across the river, threw himself over and drowned. Three others were hanged; the rest received "lesser punishments," and so ended one rebellion of 1776. For William, the incident meant heavy loss; most of his money had been turned into Negroes.

Two years later ill fortune struck harder. On the Atlantic coast, revolutionists and Tories were shouting insult, burning houses, firing on each other. William Dunbar, though hardly a political man, wanted no truck with king-haters. But he had previously known an excitable youth, James Willing, member of a well-to-do Pennsylvania family, who had operated a store at Natchez. The sprightly fellow, who liked his drink as much as the next one, had returned to the North. Now the members of Continental Congress, hearing his tales of the prosperous colonials on the Mississippi, sent him down river, to do what he could for the cause.

Roaring with patriotism, the ebullient Captain Willing slashed right and left, apparently exceeding his instructions. The Captain showed he had a long memory for Tories—a blacklist; and high on it was William Dunbar, planter. Learning that the rebels were coming, William Dunbar fled with his slaves. His house was allowed to stand but he was "robbed of everything that could be carried away—all my wearing apparel, bed and table linen; not a shirt was left in the house—blankets, pieces of cloth, sugar, silver-ware, in short all was fish that came into their net." Yet all could not be called simple pillage; Dunbar himself gives a curious instance. About to take a Tory's property, the raider learned that the man had a partner on the American side. So he carefully divided the goods and took only the Tory half! All of which proves, if nothing more, that a civil war may be one of the cruellest. In this case, Willing's heavy-handed tactics did more damage than good for his cause. Feeling against the rebels boiled in Natchez; from Pensacola the British rushed reinforcements, and Natchez stayed loyalist.

Within a year William Dunbar's property was overrun again. Spain, which had quietly helped the American revolutionists harass the Tories, now captured the Natchez country in her own name. And this time wandering Spaniards invaded William's plantation, ripped out valuables, wrecked crops, doing a more thorough job than even the Americans. His mother, thanking the fates that he stayed alive in the barbaric colony, sent her regrets and also some new shirts.

William had long been hearing about Natchez. Years earlier he had acquired land a few miles out of town. Now he moved there, and never regretted the transfer. The brown soil—a superb stretch that undulated to the blue horizon—was untouched territory to which he quickly gave a name, The Forest. As if fate had been awaiting this change, William's career blossomed. He surprised his less imaginative neighbors when, scouting about the hills near the river, he found ochre on his estate and soon was shipping it to Massachusetts.

He went further. Getting hold of an early cotton gin, he tinkered with it until he had made his own version; it would be used for decades in this region. With a frown, he watched the crude packing of the crop in bags or by a laboriously-operated lever; he came forth with a screw-press, to confine the material in a much smaller space. For generations the river people followed his method. Meanwhile, cotton seed was being burned or dragged off to rot at the swamp border. William went to work to make oil from it. He did not live to see his scheme perfected; today the processing of the seed is an industry running into the millions. From time to time he looked farther afield. How he would like to measure this or that plant, study the behavior of a fiber under heat. His scientific mind leaped ahead, speculating, asking questions. Usually he put temptation aside. In that direction lay what interested him most in life; but here his duty waited.

William's thin form filled out; the hollows in his cheeks were lost in emerging jowls. After so many anti-climaxes, life looked more certain to him. He wrote home asking his beloved sister Peggy to join him. He sent a purse, to "fit her out genteelly." Peggy set sail, and William waited several months. He sent word home, and the answer returned: Hadn't Peggy arrived a long time ago? For months he and his mother, Lady Anne, waited anxiously. Nothing was ever heard of the ship. In a letter to William, the mother expressed trust that God would "indulge me in letting me see you before I leave this world." That indulgence was denied her. With her death, his last close ties to Scotland were gone.

One bright afternoon a courier thrust a heavy envelope into his hand. Another death had occurred in the family; now no one stood between him and the title. His early training, the family tradition inclined him toward the usual course. And almost certainly it would be glorious to return now, richer than anyone for miles around. But William shook his head. The story goes that he added a comment: He wouldn't exchange all Scotland for his thick Mississippi land. So the title went to a nephew. As a matter of fact The Forest, William's plantation, gave as fine a yield as almost any feudal estate he knew. Henceforth in Mississippi he would often be described as "Sir William," though never by himself.

Meanwhile he had entered another experiment, matrimony, with a widow who was hardly less methodic than William himself. A contemporary called Dinah Clark, she was "a pattern for imitation." A likeness indicates a small-eyed, thin-featured woman with tight curls and a sharp, or perhaps merely precise, expression. Before the marriage he signed away his property interest in her estate, in favor of the sons of her first marriage. The hints of firmness are reinforced by a little tale. Going to his Baton Rouge plantation for a few days, William wrote his Dinah promptly about a party he had held, assuring her it had been very respectable; only a few had to be carried away from the table!

He could, incidentally, afford to remain away from his main property whenever he wished. Dinah, a lady ahead of her time in several respects, could supervise his Forest plantation as well as any man. The couple were congenial in other ways; together they produced eleven children.

The Spanish rulers of Natchez, observing William's skill, made him their official surveyor. He lived happily under the dons; and then, in the late 1700s, this man who had once sworn at the American rebels, learned that the new country was about to take Natchez. But much had happened since that earlier time, and now there was no bitterness in William Dunbar's heart. He accepted the Spaniards' appointment as their surveyor in the tracing of the borderline between Natchez and Spanish Louisiana to the South. For three months he struggled through a terrain that resembled glue. In one of the most richly-colored narrations of the day, he described how the high water had receded along the river, leaving the surface squirming with life:

"Objects presented themselves at every step in this animated hot bed, not of those kinds which invite and delight the view of the inquisitive naturalist; but of the most disgusting forms and noxious kinds. A few were the serpents of the waters, frequently entwined in clusters to the number of several hundreds, a vast variety of toads, frogs, including the bull-frog, and the thundering crocodile, all of hideous forms." In this season of perfervid heat, thickets to each side were "impenetrable to the stoutest breeze; the ardent beams, striking directly into this narrow passage, frequently aided by the reflection of the hills, excited a degree of heat which might be literally said to scorch." No air circulated; the thermometer showed 120 degrees. To get relief workmen frequently threw themselves into the shade of thicket or climbed the first height, "there to inhale greedily the salubrious vapors of the reviving gale."

Under conditions of staggering difficulty, they finally cleared a strip of wild dry cane, sixty feet wide. They set it ablaze and stood back to watch:

"It was a most astonishing line of fire, the flames ascending to the tops of the highest trees and spreading for miles . . . The continual explosions of rarified air from the hollow cane resembled the re-echoed discharges of innumerable platoons of musketry and mocked every idea that could be formed of the effect produced by the conflict of the most formidable armies. The scene was truly grand, aweful and majestic."

William Dunbar also took time to describe "tygers," eight feet long, that prowled the Natchez forests; turtles weighing a hundred pounds, and alligators, which went torpid in cold weather and "may then be cut to pieces with an axe without their exhibiting any powers of motion." For now, spreading himself a little, he could indulge his concern with such natural wonders without feeling he was neglecting his more practical tasks. More than that, in this day of change for the Natchezians, William found himself in a totally unexpected position. The rest of America, its interest suddenly piqued, wanted to know all about this remarkable lower river valley; and he was able to tell about it as none other could. President Jefferson, faced with the strong possibility that Congress would reject his Louisiana Purchase, needed every bit of data to back up his case; Jefferson got in touch with him, and a life-long friendship began. Celebrated scientists wrote him for information and suggested inquiries; scientific journals solicited his contributions. From comparative obscurity he had come suddenly to renown.

And the intent naturalist, who had been forced for most of his life to pass over his greatest interests, was able at last to indulge them. He had the leisure to inquire, to speculate in ways that he had always wanted. He ranged far and wide, at the edges of the cotton fields, about the bluffs, describing the dimly-known reaches of his region. At The Forest he put up a laboratory, a scientific den. He sent abroad for microscopes, chronometers, a "six-foot Gregorian reflecting telescope with six magnifying powers from 110 to 550 times." Few, having turned their backs upon the matter that most appeals to them, enjoy the opportunity to return to it, and then to find their same early zest. To William Dunbar came that rare chance.

He studied the sign language of the Indians, and tried to connect it with that of the Chinese. He dug up fossil bones along the river, measured, sketched and described them. He analyzed the peculiar soil formations and offered theories of the way the Mississippi Valley had developed. He studied hurricanes, Indian religions, New World sunsets, the lift and fall of the river. Meanwhile he pressed friends into service; they must hunt curious plants for him, bring him rock crystals, ferns with peculiar coloration, lizards, birds, snake-rattles. He made the first thorough weather observations in the river valley—a study that editors commended as a model for the world.

Isolated by thousands of miles from the great centers, William Dunbar worked away, year by year, a pioneer. He lacked instruments he could have obtained in an hour in London, Paris, New York; even more he lacked access to others who might share his concerns. Yet he did not feel himself alone, but one of a band of seekers around the globe. Observing an eclipse of the sun, he recorded his eager emotions:

"The moment approached, and reflecting that this eclipse was to be seen all over Europe and North America, I conceived that all the zealous astronomers of both worlds were then looking with me at the great luminary and center of our system. I kept my eye riveted with an anxiety known only to astronomers; with my watch at my ear, I attended to the most doubtful appearances which my perturbation perhaps presented to the eye, and upon every alarm began to count the beats that I might not lose the first instant of the impression. . . ."

Other honors piled upon him. He was called upon to preside as a judge, to serve in the legislature, to accept difficult posts fitting to few of his contemporaries. Nothing, however, meant as much to William Dunbar as his recognition in science. Jefferson named him in 1804 to take a leading role in one of the first American expeditions of inquiry, to the vicinity of Hot Springs. After that he headed a party pioneering in the Red River vicinity, and returned to tell of its breath-taking sights, giant plants, fanged animals, and strange-tasting mineral waters.

Some years before the latter expedition, William agreed with the business-like Dinah that it was time to replace their plain home at The Forest with a bigger one. Promising to remain closer to his acres, he supervised an extensive garden, a copy of Alexander Pope's in England. They saw the workmen finish the walls on the new house, the lines of pillars that they wanted on the four sides, the rails of the second story gallery. Then one day William was stricken. At sixty-one, he could look back briefly on a career that had been crowded. So much had happened since that day when he stared at an uncertain future in the family home at Morayshire. He died content.

Dinah Dunbar retired for a time, then took up her life again. First the new Forest home must be finished; she saw that the men worked at least as hard as they would have done for William Dunbar. She supervised the installation of the dormer windows, small peaked openings in the roof, the topping of the house with a captain's walk from which Dinah would watch her spreading lands. It was a magnificent pile that she finally surveyed from the distance. Those great columns faced in four directions, the sun catching the white balustrade above the roofline, the boxwood of the garden providing a richly formal design to the sides. Here the widow knew good years, watching her estate prosper, her children marry well.

---※⦂※---

In this case, like father, like grandson; or, rather, grand-son-in-law. At the same time "Sir William" lay dying, John C. Jenkins was born in Pennsylvania, son of a well-to-do iron manufacturer. Twenty-three years later, receiving a medical degree with honors, he planned to enter a doctor's career. But down in the river country, at Pinckneyville, John had a bachelor uncle, who combined medicine with lucrative plantation owning. Dr. John A. Carmichael sent a note explaining that he was growing old, his sight failing; would his favorite nephew come there, and help him in his last days?

The offer was hard to resist. It would mean deferring his own practice, for which he had long planned; but it need not be forever. Arriving, John found matters not exactly as he had anticipated. He would have little chance to treat even his uncle's patients; the Carmichael medical practice had run a poor second to cotton. There was so much money in the crop, anyone who could catch hold of King Cotton's coat-tails did so. The uncle's holdings made the young Pennsylvanian pause; the scale of affairs took the young man aback. He had much to learn, too, about Uncle Carmichael himself. That worthy, always a salty individualist, had turned into a crochety codger, on good terms with practically nobody. Half of Natchez was betting that sooner or later Uncle and John would get into a shouting rage, the way Uncle and everyone else did, and the young man would stamp off in a fury. But John, an adjustable fellow, wrote home that he had familiarized himself with Uncle's "peculiarities of disposition" and, after an initial effort or two, "acquired a tact in getting along with him that none else possessed."

The late 1830s went easily for John—a smattering of medical cases, trips about the plantations for his uncle, dinners and dancing with the Mississippi girls. A slim and handsome youth, with a quiet way about him, John was welcome at all the estates. (It need not be pointed out that he qualified as a marriage prize.)

After a while the querulous uncle was passing decisions to him; whether he planned it or not, John received a thorough training in cotton. Then the uncle died; and for John there came a chill awakening. The estate *was* vast, but it had so many strings attached that John felt himself caught in a mesh. Bad times had come; cotton's markets had dropped; the uncle's factors in New Orleans had failed. Worse, the uncle had been guardian for several heirs of another estate; when their money went, he was held responsible. Bills totaling hundreds of thousands piled up, and everybody pressed John Jenkins. A few sued, or threatened suit. To liquidate, selling heavy properties on a sagging market—that would mean tossing a fortune out of the window. John had a little of the family temper; the harder the rest pushed him, the hotter he felt. He'd be damned if he gave in. For better or worse, he was now rooted by the Mississippi, and his hope of doctoring had to be put aside again.

Another attraction, in skirts, probably helped keep John in the South. He had visited at the many-columned Forest; in the boxwood-bordered garden he met a soft-voiced, reticent girl whose unusual shyness won him. It took many months before the easy-going John was able to draw out Annis Dunbar, grand-daughter of William. They became engaged and, depression or no depression, the Dunbars saw that the union was launched in flush style.

Annis' father wrote his impressions of the evening. The Forest was alight. At the front gate guests rode beneath an evergreen arch, illuminated with torches; the lines of pillars had been festooned, lighted with candles and covered with "gimcracks," as the inexact male observer put it. The Negroes, dressed for the occasion, sang songs as the guests milled about the drawing room, the gallery and entrance hall with its sideboard loaded with drinkables for the men. The crowd grew so big there was no room for the Negro chorus, and it was sent back to the quarters. As for the supper table, the father declared he would not pretend to describe it, then went on to do so. Three cakes stood four or five feet high, with dozens of smaller ones to match. "When I first looked, I felt the creepers in my back, and the hair of my wig stood upon end." They used up two hundred and twenty-five pounds of ice, buckets of lemonade "disappeared in a twinkling," champagne "went off in a flash." To make things perfect, the minister held a "short and neat" ceremony.

The marriage proved notably successful; the couple were pointed out to roistering town bucks as an object lesson. But the amiable John had a task before him, the retrieving of a broken estate; and from the start he applied himself. A tract of land, close to Natchez itself, caught the couple's eye; it had formed part of a grant to "Sir William" from the Spaniards. Here John and Annis moved, naming it Elgin after a Dunbar holding in Scotland. It had a small wooden house, a former overseer's property. It was there that Annis set up housekeeping while John launched a kind of agriculture that neighbors called quirky.

By this time the lower South was in the grasp of its single crop; everything for cotton, practically nothing for anything else. The planters imported meat, leather, wooden implements, even corn, sometimes. If it turned out to be a good cotton year, every inch of ground would mean a golden return; and who could tell when it wouldn't be good? John Jenkins had different plans. For several seasons he had been puzzling over the wisdom of his uncle's methods. For the first time he could put his opinions to the test.

He had never lost the scientific viewpoint of his student years. He took the word of neither friend nor enemy about a plant or a planting scheme. Reading widely, he worked on new crops, new varieties of old ones, improvements of the favorites. He raised stock, fruits, nuts, anything growers attempted in other regions. To the neighbors' amusement, he

KING'S TAVERN
A Haven at the End of a Bloody Trail

GUY F. BERNARD

NATCHEZ TRACE
It Saw Murder, Torture, Death in the Dark

GUY F. BERNARD

AARON BURR OAKS
They Tried Him, and Missed

GUY F. BERNARD

insisted that even Mississippi and Louisiana soil was not inexhaustible; it needed to be renewed at intervals, fertilized, allowed to lie fallow. He had a balanced production, a range of undertakings, all going at once, that few would attempt.

John grew convinced that Natchez could become an important fruit-growing center. Nothing must be left to chance. He set aside fields, divided and subdivided, numbered every tree, kept accounts of age and production and history. He went in for tree grafting—pear on quince, apricot on peach, cherry on wild cherry, making himself a pre-Burbank of the South. Complications developed; in a place so fertile, all things thrived too easily, the parasites keeping directly behind the main plants, sometimes ahead. Out of it all, by trial and error and ceaseless recording, he produced new growths fitted to a new scene, more succulent than the originals. From Elgin's acres came wagonloads of buttery pears, massive apples, plums, apricots, raspberries. One of his prides, a pear-quince, weighed a pound and a half.

For months after the growing seasons, his guests stared as Annis had the servants bring in platters of polished fruits. It was not long before he speculated about marketing his goods outside Natchez. Making a steamboat trip to New York, he brought aboard baskets of his pears, full-grown, beginning to ripen. On the third day out, he had the fruit placed in the vessel's icebox. Arriving, he found them perfect. That proved ice shipments were feasible! Since Natchez fruit matured nearly two months ahead of Eastern varieties, they would be on the market before frost and snow had ended. This was the 1840s; he was too far in advance of his day. In later periods, men would make fortunes from schemes like his.

Meanwhile, at home, callers inspecting his cellars bumped heads against dim objects hanging on strings. They turned out to be pears. Picking the fruit and placing it in the cellar to ripen, John found it rotting. The next year he tried depositing it on cotton layers; still it went bad. Nobody could tell him why. Rubbing his cheek, he wondered if it were the contact with other surfaces that caused the trouble; and so, laboriously, he, Annis and the servants went to work, stringing the pears, one by one. The plan worked.

By this time John and Annis had put up their white Elgin house. About the original overseer's place, they constructed a wide, rambling building, a model of simple good taste. He quoted a Natchez wag: "The old house looked like an amen at the end of a long prayer." Two-storied, the building had galleries above and below, with lines of slender columns, hand-cut, that have remained for more than a hundred years. Windows, opening on the porch, had "gib doors" below, opening in two to let the breezes sweep through. Inside, Annis installed porcelain door knobs, carved furniture, and an object of long admiration, a lyre-shaped punkah—"keep people cool and run the flies off."

From a slight slope Elgin looked out upon acres of orchards, the laboratory and workshop of John Jenkins, and some ten miles of curving walks among the plantings. Tall cedars and cherry laurels outlined the main passages, with secluded alleyways of green growth between them. Near the house stood Annis' ornamental plantings, latticed summer houses, white like the house, and clusters of dark-leafed camellia trees, their broad red blossoms spotting it in the spring. All about spread the ordered perfection of the master grower, the seemingly endless lines of glossy-fruited trees.

His ingenuity and determination paid well. He counted nearly fifty-five hundred acres in four plantations: River Place, Eagle Bottom, Stock Farm, Elgin—the last his smallest, the center of his trials and errors. For a long time, however, he had to turn much of his gains to his uncle's creditors and to relatives. Regularly he groaned in discouragement. Thirteen years after his uncle's death he was writing: "I am not yet out of debt by a 'long shot.'" In bad years he grew as anxious as any around him: "December, 1844. Cotton failing. Worse and worse. What is to become of the cotton planter?" But when things turned good, they were very good. In one year he counted a profit of $45,000. And eventually he had worked himself free.

His love for Annis appeared to gain. In 1852, when she was visiting in the North, he remembered that festooned earlier evening at The Forest. He made an entry in his journal: "This day brings with it the most delightful and beautiful associations, as it is the anniversary of my wedding—which important epoch in my life happened just thirteen years ago. How many happy years, yet it seems but yesterday." Spending most of the day thinking of Annis, he suddenly worried that her funds might have run low; he jumped into his carriage and hurried to town, where he sent her a remittance. Home again, he passed the rest of the day in his room, omitting dinner, "reading over the burning notes which I wrote my bride before our marriage and subsequently."

As time went on, John Jenkins had to use some of his earlier medical training. Natchez suffered repeatedly from yellow fever and cholera; as a river port it received frequent contamination, and in the nearby swamps, dim and heavy with vegetable decay, death was bred with the seasons. Again and again his journal tells of his frantic efforts to check plagues that ran through his servants' quarters. Terror-stricken Negroes fled to the woods to die; or they fell writhing to the floor of their cabins, and a cry went out for him. He describes the sadness that struck Elgin when "our dear old Mammy Fanny" died, and the way one of their four children distressed the family by her long-continued grief, "stealing off to cry alone at the grave."

The terror grew worse: "My neighbor, Colonel Bingaman, only one mile in direct line North, lost 27 of his best hands" ... "My loss is severe since December, over 30 souls" ... "Dr. Duncan up to this time has lost 133, and every crop in 'Stack Island Reach,' where he usually makes between three and four thousand bales." He relates his frantic efforts, the rubbing of the wracked bodies, application of hot bricks or bottles filled with boiling water, the use of nauseous brews of pepper, camphor, calomel and peppermint. "The wretched quarter dogs kept up all night a melancholy howling. The atmosphere is heavy. It is impossible to eat. We keep our strength up with brandy burnt in spices. It is a good preventive; keeps stomach and bowels warm, and brandy does not affect the head." The epidemic ended, and John Jenkins returned with relief to his planting.

Several years passed and now, in 1855, a whisper ran through the region. Yellow fever had returned. Out in the country, John Jenkins believed his family safe, until a servant came with the news that his slaves were dropping over in the quarters. John hurried to prescribe, sending meanwhile for his regular doctor. Then Annis fell ill, the delicate Annis whom he had always watched with care. Day by day, John Jenkins remained at her side, noting her symptoms, speeding the servants with messages for the doctor whenever she seemed worse. Down in New Orleans, they knew of a nurse with special competence; the steamboat captain, a friend, promised to break a record to get her here. One of their sons, John, was stricken; the child asked the father not to tell Annis, so that she would rest more easily. But by now the mother lay in screaming delirium, calling to her husband for help. "God seemed to endow me with superhuman powers, for I never slept or scarcely sat down from the first moment of her attack." On Sunday, the nurse from New Orleans arrived, too late.

The haggard man had more to bear. In the next room his son John was crying for his dead mother; and other members of the household were falling sick. "I have had but little rest for the past twenty days and nights, being unable yet to sleep for any length of time." One day he went to his desk and hurriedly wrote out several documents. A day or so later he, too, dragged himself to his bed. A little more than a week after his wife, John was dead. He had suspected what was coming for him; he had managed to finish his will, and leave instructions about his overseers, fences and crop conditions.

His life, like that of William Dunbar, had worked out differently from the way he had planned it. He also had given up the thing which he most wanted, for what it seemed best to do. But he had found compensations, and also happiness.

The family looked after their four small children, and the Jenkinses stayed at Elgin until 1914. In recent years it has come into the possession of Mrs. W. S. R. Beane. Soon after their arrival, the Beanes, inspecting the cellar, saw several peculiar objects hanging there. Much later they identified them —the remains of several fruits that Dr. Jenkins had tied to strings decades ago. They had shriveled in the furnace fumes, to become mummies of pears.

Most of the Jenkins' orchards and ten miles of ornamented walks have disappeared, though remnants hang on. A weedy rectangle marks the location of the ancient laboratory. Yet the house itself, placid, home-like Elgin, has a glow in the late afternoon that seems timeless. The camellia bushes drop their red blossoms, one by one, upon the soft earth. The comfortable points of light from within make Elgin look much as it did when the early Dunbars and Jenkins walked about its parlors. A final reminder of the handsome John Jenkins is there, say some—his ghost. The Negroes maintain that, as they come past the entrance gate at dusk, there he sits. He's always real polite. Just setting, his head bowing and saying how-do, how's things?

Meanwhile the more ornate Forest has gone. The Dunbars enjoyed the use of it for years, until a bitter winter day when the slaves were clearing the heavy chimneys. Downstairs at breakfast, the family heard cries; a wall had caught fire. In the stiff wind the flames darted quickly to curtain and wall hanging. The circular stairway between the floors went quickly, cutting off the second floor with the bulk of the Dunbar possessions, furniture, portraits, jewels. The family watched helplessly, while the walls blackened, then collapsed. There remained only those columns on the four sides, their silhouettes above the smoking debris.

A century after they were erected, most of the brick pillars are there, stripped of their stucco covering, like bones of the great house, rising out of grass and weeds. They stand in futile challenge to time, seemingly hanging on for eternity. A few feet away are the remnants of the old plantings, relics of box hedges in that design taken from a British garden. Two wooden-sided buildings huddle close to the ground, beneath the lines of the columns, now stark against the clouds. From their tops grow weeds, and in them birds build nests. Between two of them, the modern generation has erected a roof, creating a garage. Found: a use for useless columns. At the borders, the trees that gave the plantation its original name are moving back, reclaiming what William Dunbar took from the wilderness.

THE FOREST

III

BLOOD ON THE NATCHEZ TRACE

A NARROW flight of brick steps leads upwards from the sidewalk. In the steady sunlight they are warm to the touch. They have crumbled at the corners and in the middle of each step the feet of men and women, long dead, have worn a semicircular depression. An iron gate that creaks as it swings opens on the little garden of the tavern-house. A bricked passage curves to the side, past a bent English myrtle, a wild peach in bright, casual bloom. In this shaded spot the borders of brick carry a soft green mold, a film of the years. And there, just ahead, stand the weather-worn walls of the tavern.

At first glance it appears smaller than it is. That is so because streets have been cut close to it, telephone poles installed, and later buildings have come to hem it in. Despite all of that, the tavern maintains its identity. It suggests a primitive blockhouse, a heavy, compact place first created as a protection against savage marauders. Half-brick, half-timber, it has a changeless look, in keeping with its rank as the oldest or one of the oldest buildings in the Natchez country. "King's Tavern," most people call it, though it has had several names. But today, as earlier, it stands as the house at the end of the Natchez Trace.

To it came the sweat-streaked travelers who had survived weeks of exhausting travel over the land route that connected

Natchez with the rest of North America. Here they met others, and refreshed by their stay, made ready to face the unknown along the line of movement that was one of the most risky on the continent. To venture along the Trace was to journey with darkness and death. For five hundred miles the passageway twisted like a slack thread around matted forest, broken valley and swamp that could not be skirted. From Natchez the line went generally northeast, between the Big Black and Pearl rivers, across the Tombigbee to the Tennessee not far from Muscle Shoals. To the North, at Nashville, the Trace joined the heavily traveled passageways to the rest of the country. In that long stretch between the two points lurked hazards of wilderness, animal and man.

For a time most of the traffic on the Trace went northeast; men used the Mississippi and its tributaries whenever they could for their southward journey. Flatboatmen, going home, were among the earliest of its patrons. As years passed, however, the Trace came into use in both directions.

Gradually crude taverns or "stands" were put up at irregular intervals. A man might hope to reach one every few nights and share the greasy food, soggy cots or other unpalatable facilities, also running the risk of being robbed while he slept. Many preferred to rest in the open, burying their money in the ground, keeping a gun under their arms, lighting fires to ward off wild animals. They had to fight the weather continually. Floods that could turn creeks into fatal torrents, or change low spots into bogs in which horses were caught so tightly that they could never escape, were commonplace. They had to take the chances that go with such isolation. Hundreds died of exposure.

But the great hazard of the Trace, early and late, was the one that walked on two feet. This was the land of the Choctaw and Chickasaw. A drunken red man might tomahawk a cotton grower with a likely horse, or a flatboatman with a gaudy prize. The experienced, however, watched for other white men. These thrived on organized plunder and carefully planned murder. Here was a trail of wealth, a magnet for those who wanted money by the quickest means—knife or gun.

Month after month men disappeared along the Trace. If nothing further was heard of a well-known individual, it was taken for granted that the bandits had gotten him. Meriwether Lewis, the explorer, was only one of uncounted thousands who met death by treachery in their travel over the passage. Through the years skeletons washed to the surface from shallow graves; or hunting parties came upon nameless corpses, rotting at the side of dried bogs. The finders speculated as to which of the outlaws had done it, then went about their business.

Toward King's Tavern of Natchez moved witnesses and near-victims, bearing tales of terror and ambush in the forest. Tossing their reins to Negro attendants, they walked through the garden at the side to the gallery. They beheld a place sturdy and unadorned. Located on a slight hill outside the town, it stood flush with the ground, a challenge to the elements. The lower bricked floor led to a second level of wood with a narrow porch, wooden-railed, and slim wooden posts. Above, a third, smaller story sat like a lookout.

Its origin is uncertain. Records traced by Mrs. Edith Wyatt Moore show it standing before 1789, during the Spanish regime. In that year the dons granted a square of grounds and its buildings to "Ricardo King," a Yankee from Long Island, whose family gave its name to the Kingston settlement outside Natchez. None of the Kings had a better source of income than Richard, or a more durable property.

Inside, guests discovered everything in massive style—thick beams, wooden pegs instead of nails, small doors and windows in the early form, every inch of space put to use. On the upper floors were private rooms; to them the ladies might gain entry along the garden stairway without risking the rougher environment below. Downstairs, however, waited the real life of the tavern. A narrow side door had been cut into the brick wall to give townspeople and male travelers quick entry into that vital chamber, the taproom. There and in the kitchen, a room with an open fireplace occupying practically a whole wall, the seeker found good cheer—a hum of quick activity, and all the news of the hour.

Year after year, tankard in hand, gaunt new arrivals sat about this taproom, to tell the latest chronicles of outrage and savagery on the Trace—the stories of the Harpes and Mason, and Murrell the daring.

At the head of the grim procession strode Little (Wiley) Harpe and his brother Big (Micajah) Harpe, a pair of twisted killers who disgusted even their allies in crime. Black-eyed, black-visaged men, they went about with a scowl, and murder in their minds. Originally from North Carolina, they were sons of a Tory who had known the bitterness of his barn-burning neighbors. Once, discussing George Washington with an acquaintance, the older brother said: "That's a brave and good man, but a mighty rebel against the King."

The name of Harpe acquired fame all along the Trace, from the Tennessee Valley to the Natchez bluffs. Sometime in the 1790s Kentucky and Tennessee began to hear about the pair. With their two women, whom they seemed to interchange when the mood struck, they joined a band of outlaw Indians in killing, stealing horses and firing farm-houses. From the start the Harpes used to take lives for the sheer delight of it—the gurgling of blood in the throat, the high whine of a trussed-up prisoner as the knives dug into his abdomen.

Settling in Knoxville, the couples operated a farm as a blind. "Little Harpe" married a preacher's daughter, thus creating a larger stock-pile of femininity for the two men. (All three ladies were enciente and none ever figured out the tangled question of respective fatherhood.) Once, when the boys went in for rather too obvious horse- and hog-taking, they had to escape with a band of neighbors after them; but not before they had killed one of the citizens. He was later discovered in the water, his stomach slashed open, contents removed and the hole filled with stones. The Harpes moved from one state to the next, doing their stint of killing as they went. Captured, they escaped but left their three women with three babies. The trio of ladies told tearsome yarns to the lay public, which was so touched it befriended them and contributed funds. Then the three women slipped away to join their men.

All of them turned up at a popular gathering place for highwaymen, Cave-in-Rock on the Ohio. For a time the Harpes did well enough in the thieves' community, helping prey on parties of river men; but then it became too evident that they were revolting fellows. They wallowed in murder for murder's sake; they stood above their victims for hours, mouths parted in fascination at each detail of suffering, as they used knives to rip out organs, or chopped off one finger, then another, or thrust sharpened bits of wood into the eyes. . . .

An incident is told of a little surprise which the brothers arranged for their confederates, who were lounging below a cliff. Catching hold of a non-professional, the Harpes stripped him, lashed him tightly to the back of a horse and forced it off the embankment. The bandits stared up to see the steed pawing helplessly at the air, the man thrashing about; then they heard screams, a heavy crunch, and horse and rider were in their death agonies. Again, the Harpes came upon a rural couple atop a hill. Without a sound, they leaped forward and kicked them off. All this was entirely too much of a good thing, and the more conventional outlaws ran the Harpes away.

Barely disturbed, the brothers moved on, gouging and slashing. They also indulged in child-killing. They were known to have cut a small girl to inch-long bits. And once, Big Harpe, exasperated at the crying of his own baby, caught it by the heels and bashed the skull against a tree, till it "burst into a dozen pieces." Later he said that of all his homicides, he really regretted that one.

The death of a confederate fixed Big Harpe's doom. Going to a friend, the grim brothers were given a bed next to a mild-mannered surveyor. The surveyor snored; angered, they crushed his head. Coming down to breakfast with fine appetite, the Harpes told the mother they would mind her baby in its cradle if she hurried the food along. The child became so quiet that the matron returned to look, and found they had slashed the throat. They proceeded to kill her with the same butcher knife and then set the house afire. Authorities offered a heavy reward; a vigilante committee overtook Big Harpe, while the little one escaped. The older man, shot, lay dying; but he took too long, and one chronicler, Robert Coates, ends the tale:

Big Harpe, his black eyes wide open, watched the mate of the woman he had murdered. Hate clouded the fellow's face. He took up the knife that had been used on his wife and child, moved slowly toward Harpe and took him by the hair of his head. Harpe, unable to do anything but move his fingers in feeble protest, felt the husband draw the knife slowly across the back of his neck, cutting to the bone. Blood spurted as from a small fountain, but the husband dug on. As the man reached around to the front, Harpe stared him "full in the face, with a grim and fiendish countenance, and exclaimed 'You're a God-damned rough butcher, but cut on and be damned!'" The man sank his knive into the front of the neck, again cutting to the bone, and completed the circle. Then he wrung off the head, as a good butcher would do, and held up the dripping thing for all to see. Even then, the eyes were open and the twisted mouth seemed to be cursing them. The head was then stuck in the fork of a tree.

"Little Harpe" disappeared, but destiny drew him to Natchez. One day, about the beginning of the nineteenth century, Joseph Dunbar Shields saw three men making a show of pricing goods among the flatboatmen in town. The smallest whispered: "Captain, there's geese worth picking down there." His friend turned: "Hold your tongue, Little Harpe. You're everlastingly blabbing. I'll have to mash your mouth for you yet, you internal villain!" ("Internal" is Judge Shields' word for it.) Within two months all Natchez knew that a new, well-integrated band of gangsters had settled on the Trace.

The younger Harpe was only a member, controlled by the leader, Sam Mason. Here was an enigmatic individual, a careful thief of good birth, who generally operated by efficient planning rather than bloody impulse. A Virginian, he had served honorably in the Continental Army. Some claimed him kin to a signer of the Declaration of Independence. A strapping fellow with a gift of convincing speech, he had a snaggle-tooth that gave him a slightly sinister look. Winning too great a celebrity in other parts, he had moved down toward Natchez.

Introducing less wasteful methods than his predecessors, Mason worked through spies and agents. In Natchez he had a representative whose identity went unsuspected for years. Regarded as an honest merchant, Anthony Glass was seen often at King's Tavern and other popular places, talking trade over a drink. He was a fence, who kept runners ready, to speed tidings of impending movements to listening ears.

Growing bolder with success, the gang frequently identified themselves as "Mason's Men." Several times when they killed a man, they scrawled cards in his gore, proclaiming the work to be theirs. Mason enjoyed confronting an individual in the forest, announcing who he was and watching the victim tremble; not infrequently he would let him escape in a shower of bullets. A mail rider told how he often came upon the long-toothed Mason, who talked frankly of his calling. A "fine looking man, rather modest and unassuming ... he was always anxious to hear what they said of him." During these years the blood-hungry Little Harpe stayed more or less quiet. Occasionally he was able to catch a wretch and cut him in half, or chop off hands and feet; but usually he was restrained. He was biding his time, planning bigger things.

Along the river just outside Natchez, Mason had his eye on a point of new operation—a peculiar, to some awesome, phenomenon called "The Devil's Punchbowl." Far in the past, a great cup-shaped hole, about five hundred feet wide, had formed in the soft earth of the river bluffs. Slowly it seemed to widen, as gullies formed along its sides and rows of trees hurtled into its depths. Thickly grown, it provided a dim, almost impenetrable place of concealment. Natives thought a heavy meteor might once have plummeted here, sinking into the earth. Steamboat men claimed that their compasses behaved crazily when they passed.

Inevitably the "Punchbowl" became a spot to be gossiped about, and feared. Hundreds were certain the vicinity contained buried gold; at intervals men with picks and shovels climbed warily about it. Early Spanish and French pirates were supposed to have secreted their treasures in the depths. Daring runaway slaves headed there and hid for days. Through the years men who had reason to dodge their fellows headed to the "Punchbowl."

By this time Sam Mason went to work. Here he established several intelligent assistants and coached them. At the water's edge they posed as farmers, holding up produce for the flatboatmen. Or one might cry piteously for help, saying he was being beaten to death. Sometimes a girl was assigned to the task; nothing stirred folks like the shriek of a female. Once the fools stepped on shore, a few hatchet strokes did the rest. The naked bodies were hauled to the edge of the Bowl and sent hurtling down. Sometimes Mason's men would start a couple of them moving at the same time, and bet which corpse would hit first. For years the Masonites slipped in and out of the Punchbowl.

Early in 1801 Colonel Joshua Baker and friends left Natchez after a big sale of produce. Along a creek four men confronted and robbed them. The take was twenty-five hundred dollars, plus horses and equipment. Showing remarkable daring, Mason and his son turned up in Natchez not long afterward, assuming the roles of cotton growers. A member of the Baker party pointed a finger: "That's them!" Thrown into jail, the two Masons were sentenced to twelve hours in the pillory and a flogging of thirty-nine lashes. (A remarkably light sentence.) As he sat through his public exposure, the fang-toothed man shook with rage and managed a striking imitation of rectitude. A witness could "never forget their cries of 'Innocent,' at every blow of the cowhide which tore the flesh from their quivering limbs; and until the last lash was given they shrieked the same despairing cry of 'Innocent,' 'Innocent!'" Freed, the pair got drunk, stripped themselves and rode through the town, yelling like Indians, making threats of vengeance.

In the following year Mason's operations became a general scandal, the subject of comment in many states. Something had to be done. Governor Claiborne issued a proclamation against the "pirates" and "desperate villains" and offered a reward. The region was stirred, militia joined the search, but the gang escaped to Spanish land upriver. Taken at New Madrid, they managed to blast their way out. Thus far Mason had eluded practically everything. He had not, however, reckoned on betrayal from within. And the traitor turned out to be the brooding Little Harpe. He kept in mind the reward for Mason, and finding himself alone with the master and another party member, he whispered his scheme. Pouncing upon the sleeping Mason, the pair sank a tomahawk in his head. Little Harpe would have preferred a subtler method. Still, better this than nothing. They sliced off the head so that they could prove Mason was dead, and plastered it in blue river clay for preservation.

Riding into the town of Washington, presenting themselves

as honest farmers, the pair handed up the grisly relic. Despite the clay, the head had not remained entirely fresh. Many were dubious that it was Mason; besides, the public treasury was bare. The gentlemen must wait. They waited too long. From a crowd a barkeep stepped up: "That's Little Harpe himself!" The barman had had a horse stolen by the villain; look, he recognized his horse! Yet this did not seem a full identification, until a riverboatman moved forward. He knew how to make sure. Years ago he had gotten into a scrape with Little Harpe and stuck a knife into his chest. If this was Harpe, they'd find a scar under his left nipple!

The prisoner bared his teeth: They'd better keep their hands off him. The mob pushed closer. He struggled as two sheriff's assistants ripped his shirt off. For a moment they made out no mark on the black, matted chest. Then the sheriff pushed aside the hair, and there was a thin white scar. Early in 1804, near Springfield, where Andrew Jackson and Rachel were married, they hanged the pair. Pointed poles were raised, and the heads stuck up in warning.

John Murrell came last, and reached highest. A racy, remarkably comely fellow, Murrell had deep eyes, a well-chiseled nose, and glistening blue-black hair. He dressed with a taste beyond that of the river gamblers, though he never stinted the diamond studs, and his waistcoats showed several colors. The ladies loved him and his taste in women was catholic.

He served an apprenticeship in elegant scoundrelism, traveling and observing men and the means of trimming them. He was born in the same year that Little Harpe kicked the air on the gallows platform—the birth occurred in Tennessee, practically on the Trace itself, in his father's inn. As ever, maternal influence was strong. By Murrell's own story, his mother was a prostitute, who taught him to rob guests with whom she had just lain. In his early teens he went on to higher things, as a young fence, a transporter of stolen horses. An authority taught him to kill, with illustrations in the field. About the New Orleans dives and in Vicksburg's restricted district, in the "Gut" of Memphis, the boy became known as a rising rascal.

Men of crime took to this engaging villain; some of his best friends were cutthroats and grafters. He cultivated good-will among thieves, eventually making full use of his connections. He expanded, developing refinements of old techniques. In a Natchez bawdy-house he met a man dressed as a minister, who taught him a fine act. Murrell practiced Biblical quotations, convincing sermons, ways to set a frontier audience jumping in religious spasms. With this as a front, he had an easy time along the Trace. Looking holy for several days, he allayed suspicion until he had a man on a horse ahead, his fingers on the trigger. In addition, he gave sermons while helpers picked purses in the crowd. Widening his ventures, he passed out counterfeit bills from the pulpit, asking for change. Who would turn down a minister? By the time the fraud was discovered, Murrell was miles away.

After a little, he moved into another field, slavery. He sidled up: Would Sam like to be free? Then meet him after dark at the turn. . . . In the next town, after selling the Negro, he started off. A day or so later Sam had escaped again and was riding at Murrell's side. This went on until too many people were hunting the black man. Then Murrell blew out the victim's brains. Now he had to find a new subject and carry on as before. Sometimes he captured a family of three or four, and had to shoot them all in the woods. From this he worked a kind of Murrell underground railroad—a savage travesty on humanitarian organizations evolved to help slaves to freedom.

From a farm near Jackson, Tennessee, Murrell looked farther ahead. He studied the law, ways of evading statutes. He placed respectable-looking agents in towns; there are hints that, like later American men of crime, he developed tie-ins with public officials. When confederates got into trouble, he generally brought up five or six men to swear the opposite of what any victim contended.

Once, however, his brilliance came to naught. He was caught, and on an embarrassingly small count. For stealing a steed or two, too publicly, he received a year's sentence, and his thumbs were ordered burned with the letters HT—Horse Thief. Lips twisting, his deep-set eyes showing his contempt for his captors, he sat silent as his flesh smoked and burned under the brand. He walked defiantly into prison, and he came out the same way.

This time he would outshine anything he had done to date, with a scheme the nation had never imagined—a vast slave rebellion, directed by a band of his own plunderers. The motive, it need hardly be observed, would not be freedom for the enslaved, but a spree of pillage for Murrell. Beyond that, he seemed to think of himself as the new ruler of a new South, organized like a bandits' empire. Beyond doubt the man had become unbalanced; nonetheless he showed himself a dazzling plotter. He planned a Council of the Clan of the Mystic Confederacy, while several thousand assistants prepared far in advance for rebellion day, Christmas, 1835. There were "degrees," oaths and ceremonials. Murrell slipped about, presiding at secret meetings, laying the basis of a military organization. In Natchez, New Orleans and elsewhere in the South—they'd all strike at once, and the world would see.

An outsider met Murrell; for whatever his reason, the youth joined the band. Murrell was jolted when the newcomer denounced him and gave out the names of certain leading followers. Arrested, Murrell escaped jail, was recaptured, and went to trial. There he put up a resourceful fight, using all of his legal skill. But he received a ten year sentence for Negro-stealing, and served practically all of it. Returning as a broken man, Murrell disappeared into a mist of contradictory legends.

Other henchmen decided to carry on as best they could and quietly advanced the time of their "uprising" six months, to

July 4 of 1835. Shortly before then, on a Mississippi plantation, a woman heard her nurse arguing: "But this is such a pretty little baby to kill!" The story came out, and a wave of violence spread over part of the South. Negroes were shot, whites hanged, all without trial. Some of the victims had been part of the wild scheme; others were entirely innocent. July 4 brought no uprising. The golden day of the outlaws had ended.

Of all who wandered into King's Tavern none could claim greater rank as a bizarre individualist than Lorenzo Dow, "Preacher of the Natchez Trace." Though the plantation sections are customarily pictured as high Episcopalian, the evangelical faiths made thousands of converts throughout the Natchez country. The first quarter of the nineteenth century saw the beginning of that almost frantic turning to religion that has since been called the Great Revival.

From his first days Lorenzo had been set apart. Born in Connecticut, he had five brothers and sisters: Ulysses, Ethelinda, Mirza, Orleana and Tabitha. At four, he said, he knew spiritual experiences, dropping into "muses about God." Spindly, unhealthy, he had coma-like seizures in which he spoke to Him in Heaven. As a youth, he was whirled into the sky, where God told him to preach. His first efforts singed his listeners; what came forth was full of thunder and broken cries. Several times they asked him not to come back. He meant well, but . . . Yet the boy had an almost savage courage and good ingenuity. He hit on a device to "hold" his crowd; gathering the flock in a meeting hall, he locked the door, backed against it and preached. Launching a career as an itinerant, he made conversions by the score. Admitted on trial as a Methodist preacher, he shifted about, startling audiences, then winning them by his furious words.

Lorenzo was long, lank and pale-faced, with pinched features. He never cut his hair, which fell in a red-brown maze below his shoulders. He never shaved, though he was made significant gifts of razors. Through his life he was sure that Satan pursued him in person: "Oh! how can people dispute there being a devil! If they underwent as much as I do with his buffetings . . ."

For a time he felt sure God wanted him to head for Ireland. Catching hold of a skiff, he stuck up a bush for a sail, and made his way from New England to Canada, where he went aboard a ship. The Irish Catholics listened to him, goggle-eyed, and reached for their sticks. Lorenzo was delighted at their beatings and the riots that he caused, for it proved the Almighty was testing him. Returning to America, he had the inspiration of a lifetime. He would go South. Through Alabama, Georgia and Mississippi he made a slow progress. He liked the raw wildnesses, the towns and the stopping points along the rivers and the Trace. And the people came to like him.

Through heat, through downpour, he pushed on, ever humble, ever fervent. Miserably poor, he nevertheless got along. His feet stuck out of his shoes, his threadbare clothing was falling off; from a distance he looked like a bunch of hair on a sorry nag. Men who came upon him suddenly on the Trace were sure the Devil himself had burst upon them. When he went from house to house, matrons fell back in fright. Through the mazes of whiskers his small eyes gleamed, and a voice cried: "A crust of bread. A crust!" Getting the bread, he walked to the pump, dipped it and sang a hymn as he munched. Finishing with thanks to God and the housewife, he jogged away.

The Mayor of Natchez, after much thought, agreed to let Lorenzo preach. In 1803, at Kingston settlement, Dow determined to have a church. For the land he gave up his sole possession, a watch. It became the first location in the territory to be deeded for a Protestant house of worship. He provided that he himself would be barred from it if he ever opposed the church doctrine or discipline. Bishop Charles B.

Galloway termed this the only known instance in which, by giving property, a man guarded against his own defection from a faith.

In the Natchez country Lorenzo perfected his techniques. Once he gave out a startling announcement. His topic was "latest news from Hell." The crowd gathering, he quoted the Bible: "And in Hell He lifted up His eyes . . ." Again, as if idly, he opened the good book. "'I can do all things,'" he read, and looked angry. "Ah, no, Paul," he cried to the prophet. "I'll bet you five dollars you can't." All ready to show up Paul, he tossed a bill on the pulpit. Then he read on: "'. . . through Christ which strengtheneth me . . .' Ah, Paul," he grabbed up his money. "That's a different story!"

It was near Natchez that Lorenzo's resourcefulness almost came a cropper. For an open air meeting he secretly placed a little Negro in a pine tree and gave him a horn. Lorenzo's subject was "Judgment Day." Pointing his finger, he approached the sepulchral climax. "And you," he asked, "suppose you found this your final day; suppose, at this moment, from the sky there came the blowing of *Gabriel's Horn?*"

As if from the heavens themselves there issued a terrible blast. Men ran for the trees and children were trampled as mothers fell whimpering. When the truth came out, farmers took whips to the little Negro and Lorenzo, too. Without a sign of fright, the minister shouted: "That shows you! Now, brethren, if a boy blowing a tin horn can do that to you, how will you feel when Judgment really comes?" He won.

His followers were surprised to hear that Lorenzo was getting himself a wife. She was a match for him in almost everything except beard, said those who knew her. A little earlier in New York he had met Peggy—"Peculiar Peggy" as several termed her—a frail girl who thought mainly of religion and Lorenzo. His wooing must be granted high place among idylls of eccentricity. Invited to her relatives' house, Lorenzo looked hard, and she blushed. Already, she said, she had heard of him as a "singular character." Lorenzo stayed all night at the house, came back next evening and suddenly, without preliminary, he proposed—in the presence of her sister. "Do you think you could accept of such an object as me?" Shyly, Peggy slipped away.

After a pause, Lorenzo returned and asked again, ending with this remarkable sequence of sentiments: He was going to the warm countries, where he would probably die. But if he lived, he hoped to be back in a year and a half. If she lived and stayed single and found none that she liked more than she did him, and if she were willing to give twelve out of every thirteen months to travel in foreign lands ("and never say, do not go to your appointment, for if you should stand in my way, I should pray to God to remove you, which I believe, he would answer"); and if Lorenzo found no one that he liked better than Peggy.... Achieving this grand climax, he concluded. "Then perhaps something further may be said on the subject."

So saying, he was gone for two years. On his return, he found Peggy still waiting, and he married her. They had one short evening together. Before the next dawn, Lorenzo was heading once more South. Eight more months passed before his second meeting with his bride. This time he took her with him to Natchez, settling her in a cottage near Port Gibson. Then and always he called her "my rib." He and the rib enjoyed an almost idyllic stay in the Natchez vicinity.

However, snakes did grow in the garden of Lorenzo's happiness. His brother-in-law, a backslider, got into financial trouble for which Lorenzo was blamed. Peggy's sister ran off with a younger, more athletic man. Holding firmly against their critics, Lorenzo and his rib stuck it out. But the climate disagreed with both, and they eventually left. Later he came back to Natchez, but his febrile spirit had slackened; even a Lorenzo will wear. Peggy died first. Following her by several years, Lorenzo was buried by the Order of Odd Fellows.

For years the Tavern at the Trail's end continued to draw the wearied to rest in the narrow rooms, or to convivial joy in the downstairs barroom. Stories, vague but persistent, have come down of killings in the doorways at dark of night, attempts by marauders to raid the house. For many years the door to the bar bore bullet holes, and the windows had bolts thicker than ordinary need would indicate.

The King family sold the property about 1817. Another owner operated it for a time, but eventually it was taken by a family that has maintained it as a home for nearly a century and a quarter—the Postlethwaites and their descendants. Two Postlethwaites, Sam and Henry, arrived from Pennsylvania before the War of 1812, to prosper and help run the town. When Henry died of yellow-fever in 1823, his widow and children went to the former tavern. The nearest houses were some distance away and daily the family beheld Indians trudging along a narrow pathway outside the town. Slowly the vicinity built up as additional roads were cut, then city streets. Today the inn is surrounded by modern structures that look like pretenders beside its strength and age.

Currently, Mrs. A. C. Register and Mrs. Jean Register Modisett live among the tokens of their family's past. Mrs. Register, energetic in her eighties, speaks in lively style of the old hostelry, and the way the Federal government has recognized the richness of American history bound up with the old Trace. Interest in the roadway has revived in recent years; historians and park officials have revived the half-lost route, running it through fields and along lakes and hills.

The Trace began to fade as the last century advanced. Towns rose in the old wilderness with new roads connecting them. Railroads established different patterns for cross-country travel. The unused sections grew up with thick grasses, and the woods reclaimed their own. All that remained of the Trace were small stretches in local use, sections beneath a hill where a few ruts had never lost their identity, or the recollections of aging pioneers that "she went through there." Now a long parkway and national highway will follow four hundred miles of the course, from Natchez to Nashville.

Mrs. Register does not conceal her pride that her house has a part in that story. She shows the kitchen in which swings an original crane, the ancient weatherboarding of the gallery, the first cypress blinds, and also a jeweled dagger. An early chimney broke apart a number of years ago in the Tavern, and the weapon fell from the bricks. There was a mystery, also, about a skeleton that diggers discovered in the basement when they made repairs. Too much time had passed to make any inquiry about it, and the family had it taken away.

More tangible to some in Natchez are the Tavern's haunts. At the proper moment, on a still winter evening with a crescent moon in the sky, the understanding ones see wraiths of wretched travelers riding silently on the empty street. Bringing their ghostly horses to a halt, they knock on the door, and knock and knock. Turning wearily away, they ride off into the shadows. A neighbor has an explanation: "Dey de poor folks dot got themself kilt after dey was turn' away at de inn. Who kilt 'em? The Harpes." She pronounces it Harp-*ees*. Which may not be a bad word for them.

EDGEWOOD

IV

MR. AMIABLE AND MR. BLUNT

THERE are always at least two ways of doing a thing, the indirect and the direct, the suave and the blunt. The history of Natchez probably worked out somewhat differently from what it might have because two men, representing these opposite approaches, came to Natchez in the late 1700s. The suave gentleman ended as the most popular figure of the countryside; the blunt gentleman got himself practically run out. Which indicates, perhaps, that a good-humored smile may yield more than a frown.

Stephen Minor liked everybody, and everybody liked him, including people who, by all the rules of reason, should have been his enemies. Pre-eminently he is Natchez' man of amiability. Born in Pennsylvania, one of eight boys, he received a fashionable education that provided polish, a commanding presence, and an ease in any company. Dark-haired, dark-eyed, a husky-framed individual, Stephen could laugh when others fretted, and remain at ease when most men shouted out their rage. During his lifetime he made good use of these qualifications.

Before he was twenty, in the unsettled beginning days of the American Revolution, he was traveling West, apparently undecided what he wanted to do, or where he would do it. At St. Louis he met a Colonel Howard, Irishman in the service of Spain. The expansive Irishman invited the youth to dine. Later it would be said that once Stephen was introduced to someone, he had to work hard to keep the stranger from being impressed. They enjoyed several more meetings; over a cup of rum, the Colonel threw out a suggestion: Stephen knew, didn't he, that Spain was helping the colonials against England? Stephen nodded. Well, the Colonel was sending several dispatches down to New Orleans. Would the boy like to go along and see the country on the way? Stephen, ever adventurous, certainly would.

With several others Stephen floated down river by flatboat, passing low spots and hills in which Mississippi pirates kept an eye out for promising prey. In New Orleans Governor Galvez, an ambitious young Spaniard whose eyes sparkled at any chance to humble the British, extended a quick welcome. Like the Colonel, Galvez was impressed; he had Stephen call several times and they talked about the military stores that Galvez was allowing the Americans to gather. Stephen strolled about the pungent Creole city, dabbling in its offerings; New Orleans would always be an inviting place for a twenty-year-old of good appetites.

His first errand completed, Stephen was invited to accompany the party in taking American supplies up the Ohio and Monongahela. His partners regarded him as an asset with his songs and tales, his way of taking mishaps with a grin. Besides he had a pair of fists that he could swing with precision when necessary, although he seldom had to resort to them. The caravan had a good time en route, somewhat too good a time perhaps, considering the number of times they tarried at inns. Passing through Natchez, they struck East. Stephen seldom knew an illness, but now a chill struck him and one morning he could not rise. The party had fallen behind schedule. Sinking back, Stephen told them to go ahead; in a day or two he would post behind them.

The next morning as he lowered himself into a tub of tepid water, the servant burst into the room with startling news. On the road, a few miles off, Stephen's party had been ambushed by bandits and every man among them killed.

Stephen, left high and dry, wondered what he should do next. He remembered sprightly New Orleans, and its opportunities for an enterprising individual. Returning to report the tragedy he had missed, he was ambling along a balconied street when he heard his name called. A carriage halted, and his friend Governor Galvez beckoned. Over liqueurs Stephen learned what the Governor planned. The military winds were shifting; Galvez was preparing a stabbing attack on the British possessions in the South. Wouldn't young Minor want to join the effort? Stephen, scouting about, counseled with other Americans who were finding adventure, and profit, in Spain's favor, and accepted. As an officer of the forces that marched on Mobile, Stephen showed a quick skill with the gun, and a mastery of his men that sped Spain's victory. Galvez, advancing him in rank, swore him in as a subject of His Hispanic Majesty. The course of Stephen's life had been altered.

When war ended, Stephen remained in New Orleans, liking the place more with every month. Clearly Don Esteban Minor was a man to watch. Many faces clouded as rivals beheld the good-looking upstart, going everywhere in official circles. A change was pending up in Natchez which brought the bland Don Esteban a new assignment: aide-major or adjutant of the military post.

At Natchez he made a quick conquest. "Sir William" Dunbar called him a "lively, agreeable man" and welcomed him to his house. Stephen found himself the only individual of American heritage in the higher Spanish service, stationed in a place whose major population was English-speaking. The Governor called upon him for advice and suggestions; unobtrusively Stephen fitted himself to the situation, beginning to function as a kind of assistant governor. Here was a position where a fatal slip might occur at any moment. He must offend neither Spaniard above nor too many Natchezians below. A word too many over a glass of ale, or too few in responding to a toast, and he might be lost. As somebody said, the Spaniards might be bribed, but their pride should not be offended.

Don Esteban had met his career. Deftly, in behalf of his former fellow-countrymen, he would suggest that the Governor exercise a particular liberality. With equal deftness, he caught the ear of the other side: Might it not be wise to temper a request, asking less and getting it, rather than demanding much and receiving nothing? Indicating his success, "Sir William" wrote again: "Major Stephen Minor, though yet in the pay of Spain, is a sincere friend of his native country." Governors came and went, but Stephen stayed on.

The dons maintained as ceremonial a life as they could manage—military marches, full-scaled banquets, balls at which braid shone in the candle-light. In the social setting, this Spaniard-by-adoption proved an asset—personable, gallant, and a bachelor into the bargain. On one such evening his glance, which missed little, was drawn to a highly eligible subject of His Majesty, Martha Ellis of the White Cliff Ellises. With the Governor nodding approval, the marriage was eventually performed. In due time, he became the father of twins, and the smiling Spaniards congratulated him on his prowess. A miniature shows Don Esteban at this period. The face looks forth with a combination of alertness and benignity. His coloring dark, the hair beginning to recede at the temples, he stands on display with an ornate coat of blue and gold, red collar and lining, gold star on chest, braid on everything else that shows.

Tragedy struck, a double one; his wife and one of the little girls were taken ill, and died. The depressed widower went about alone for a time, but soon practically every belle had decided to allow herself a go at him. With each year Stephen emerged as a greater prize. His rank brought great land grants; by now he had a plantation which would grow until half the town's outskirts were in his name. Before long he married again, taking one of the young, highly-placed Bingaman girls —of a family we shall meet later. This bride died almost at once.

After a proper interval, Stephen took a third wife, in a union that lasted the rest of his life. Katherine Lintot, originally of his native Pennsylvania, was a cool, long-faced blonde ten years his junior, a match for him and more. "She had a strong personality," a descendant explains. "You knew it the moment you met her. Before anyone around her did anything, they asked if she'd mind. If there was a chance she would, they didn't." In her portrait Katherine stares right back, crisply competent. The easy-tempered Esteban liked it that way. With a steady hand, Katherine installed new household helpers, fixed rules for their living and took over management of their finances. Esteban didn't mind that, either.

The bride acquired a name, "The Yellow Duchess." She had the courage of her idiosyncrasies. She liked the color; she would have it always about her, no matter what anyone thought. For every costume she adopted an all-gold ensemble, complete from tiny shoes to feather in her hat and flower in hand. Handkerchiefs, bangles and, said the informed, her underpinnings were all of that hue. The Duchess' drawing room glimmered with yellow walls, yellow carpets on the floor, mirrors and cornices of gold, sofas and chairs to match, mantel of a tawny shade. Artisans upholstered her coach in a golden cloth and painted it in two shades of yellow; she hunted about until she obtained four claybank horses—the closest she could approximate the proper color. She even picked attendants who were pale mulattoes of yellowish pigmentation.

When she rode by, gold fan in hand against the sheen of her satin dress, two outriders at the back, clinging to the straps, Natchez knew something important was passing. On one such trip occurred an incident which afforded her children subsequent amusement. The Duchess had weak eyes but, like women before and after her, she had no thought of wearing disfiguring glasses, even gold-rimmed ones. Or was it simply that she liked the feel of a lorgnette? Anyway, she kept one ever about her. One day, as her carriage tilted along, she lifted the implement to inspect an approaching vehicle. The occupant of the other carriage, an overseer's wife, recognized the Duchess, and didn't like the gesture. Almost simultaneously she pulled out an iron key, to give the Duchess a hard survey through its loop. A golden mulatto nearly fell off the carriage.

The Duchess had her defenders, who found her warm-hearted and generous when her interest was aroused. Even they, however, admitted that with her a certain meticulousness was the original virtue. "Everything must be so—a chair not an inch out of the way, the salt-cellar filled just that high." She was never satisfied with a servant until she herself had trained him for six months. If he failed to meet her standard by that time, she sent him to the fields and set to work on another.

Thus it was that Katherine Minor grew disturbed when Stephen had to receive an Indian chief at a conference, with supper to follow. At the last minute she discovered that the chief's wife and a group of squaws were expected to join them. Peering through the window at the blanketed, dusty females, Katherine sniffed. Not at her table. For once Stephen's diplomacy did not work. She pointed out the richness of her French china, the quality of the cloth. A chief and a few of his men—that she would bear; the women, no. To Stephen's relief, a compromise was reached. Servants hurriedly prepared an adjoining room, with heavier table, thicker linen, cruder utensils; the women were escorted there.

The chief's squaw seated herself, her stolid face showing no wisp of emotion. She rejected the first course, a well-spiced gumbo. A pause followed; in the main room an enormous side of venison was carried in—the pièce de résistance, an imaginatively prepared object, seasoned with the Duchess' best herbs. That lady's face brightened; in spite of the early awkwardness, the affair was going well. After a few pieces were sliced off, Katherine Minor gave a side glance into the squaws' room and ordered the servants to take the meat there.

The chief's wife let her eyes shift from the Yellow Duchess to the meat and back. As the servant bowed, she reached out with both hands, caught up the venison and thrust it into the folds of her blanket. Signalling to her women, she rose, and all of them walked across the room, their bare feet slapping the polished floor. "Ugh," she grunted to Stephen. "Good meat." Padding past the Duchess, she ignored her and her retinue did likewise. The ladies ate their venison outside, squatting on their haunches. This was one triumph of which the Duchess did not boast.

After a time came a new Governor, who would be involved with Don Esteban in affairs larger than either realized. Most glittering of Natchez' Spanish officials was Don Manuel Gayoso de Lemos. Educated in England, he spoke the language with ease; soon after arriving, he married a Louisiana girl. A rich man, extremely social, he revealed himself as a lover of good things. Though a Spanish official, he was, amazingly to some, not a hunter after a fortune. To add to his rare qualities, he could drink any Natchezian under the table. Who could ask for more in a Governor? Certainly not Don Esteban. The two men got on famously.

Don Manuel gave a new flavor to Natchez. He laid down the outlines of the present city, a square along the bluffs and streets spreading from the river—a village with a Spanish tone. At the same time he created a little court of happy extravagance. For a court a setting is required; for that he erected an establishment that would long stand as the White House of the district. Creole in style but considerably more elaborate than the usual such place, it was galleried all around, of heavy brick below, wood above. Over it swung a long hipped roof, shingled and expansive. The upper story, in the European pattern, had the main chambers, drawing room, dining hall, reception room. The lower floor, flush with the ground, had the lesser quarters, storerooms and, surprisingly to some, the stables.

A drive circled before the house, to lead beneath the gallery. Through a wide doorway, carriages rolled to a cool, protected tunnel, and guests went upstairs through an interior staircase. Flooring was of white and yellow flagstones and, like the furniture and draperies, was brought from Spain and transported laboriously upriver and overland to the site. The days went quickly behind the wide, airy gallery. In the fragrant greenness of the rear courtyard Don Manuel and his Louisiana wife sat with their friends, reflecting how good life could be in this land.

Governor Gayoso christened his house with a name it never lost—Concord, in token of the kind of harmony that Spain sought among these distant colonists. For a time Don Manuel and Don Esteban could feel they had all the concord they wished. The Governor gave bubbling banquets in his Creole home, the planters made bows and toasts, and Don Esteban moved smilingly among them. Yet all was not as easy as it looked; turmoil rumbled in the distance.

The fate of Natchez hung in an uncertain balance. For years the rambunctious new United States had been insisting on its claim to the vicinity. At the Revolution's close, England recognized that it belonged to her former colonists; in defeating her, they had won what had been hers. But Spain, having moved in on her own, was not to let herself be influenced by a little thing like a peace treaty between two other countries. She held tightly to the Mississippi's East bank as far as the site of Memphis.

Then, in 1795, Spain found herself temporarily in a tight place. Courting American good will, she reluctantly signed an agreement giving the Natchez area to the United States. The news caused surprise among the Natchezians, but knowing Spaniards nodded with a smile. Two years passed. In Washington and Madrid, American officials pressed Spain without

REBER HENDERSON

CONNELLY'S TAVERN
A Mere Quaker Made the Spaniards Look Foolish

CONCORD — EARL M. NORMAN
Its Duchess Wore Yellow Down to Her Pantaloons

CONCORD TODAY — REBER HENDERSON
Its Superb Stairs Climb to the Empty Sky

success. Repeatedly the transfer was delayed. Spain began to violate another provision, closing the Mississippi's mouth to American traders. Spain was working for time. Conditions had changed; she was looking toward bigger stakes—the collapse of the whole United States. In this play the urbane Governor Gayoso held a number of cards.

Secret Spanish agents, some in the American Army itself, were spying and fomenting trouble. In Tennessee and Kentucky men snapped out their hate of the Eastern seaboard merchants. Those Easterners were agin' our West; God damn 'em, we'll form our own country! Spain had reason to feel that the loose American confederation would fall apart, and she would be there to catch some of the pieces. In this furtive scheming Governor Gayoso was spreading out his Majesty's gold, dispatching messages in cipher, making quiet upriver trips. In the shuttered court behind his Concord, he received hundreds of callers, reporting, questioning, whispering.

How much Don Esteban Minor guessed of all this we have no way of knowing. Certainly the American-born Stephen found himself in an odd position. He probably surmised that certain visitors were selling the country, which he once called his, into Spain's hands. Of course, Stephen had openly changed his allegiance. Still, for the first time the United States and Spain faced each other in conflict; and he must have had moments when old emotions started unexpectedly within him. On the surface in Natchez, all remained graceful, punctilious. But Americans watched Spaniards, and Spaniards kept their eyes on their alien subjects.

Toward Natchez there moved a newcomer who would shake the place as it had never been shaken. Andrew Ellicott was a big-stomached, big-bottomed fellow with a cherubic pink face. A Quaker, he came from Pennsylvania like Stephen Minor, and he had the same military rank. There all resemblance ended. Where Stephen smiled and shrugged, the chunky Major Ellicott stared coldly with his pale blue eyes, and kept his cupid-like lips tightly closed. His forte was firm intention, bluntly expressed. He had a will to finish what he started, a dislike of Spaniards, a deep inclination toward democratic self-rule. And this Quaker enjoyed a good, fist-swinging fight.

A surveyor and astronomer, Andrew Ellicott had mixed with many men in several careers. He made the first authoritative measurements of Niagara Falls, laid out some of Washington, D.C.'s streets, served as America's surveyor-general; not to mention mediating several border disputes. In 1796 President Washington asked him to go to Natchez as American commissioner to fix the long-disputed boundary with Spain. He was to be prudent and prevent an open break if possible; but he must do everything necessary to bring American control. A great deal of the nation's future might hang on his behavior. It was a prickly assignment, and one that would become a duel between Ellicott's way and that of Gayoso and Minor.

For five months of a gruelling fall and winter, Ellicott and his military and civilian helpers labored South by land and river, now blocked by ice, now caught in river shallows. Later they considered this the easiest part of their task. When they reached New Madrid, the Spanish commandant tried to hold them. He'd been told not to let them descend until the Spanish river posts were evacuated. That wouldn't be until the spring waters rose, Governor-General Carondelet had said in New Orleans. They palavered; Ellicott's cheeks quivered a moment, and then he announced quietly that he would push on regardless. The commandant, fumbling, observed that since the waters *had* risen, half the objection was eliminated. And so they moved ahead.

Wherever they stopped, the Spaniards shrugged politely; they knew nothing, señor, of any plans for leaving these posts. Ellicott's short, stubbed nose smelled something gamey. Near Walnut Hills (Vicksburg) he was handed a polite message:

Governor Gayoso of Natchez regretted that he lacked vessels for evacuating the forts; to prevent "misunderstanding" he asked Ellicott to leave his troops above there. The Quaker consented; he could be polite, too. Taking only his civilian attaches, he proceeded to Natchez, where he dispatched a note, announcing his arrival to start the survey, asking when he could present credentials. Gayoso replied that he "learned with pleasure" of Ellicott's presence; that was all. Ellicott tried again—When? The Governor indicated that his feelings were hurt; Ellicott had "surprised" him, giving no time for a formal reception.

Reception or no reception, Ellicott persisted. More exchanges, more explanations, and finally a meeting. There three men sized up one another—the plump, sharp-eyed American, suave Gayoso, Stephen Minor the happy-mannered. Repeatedly Ellicott's eyes met those of Minor. By most standards these two should have despised each other; instead, they got on famously. In common with many before him, Ellicott found it impossible not to make friends with this man. Promptly, too, he recognized the fact that Minor knew more about Natchez than Gayoso ever could, and he acted accordingly. Adroitly as ever, Minor became an intermediary between the Governor and the American—a significant pause, a lift of the hand that conveyed a meaning. Eventually accounts spoke of "Major Minor, Mr. Ellicott's friend," and "Stephen Minor, in whom Ellicott had confidence." Yet they remained on opposite sides, and none could charge Stephen with breach of Spanish confidence, or tale-telling. Truly it was a miracle of tact.

After long conversation a date was fixed for the survey, weeks hence. But a friend slipped Ellicott a note: In New Orleans Governor-General Carondelet was saying he would delay and delay until the treaty became a dead letter. So that was it? Ellicott puckered up his deceptively babyish face. Picking a hill that dominated the town, not half a cannon shot from the Spanish fortification on the bluff, he erected a camp and lifted the American flag. The Spaniards, furious, sent a messenger; the Governor wanted the flag down. Ellicott refused. The flag stayed.

What to do now? Ellicott strolled about town. Near his camp rose a building with which he quickly became familiar, Connelly's Tavern, a place that would see history in the shaping. Two years or so earlier, Patrick Connelly bought an imposing structure built into the hillside, powerfully constructed, heavily timbered.* Ellicott speculated over the location as he surveyed the double galleries across the wide front, where a retaining wall held in the sloping soil; and the moat or bricked court, cut deep into the hill at the rear.

Part brick, part wood, the Tavern reflected a French and Spanish tradition. Slender colonnettes, above and below, supported a downsweeping roof that all the town knew; from its high galleries, with a narrow flight of stairs tucked into the side in the Creole manner, a man could survey the Esplanade below and the river beyond that. As the trade required, the Tavern had a dual personality. On the lower floor all looked plain and heavy—the bar, kitchen, tavern room for roisterers and sleepers who rolled up in blankets and rested where they could. Above waited the airy elegance of delicate mantels, French windows, ornamental moldings. Mr. Ellicott, pipe in hand, walked in and indicated he liked a drink on a warm night. Before long, sitting around, keeping his eyes open, he knew the Tavern upstairs and down.

Connelly, the host, liked the direct, untalkative American; he passed on the information that would reach the ears of any alert hotel man. In the rooms of the Tavern, Andrew Ellicott formed many of his plans. There, too, he received much advice, which he often didn't take. If there was anything the Quaker received above all else, it was advice. Delightedly, he discovered a strong pro-American sentiment in Natchez. The

---

* Mr. Connelly is sometimes pictured as a genteel soul. Records show that he was charged once or twice with wife-beating, which might indicate something else.

town simmered with rebellious spirit, all undirected, all disorganized. This one wanted the Spanish fort stormed, and offered to raise men for the job; the other would merely kill Gayoso, Minor and associates. Late one evening Ellicott learned something more. A mysterious minor officer in the American Army called, with peculiar hints; immediately a leading old-line Tory of Natchez followed, with much the same purpose. Ellicott put things together; this pair, and others in Natchez, must be working with British officials who, he already knew, were hoping to effect an invasion of the central Mississippi Valley through Canada! More than that, he received strong hints that France, about to take Louisiana again, was planning to march upriver to Natchez as well. The plot not only thickened, it developed sub-plots.

Meanwhile came more lessons in the Spanish art of evasion. Again the survey was delayed; work could not start without Carondelet, and Carondelet couldn't leave New Orleans. From the Creole city arrived a gracious request: Wouldn't Señor Ellicott visit there as Carondelet's guest? Mr. Ellicott would not. The treaty said the commissioners should meet in Natchez; in Natchez he'd stay. A friendly invitation arrived from Governor Gayoso: Wouldn't Mr. Ellicott be his guest at his plantation? With equal friendliness, Mr. Ellicott declined.

Ellicott's camping ground drew the attention of bands of well-liquored Indians, screaming curses and threats. The Quaker, suspecting that the Spaniards were stirring the red men, told Gayoso about it, and announced he was bringing his American soldiers from upriver to protect the camp. Gayoso, for the first time really disturbed, made speedy protest. Spain would be insulted if the soldiers arrived. Then, turning adroit again, Gayoso suggested that Ellicott and his soldiers go *below* Natchez to the place where the survey would start. The big Quaker grinned behind his hand. So they wanted him out of the city? Obviously he was making the inhabitants think too much about American rule and similar upsetting subjects. Finally Stephen Minor stepped forward, and they compromised. The soldiers went below; Ellicott and staff stayed. Having prevented a break, Stephen went about with his usual good-humored expression.

Ellicott almost purred to himself when he noticed that Spanish artillery was being removed from the river forts. Then a little later he saw that the artillery was being wheeled right back! Now a gun was trained on his tent. Down in New Orleans, Governor General Carondelet told a friend that he would "give the Americans lead and the inhabitants hemp."

This time the Quaker really went to work. A skillful sampler of opinion, Ellicott also knew well how to influence it. He dropped a word, he hinted, he pointed out. Suddenly, he reported, he found the pro-Americans so aroused it was hard to keep them from "acting offensively ... A general commotion in favor of the United States would take place in the course of a few weeks." More American troops moved downriver; Gayoso made nervous objection, then, seeing it was too late, agreed to let them come. The Americans marched through Natchez, while flags waved, crowds grinned and jigged.

But Gayoso had his own weapons. He issued a proclamation designed to wring tears and stiffen backs. His people were being beseiged by "busy and malignant individuals," unnamed, though clearly he meant outside American agitators, who were trying to disturb them in their attachment to the King. Also, he said, Spain couldn't leave now; the British were scheming to take Natchez. . . . There was truth there; but certainly Spain was a well-smudged pot calling the English kettle black. Ellicott was delighted; the Natchezians became angrier than ever toward Gayoso: "After the appearance of the proclamation, the public mind might be compared to inflammable gas; it wanted but a spark to produce an explosion."

In a totally unexpected fashion, the match was applied to Ellicott's "inflammable gas." In rode a traveling minister, Mr. Hanna. He asked permission to preach at Ellicott's camp. This was against Catholic Spain's rules; but Esteban Minor saw no harm in it, and the diplomatic Gayoso thought it wise to agree.

A crowd attended and Mr. Hanna made a solid hit. Afterward talk flared about religious freedom and such. Also, it seems, some patriot passed the bottle around. Glowing with new emotion, the minister staggered around town and rather carelessly got into an argument over doctrine with a handful of Irish Catholics. They used a brick on Hanna's skull, whereupon he stumbled over to Gayoso, demanding punishment for the Papists. The Governor suggested that he pause and consider the circumstances. Declining, the well-oiled man of religion shouted a threat, and the Governor ordered him to the stocks.

The "inflammable gas" spurted high. Spain had insulted a good American; to hell with Spain! Men waved fists, collected sticks and guns and converged on the Governor. Gayoso and Esteban Minor consulted, and the Governor did a thing he probably regretted long afterward. Beckoning to Esteban and other assistants, he scampered to the fort for protection. The crowd milled about, and now the Spaniards couldn't get out. For two humiliating weeks they stayed cooped up there, while the Americans talked of storming the place.

Ellicott was putting his time to good use. If the good people really wanted the United States to help them—he let his eyes slip from one to the other—why not show it? Declare themselves firmly American, pledge their allegiance, call for an election! Here was subversive democratic propaganda, inserted by a resourceful agent provocateur. The citizens agreed with a whoop. Meanwhile, strengthening forces, they marched up and down in militia companies before the eyes of the dons. Poor Gayoso, with Minor at his elbow, asked for a conference with Ellicott. It was the Quaker's turn to do a little dillydallying. By letter Gayoso protested the circulation of the traitorous petitions. Traitorous? Ellicott threw the word back. Why, sir, Natchez was American territory. These were Americans, exercising American rights!

Gayoso sent out a proclamation, asking for an exercise of reason. The citizens ripped it to pieces; this liberty was heady stuff. Gayoso pleaded for an interview; Ellicott agreed to meet him, and Esteban Minor provided a place, the Minor country plantation. Spain's Governor, who had once walked in braided splendor about these streets, crept out of the fort along a mosquito-thick canebrake, and through a cornfield to Minor's house. The democratic Mr. Ellicott was touched: "My feelings were scarcely ever more affected than in this interview." One gathers that Mr. Ellicott almost cried to behold "the humiliating state to which he was now reduced, by a people whose affections he courted, and whose gratitude he expected."

Under Ellicott's guidance the Americans, beaming with success, took the republican step of naming a committee. On it was one whose presence might have caused eyebrows to lift —Bernard Lintot, father-in-law of Major Esteban Minor. Stephen now had connections on both sides! And Stephen's superior, Gayoso, could only look on while the committee went to work.

At last Andrew Ellicott was able to mark the border line, cutting his way through brooding swamp and forest. The Spaniards, formal even in defeat, lined up for a ceremony. Esteban Minor, still in uniform, stood proudly at attention; having regained his courtliness, Governor Gayoso gave Ellicott a tribute—a kiss in the Spanish style. The Quaker, who hadn't used a razor in two days, rubbed his bristly jowls and set down in his journal that he didn't think much of this custom of men's kissing one another.

Everything was over but the voting, and the democratic squabbling to follow. Gayoso was called down to New Orleans and a new post. Spain planned to send another Spanish subject for the final days of governorship. But by this time the mention of Spain made many Natchezians hold their noses. They announced that they wouldn't take the man. The honor went instead to one who had bowed and smiled his way through it all, Esteban Minor. No American-born individual had ever held such a post in the New World. Who could say that amiability did not have its reward?

Suddenly Andrew Ellicott knew it was time to go. He had made enemies aplenty, among Americans as well as Spaniards; he had offended a large faction among the citizens, and had been branded an officious upstart, trying to run things. (That, it would appear, was more or less what he had been sent down to do.) Still, such is often the lot of the agitator, after the agitation has worked. Andrew packed and made the rounds of the town, staying longer than he had planned at Pat Connelly's Tavern, where he had labored harder to plant his seeds than most people realized. Among those who bade him a warm Godspeed was his friend, Esteban Minor, in his capacity as Governor of Natchez.

Spain had another post for Don Esteban. But one day, no less composed than at any other time, Don Esteban knocked on an official door and took an oath as an American. It marked his third citizenship. Born a British colonial, he had shifted to Spain and now to the United States. Hereafter he would be plain Mister Stephen Minor; or, perhaps, not so plain. He and his Yellow Duchess made Gayoso an offer, and eventually took over the Governor's magnificent Creole home, Concord of the sloping roof. If the name of the house now appeared ironic, nobody noticed.

Here the Duchess proceeded to make her place an almost regal center. To her whole house Katherine Lintot Minor could now apply the splash that she had given her golden chariot with claybank horses and pumpkin-colored mulattoes. After some years Concord seemed to her too small and plain; for a daughter's marriage she extended and elaborated it in several ways. She added a large front portico with four columns extending from the roof to the ground below, and placed it, in a highly unusual pattern, beyond the line of the old gallery. From it in a stately design led a double flight of curving iron-railed, marble stairs, probably the finest outdoor stairway the river country ever knew. The wedding party, under the Duchess' supervision, moved ceremoniously up the passage. The effect was as she had planned it.

At Concord Katherine stayed yellow-haired, yellow-gowned, and yellow-pantalooned to the end. And it was about her Concord that there centered the story of the enigmatic Philip Nolan.

THE BURN

⸺ V ⸺

A MAN WITHOUT A COUNTRY?

IN THE many lights of Concord's drawing room women's jewels glimmered as they moved in a stately dance, and the hum of voices almost covered the tinkle of the musicians. The unending pound of winter rain against the long windows gave a sensation of added intimacy; the occasional opening of the front doors, with the flurry of damp air that followed, heightened the impression of friendly warmth inside.

Beyond question the belle of the evening was the petite green-gowned Fannie Lintot, red-headed younger sister of Stephen Minor's wife. Katherine, the Yellow Duchess, looked on approvingly as Fannie's small, well-shaped features came into view. Fannie could pick any plantation youth she wanted, if only she'd make up her mind. It was high time for her to do so. She was nearly twenty; already she'd let four or five slip away because she hadn't shown enough interest.

At the doorway the hostess noticed a stir, and the portals swung open. Who would be arriving so late? She saw Stephen extend his hand; beneath the chandelier a stranger came into sudden relief, and the Duchess' attention was taken by a compelling figure. He towered over all the men about him, a strapping, heavily-muscled individual, apparently in his early thirties. Beneath the black hair, the face looked well-bronzed, as if from years in the sun; the features, though irregular, had a dark strength. The young giant divested himself of his wet cape. As Stephen made a remark, the caller's mouth parted in a laugh; the teeth, made whiter by the brown complexion, shone for a moment, and then the face quickly grew serious again.

Stephen and the new arrival moved toward her; and just then her sister Fannie slipped her arm through Katherine's. As she patted the little hand, Katherine felt an unaccountable twinge—mild alarm, or was it annoyance? For some reason she wished Fannie were elsewhere, with one of the dozen boys who would like to dance with her. Fannie's soft blue eyes were passing casually about the crowd, when Katherine saw that they had met the newcomer's, and halted for a long minute. She seemed about to say something to Katherine, then changed her mind. By this time Stephen reached them: "My dears, Mr. Philip Nolan."

So that was who he was. For months the men had been talking about him—the daring, rather puzzlesome Irishman, who had been mixed in various exploits over the Mexican border. Philip Nolan had friends in high places, Katherine knew; he moved in and out of the Spanish representatives' offices. All the men admired Mr. Nolan's skill in capturing and taming herds of wild Spanish cattle and bringing them back to American territory; but there'd been some trouble about it, and a lot of gossip. . . .

Philip Nolan dropped his head in acknowledgment of their introduction, and Katherine was surprised at the voice, a softly-modulated baritone. She had expected—well, less cultivation. This man, she suspected, would have been at home anywhere in society. He had looked from her to her younger sister; there was a brief, awkward pause. A servant approached, to ask Katherine a question. By the time Katherine turned back she heard Fannie tell one of the Natchez boys: "I'm sorry. I've already promised Mr. Nolan—" Katherine had heard no such promise, but before she had time to say anything more, the pair had danced away.

Fannie Lintot felt herself almost swallowed in the man's

arms; the top of her red curls barely reached his chest. For a moment or two she was at a loss; Mr. Nolan did not chatter on, or whisper compliments in the usual manner. Then she was glad he didn't. His dark brown eyes caught hers; his hand, thatched with wiry hair, held hers in a tight grip; he seemed not to realize that there was another person in the room besides her. He was entirely devoid of small talk; she asked questions, and he replied.

Yes, he'd been born in Ireland—Belfast. Oh, he'd lived all around, mostly in Kentucky. That was why he liked horses so much, he imagined. He'd been in the Revolution, practically a boy at the time. That was all he said about his earlier life; later Fannie discovered that few learned that much. Now, as his somber face lit up momentarily, he was telling her of his experiences among the Indians in tracking down Western horses.

"They're a strange breed of animal," he explained. Some claimed that the first Spaniards in Mexico, centuries past, had introduced them. By this time they covered miles of territory, stampeding in a moment—nervous, tricky, fine beasts. Almost rapturously, he spoke of the silent evenings on the plains, his camps along the quick-running streams, his months of fishing and hunting with the Indians.

Why, yes, he assured her when she looked up in astonishment; he got on very well with the red skins. He spoke several of their languages. It was the white men, not the Indians, who were unreliable, treacherous. The man's face clouded, and Fannie knew that Philip Nolan had suffered in his earlier days. He was, he admitted a moment later, a true wanderer. He felt driven to move about; the same faces, same things day after day—for him nothing could be deadlier. The music ended, and one of the Dunbar boys came up to claim her for the next dance.

During the next few days, by deft questioning, Fannie Lintot learned more about the mysterious Philip. Her plantation cousins knew him as almost a legendary person. So great was his physical strength that with one hand he could lift from the saddle a bag of two thousand silver pieces and carry it across a yard. A familiar visitor to the taverns, he enjoyed a good fight. Hadn't she heard of the time he picked up four troublesome wights by the seat of their britches and tossed them into the road? The men hailed him for another feat; nobody in the Southwest was so adept with fist or tongue in quieting Indians who had taken too many swigs. Despite this, he remained a favorite among the tribes, a friend respected and trusted.

Very much a man's man, Philip Nolan was a careless, unconventional figure; he lived heavily, played heavily. He enjoyed the races—anything to do with horses. He liked gambling in any shape; he took in big sums and lost them with the same ease. Many admired him for his bravery, his daring in taking risks. Sometimes hints appeared of a wild streak in the fellow, an unsteadiness of purpose. For months he would be quiet, earnestly at work, and then he would kick over the traces. He seemed always to yearn for far places, for long trips into the wilderness. None called him the plantation type, yet he was well respected by many of the Natchez business men. Once Philip Nolan gave his word, he did a thing, no matter what it cost him.

This, and more, came to Fannie Lintot's ears. She asked one more question: "Mr. Nolan, is he married?" Her informant smiled archly. "Indeed, no! Not the type, my dear."

A week later, at another party, she did not have to look up as a heavy footstep approached; she knew who it was. In the latticed summer house she set out to find more about Philip. It was true, he told her, that General Wilkinson of the American Army had taken him as a protégé years ago; he had been the General's agent in trading operations between New Orleans and Kentucky. Then, nearly ten years past, Philip had gotten a contract to provide animals for the Army; and that was where he first got into a little difficulty.

"What was wrong about that?"

For the first time that day, Philip's face broke into a grin. "Miss Fannie, you don't understand . . ." He resumed: The Spaniards kept jealous guard upon Mexico, the jewel of their New World possessions. They wanted no strangers wandering over their lands, learning about them, their wealth, or their geography. It was hard for most Americans even to get across the borders. Rules from the court specifically forbade trade between Mexico and the United States; but like all such regulations, they might sometimes be overlooked. Philip had experience with Spanish officials; and he also had connections. Before too much time had gone by, he had a heavily scrawled document, a passport with the signature of the Spanish Governor, Miro of Louisiana, giving him authority to hunt horses.

Grudgingly, the Spaniards allowed him to enter. There followed happy, productive months. The Indians helped him trap the horses; he lassoed them with skill and precision, and rapidly he built up a good supply. Then, overnight, he was hauled before an official; no charge was filed against him, but it was hinted he was a spy. The authorities confiscated the animals; his long effort had come to nothing but humiliation and poverty.

That was when Philip Nolan gave up his fellow white men. His eyes icy in their hate, he told her how he joined the Mexican Indians, living with them, hunting with their braves. "That lasted for two years. . . ." Philip sat silent, his hand rubbing the sleeve of his coat. "Well, I couldn't make myself an Indian, altogether, and I had obligations at home." He started back to the United States, catching more horses on the way, and he managed to get them out. In Natchez and New Orleans, things improved for him. He enjoyed a time of easy respite; then once again he wanted to go West.

He had what he called a stroke of luck; the new Governor, Carondelet, was turning out to be one of his warmest friends. Carondelet gave him a new passport, strongly worded and impressive. Staying for a time in Natchez, Philip soon found financial backing. Stephen Minor and his brother John, who had followed him to Natchez, had taken an interest.

But meanwhile, Philip's next expedition had been ready. At the last moment a hitch developed. For some reason the urbane Governor Gayoso of Natchez seemed to turn against Philip. He bowed blandly and even presented him with a mark of friendship, a portable sextant; but Philip had reason to suspect Gayoso would try to injure him. Affairs were growing more risky.

Gayoso set a trap. After Philip left Natchez, Gayoso sent a message to the Spanish Governor in the West to arrest him. Nolan, he said, had tricked Carondelet into giving him a passport. The man was a non-believer, a hypocrite—among Spaniards he called himself a Catholic; among Americans he laughed at the mother church. A noose was set and only a lucky accident prevented it from being sprung.

The Mexican Governor had just died. His temporary successor, expecting that another would promptly be named, did not open official letters. Thus Philip caught all the horses he needed and slipped back with a thousand head of superior animals. Now he was at the high point of his career, a lion of the adventurous youths along the river, a name that implied excitement and daring. This time the petite, soft-faced Fannie Lintot had heard enough. She said nothing, but she knew that if she could, she'd see a lot more of this Philip Nolan.

After that, she carefully arranged for them to meet at intervals. She had to be wary, turning aside the questions of her sister Katherine. Months passed and when she saw Nolan she rejoiced with him over the recognition he was receiving. Andrew Ellicott, "Sir William" Dunbar and others had been taken with the man and his obvious knowledge of the West; word passed to President Jefferson, who unexpectedly wrote to Philip. For a long time, the President explained, he had been hearing about the large herds West of the Mississippi and he was curious about such animals, their history and habits; Philip, as far as he knew, was the only person who could provide information for an untold chapter in the history of the horse. After a time, Philip went to Philadelphia, where he had a long conversation with the President. In a letter which later came to light, Daniel Clark, one of Nolan's friends and business associates, cautioned President Jefferson not to reveal the source of information which Philip might bring; it might prove fatal to the man.

There is something rather strange here. Was abstract science, in which Jefferson was much interested, the only reason for the President's concern; or was he hunting information of another kind about Mexico? Over much of this there hovers the shadow of Nolan's sometime protector, General Wilkinson, the ever-active intriguer who allied himself so closely with the Spaniards at one stage of his mixed career. Philip remained loyal to Wilkinson; when he died he carried with him more than one Wilkinson secret.

But with this the love-smitten Fannie Lintot had no connection. Her Philip was touching shoulders with the great, and she was happy. They saw more of each other than ever. He had a poise that Fannie found appealing; frequently she wondered what he was thinking. She found him moody, earnest, and playful in turn. He had a tendency to moments of brooding despair. A fatalist, he felt that one day he would be wrecked by an unfriendly fate, but meanwhile he would get what he could from life. When he felt thus depressed, Fannie smiled and reasoned, won him back to good temper, and turned the conversation to fresh topics.

One morning, breaking off in the middle of a rare laugh, Philip caught Fannie's hands and asked the question for which she had been waiting. She gave him her answer at once, then took him with her to her house. This was the step she had been dreading; by this time, she well understood, the family had begun to suspect her intention. Pushing back a loose lock of her bright hair, Fannie took Philip in to her father. Philip started to talk, awkwardly, haltingly. With a nervous smile, Fannie finished for him.

The silence that followed was long. At last Bernard Lintot spoke, and they realized he had pondered his words in advance: He hated to say this, but surely Mr. Nolan must understand . . . social rank, position in the community. And Mr. Nolan, he hardly led a steady life, moving from place to place . . . Philip interrupted; the older man flushed. In a moment the bitter word was thrown out—horsetrader! His hand trembling, Philip muttered his reply: The family wasn't above dealing with him, was it? It must be he hadn't earned enough as a trader. How many horses did the Lintots want for their daughter?

The two men stared furiously, until Fannie cried out that she'd made up her mind; she didn't care what anybody said. She'd marry Philip if she died for it! Then she ran out, high heels tapping on the polished floor, and Philip strode after her. For a day Fannie remained in her room, and tension ruled the rest of the house. After that, dressing with care, she called the carriage. Her hands white within her muff, she went to her father: "I'm going to see Philip. Don't try to stop me." Thus it was during the ensuing months. They met at parties, on the Natchez bluff, on rides with friends along the deep-cut roads on the outskirts of town. The family has preserved a letter that Philip wrote her, in the stilted language of the day: He had met her father again, and he "did not give me the most distant invitation. I lament that love and friendship should suffer so much through his caprice, prudence or pride. Perhaps I will see you here today at the hill. . . ."

Fannie finally threatened to elope to New Orleans or Kentucky. Reluctantly the family gave in, and hundreds came to Concord for a wedding not noticeably less gala than any other held there. There was a look of serenity on the face of the tiny bride, her red hair piled high on her head, as she stood beside her giant of a groom.

The first months were calm and, perhaps to the disappointment of the gossips, very happy. Friends watched closely for signs of stress; they were never to hear Fannie in complaint against her husband. She saw fewer of her intimates, but she had expected that, knowing her life would be different. The couple were often alone in the evenings, and for this Fannie felt grateful. This was a marriage that would require effort to keep it going. Philip, the family admitted, was applying himself to the business of horses and the maintenance of his stock. Philip's friend, Daniel Clark, wrote to express hope that the union would "reclaim you from your wandering way of life." He suggested that Philip attend strictly to his affairs and "think not of horseracing; you will lose time and money by it." (Clark knew; *he* always did.)

A portrait shows the Philip of this period, in elaborate dress with queue, high stock and ruffled shirt. The brown eyes look out with candor, but there is a hint of his inclination to moodiness. Occasionally Fannie came upon him in a spell of despondency and she managed usually to bring him around. Then suddenly her heart beat heavily at her husband's words. He began hinting of another expedition to Mexico; he had received indications of favor from certain forces that controlled the border, and certainly many planters and merchants wanted fresh supplies of animals.

Gently Fannie tried to reason with him. Matters between the two countries were more hostile than ever. Didn't he remember the last time, when he escaped by an inch? His enemy, Gayoso, was now Governor-General of New Orleans and more unfriendly than before. Absently Philip nodded, and continued to plan. She had a last weapon: She was going to have a baby, she told him. But this gave him still another reason, all the more cause! It would be the last time, one final deal, and the best of them all. He'd be back before the baby came. Just watch!

The young wife might have blamed Natchez, if she wished. The planters and merchants came forward with money and advice; nearly everyone liked the plan, or the chance of gain he saw in it. Then Fannie heard hints that this was to be more than mere horse-trading. Philip and his backers, it was whispered, were working for bigger stakes—a scheme of conquest, to rally Nolan's Indian friends against the Spaniards and set up an American outpost in Mexico. A few said the party would hunt mines and defy the Spaniards to dislodge them. One or two claimed that Wilkinson stood behind the same thing. Nobody could deny that the Spanish officials in New Orleans were trying frantically to find out what was the purpose of the project. Philip listened to Fannie's tearful questions, then shook his head. No, it wasn't true. He had no such ideas. She mustn't worry.

Yet she could not close her eyes and ears. Captain José Vidal, commanding the Spanish post over the river in Louisiana, charged that Nolan had hostile designs and called on American officials to stop him. The new American Governor asked the Mississippi judges to take up the matter. At the hearing, followed closely by cheering pro-Nolan Natchezians, it was brought out that he was carrying guns, compasses and other equipment. Philip retorted that there was nothing to this; why shouldn't he take such equipment? The case was dropped, and Philip rushed his preparations. Fannie stood in her doorway, waving slowly as the expedition moved off.

The party marched quickly through Louisiana, evading Spanish parties on the alert against them. They met one body of Mexicans, outfaced them and sped on. Soon they were in the open country, beyond the Trinity and the Brazos, shooting wild game, hunting deer. They lived well for a time. Spain's few settlements lay far behind; the green earth spread all about them. Not far from the Brazos, Philip put up a log block house with a corral. They lassoed horses, penned them, started the process of breaking the animals. Matters moved more slowly than he had hoped, and he began to worry.

Meanwhile his ancient enemy Gayoso had struck, sending word to Mexico that Nolan was a "highly dangerous man," who must be taken. From the presidio at Nacogdoches, a force of a hundred and fifty men, bearing a swivel cannon, began a trek toward the Americans. Affairs were going more and more poorly for Philip. He had obtained far from enough horses; long months had gone by, and for weeks they had been living off the only source of nourishment left to them, the flesh of the steeds they had caught. A listless discouragement settled upon them.

Before dawn one morning the enemy party crept upon the encampment, overpowered the guards, and demanded a surrender. Gaunt and bearded, Philip refused; he had a supply of rifles and muskets, and he and his men poured fire upon the Mexicans. The enemy rolled their cannon into position and the first discharge blasted the blockhouse. Shot through the head, Philip died there on the floor. For a time his followers fought on, retreating to a creekbed for a last stand. Finally they agreed to a parley and, promised fair treatment, they surrendered.

The Mexicans dragged forward the emaciated figure of Philip Nolan. Lifting the bloodied head by the beard, an officer used his sword to slice off one ear, then another, to be taken to his superiors. Philip Nolan's fellows averted their eyes; he had been right when he assured Fannie it would be his last expedition.

Some have said that, in giving up, Philip's men were pledged their eventual freedom; if any promises were made, they were not fulfilled. At Nacogdoches, they waited a long time for word to come from higher Spanish authorities; then they were shackled and taken to San Antonio. Years elapsed and they were shifted from one filthy cell to another, though eventually they were allowed the freedom of several remote settlements. A judge, passing on the case against them as invaders, freed them. But military officials objected and the matter went to Spain, more postponements resulting. One by one the men were dying. Finally the King ordered a token punishment; one of each five would be hanged, the rest imprisoned for long terms. Their number had dropped to nine; a single man would be killed. The Spaniards brought blindfolds and a pair of dice. Each man threw; one made a four, and was led to the gallows in the crowded plaza of Chihuahua. Only one, the youngest, got back to the United States, long years later.

—◦❦◦—

Meanwhile Fannie Nolan had waited. She would not give way to her fears, she told herself; Philip had warned her there might be delays. When months went by, she knew people were whispering, calling her a deserted wife. They'd always had doubts about the man—a no-good, a wastrel. Then one or two other wives who had stayed in Natchez looked at her as if she were responsible; this was harder to stand. Fannie's eyes clouded. The baby was nearly due.

Her father, a new fear in his face, stayed close, assuring her repeatedly that Philip must be alive, or they would have heard. Sometimes, in those grim days, Bernard Lintot asked her forgiveness. If he had been too harsh that previous year, he was sorry. She went to live with a sister, Mrs. Samuel Steer, near Baton Rouge, and there a sickly boy was born. Broken, weeping whenever she thought of Philip, Fannie did what she could for the baby. Finally, the news of her husband arrived from Natchez, and they could not hold it from her.

Less than three months after Philip's death, his wife breathed her last. She died with a hint of a smile. "If there is a heaven above for the reward of suffering innocence," the witness wrote, "she must be there; else we stand but a poor chance that are left behind." The time was July of 1801.

William Dunbar commented: "I am much concerned for the loss of this man. Although his eccentricities were many and great, he was not destitute of romantic principles of honor, united to the highest personal courage with energy of mind, which under the guidance of a little prudence might have conducted him to enterprises of the first magnitude." Why had he gone on this last adventure? The mystery has never been solved. Some feel he was the continent's earliest filibuster, the first in a long line of Americans who would die in an effort to expand the country's limits, by whatever means occurred to them. Many more from Natchez would follow him as the years passed.

Such was the Philip Nolan that the Minors described as they sat about the gallery of Concord during the afternoons. But fate, which had already played him false, was to do a disservice to his memory. More than fifty years later, Edward Everett Hale wrote a short story, "The Man Without A Country," a fictitious account of a young American officer involved in treason. As most high-school graduates should know, Hale's character cried out: "Damn the United States! I wish I may never hear of the United States again!" That, of course, became the sentence. He spent the rest of his life sequestered on American vessels, never to hear a reference to the nation.

The story, preposterous as it is, appeared during the Civil War and had an astounding success, printed in hundreds of thousands of copies, translated, pirated in other countries. Though he described things which never happened, Hale used the name of Philip Nolan for his central figure, and by a mere accident. Reading General Wilkinson's memoirs, he was struck by the name Nolan; for the character's first name, he thought he picked one that came to him out of the air. As has happened in many such cases, his memory played him a trick. Discovering what he had done, the author expressed his dismay. Feeling he owed something to the dead Nolan, he visited the Minors, took notes and eventually wrote a novel based to a degree on the man's life—"Philip Nolan and his Friends." However, this work received not a fraction of the recognition achieved by the earlier effort; and the false Philip Nolan goes marching on.

Old Concord, mother house of the Minors, remained in full operation until 1867, when the family had come to find it a burden. For years it continued in possession of the Minors, empty, and untenanted. Too big for a residence, it became a school, then a place for community parties. In a dismantled coachhouse a curious visitor once found a relic of the Yellow Duchess, the bleached wreck of her golden carriage. The top had fallen apart; the step that had unfolded to the ground for milady's step hung like a broken jawbone, and the sun outlined shreds of yellow cloth, clinging at the corners.

Toward the end of the last century Concord came into the hands of a wealthy young man with the means to restore it. With his wife, George M. D. Kelly arrived in Natchez. Mrs. Kelly looked forward to her first sight of this place of theirs, one of the historic establishments of the lower valley. A few days afterward she beheld it, for the first and last time, aflame.

The fire company did what little it could to check the blaze. In the crowd stood men and women who had danced in the big rooms, who had watched christenings and marriages and deaths within these thick, ancient walls. At last, the long roof and the sides collapsed, but yet something hung on; and people would make trips there to see it and understand something of the majesty of the original. That double flight of curved stairs, marble-topped, with the swerving ironwork railings, was untouched by the fire. It is an ironic sight, the imposing approach, leading to nothing but the clouds above. Beneath stands the old passageway through which Esteban Minor's carriages rolled. Today it grants entry to a stretch of weeds.

The place on the hill patronized by Minor's friend, Andrew Ellicott, has had a spectacular career through the years. Pat Connelly gave it up about the beginning of the American regime; after that it was alternately a house and an inn, then a school, a run-down residence, and finally a tenement. For decades it stood in bedraggled grandeur, rooms partitioned into cubicles, brickwork sagging, surrounding growths gone wild with neglect. Warehouses and sheds crowded it as industrialism encroached upon the old Spanish Esplanade; the old tavern appeared only a step removed from ruin. Then in 1936 the Natchez Garden club, acquiring it, made a thoroughgoing restoration. Out came the additions, the cubicles and layers of dark paint. The essential parts remained intact. Much of the early glass, brought from abroad, was uncracked.

Investigating, some concluded that the inn had been constructed of ship's materials, left when vessels were dismantled at the Natchez waterfront. Such readily available, well-seasoned wood was used in many instances. The ceilings are excellently vaulted, and may have been the work of shipwrights who serviced the port below. Today Connelly's Tavern looks much as it did when Ellicott and Minor walked inside it. Downstairs is the central tavern room and brick-floored tap room with hand-made chairs and benches and an antique bar. The kitchen retains its heavy fireplace, candlestick molds, heating pans and iron spiders. Upstairs waits the luxury of the privileged—four-poster beds, slave-made; a counterpane with the date of 1812; a trundle bed for a child, to be slipped beneath a bigger one during daytime; a bedspread whose cotton was grown on an older plantation, spun there into thread and then handwoven.

The walls hold copies of rules dating back to Connelly's day. However elite the gentlemen guests, they must obey regulations. No more than four to a bed; in case one sleeping companion robbed another, the management could not be held responsible; a guest must remove his shoes before retiring. The era was a less fastidious one than the present. Some, careless or completely fagged after a harrowing journey, were known to throw themselves in complete attire across the nearest bed. A custom at the inn, it is explained, was the immediate appearance of a slave with hot toddy and hot water, and an offer to wash the traveler's feet for him—a proposal prompted by more than courtesy, no doubt!

{VI}

PURITAN IN THE SINFUL SOUTH

HE WAS the kind of man who, as an intimate wrote, held himself so erectly that he looked even taller than he was. He was confidently correct in all things. And during the greater part of his life, practically everyone praised him, and practically no one got along with him. Winthrop Sargent of Massachusetts spent much of his adult career working with extreme conscientiousness, and experiencing a haunting sense of unhappiness. For fate had made him a tight-jawed Puritan and then put him in places where the Puritans drew both shouts of derision and stones.

The world seemed to brighten that morning in 1798 when the sharp-eyed man of forty-three received news from his government. The advancement he was waiting for had come through. He was to be the first Governor of the new American Territory of Mississippi. Sitting in his office in the Ohio country, he breathed a sigh of relief; and if contemporaries are to be believed, those about him did the same thing.

Life had begun well enough for this personable son of a respected shipping family. Born in Gloucester, he finished Harvard and went to sea at twenty as captain of one of his father's vessels. Home after several years, Winthrop joined the Revolutionary Army, surviving the icy months at Valley Forge, and emerging a brevet-major at twenty-five. For the officer, prospects looked temporarily good; then the bottom dropped out. His father suffered reverses, and Winthrop had to scratch for himself. He considered joining Holland's army as a mercenary; George Washington wrote a letter of commendation. But neither this nor several other projects worked out. By the time he reached thirty, long conditioned to command, he had nothing to command.

At an early date he discovered himself resenting the entrenched East from which he had come; with his friends out of uniform he talked of the beckoning frontier where "the veteran soldier and honest man should find a retreat from ingratitude—never more to visit the Atlantic shores." In time he saw himself as a perpetually wronged person; the attitude became a fixed one, adding to his troubles.

He and other war veterans formed the Ohio company to develop the Northwest; though scandal later was attached to it, Winthrop was never blamed. From a post of surveyor he won office as secretary of the Northwest Territory and for long periods served as acting governor. For twelve years he performed duties with honesty and zealousness. But, though he had welcomed the challenge of the assignment, Winthrop Sargent found the frontier alien and unfriendly. The loud buoyancy offended his New England spirit; the zest of living shocked his feeling for rigid decorum. Because they did not do things his way, he quarreled with those above and below him. To make matters worse, Winthrop possessed a strong streak of Army; when a citizen did not step forward to follow an order, the word "insubordinate" came to his lips. He lacked both tact and the common touch. His way was not rendered easier when his young wife died in the West, following the birth of their first child.

Soon after word of his new appointment, a friendly tip arrived from the Secretary of State: The Mississippi Territory would present problems; Winthrop should be firm but also conciliatory. He could well follow the example of former

Governor Gayoso, in establishing good social relations, fitting his manner to the people's. Cautiously Winthrop Sargent replied that it might not be in his power to do so, but he would try to "conciliate and attach all parties to the United States." Alas for pious hopes! Winthrop was the last person in the world to "conciliate" Natchez in normal times; at this moment a special kind of concentrated fury was brewing for him.

Preparing to leave the Northwest, Winthrop Sargent fell violently ill. Doctors held grave consultations. The long years of work had told; the man needed a full rest—a trip to Europe or months at the Eastern watering places. That same day the post-rider brought a new message from the Secretary of State. Mr. Sargent's presence in Natchez was required more urgently than ever. Could he go sooner than he had planned?

Within a week, sustained by his ambition and rigid sense of duty, Sargent was lying on a crude bed in a rocking flatboat, almost in delirium. Under what he later called a "vertical sun," he further sickened and nearly died. In moments of calm, he ordered the crew to speed up. Reaching the river town, he felt only slightly better; his first view of Natchez was in a blur of nausea. They took him to Concord, where he began slowly to recover.

From the first he found Natchez' climate almost unbearable. He had never known such blasts of heat, or such heavy rains that left the air only more steaming and hostile. Sweat poured down his frame morning and night. He cursed the whining mosquitoes that circled him, getting into ears and nose. How could men work here without suffering sun-stroke or dying of exhaustion?

His state of mind hardly improved when he heard what was happening in the territory. Laws, especially in regard to land, were hopelessly confused. Who owned what? Would the Americans follow the Spanish land grants? What about conflicts between earlier British property dealings, and Spanish ones? Men rushed about, claiming squatter's rights to land they had never before seen. Newcomers were slipping in from Spanish Mexico, French Louisiana and elsewhere. "Diffused over our country," the bewildered Sargent wrote, "are aliens of various character, and among them the most abandoned villains who have escaped from the chains and prisons." As for the natives, they showed a "refractory and turbulent spirit, with parties headed by men of perverseness and cunning. *They have run wild in the recess of government.*"

Beginning to hobble around, Sargent met little to praise. His eye surveyed the teeming under-hill harbor, the sprawling Spanish shops, the thronged roads to outlying plantations. His upright soul writhed at the improprieties. For Natchez, with its Creole air of ease and relaxation, was hardly a prim New England village. People attended mass or morning services on Sunday, then went about, paying social calls, picnicking, enjoying themselves. Stores stayed open, fruits and sides of meat and trinkets hanging in the sun, hawked by the proprietors. Bars operated full time. Indians came into town, poured down as much fire-water as possible and fell in a stupor in the road. Negro slaves, managing to get passes into town, met in groups near the river, took to high jinks and any liquor that came to them. In the warm afternoons the planters did not stream perspiration as did Mr. Sargent; they took their rest on their galleries and during the cool hours afterward, they enjoyed leisurely dinners and visits. Also, they liked races; they made bets and they gambled.

Winthrop Sargent was appalled. "Natchez . . . has become a most abominable place," he reported. He saw more than really existed; he piled horror upon horror. Yet in some respects conditions undeniably had turned worse. Robberies increased day and night; murder had grown common. "Every day and hour multiply complaints, some amounting to felonies and very high misdemeanors . . ." As soon as he could drag himself to his office, the Governor addressed his fellow-citizens in a friendly tone. Matters were complicated, he admitted; he would get affairs going as soon as possible, but meanwhile he appealed for order. He did not speak his full mind because, secretly, he had grown frantic. Under the territorial system, the Governor and three judges were the government; they adopted laws and enforced them, without the help of legislators or anyone else. But Sargent was no lawyer. One judge had arrived, and he knew practically nothing about law. Long months must pass before another, only slightly more qualified, showed himself. The third, best of the lot, waited until the following summer, then didn't like what he saw, and he went home.

Sargent lacked even laws to guide him. Months earlier he asked the State Department for copies of those in other parts of the country. He received nothing. One of the judges found his boat too small for lawbooks, and left them behind. They needed a printing press, and its arrival was long delayed. (Spain had never permitted so subversive an instrument in the colony.)

The Indians, always a problem, grew worse. He couldn't learn what Washington officials wanted done about them. Should he placate them with gifts, and if so, where would he get the gifts? The Indians, like some natives, were "running wild," swooping down on unprotected houses, forming delegations with grandiose demands and threats. Sargent feared that they might unite with the hostile French or Spanish or British to burn out the settlement.

At best the task called for an adjustable man with a thick skin. Mr. Sargent was hardly one to make easy shifts, or draw on the help of friendly natives. Without effort, often without knowing it, he won enemies on all sides. Citizens called with good will and left spluttering. William Dunbar wrote a friend: "I am on as good terms as it is possible to be with a man of his phlegmatic and austere disposition. However good his intentions, it is impossible that a man so frigid and sour can give satisfaction to a free people."

In at least one direction, however, Winthrop was solidifying himself. He made friends with the well-placed Williams family. They invited him to their plantation outside town;

and for the first time he had respite from his harassing troubles. On the breeze-swept gallery, sipping his punch beneath the trailing vines, he settled back to watch the moon rise over the darkness of the magnolias. For weeks he had been jumping at the perpetual noise about him—unruly clamor on the street, shouting exchanges at the market place, drawling cross-comment among his petitioners. Winthrop was not the first Northerner to shudder at the well-developed art or habit of Southern conversation. Tonight, he thanked his New England God, people were quiet; the sheer novelty was a balm.

He dozed, and opened his eyes to see a handsome, smiling woman sitting opposite him. The Williamses, sorry for Winthrop, hadn't disturbed him. Leaping to his feet, he apologized. Maria McIntosh Williams, a recent widow, looked at him with amusement and sympathy. In their small circle the Williamses talked of things that had nothing to do with Natchez and his troubles, and Winthrop sighed his gratitude.

The widow Maria proved herself a well-traveled, intelligent and observant woman. They had seen the same things in the East, and they found three or four common acquaintances. A little later he noticed several well-behaved young men and women in the summer house. When he discovered that they were her children, his respect grew. This man who liked order in everything considered docile youngsters a major blessing. When the evening ended, he found he had spent most of his time exchanging pleasantries with the widow; as he went to bed that night, he remembered Maria's last, half-humorous suggestion: If Mr. Sargent would only relax a little, he would not find matters so difficult. For the first time in months, he had a restful night.

When the Williamses repeated their invitation, Winthrop accepted with happy anticipation. He was not disappointed. At the evening's end the awkward New Englander asked permission to call on the widow. Following that occasion, he did not sleep so well; the widow Maria's expressions, her gestures and tones came back to him. After all, he told himself, he had been alone for eight years; none could claim he had not waited long enough. After many preliminaries, including delicate hints to her brothers, he asked Maria for an answer. Her "Yes" opened a prospect of new happiness that Winthrop had never expected.

Had Winthrop Sargent's identification with the Williamses occurred earlier, there might have been hope for him among the Natchezians. But it came too late. Even the sight of a less forbidding Governor could not halt the tide. By this time he had thrown together a set of new laws. He issued a proclamation forbidding citizens to sell liquor to Indians. He ordered newly arrived non-Americans to report within two hours to a justice of the peace. He set up a tax of eight dollars for a wedding license, eight for operating a tavern, four for a passport. Too, he put up the territory's first public building—significantly, a jail.

Some of the measures were necessary; others represented a Puritan method of justice, a harsh "thou shalt not." Under the Spaniards, Natchez had grown accustomed to a far more tolerant rule, and the opposition had a new hinge on which to swing their condemnation. The man was a fanatic, a usurper of powers! Who did he think he was, God, or the President?

Citizens leaped up, fists flying, eyes bulging. Did this fellow mean an owner to pay for a passport every time he crossed the river to his plantation? (Obviously Sargent didn't intend this, but it made good fuel.) Marriage fees—what wouldn't the fellow be trying to tax? His penalties were outrageous. Arson could bring confiscation of an estate, whipping, pillorying, long imprisonment. What would he try next—witch burning in the New England manner?

Sargent cried out that he had done the best he could, following custom of the Northwest territory in some instances. True, there had been mistakes; but he denied most of the accusations. No matter what his diplomatic wife said, he could not restrain himself. He retorted that the opposition tactics were "systematically calculated to sap the reputation of a declining

GLOUCESTER
The Puritan Blushed at Wild Natchez

EARL M. NORMAN

MAGNOLIA VALE
Next Door, Quivering Sin on the Mississippi

EARL M. NORMAN

life, the morning and meridian of which have been most faithfully devoted to the honorable service of my country."

Citizens' agents went to Congress, insisting that Sargent be removed, that the Territory be advanced to the "second degree," given the right to elect a legislature to act with the Governor. A Congressional committee, investigating, ruled that while certain irregularities had resulted from Sargent's incorrect opinions of his powers, no "impure" intentions were involved. But his opponents scored when a legislature was ordered elected. At once Winthrop clashed again with his enemies; he claimed that the election was rigged. (It all has a fairly contemporary ring . . .)

In Washington, Sargent's Federalist party went out and its enemy, Jefferson, came to power. Winthrop knew it would be wise to present his case in person. He almost broke an overland record in getting there, only to find a new man already chosen. Jefferson spoke tactfully; however meritorious, Sargent's administration had "not been so fortunate as to bring the harmony and mutual attachment" that a new territory required.

His world in pieces, his political career at an inglorious end, the Puritan went home to Massachusetts to ponder whether he should bring his wife and her children North, and take up life in a place that, at the least, would not jar him as had Natchez. On the one side were the angry files of his opposition calling him everything from Nero to blockhead, and the strangeness of Natchez life, its discomfit, informality, profligacy. On the other side stood the lady, and then, too, he remembered the quiet evenings, the restful hours on the calm outskirts, and their visits with the neighbors. After long communion with himself, Winthrop made his decision. He would go back, as a Mississippi cotton planter in his own right.

The Widow Williams had been the possessor of an ample plantation; to this Winthrop added his own means. They quickly had a flourishing establishment in operation, and he was riding his acres like any of those with whom he had quarreled. He had spoken sadly, in controversy, of his "declining life." He showed this to have been mere rhetoric; he and the widow produced two boys in succession.

In his new phase Winthrop never became a wildly popular figure, to be hailed on the street, and invited to the hotel bar for a drink. But he turned into an opulent grower; he got on well with his fellow planters, and he was one of the commissioners who founded the Bank of Mississippi. Then, as a final step, he proceeded to give Natchez one of its most Southern of Southern mansions. The house at which he had first seen Maria appealed particularly to him. Comparatively new, built about 1799, it had gone out of the Williams family, but whenever he passed he remembered his original peaceful evenings. Acquiring it, he refashioned it in his own way.

In the center of several hundred acres of wooded park rose a compact, two-and-a-half storied house of warm red brick with a white front. For the expanding Sargents, it must be enlarged. The original house had a graceful doorway, deeply recessed, with delicately styled white woodwork above. Winthrop doubled the width of the building, and this left the door out of balance; so he duplicated it at the other side, giving a house with two identical entrances. The visitor was frequently puzzled which to try first.

At front and back the transplanted New Englander installed galleries as ample as those of any other Southerner. The first lifted itself high, a two-storied Grecian portico with pediment and delicate oval light in the center. The columns, each resting on a rectangular base, were Doric and imposing. These and the wooden railings of the two galleries and the balanced doorways gave a shining whiteness in contrast with the red of the bricks and the bright greens of the shutters and lattice work at the sides. A wider porch, at the rear, had five similar pillars. Along three sides, Sargent's slaves dug a dry moat with a protective railing; the basement floor had thickly-barred doors and windows. Additional bars at the two main entrances provided the protection of a fortress.

Inside, from each of the two great doors, a long hallway led through the house; a cross-hall gave entrance to an octagonal room at both sides. Just beyond each front door, carrying out the balance, rose a curved stairway, leading to the upper floor. The many passages had arched connections, fanlighted, ornamented, giving an additional richness. Despite its considerable width, the house remained only one room deep; the first floor had three main chambers, drawing room and dining room in the octagonal side extensions, and a library in the center. But some of the hallways and connecting passages were the size of full rooms in ordinary houses; and in 1808 a traveler declared that the establishment "bespoke more taste and convenience than I had yet observed in the territory." Yet, as if to show he had not entirely succumbed to Mississippi's charms, Winthrop called his house by the slightly incongruous title of his old town, Gloucester.

In these later, controversy-free years, Winthrop divided his hours between his cotton fields and his library, his office and drawing room. There the good-humored Maria received guests as she had always done; among them she counted many who had swapped abuse with Winthrop in the heated days. She brought her husband together with one such man after another; she had learned, long ago, the art of quieting a New England conscience, and also temper.

Twenty years after his arrival here, while making a seaboard steamboat trip, Winthrop died unexpectedly. The cause was a seemingly unpuritanical one: gout. With his last testament he gave Natchez a prod or two, demonstrating that he still had reservations about the place and its life. In a document filled with peppery passages, he asked that his body be "speedily and without parade borne to the willow yard by my own blacks, attended only by half a dozen friends, neighbors or acquaintances, and committed to the earth, and that no mausoleum but some simple stone proclaim me dead."

He left more than 25,000 acres of land in Louisiana, Mississippi, Virginia and Ohio, together with cash, bank stock and other assets; he gave highly specific instructions how the estate should be handled to increase its value. He provided trusted administrators, but arranged for a check to be made upon them. A well-bound blankbook must, for instance, be available with a record of every proceeding, for inspection at any time. Winthrop Sargent hadn't lost all his suspicion of the world.

He wanted no pampered sons; their money must not keep them from working hard for their training. The widow was to see that they finished their education, "giving them such decent economical provision as may insure exertion and industry on their parts." Eventually the house, Gloucester, should be leased. One of the boys might wish to keep it, but he added: "'Tis a costly establishment and unprofitable plantation, and in a climate suited only to the winter of life. From the probable state of society and physical causes, it cannot be considered a proper residence for them till they have passed the meridian of their days." Climate and "state of society" notwithstanding, Winthrop went to the grave still a man of Massachusetts. But Natchez couldn't understand the word "unprofitable" which he applied to Gloucester. Certainly cotton had done well by him.

He wished the boys to be taught law at the University of Cambridge; and here he disclosed his opinion of the average attorney. He was making ample provision for them, so they would not have to "prostitute talents in bad causes." Another provision was stern. If either son, or his legitimate descendants, became "debauched or drunkards or gamblers, or be guilty of other intemperance or infamous conduct," he wanted them reduced to five hundred dollars a year for common food and raiment. Only if they gave full proof of "restoration to rectitude," might they get back their inheritance. As for Cambridge, it received part of the estate—provided the money went "not only to promote literature but to put down the immorality and vice which is generally believed to be increasing from the sufferance of a kind of college taverns—places of trust for ardent and inebriating liquors and gambling"!

One of the boys died early; the other, George Washington Sargent, led a life as upright and quiet as even his father could have wished, and not in Natchez for the most part. Shortly after Winthrop's death the widow sold Gloucester for twenty thousand dollars and went to Philadelphia. A quarter century later, when the house changed hands at sheriff's auction, there stepped forward a man with a face vaguely familiar to the Natchezians. George Washington Sargent had come back to take his father's house.

The town people liked the second Sargent; for him Gloucester provided a serene fifteen years in the red brick place with the double entranceways and thickly-barred openings. He enjoyed the house and the many acres of wooded passageways, staying through the Civil War and part of the reconstruction. One evening, he heard a noise and made out dim figures in the yard. When he received no reply to his call, he hurried to a back doorway and opened one of the guarded doors. He started down the stairs, but in a moment was rolling forward, a bullet in his body. The killing is attributed to roving soldiers.

The son's body was taken to the family graveyard across the road, where he was placed next to his father in that "willow yard" to which the slaves had carried the New Englander. The Natchez country and the Sargents, it would seem, had never really gotten along.

For a time Gloucester saw dim days of neglect, during which the carved archways grew dingy and streaks of stain marred the paneled walls. About 1923 Mrs. James Surget restored it, with a splendor of ornamentation unknown in the days of the first Sargent—classic French mirrors, chandeliers of Bohemian glass in many colors, oils of nudes and voluptuaries, scenes of bacchanalia that would have stirred the correct Winthrop, but only to a temper.

During the past century and a half the brick walls of Gloucester have faded slightly, and the decades have left their imprint—markings at the bases of the firm columns, the slight sagging of a frame that nevertheless holds as well as ever. Inside most of the early wide planking remains, worn by successive generations. The library holds early volumes, including first editions that have become collectors' items. The arches and interior fanlights have lost little of their original rich effect. The heavy iron bars, put up by the careful Winthrop Sargent, have never been removed. The present owner, Mrs. Lennox Stanton, points to a name scratched in the original opalescent, wavy window glass. In an idle moment, Julia Sargent cut her name there and then added the figure of a horse. Surely she, like anyone else, would have thought this glass the least permanent part of the house. But her signature has survived her, as well as the horse that prances on toward eternity.

BONTURA

⋅❴VII❵⋅

HELL UNDER THE HILL

"For the size of it there is not, perhaps, in the world a more profligate place." John Bradbury, shaken by what he saw in Natchez, said this in 1810. Hundreds echoed him in their horror or delight, or combinations of the two.

New Orleans frequently proclaimed its riverfront to be the wickedest locale in America. Vicksburg asserted with warmth that its underworld could outshade and outstrip anything the Creole city offered. But for nearly fifty years authorities in such matters gave Natchez Under the Hill the crown for flaming, free-wheeling gaiety. Up and down the Mississippi, native eyes brightened at the tales of glittering good times to be had in lower Natchez. Whatever you liked, whatever way you liked it, Mister, you got it in Natchez. It was hell on earth, with bells attached.

At the foot of the bluff the Mississippi had built an irregular shelf of soft earth a half to three quarters of a mile long. Over it narrow streets criss-crossed in haphazard fashion. Jerry-built, weather-beaten shacks filled practically every square foot of ground, extending to the water's edge, where they perched on stilts. No flowers, no grass grew in this mud; the alleys were dank and dark, a green scum covering the wetter holes.

At the landing hundreds of vessels moored in a bobbing, shifting line—flatboats like heavy rafts with huts on top, laden with wheat and corn, turkeys and pigs; keel-boats, sturdier, more elongated, big enough for crews of twenty-five or thirty; barges and skiffs and sea-going vessels as well. Their crews cursed each other as their crafts jockeyed for space. At the wharves, yellow-skinned hawkers told of the joys beyond, pointing to Silver Street, the main thoroughfare under the hill and the toughest on the Mississippi. In doorways, on the roadways, leaning over the landing itself, were agents on the lookout for prospects. Few establishments were ever closed or silent. There was a consistent pound of tinny pianos, high laughter of women, and clatter of games. Parrots squawked; half-nude girls bent out of the windows touting their charms.

Drunken men, white, black or red, lurched past. Soldiers, lawyers, merchants ogled, grinned and exchanged comment. A naked sailor, crying that he had been rolled, ran into the street after a shrieking mulattress. Several people laughed, and everybody stepped out of their way. That was *their* business. Under the Hill you kept to your own concerns.

On an upper gallery a screech of agony rang out, and two men wrestled for a knife on a tin half-roof. Both rolled off. One walked away, leaving a twitching figure behind, the intestines hanging from a ripped stomach. The witnesses turned away for they knew the victor, and they knew better than to remember what they had seen. Through the crowd sped carts and drays. Lines of cattle stumbled under drivers' whips, and files of slaves trudged up the narrow ledge of roadway to the hill above. All was hot and sweaty, congested and stinking; from the earth arose a vague effluvium of squalor and musk and decay.

In this paradise of individualism, a man took what he wanted or what he could grab, and told the world to take a flying jump. He kept what he caught, until a hardier bucko came along and strangled or gutted him for it. Natchez under the Hill grew out of geography, an hour in the American story, and a temperament touched by the Southern climate. Natchez was a river town, a cross-roads capital, a frontier and border settlement. It teemed with money from cotton, from trade in black men, from commission business.

Gambling got into the blood; it was a drinking place, a fighting place, a killing place. Above all presided the careless spirit of the frontier—the r'aring humor of the Mississippi bully, the quivering truculence of the river rat, a man who picked a fight because he didn't like the cut of another's trousers, or the way he spat, or simply because the battler had waked with a belly cramp.

Through the Spanish regime the river landing had remained a more or less quiet spot. A few jaws broken, stray shots exchanged as American and Spanish temperaments clashed; that was all. With the 1800s it came into its own. The full force of migration was unleashed, from all of the East and North. A nostalgic native lamented: ". . . all of the bad reputation which Natchez acquired was after it came into the hands of Americans." The explanation, however, was the inevitable force of human movement, not a matter of nationality.

Along the bluffs a baronial civilization lifted its head. We live up here, in Natchez proper; they're below, in Natchez improper. . . . The secure and stable element rested in the breeze-swept heights, the precarious existence in the musty depths. Through the years many men who owned the pillared establishments earned part of their income from under the Hill. Oftener, too, than some would have it known, upper and lower met. If a plantation miss or madame proved altogether too lady-like, there was always a good-humored girl of white or yellow or saffron coloration in the shacks at the water's edge.

Certain discreet operators maintained attractions open only to an approved few. Curtains would part and reveal ladies, "direct from New Orleans," or Paris, the possessors of specific whispered-about attributes. They postured, they circled, and frequently the plantation gentlemen were fighting, even like the lesser breed downstairs, over which one went to whom.

The main customers of the barrel-houses and dives, however, were the boatmen, tired of their long isolation on the water, bursting for action. Raw-boned, red-faced, they surveyed the field over their bottles. When they opened their mouths, they made sounds that listeners remembered for months. Loud, boastful, they had majestic command of pungent phrase, of sulphuric oath and obscenity. When they fought, no rules prevailed; the best man won in any way he could. The loser might end up with his nose bitten off, his private parts a bloody pulp or himself a corpse in the river.

An early observer told how he beheld a powerful river man swinging his arms in challenge to the universe. He was a "roarer." He hadn't had a fight in a month. He was getting lazy. He dared anybody to "scrape the rust" off him. For a few minutes the bruiser found no takers, until a "little stubbed fellow" looked up dryly: "And who might you be, my big chicken?"

"I'm a high-pressure steamer!"

"And I'm a snag!" The tiny one pitched in, and the great man fell sprawling. A shout rang from the crowd; that steamboat had been well snagged. The boatmen's spirits rose; they moved in for a closer view. One shoved another, who shoved back; a free-for-all broke out. The net result, our friend concludes on a casual note, was that "several houses were torn down."

When several keelboats arrived at the same time, excitement popped. The girls were awakened and Negroes called in for music. Dice rolled and sleek gentlemen eased over to tables with packs of cards in hand. All available men, pimps and shackbullies, were summoned. From outside came shouts, and a stampede began. Fists pounded, and feet kicked open doors. A fight or two started when bullies, jostling at the entrance, decided that they didn't like one another's looks, anyway. These differences were settled with a scuffle or the timely use of a gun butt and the boys shoved forward, reaching for liquor, slapping the first female rear that hove into view.

Some of the women, catching the combative spirit, soon were whacking each other, pulling at dyed curls, and shrieking until separated. After a time the boys had enough to drink and they lurched away with their girls. By the time the evening ended, if several jaws had not been broken and an eye or two gouged, the management knew that a business recession had arrived.

Meanwhile, outside, stealthy figures crept about in a gray fog that rose from the river. In the still water near the landing eyes caught dark floating objects. Nobody did anything about the bodies; some fellow had caused too much trouble and had been quieted, that was all. The next morning a shanty-boat dweller, some miles downstream, would spy it and drag it to land with a rope, hoping for a reward. Frequently he got none. No, sir, nobody knew nothing about it. There was little curiosity under the Hill about murder.

The spot had its natural leaders. Best known was the bearded, immensely tough Jim Girty, who withstood fate and the knives through many years. Impressed citizens made up folk-lore about him: He didn't have ribs like you and me, that you could shoot through or cut in. No, sir, he got thick bone like a man's head, only thicker. . . . So endowed, Jim ruled his roost. His woman, Marie Dufour, ran a bawdy house of good reputation. She kept it good; for Marie, a pink blonde Amazon, could open a bottle with her teeth, and shoot off a man's nose at a hundred feet. Jim and Marie loved one another if only for their unchallenged strength and their cold scorn for the universe.

Eventually several individuals elected to test the belief about Jim's no-ribs. On a dark evening they ambushed him. Jim cursed and reached, but they had reached first. Guns exploded, girls screeched. Marie thrust forward, firing, and two of the men fell. But Big Jim was on the floor, and silent behind his beard. Marie turned him over, and his mouth sagged. He *had* had ribs, like anyone else. Moaning, Marie thrust her gun into her mouth and sent the bullet crashing through the top of her head. That evening, several places closed for the first time in years. There'd never be another Jim and Marie.

When steamboats arrived, revolutionizing river traffic, Natchez under the Hill throbbed for a time with added life. The waterfront was crowded more than ever, but now the ornate white palaces of jigsaw and plush ruled the landing. The glow of their lights dimmed the flatboats and keelboats; in their wash the pickings of waterfront life grew fatter. Over and over cannons boomed to let the town know a packet was arriving or leaving. Negroes and Indians formed raffish musical bands to "serenade" new arrivals for their pennies. So many gambling houses and bawdy rooms appeared that there was no room left. The line overflowed along the road up the hill; others thrust themselves far out on pilings at the riverside. And Natchez became a stamping ground extraordinary of the professional gambler.

This gentry worked according to world-old principles. Every man, especially if he were prosperous, liked to talk about himself and his business. First and foremost, a gambler had to be a good listener; stepping aboard, he needed only a few hours to find out what he wanted to know about any passenger. Planters made ideal prey. Generally they were traveling to town to settle with their factors. On the down trip, a skilful gambler worked slowly, carefully. Apparently by mere chance, he got off with the man he had picked, went to the same hotel, and looked over to discover his new friend at the bar. A reunion followed; others joined them. In a good-natured card game, the planter won several times before they broke up.

Finishing his business in town, the planter collected his thousands. On the trip home, a voice hailed him—his same friend. This time, in two or three quick games, the grower lost everything. At the next stop the little party of players disappeared, and that was all there was to that. Except, perhaps, for the planter. Knowing he had been plucked, he might wait for years and then, meeting up with the gambler, shoot him on the spot. At least as often, he walked to his cabin on the boat, sat in the dark and blew out his own brains.

Most of the outsiders who caused annoyance under the Hill found it the last they ever started. Once, just as a steamer was about to leave, a pistol shot rang out. A passenger, who had just returned to the upper deck after a stop on shore, slipped to the deck. The vessel was backed in, the corpse placed on the wharf. The captain called a sheriff's helper, told what he had seen, and the steamer chugged off. A brief inquest brought a verdict of murder by persons unknown. Again that was all there was to that—except for a family far away, that would forever curse the name of Natchez.

The Irish actor, Tyrone Power, in 1836 pronounced the under-hill establishments "more obscene in their appointments than the lowest of the itinerant hells found at our races." Things, however, had a "bolder and more swashbuckler-like air"; for Natchez, always, the romantic touch. Strolling one night on the bluff above, Power heard a fight in the depths. "The tumult grew in loudness and fierceness. Men's hoarse and angry voices, mingled in hot dispute, came crashing upwards as from the deeps of hell. I bent anxiously over the cliff . . . a louder burst ascended, then crack! crack! went a couple of shots, almost together; the piercing shrieks of a female followed, and to these succeeded the stillness of death. On one hand lay the town of Natchez, sunk in repose; the moon at full, was sleeping over it, in as pure a sky as ever poet drank joy and inspiration from." Before him, luminous in the half-dark, flowed the Mississippi, careless of Natchez above or Natchez below.

The gambling fraternity used the time element, like everything else, to assist its operations. When a steamboat disgorged passengers for a short night stop, the houses received them with delight. The proprietor kept his eye on the vessel's loading operations. At a climactic moment the rows of money piled high at the tables; nerves grew taut. The steamboat bell sounded to summon back the passengers. Then someone doused the lights, and while they were out, attachés scooped up all the cash and ran. It was too late to protest, and what good would that do? The passengers rushed out; but the house wasn't finished with them yet. A rope was suddenly lifted across the narrow street, tripping them. Watchful men, who had already taken their measure, caught them in the dark, ran through their pockets and scurried away. To have followed them through the murky labyrinths would have been hopeless, perhaps fatal. The victims could only curse and leave.

One of Natchez' most famous yarns, however, concerns the way the situation was reversed. Hot-tempered Captain John Russell became increasingly annoyed at the gambling crowd. On an upriver trip from Baton Rouge, he was carrying a delegation of ministers. The party stopped at Natchez where a young recruit, carrying his organization's money, was drawn toward a gaudy establishment near the water line. Stepping in for a few minutes, he was stripped of his funds. The minister went to Captain Russell. The captain, with a warm oath about preachers, marched back with him.

Russell, his snowy hair bristling, told the proprietor he wanted that money. The gamblers laughed derisively. Wasn't that just too bad? The captain grew red in the face. They'd regret that. See his steamboat? They knew how powerful an engine he had in it. Well, if they didn't come across, he'd use it to pull the whole thieving building into the river. The fraternity remained amused. The captain summoned his black crew, who went to work on the flimsy blocks that formed the base of the building. *All right—let 'er go!* The bell rang, great wheels churned up a foam, and slowly the vessel drew away. The building groaned and the inmates heard a sound below, as of ripping and tearing, while a crack broke out in the cheap ceiling plaster. Shouting curses and protests, out they ran.

The preacher got his money and thereafter kept out of gambling dens.

Only one man ever chose to defy Natchez Under the Hill by establishing a plantation way of life beneath the bluff. For years, within sound of the brawling, the Scotsman Andrew Brown held his own, swearing that he'd outlast it all. And he did. A lean and long-faced man in a heavy black suit, with the domed forehead and the look of a pedant, he arrived with his wife in 1820, at the age of thirty-one, and created a stir the first day in town. On his earliest business calls he made it clear he was an individual of firm Presbyterian principles. Pressing his thin fingers together, he observed that he didn't altogether believe in slavery; he wanted little to do with it. His listeners exchanged glances; this one would hardly last long in Natchez!

Also, Andrew Brown talked primly of "science," of doing things only after prolonged study. Plantation management, he hinted, struck him as a reckless, wasteful operation. He had, for a man, another unusual interest. Frequently he stopped to admire plants and shrubs; he knew as much about them as most professional plantation gardeners. In the lapel of his dark, correct suit he always wore a blossom. Practical Natchezians shrugged.

Announcing himself as a builder, Andrew obtained a few assignments. He infuriated the owners by doing nothing until the final tiny detail had been settled. At last, however, removing his coat and ripping off his black stock, he shed his austerity and stepped spryly about. Whatever his Presbyterianism, when he grew angry he could spit out his oaths as violently as any river boatman. He won the reputation of finishing his jobs, not on time but far ahead of it. More than that, Andrew Brown proved himself a true Scotsman by never losing a penny on a project.

Slipping quietly about the town, Andrew asked questions

and inspected things. While others spoke of cotton, he busied himself with everything except cotton. He found one Peter Little doing well with Natchez' first sawmill, operating on another ledge of ground a little distance from the river landing. As a builder he became a customer of Mr. Little. One day, planting his tall hat on his head, the lean-jawed Mr. Brown called on Mr. Little. How would Mr. Little like Mr. Brown to work for him? Mr. Little would; after a time they became partners. Eventually Andrew Brown bought out Peter Little to become the town's lumberman.

The fine new Little mill wasn't fine enough. So Andrew Brown put up one with four times the capacity, including new saws of tremendous size. He dug a canal across the mud flats to float logs to the river. His associates were skeptical. They felt there would never be need for anything like it. Then all at once Andrew was taking more orders than his plant could handle and devising further expansions. He had been the first to sense the booming demand for lumber, for steamboats, plantations and new buildings. He had spied almost inexhaustible sources up and down the valley. For a century and a quarter the sawmill under the Natchez cliff was to operate without let-up.

Though he insisted he still opposed slavery, Andrew compromised by using slaves. (White artisans had no wish to compete with labor that could not bargain for its hire.) His black men grew extremely able on the job. He sent one to Pittsburgh for training in iron work. As the servant left, the black-frocked master expressed his full confidence in him. The slave made no attempt to flee to freedom then or during subsequently long journeys about the country. Such is not the usual picture of bondsman and master.

Andrew got on well with his dark men. He told a story on himself: Joe, a colored helper at the mill, had had a glowing evening the night before, and his hand quivered badly. Andrew called out "Joe, that file you're using—it's drunk!" "Yessir," was the answer. "And if you been where dat file was las' night, you be drunk, too." Andrew guffawed with the others. Two of his mulattoes handled sales of lumber on short river trips. Bands of Irishman manned the sweeps. The mulattoes, better educated, took over supervision, handled sales and paid off the crew, all without friction. Then, after the payment, the mulattoes would shoot craps with the Irishmen and win back half the cash. Again, it is an untypical view.

To and from the rowdy landing place under the hill strode Andrew Brown, nose high in the air, scornful of the "citizens." Three years after he set up his new mill, he put on his black coat with the blossom in the lapel and walked slowly over the ground near his property. Workman started out with measuring rods, laying foundations. When friends asked questions, Andrew admitted solemnly that he was building a house. The townspeople hooted. That location, full of miasmas and crawling with such neighbors! But they made trips down the road to look.

Andrew worked with his usual exactitude, losing not a dollar's worth of value, producing a many-roomed establishment in a pattern that appealed to his instinct for wise use of space. A wide stuccoed-wooden structure, two-storied, it took the shape of an E, with three wings to the back; before it stood a simple, neatly balanced gallery with a double set of four Doric columns, supporting a tasteful shingled roof. The professional builder saw that there would be light and air in practically every room. The house itself could be divided into a series of separate apartments. Rear galleries opened into an expansive courtyard, bordered by a thoroughly untypical three-storied wooden fence, the highest Natchez ever had. It was a rectangle that enclosed a yard, chicken house, smoke house, wine-press and storage house.

Even from the nearby road along the hillside, the Browns had full privacy. Only the two-storied, columned front was visible. Another court, a small open one, was created before the house, its outer corners guarded by a set of statues, depicting the four seasons. Like primly posed figures awaiting a signal to begin a quadrille, they looked out upon what was to become a Natchez wonder, "Brown's Gardens."

For a long time the flower-loving Scotsman had been planning what he would grow. He had fifteen or more acres with which to work and upon them he lavished all of his feeling for green things. At the entrance he built up two mounds of earth, each topped by a tree; between them he put an arched white gateway. From there to the house was a distance of some twelve hundred feet. Along it he set an avenue of magnolias, interspersed with shrubs. In proper season the petaled heads of the creamy blossoms hung like white lanterns among the leathery leaves.

At both sides of the aisle of trees were circles, quarter circles and triangles of growth, carefully and precisely separated. Cherry laurels, oaks, magnolias and poplars were interspersed with both plain and showy shrubs. Walks twisted among plantings of camellias and rose bushes in graduated shadings from white to scarlet, some climbing over lattice work, forming arcades of color in the distance. Orange trees flowered near the foot of the hill. Wisteria dropped at the corners, and along brick paths the coral of crepe myrtle spread in waves. Between the box hedges, Andrew Brown and his gardeners developed secluded spots in which trees met overhead. Near the house several high natural mounds raised themselves; atop one of them he constructed an "outdoor living room," a circular, topless retreat, with benches inside and a round of tall cherry laurels to shut out the world. The winds brought the sharp cool scent of the sweet olive trees, which were to be called the finest along the Mississippi.

In the evenings when the Browns gave a party, the whole of their estate provided the setting. On one side rose the sharp lines of the brown cliffs, the vines and trees pressing close to the edge of the cultivated land below. In the other direction the Mississippi coiled by like a silver giant. Between water and bluff, strings of lamps extended among the plantings, outlining the "outdoor living room" and the avenues along which the couples strolled.

Passengers on steamboats hurried to the rails to look at the ordered beauty below the bluff. Vessels delayed their departure so that visitors could have themselves taken to the gardens. Andrew Brown's acreage assumed a great deal of the character of municipal property. It became a showplace for visitors, a Sunday afternoon parade for the natives. Callers found the high-domed Andrew there, puttering about the hedges, speculating about new plantings. Here was another universe from that other one below the hill—a spot of placid retreat, apart and remote from the rest of the town. On many an evening, a short way from the quiet house and its flowers, riots were breaking out on the river front. From a point on the cliff, an observer might look in two directions, at the high life and the low.

At Brown's Gardens two children grew up, Andrew Brown, Jr., and his sister Elizabeth. The son joined the father in the business, but died while still young. Not long afterward Mrs. Brown also died. In a year or so Brown married a capable widow of Jackson, Mississippi, who had already brought seven sons into the world. She had supported herself by operating a girls' school. With her spare funds she had sent her favorite boy, Rufus Learned, to school in her native Maine. And now Rufus returned in his early teens to find his mother remarried, and the mistress of Brown's Gardens.

The story shifts to this youth. At seventeen Rufus was a good-looking boy with black hair, a hint of brisk humor in his gray eyes and the beginnings of a bristling moustache. The young man also had a will and a temper. He liked his stepfather well enough; he could take Natchez or leave it. His glance darted quickly and without interest over his thin stepsister Elizabeth, less than half his age. It was time for Rufus to go North again to enter Bowdoin College. With polite goodbyes he started forth, without mentioning the project that was uppermost in his mind. In these early '50s, stirring tales were coming back of gold on the West Coast. The more Rufus thought about it, the more interested he grew. Reaching Maine, he turned quietly around, and the next the family heard of him he was on a sea voyage to California.

Arrived at the West Coast, he shoveled and dug, with some success. But, flaring with an almost habitual annoyance, he decided he had gone too late. New strikes were reported in Australia; that was the place. Showing a firm organizing ability, young Rufus called together a hundred and fifty men, bought a sailing vessel with their funds and led the party forth. Arriving at Hawaii, many of the party added the willing girls to their avocations; tropical climate, rum and maidens proved more alluring than prospects of gold, and they quit. But Rufus held to his purpose, (after rejecting the offer of a chief's wife for a second-hand shotgun). In Australia the expedition hit a good vein of gold and things looked up, until a gnat in his eye changed Rufus' destiny. He nearly lost his sight, and when the doctor insisted on a year's rest, he decided he could get that in Natchez.

He received a quick welcome at Brown's Gardens. His mother, though happy as the chatelaine, had a new pensive look. Of her many boys, he was the only one left. Now she was afraid she might lose him, too, and she asked him not to leave America. His future, she pleaded, surely was here, at his home. Reluctantly Rufus sold out his Australian interests and moved restlessly about Mississippi, buying a sawmill with his own capital, trying various enterprises. His bad eye bandaged, his temper short on many occasions, he seemed uncertain as to just what he wanted to do. This he knew—he didn't intend to depend on his step-father.

One of the surprises of his return was the sight of his stepsister. The once-scrawny child had bloomed in a way he would not have thought possible. Her portrait presents an amply-endowed brunette of brooding beauty, black hair in severe style, black taffeta and lace, hands folded before her. The picture has a Mona Lisa-like quality, and as far as Rufus was concerned, Elizabeth must have been a rather enigmatic miss, hardly the milk-and-water belle of tradition. The boys of her own age crowded around, and Andrew Brown and his wife looked on approvingly as Elizabeth tried to make up her mind. She saw her older stepbrother at intervals. Sometimes they got along famously, again they quarreled. Apparently they were a little alike in mind and spirit.

Civil war approached. Rufus, no believer in secession, voted firmly against it. But when Mississippi quit the union, he stepped forward, moodily as ever, to volunteer. There was nothing enigmatic in Elizabeth's attitude toward the war. She fought with her stepbrother because his feelings did not boil as hers did. His sharp temper snapped; then, recovering, he kissed her with a grin and left.

Now Elizabeth waited with her aging father and stepmother to see what would happen. Brown's Gardens occupied a site in which the Federals would naturally be interested. Union forces took over the sawmill, while Andrew Brown walked among his great plantings and watched. Some thought the mill would be burned down, until Brown, an earnest Mason, found a fellow Mason in high place among the Union men and persuaded him that, after all, it would be wise to keep the plant and operate it for the Federals. Old Andrew had not lost his cunning, or his sense of economy. And how did the Confederate Elizabeth act? There was danger that the house, too, might be taken, and for a time it was occupied in part. But Elizabeth decided that, whatever happened, *she* wouldn't be the cause of their losing their home. She smiled at the Federals, went to their dances, and kept her status as a belle.

War over, a leaner Rufus Learned returned, to find trouble. The property was in fair enough condition, but the lumber had been used up, and all the elderly Andrew had was $175,000 of unpaid bills, due from the government. Try as they might, they could never get payment, and bankruptcy was indicated. Rufus, still young, despite the lines at the corner of his eyes and the gray beginning to show in his moustache, listened angrily while lawyers argued. Jumping up, he announced that this time he'd do what his stepfather wanted, and try to run the mill. He liked a fight, and he'd give 'em one. His first task was to persuade creditors to wait. After hot arguments they agreed to delay a little.

Ironically, Rufus' first important post-war customer turned out to be the government. The Quartermaster-General's department wanted a large supply of timber at "St. Louis value plus freight." The nation's economy was still shattered; Rufus hardly knew what the figure meant. But this time, in any case, he would be paid. He took the chance—and realized a phenomenal profit. The Federals had taken; the Federals gave. There remained the matter of the luscious stepsister Elizabeth. Their marriage took place soon afterward.

When Andrew Brown died a few years later, at eighty-one, his stepson assumed direct command. And when the widow also died, Rufus had a free hand. He exceeded even Andrew, launching out into cotton mills, ice companies, railroads, banks and steamboats. The Learneds became Natchez' richest family of the 1880s and '90s. He changed the name of the estate to Magnolia Vale, so famous had become the majestic magnolia trees of the gardens. The plantings continued to thrive; in the evening, sitting with the family in the gardens, Rufus pointed out his vessels as they passed, tooting their whistles for the master.

At Magnolia Vale Elizabeth mellowed before Rufus did. He never lost either his firmness or hot temper. Conducting rate fights with rival steamboat owners, declaring war on any competitor, he saw to it that he always won. When automobiles came on the scene he acquired one of Natchez' first. Too old to drive, he sat in the front seat with his chauffeur and did the managing. He liked speed. When the driver grew too cautious, Rufus Learned reached over with his foot on the accelerator. "You just attend to the steering," he ordered. "I'll handle this part of it." Recognizing his shiny machine, pedestrians would run to the side of the road. Whenever he met another car, he would have to pass it, no matter how long it took, or how many appointments he missed. Then the old man gave the other driver a triumphant glare, and had the car turned around.

One of Rufus' battles, and his hardest, was with the Mississippi. Years earlier, his land along the river had begun to crack and slough off. The earth was sinking, gradually, imperceptibly, in certain areas. It became all too evident that the river was tapping the shore by underground drainage. Many grew certain that all the property—gardens, mill, Magnolia Vale itself—would eventually tumble in. Not Rufus Learned. He put up a breakwater and worked over the bank. After a fashion he succeeded, for the erosion-like process slowed down. But the mill had to be given up, and a new one built on ground long occupied by the gardens. The wonderplace was being whittled away, and old-timers looked on with sadness. There, where they had walked as children the river now washed. That spot where their party had sat under Brown's trees and sipped sangarees, was now ten feet deep. . . .

The house itself seemed endangered. Near it a rectangular section of earth, more than a hundred feet long, was gradually declining. The building settled irregularly, beginning to crack. Rufus decided on a peculiar operation. Hog chains were run through the building to keep it from falling to pieces. Concrete piers were sunk in the earth; between them and the sills of the house engineers installed iron plates and rollers. The house would now "ride" on them. The residents, if they were imaginative, might feel that they were sitting on top of a bowl of jelly. But Magnolia Vale stood.

When Rufus died, his son, Andrew Brown Learned, took over. He moved up on the hill, and for a time mill officials lived below in the fading surroundings of the gardens. Finally it became clear that Rufus had won his fight. The river made a small change in its course; no longer did it eat into the bank, and the house was secure. A few years ago another member of the family, a direct descendant, Howard Peabody, returned from wartime Naval duties to live there with his bride. The plantings received attention again. With a smile the family noticed that callers, passing the depressed area, assumed it was a carefully contrived sunken garden. Man could not have managed a finer job of it.

Then, during the Christmas season of 1946, flames achieved what the river had failed to do. The young Peabodys had a holiday party for orphans, and fireplaces, unused for years, were lighted. Afterward, in the night, the house went up in smoke along with the furniture, paintings, and rare books dating from the days of the scholarly Andrew Brown. Much of Brown's Gardens, however, can still be seen. That long central passage of twelve-hundred feet has been reduced to half, but the width of 350 feet or so is little changed.

Descendants of those first roses bloom in the spring air, with camellia bushes almost as high as the house once stood. The stately magnolia trees still spread their branches. Near the site of the house rise sweet olives nearly forty feet high, the tallest that I have ever seen. On one of the mounds a circle of cherry laurels remain, no longer as carefully trimmed as in former days, but so high that they touch above. The old "outdoor living room" is more private than ever. It is possible, even now, to realize the scale and richness of this great sight of the river country.

Yet a triumph can be counted for Andrew Brown and his successors. They have won over their neighbor, bawdy Natchez Under the Hill. The fate that almost took their shelf of earth long since practically destroyed that place of garish festivity. As early as 1820, or before, the Mississippi began to strike at this point with a strength even greater than it turned upon Magnolia Vale. Year by year, sections slipped into the water. Another natural force made itself felt. The hurricane of 1840 cut into the earth, killed men and women along the ledge of earth, wrecked steamboats and flatboats. Through the years, too, clashes occurred between the townspeople above and the residents under the Hill. "Clean-outs" took place when townsfolk descended on the place, to run men into the river, lynch them and burn their shacks. On a few occasions despised denizens were tied in flimsy canoes and set adrift, to float to their death or perhaps a lucky rescue. It didn't much matter which. In the course of time things quieted all along the Mississippi. Under the Hill grew more circumspect.

Recently I revisited the once-flamboyant settlement, or what remains of it—a single passageway with a few tired, dusty shops, groceries, deserted bars and rooming houses. For years those who had establishments here received trade from the ferry landing. Now, however, a high bridge spans the Mississippi between Natchez and Vidalia and there is a little reason to drive to the place below.

This passage had once been Silver Street, the wildest block along the river. Now it has become a silent place, its air disconsolate, as if it remembered its bawdy glories. The morning that I was there had dawned gloomily; the scene shared the pervading dull grayness. Old Silver Street had much of the quality of a ghost town. A fisherman plodded slowly toward the water, a line over his slumped shoulder. A boy, his eyes on the roadway before him, went by with a loaf of bread. On one of the galleries three or four children played; down the way, several girls were running. Children had not been plentiful in the old Under the Hill.

VIII

THE GOLDEN SURGETS

"I suppose you've heard what they say—we were once pirates...."

The gentle-voiced woman paused. At the window the yellow damask curtains stirred lightly, and her bright eyes followed the sweep of the lawn, where the birds sat silent in the midsummer heat. She sighed: "Since we have the reputation.... I hope we were good ones."

For generations the Surgets have been denying, with or without heat, some of the traditional versions of their beginnings. During all that time the Surgets have been making their own history, only slightly less tempestuous than that attributed to their ancestors. Though much has been said of the Surgets, few have accused them of being quiet people.

"Yes," the gray-haired matron nodded. "We've usually been ... well, intense. A friend used to tell me 'There's something about a Surget.' Sometimes I was afraid to ask just what she meant!" She looked behind her for a moment as if expecting a dead relative to contradict her with a well-recognized Surget bellow. Down the road creaked a wagon, bearing a grayish load of cotton. Inside the dimmed hallway, a line of earlier Surgets stared down toward us, most of them with that certain intent look.

Some hundred and seventy years ago, far off in Normandy, Pierre Surget received the news that his family had decided he would become a priest. He cried out: *"Mais, mon père..."* He had no vocation; it would be a prison. But Monsieur Surget was adamant; Pierre knew it was hopeless. Up in his room, his decision made, the boy stared with red eyes into the dark. He would be sorry to leave because there was a girl, the bright-lipped daughter of a merchant. The present Surgets, members of the well-to-do business class, had always wanted a priest in the family. Well, Pierre muttered, let them look elsewhere! A bundle under his arm, he dropped to the ground outside his window.

A little later, with his friend Auguste, he stood at the dock. Auguste had needed some persuading. Now they argued with the officer on the deck above. Finally the man nodded and at midnight the boys watched the lights of La Rochelle disappearing in the distance.

Weeks afterward, the new cabin boys stood suddenly at attention. The crew had grown rigid with excitement; a cannon had been dragged out, and now it quivered as a ball was fired. The two boys realized then that they had shipped aboard a privateer's vessel. Auguste got sick; Pierre turned away from him, his eyes glowing. This was excitement, adventure. The other vessel tried to answer fire, failed in the race that followed, and the crew made a swift, expert sweep upon the prey. Pierre's cheeks flamed. When would they get another? The sailors, laughing, pushed him away.

It was not long before the answer came. Their vessel was captured by an armed British frigate. When the enemy climbed aboard, the officers questioned the two youths, and motioned to them to step aside. At the British port, they were allowed to leave.

"Well?" Auguste appealed to Pierre. "They said they'd help us get back—"

Pierre, his eyes on the file of his former seamen-friends, spat out his contempt. "Go home and *be* a priest!" He walked off.

That same day ashore, he sniffed about a heavy vessel and spelled out the words New York. When the ship pulled out, Pierre crouched in the hold, a stowaway.

Pierre Surget kept his back turned on his family. For years there was to be a Surget tradition of seamanship. Added to this was, no less, a tradition of steady garnering of funds from the sea. On occasion Pierre roistered; but, pipe in mouth, most of his cash in pocket, he always went back to the water. Before long he became a mate, then captain; after much balancing of accounts, he had his own ship. It leaked a bit, and it smelled more than that, but it was his own.

A little later, after some consideration Pierre made a further acquisition, a wife. A stout-faced girl with steady blue eyes, Katrina Hubbard of Red Bank, New Jersey, was the daughter of a Dutch Reform minister. The union was a successful merger of Saxon and Gaul. Blonde Katrina's heavy frame plodded obediently behind her wiry husband's, and when Pierre thought it wise to take their ship and hunt greater opportunity, Katrina nodded and packed.

Down toward the Gulf of Mexico they sailed, along the sandy shores and up the coils of the Mississippi. For a time they stayed at New Orleans, living aboard their vessel for economy's sake. Neither had any thought of joining the easy-going life of the semi-tropic town; they were developing what would become a Surget affection for the intact dollar. Their first child was born there, on the water. Seeing a better chance at the upriver settlement of Baton Rouge, Pierre moved there. Again along the Mississippi's bank, Katrina had a child. More and more frequently, her husband had been hearing of the place called Natchez. Then in 1785, standing at the prow, Pierre rounded a curve and beheld a sight that quickened his pulse.

Ascending the hill, Pierre appraised the teeming fertility of the sparsely settled countryside; out of this soil, rich beyond anything he had known in the frugal acres of his home, he would draw the living he wanted. Some six miles from the little settlement, he saw the place he wanted. Who owned this ground about Second Creek? A band of Indians, he learned; but they had refused to sell. Pierre asked to meet the chief with whom he spoke long and beguilingly, pointing to a cargo of pig iron in his vessel. As Katrina stared up from her place beside the hickory-bark cradle, Pierre made many motions. She wondered idly what the Indians could do with unprocessed iron. Apparently the chief had no time to do likewise. The cargo fell into the Indians' hands, their land into Pierre's. How the red men disposed of the metal is unrecorded.

For a start Pierre erected a store at the foot of the bluffs, but he had visions of a life in the broad acres beyond. He paid a call on the Spanish officials, and reached an understanding. Hereafter his activities would be followed with a friendly eye. Soon Pierre had a nucleus of bondsmen to work his acres, "brute" slaves fresh from Africa, and others from Jamaica, Cuba, and the Indies. Pierre expected his males to do well by their wives and the Surget menage, producing children with goodwill and regularity. He set them an example, for in time he had eleven.

Soon he was asking more land. Expansion was the rule; more slaves meant more miles of earth; more earth, more slaves. He received a handsome grant, twenty-five hundred acres. He would want more, but this would do. He laid out a neat house, his Cherry Grove. Strong-timbered, it nevertheless was small, only five or six rooms without elegance of style. That would come with later years; life at Cherry Grove meanwhile had a simple flavor. Pierre rode about his acres, talking with overseers, visiting gins; Katrina supervised the household, checked supplies, watched sick slaves. In the evening they visited among the neighbors, most of them of British descent; they drank rum and wine, enjoyed turkey and venison. Entertainment was full, but hardly of ornate magnificence. The great social tradition was only in the early stages.

Pierre approached sixty. Now and then the dark, lean man sat alone, pipe in hand, counting his returns. Sometimes he seemed to listen, as if for the sound of the sea. It took a long time to get the salt out of a man's veins, he said. Katrina, more placid than ever, smiled and made no comment.

Late one afternoon in 1796, Pierre peacefully died. They buried him in the graveyard of Cherry Grove, and then Katrina took up the burden. She had watched Pierre in silence, but she had learned. Perhaps the three oldest boys, in their teens, expected that they had only to wait a few years before all would fall to them. Katrina reflected. At their age, Pierre had been scurrying after his own fortune. Would the boys value what came too easily? She settled her firm Dutch jaw.

At breakfast, she glanced up from her grits and eggs. It seemed to her, she said, that it was time certain people struck out for themselves. A silence fell; the brothers exchanged hot glances, and the widow went on to talk of the weather. Within a day, the oldest boys had gone. One of them, the excitable Jake, wiry and dark like his father, took it hardest. He boomed out, in typical Surget voice, that he'd never come back unless as a rich man.

Frank and Jim set themselves up in Natchez. The mother gave each a small start, but it would be up to them. Jim, of all the peppery Surgets, seemed to be the most easy-going. Light-haired, squat, he looked more congenial than the rest. He would work so many hours, and that was all. Yet he prospered. It was, however, the brother Frank who surprised the countryside. Still growing, he stood six feet tall, with strong black eyes and black hair, handsomest of the lot. Outsiders might have thought him destined for the role of rakehell, accomplished pursuer of neighborhood maidens. But Frank had inherited, above all, Surget ambition and also the Surget habit of retaining their gold. He became the quiet, plodding one. Few in town saw him, for Frank was too busy. Canvassing the field, he picked a "born manager" (the family word for it) for a wife. The neat, sharp Mrs. Frank Surget worked no harder than her husband, which meant that she worked as hard as three other women.

She woke her family at four in the morning. Though she herself sometimes nodded at the table, she never missed the early hour, and saw that none of the others did. She had a saying: "Frank has the money to make; I have the money to save." More and more their party-going friends passed them by; and that seemed to be what Frank Surget wanted.

Up North somewhere, Jake wrote no letters and answered none. Like his father, he turned to the sea. "Hardly the way to get rich in a hurry," said the cotton Surgets, remembering Jake's angry assertion on his departure. Again like his father, however, Jake let few chances go by. After a time he signed on a ship as second officer. The florid captain brought his wife, a lady as jovial as her husband. The trip proved arduous; by the time the vessel returned the captain was dead; Jake had assumed command of the ship and also the wealthy widow. Now Jake could go home again, with his new wife.

Back at Cherry Grove, the Surgets clustered about the proud Jake and his amiable lady. Old Katrina had died, and the family had come through more happily than she had hoped. For a time Jake and his brother Jim, the good-humored one, occupied Cherry Grove together. Subsequently it became evident that Jim was less of a sober-sides than Jake. Jim liked a good time and the place to enjoy it, he felt, was home. Sunday dinner was the climax of Jim's week, when most of his guests enjoyed the meal so much that they had to be rolled from under the table and taken home afterward. (These, of course, were the hard-drinking days.) The brothers had a tiff or two, then a howling difference of opinion, and the quivering Jake proceeded, as Natchez says, to "divide the house." Taking a piece of white chalk, he went from gallery to hallway, to dining room and down the back stairs. "Now." He flung out the words. "You stay on that side, and I'll stay here!"

Matters worked out that way. One side was filled with Jim's things, the other with Jake's and his wife's. For several years the brothers did not speak, ignoring each other on the steps, on their way to and from the dining room. The good-natured Mrs. Jake made a few protests, then settled down to enjoy her half-house. The division extended to the yard: Jake's chickens could not contaminate themselves with Jim's. (Who'd know whose eggs were whose?) A Jim Surget cow had not the briefest contact with a Jake Surget bull; a Jim Surget Negro had to creep around the back at night to meet a Jake Surget girl.*

Eventually the brothers tried separate establishments. Distance did the trick and they got on famously. By this time Jim had married and gone to work to perpetuate his line. It remained for one of their sisters, however, to give Natchez a son who became a free soul extraordinary, an authentic *jeunesse dorrée* of the river, Adam Louis Bingaman. . . . Over the name elderly Natchezians indulged a quick smile; then usually there followed a regretful pause. At his birth the gods endowed him with a handsome face, an admirable physique, as fine a mind as anyone's; and then they forgot several other qualities, among them the balance without which the rest might eventually mean little. "He was," says a grand dame, "our Lord Byron."

A. L. Bingaman came of mixed stock. His grandfather, Christian Bingaman, was a German who served in the British Army, then came to Natchez to acquire a plantation. Growing up in a family of many tongues, A. L. had opportunity to become a linguist, and he did. He also had opportunity to learn firm management, and he didn't. It would be years, however, before the latter fact was evident.

He was a boy in the early 1800s, as Natchez' wealth began to pour forth. With the expanding estates came spreading elegance. A. L. enjoyed casual study under a succession of tutors, long rides about the countryside, visits that lasted for weeks, parties, receptions, races. His father died when A. L.

---

* Similarly, two Natchez sisters split over their devotion to a dead mother. At her grave one took a stick and drew a line down the center. "This side's mine, that's yours." Each brought flowers to her half.

EARL M. NORMAN

LINDEN
A Plantation Applecart Overturned

LINDEN
Its Punkah Is One of the Region's Oldest

REBER HENDERSON

LINDEN
The Doorway Is Notable for Its Grace

EARL M. NORMAN

was a boy. In his early teens he found himself the favorite of mother, aunts and uncles, cousins and neighbors. He had a persuasive smile, a happy manner. In his eye, in his deep voice was an assurance that the patriarch Pierre had never possessed. Had they heard the way he met the lady at the gate the other day, swept off his hat and escorted her through? At sixteen A. L. was the junior gentleman from the tip of his pointed French leather boots to the top of his beaver hat. Now and then an aggrieved cousin complained of a too-quick observation or a witticism with a barb. A. L. apologized, then went ahead, more and more spoiled with the passing seasons. The family would admit the boy was a bit high-spirited. But would they want his fine will broken?

Inquisitive about everything, A. L. Bingaman smoked early; tasted hard liquor at seventeen and stood up under three glasses. He also courted and chased the ladies of Natchez. In spare moments he finished his classes. His ambition was Harvard. The aunts protested. They would never consent to it, never. Massachusetts indeed, so far off, and so frozen! A. L. bided his time and eventually, as he had known he would, he went to Harvard.

Here he was even more his own master than in Natchez. Those who didn't like him and what they called his grand manners—they could go their Yankee way. None could deny that he did brilliantly in his studies, though he hardly let them interfere with his more important activities.

Word flew back unexpectedly. At nineteen, A. L. had decided to get married. Upset at first, the family was reassured. Julia Maria Murray was of A. L.'s age; her mother had been a Sargent, sister of Winthrop, sometime American Governor of Mississippi. As a Gilbert Stuart portrait testifies, Julia had a soft loveliness. From her poetess-mother she inherited a quick mentality, and everything indicated a highly desirable union. After the marriage, the rich young student resumed his education in Massachusetts. Then came evidence that something had gone wrong. The couple quarreled with increasing frequency; between New England and the new South the difference could be more than geographical.

At the Bingamans' Fatherland plantation, a sister looked out the window. Down the highway rode A. L., alone. The deep laugh pealed out; A. L. distributed kisses, handed around gifts, talked spiritedly of everything except his bride. Oh, yes, he replied, Julia was well; and this peach cake—he'd tasted nothing like it since he left Natchez. After supper, as the family sat uneasily about the gallery, up came the mild-tempered Jim Surget of the chalk-line incident. He and his nephew usually got on well. Alone with A. L. in the library, Jim showed his Surget will. In a few hard sentences he told the youth what he thought. "And, sir," he ordered, "you'll pull right out and bring her here."

Oh, no, he wouldn't, A. L. Bingaman asserted. Then, said his uncle, *he'd* do it. Jim Surget, without further word to A. L., started on the long overland journey by horseback, advancing slowly northeast. In Massachusetts, he taxed his persuasive powers to the utmost. Julia listened, shook her head, then gave in. They left together, the young wife riding on a pillion behind Jim Surget. Weeks later, they reined in at home. Julia, her lips paling, clung for a moment to her companion's coat. The door opened and Adam walked quickly down, a composed smile on his face, and took his wife in his arms. "It was just like that," the storytellers add.

Julia, who often said she could "do anything I set my mind to," went to work to become one of the Surgets. Soon she presided at meals of the kind favored by her banquet-loving husband. She visited scores of relatives, laughed at the Surget stories, and listened attentively to the elders. The first child was on its way. So Julia's mother, a widow, joined her, and stayed. The two women of Massachusetts applied themselves to their duties, but it is evident they were never very happy. Natchez was so different from what they had known, its style freer, its gestures less restrained. Julia Murray of New England never accustomed herself to the river manner—the easy way in which her husband brought a band of friends, with a casual greeting: "We'll have thirteen more for tonight, dear." Most Natchez hostesses would have thought nothing of finding something extra in kitchen or chickenhouse. Julia clenched her fists. Other things made her shudder: the searing heat, the perspiration that ran into her eyes; those all-too heavy meals, and the long hours of talking afterward. She was appalled at the hot tempers among the men and the murderous duels, not to mention the torrential rains and the wild, almost uncontrollable spread of green over everything.

Yet life must have looked at least secure for Julia. They had several hundred slaves, three plantations, and more to come through inheritance. Too, she had to admit that when he was in the right mood, A. L. could be a compelling fellow. A great reader from his early days, he collected magnificently embossed volumes of Greek dramas, Horace, Homer, collections of English poets. He could enjoy days alone in his library. Visitors spent hours ranging about his collection. Strangers listened in amazement to his stories, wild or whimsical. He turned from Greek to French, from a slave's anecdote to an imitation of a Harvard professor. With it all he showed a rare charm, a spontaneous sparkle. He would take a companion's arm, give a wry smile, and no matter what he had said or done, the other would be his. Did he have too many talents? Julia sometimes asked herself if everything came too easily to him.

A picture of Bingaman at his florid best is offered by the historian Claiborne. Edward Everett was guest at a dinner given by Samuel Davis. Over succulent game and gravied meats, conversation darted nimbly from one subject to another. Mr. Everett recited passages from Dante. At 11 o'clock the ladies left the table; then came cobwebbed bottles of Madeira and Amontillado, imported by the Bingamans during George Washington's administration. Mr. Everett gained in fluency, "the warm sunny tints of the generous fluid coloring his thoughts and language." At one o'clock the guest reached a climax, reciting in the Cervantes original, Sancho Panza's eulogy to sleep.

As he sank back, it was evident that Natchez must reply; and who but A. L. Bingaman? Rising, the gilded one paused. Which language to use? Spanish, or French, German, Latin, Hebrew, Greek? Lifting his eagle-like head, a hint of a smile on his lips, he rolled out an address in a tongue that for a moment, only one or two could place. Then the rest recognized it. It was Indian, the Choctaw dialect, a language soft and compelling:

"Mingo of the Massachusetts, farewell! Return to the wigwams of your fathers, where the great water rolls its billows and the voice of the Great Spirit thunders along the shores. Tell them that you have seen the Great River and that in every hamlet on its banks you have found men of the Massachusetts tribe, wedded to the daughters of the land, prosperous and happy. . . . Sachem! May sunshine light your path, and peace go with you to your hunting grounds."

An oil painting reveals him in Byronic pose and expression, a slender throat above an open collar, dark eyes dominant and a little haughty. The full, sensual lips are slightly curved, the nose held high. So he must have looked when he made his toast.

Turning to politics, A. L. Bingaman was re-elected several times to the legislature, serving twice as speaker of the House, once as president of the Senate. He hoped for more, the Governor's chair, the Senate in Washington; yet some of his habits might have made him a target in such races. He loved the military and organized his own company, the "Bingaman Blues." Blithely he continued to function as speech-maker extraordinary, toastmaster-general of his scene. Meanwhile another interest haunted him, one of which Julia could not approve. He grew increasingly absorbed in his love of the track.

Natchez of the 1830s found itself one of the prime Southern racing centers. The actor Tyrone Power remarked: "The passion for the turf is yet stronger here, if that be possible, than in the North. . . . Visited the plantation of Colonel B——n, where I saw three or four very likely racers at exercise; amongst others a horse called Hardheart, whose time for a mile, they declare here, has never been matched. One or two persons are this very year going to Europe for the sole purpose of importing horses of high reputation." The leader of Natchez' horsey set was A. L. Bingaman. Along St. Catherine's Creek he and his fellows maintained a course, the famous Pharsalia. Though removed from most populous centers, the track won a high reputation. There was no reason why it should not have done so.

A. L. Bingaman went almost annually to the Continent to observe at the better meetings and study the horseflesh. Natchezians smiled when he promised to be back with the finest pair he found. They knew he would return with a dozen, at five and six times the cost he had planned. Furious rivalries grew between him and his friends. The gentry gathered regularly for the matches, the beribboned ladies with their umbrellas, staying in their carriages within seeing and shouting distance. Thousands were exchanged in the betting, tempers were lost and duels held as a consequence.

Jockeys were smaller Negroes of the plantation. The stable staff regarded itself as several notches above field hands; on a par with, perhaps higher than, house servants. Some jockeys won Southern fame; planters offered thousands for them, but an owner would seldom trade. It was a matter of pride. That was *his* nigger, flying *his* colors. Among the Bingamans and Surgets, dynasties of handlers developed—a father who was a jockey, a son who became a trainer and begot a boy perfect in size and temperament to ride the Master's best.

The mare Brittania was brought to Natchez in a specially padded stall on a sailing vessel. When traveling portrait painters came here, the Bingamans and Surgets not only had their own features immortalized, but those of their horses. Eventually Troy, the specialist in equine studies, did Brittania in oils. Today the pictures of the horses remain on the walls of several families; and near them stand one or two descendants of the Negroes who handled the mounts for A. L. Bingaman. "It's in my blood," a gnarled, moustachioed retainer told me. "It can't get away from me. My pappy, you maybe hear of 'im? We all Surget and Bingaman men." He paused, and his yellowed eyes lighted. "Mister A. L.? Don't you believe half the thing' you hear on 'im. Them that says it ain' *this* little to 'im!" He indicated the tip of his brown finger.

At the track and away from it, A. L. Bingaman had a vast influence on the neighborhood youth. He led gargantuan drinking parties, took friends on jaunts to Baton Rouge or New Orleans or New York. His peccadillos became the style, his oaths the rage, his attitude a contagion. If he put a feather in his hat at Pharsalia, the following Sunday found half the dandies doing the same. When, with sweeping gesture, he reversed a woman's hand to kiss the palm, three-quarters of the gangling localities tried to follow suit. He always earned a smile whereas some received a giggle or a face-slap.

Freely he endorsed notes for any who asked. Among the Natchez gentry, a man's word was supposed to be his bond. Refusal to endorse a note might be regarded as an insult, calling for a resort to arms. A. L. Bingaman fought duels, but not over such prosaic matters. . . . With the years, gradually, there developed a certain willfulness, a delight in shocking the less joyous. Also whispers spread: A. L. was giving less and less time to his plantations. "There's no fertilizer like the footsteps of the master," the saying went. The Bingaman staffs went lax, and fields grew unproductive. A. L. had strokes of what he called poor fortune; he announced that he would accept family loans. Relatives responded, but soon he needed more assistance, and was taking help from outsiders. He was digging deeper into his holdings, and those he had expected to leave his children. But the banquets, the purchases of horses, the champagne and ebullient gesture went on.

After eight years Julia had a second child, and a third. No

more. Then Julia died—some said of a broken heart, others insisted it was yellow fever—and the last child went with her. After a proper period of mourning, A. L. went forth again, resuming his life.

More years passed and more mortgages fell due. A. L. Bingaman still drank deep of life's gifts. Creditors scowled; cousins, scandalized over the stories, did likewise. A. L. shrugged and snapped his fingers. One day an old friend advanced upon the Fatherlands, determined to collect a heavy debt. As he stalked past a servant, A. L. came to him, beaming: "My friend, how *are* you? Why haven't I seen you? It's my fault, I know, I know." The arms went around him; into his hand was thrust a glass. By the way, the friend must accept a gift, this volume that A. L. had just received. . . .

Pressed into staying for supper, the friend did not arrive home until noon the next day. His wife met him at the door. Turning slightly green, the husband confessed. He had gotten nothing, dear. He had, in fact, loaned another thousand!

By this time the stress and strain were leaving their mark. Another likeness hangs in a Natchez home; only after a minute or two of study did I convince myself it was the man of the earlier Byronic pose. The eyes are faded, worldly; the face has heavy lines, the mouth a look of disillusionment, almost of contempt. However the artist intended it, the portrait stands as a commentary upon the man.

Inevitably the day arrived when he could borrow no more. He gave up one property, then another. The South was fighting the North, but he could not blame this for his troubles. At last he felt he had to leave Natchez. So often had he gone to New Orleans, the good-time town, that it was not difficult to follow the old trail. There his existence trickled away in a small apartment. In a drawer he kept a few possessions, fine garments, badly laundered, pictures and, most important perhaps, some of his embossed books. Those last became his solace in these lack-luster hours when there were few whom he knew on the streets of the city.

He walked slowly through the French quarter. A few years back, bringing his horses to New Orleans, he had sauntered confidently along these narrow thoroughfares. His blooded stock, where were they now? And then he reflected: It was along these same streets, less than a century earlier, that his grandfather Pierre Surget had moved, when he was establishing the fortune—the fortune which he, A. L. Bingaman, had shared, and wasted away. One day his friend Claiborne met him, and they matched recollections of bygone years. With tears in his eyes, Bingaman confessed that he had sold most of his volumes; "he referred to them as men refer to the loved and lost." Then he walked away.

A few weeks later, when word came that he was dying, a relative and a friend went to his bedside. Greeting them with a smile, he quoted something in Latin about life's futilities. For a few minutes he spoke feverishly of his horses, and ended by whispering: "When it's over, will you lay me some place where I can hear hoofbeats, now and then?"

They buried him in a New Orleans cemetery that had once been a race track, over which his steeds had run. His belongings were scattered. One of the portraits turned up at a racing stud, where a family connection found it. A few rings, a tie-clasp or a well-favored book appeared intermittently at a second-hand shop; a dark girl came forward with a small jewel: "He was kind to my mother." One of his children wrote in the family Bible: "May the Almighty God have pity upon one who was more 'sinned against than sinning,' is the earnest prayer of his desolate and loving daughter."

IX

ALWAYS INVITE THE RIGHT PEOPLE

As they talked of the other Surgets, few Natchezians paid attention to the earnest Frank, grubbing away his days in the country, trying to teach his children to do the same. Gradually, however, commission merchants and land officials realized that, no matter how plain his house looked, or how drab his costume, Frank was outstripping everyone around him. His little world, well-plowed and heavily-seeded, was blooming beyond even his own hopes. He was becoming one of the most affluent men of the region. But by this time the handsome Frank, whose dark looks had once made the ladies turn in his direction, had grown old. Still he insisted on living quietly in the rural stretches, rising early, going early to bed, thinking of tomorrow. Tomorrow, apparently, would be little different from today.

Then Frank Surget and his wife died. The children remembered their long, hard routine, remembered it so well that they wanted to leave behind whatever reminded them of it. In this they were led by another Frank, Frank the Second, a son as unlike the father as any could imagine. Where his father had been dour, he was gay. Where the first Frank had applied himself relentlessly to the acquisition of a fortune, the second concentrated on an easy enjoyment of it. Physically the Second Frank was not quite as prepossessing as his father, but he inherited a share of Surget good looks, the same aquiline nose, and a wit of his own. He also had a practicality about him that others—for instance, A. L. Bingaman—had lacked.

For the bright-humored Frank the Second, the countryside had the charm of a desert. At four in the morning, the hour when his mother had once summoned the family from their beds, he was now sound asleep, or just going to bed. He had the means of indulging himself. From the hard-working father came an estate that made the son, overnight, a millionaire. It included no less than thirteen plantations, miles of the river bank in Louisiana and Mississippi, and other properties along lake and bayou. Moving into town, the new Frank set out to have a happy, relaxed time of it.

When Frank wasn't having a party, he was planning one, and when he was doing neither, he was on his way to Europe. His interests and his circle of friends widened beyond the American borders; Frank the Second styled himself a citizen of the world. When he returned, he talked gaily of the new French styles in waistcoats and the latest in court manners. But most Natchezians liked young Frank. With all his money, he wasn't unkind or haughty; and he remembered his old friends, invited them to his festivities and helped them, when they needed it, quietly and unostentatiously. Few as rich as Frank, most people said, would have behaved half as well.

Now he took a wife, the graceful Charlotte Linton, who brought him not only beauty but an extra fortune. Immediately after the marriage they acquired the princely setting of Clifton, set like a palace on the town bluff. Several years earlier the Postlethwaites—the same family that was connected with King's Tavern—had erected the red-brick manse. Samuel Postlethwaite had died there of yellow fever. Now Clifton had a master and a mistress who could maintain it.

From the shanties under the Hill many pairs of eyes sought out this serene house that seemed perched in the clouds. When a mist settled upon the river, Clifton looked as if it were riding a gray ocean, suspended in nothingness. It was the first sight of upper Natchez that came to thousands of visitors, and the last. The clean white pillars supported a white roof line and, atop a hipped roof, an immaculate captain's walk dominated the surroundings. To side and back was extended a file of smaller buildings among the gardens and bordered paths that followed the curve of the hill.

Frank the Second, not content with what he found, embellished it. A glassed conservatory on the hill-top, a half-hidden grotto and rock garden, a box-hedge with a maze for the amusement of guests were added. Pools were dug, to be overhung by inclined oaks and willows that trailed their hanging draperies in the water. At the bluff's edge benches were placed from which the guests might inspect the river and land below. Sitting in the gardens beneath the trees, visitors saw the red house in full illumination, the tall pillars a challenge to time and man.

Inside, Frank conducted friends about his ornamented hallways. He had become a great collector of Spanish, Fleming and English works, both religious and profane. His pictures hung everywhere, between rare teakwood furnishings and statuary and the curved intricacy of rosewood and mirrors. Here was one of the greatest collections ever known on the Mississippi. At the garlanded doorway stood the smiling Charlotte Surget, at her queenliest.

For the Frank Surgets and their many relatives the days were bathed in a silver light—except, of course, for that nettlesome subject of dissension over slavery. Frank, never one who liked controversy, talked little about the matter, but he made no secret that he did not side with the fire-eaters who clamored for secession. In that direction he saw only ruin. A Whig and a conservative, he looked on the secessionists as radicals. He asked how an underdeveloped agricultural region could hope to win over one industrialized and highly organized. In addition, a certain part of his wealth was in the North and in Europe; there he had banking and financial ties. In time Frank became the arch example of the Natchez planter who had little to do with Confederate purposes. Like a number of others, he claimed a kind of "neutrality." He had had no part in bringing on this war; above all, he wanted to protect Clifton for himself and his family.

Natchez, he argued realistically, was in a precarious position, perched above the river, available to gunboats of both sides. The nation knew it as a cotton center, stuffed with the commodity that grew rapidly more precious than gold. On the fate of cotton, many argued, hung the fate of the South; campaigns were organized to take or protect it.

The town fell to the Federals. A clear-eyed spectator came to Natchez, Mrs. Walter Q. Gresham, wife of the Federal commander, and she has left a sharp account of the unconventional situation that followed. Many of the major planters, among them Frank Surget, did what they could to save their cotton and their other property. Regularly Frank invited the Federal officers to his lustrous Clifton; they got on well and, as Mrs. Gresham describes it, the Union men regarded Frank as practically one of them. Still, another problem developed for Frank. In nearby Woodville, which the Confederates held, he had at least five hundred bales of cotton, worth some hundreds of thousands of dollars. Wanting to preserve them, he "finessed." He explained to his Federal friends that he must exercise care, or the Confederates would take his cotton. The Federals sympathized, and so Frank walked a narrow line. A slip in either direction, and there might be trouble.

The war went on, and Lincoln issued his amnesty proclamation, granting pardon and full privileges to Southerners who declared allegiance to the Washington government. Federal commanders were suggesting that the natives do so. Certainly Frank would have difficulty avoiding the course? But Frank didn't. The Federal official told him: "The time will come when you can take the oath without running any risk of having your property outside our lines destroyed by the other side. Until then, continue as you are, and come and dine with me this evening." Here was success indeed; the Federal was counseling the Southern planter against coming out for the Union side!

Frank's situation strengthened. When a new Federal commander insisted he go the whole way, Frank had an answer: "There are two things you can't make me do. You can't make me take that oath, and you can't break me!" The Federals won increasing victories, and Frank decided to cross the Rubicon. But the Federals then demurred. Frank rose, threatened to apply to Lincoln himself to make the Union man swear him in—and won.

He and his wife continued to entertain the Federal officials while all Natchez looked on in wonderment. Whenever he sat with the younger Surgets, Frank told himself he was protecting them, guarding Clifton and his other Natchez properties for their future use. One day he planned a fete for all Union officers in the town. Hints went out of the elaborate preparations, of the delicacies being assembled from one Surget farm after another. It would be Natchez' most gala wartime entertainment.

For hours that evening Frank moved about his drawing room and garden, pointing to his rare paintings, explaining the origin of his statuary, leading friends from conservatory to ballroom. The Surgets strolled about with their friends, a little proud of their great place, of their rank in Natchez. When Charlotte Surget, her hoop-skirted figure silhouetted in the doorway, bowed to the last of her guests, she could indulge a smile with her husband. The affair had turned out well, hadn't it?

The next day the couple knew suddenly that the affair had not turned out well at all. A messenger thrust out a note—an order to vacate their house, signed by the chief Federal engineer. They blinked. Of all the Union officers, Frank had accidentally omitted the chief engineer! Working so hard to please every Federal, he had antagonized one of them and very much the wrong one.

When Frank bustled into his office, the engineer frowned. The order must stand. As he heard the next words, Frank swallowed hard: They were going to tear down the whole house; it was in the way of their fortifications. In vain did Frank argue: With all the hill, couldn't they take some other spot, a hundred yards off? The man couldn't do this. As he went on, he realized there was no need for a fortification of any kind; the Federals had full command of the river. . . . At last, as he met only silence, he knew that his protests had been hopeless. All he could do was beg for time. Couldn't they have a month, two weeks? Think of what had to be moved. . . . The engineer rubbed his nose. Three days.

The Surgets scurried about. Charlotte Surget directed the servants, stuffed clothes into boxes, brocade curtains into trunks. There was so much of it, filling room after room. She heard a crash; one of the best sofas had smashed against a banister. Legs of delicate chairs cracked; woven goods ripped on nails. Relatives ran in, offering carriages and wagons to carry things away, to the bottom of the bluff, to temporary storage places.

Charlotte Surget remained on her feet through most of the three days. Servants worked in shifts, under candlelight. How different a scene from that of the recent evening, also in candlelight; but she tried not to think of it. Rain fell, whipped in several directions by the wind; sets of rosewood were unprotected in the downpour. They could never hope to cover them, and so they went back to their task of removing the rest. In the morning they found that several of their best pieces had disappeared. Charlotte stood there, crying a moment; then, wiping her eyes, she returned to work.

The hour approached. Only a few items remained—broken pieces, unwanted chairs. The Surgets called their assistants and gathered in the hall; their ears caught the sounds of men moving outside. The house would be removed by the quickest method—dynamite. Frank Surget groaned when he heard that. For a moment the family hesitated, then started forward. At the great fanlighted door, the wife paused; mechanically, almost blindly, she locked it behind her. Somebody snickered; Frank Surget's face contorted, and for the first time he sobbed. They were led beyond the fence of their estate, and there they turned to watch. Soldiers ran about, shouting, attaching wires.

"Everybody back!" came the signal. From the distance Clifton had never looked so serene, its hundreds of panes of glass shining in the morning light. The sun made the whites of the pillars almost luminous, and sent another set of them, in black shadow, across the brick front. The place seemed prepared for a guest.

Suddenly, came a sound like a muffled roar within the earth. A woman gave a high scream that ended with a gasp. Glass broke over the crowd; the building shook, and hunks of plaster flew toward the sky. Yet Clifton still stood. The officer rapped out a second command, and this time there followed a heavier blast that made the ground quiver. Thick yellowish dust rose into the air, and when it cleared a little, long cracks zigzagged through the red brick walls, and several window frames had fallen out. But again Clifton remained with its pillars and its cupolas. A third attempt, and a fourth; a few sections slipped further, yet nothing more happened. The orders were changed, and men moved forward with ropes to be attached to the columns, and picks and other tools. It would take a longer time than they planned, but they would do it.

Out in the garden, light charges were set up among the pavilions, the grotto, the glassed conservatory. The crowd shuddered as a boom rang out, and broken bushes flew upward. Clusters of camellia blossoms, whirling toward the sky, changed direction, to fall tattered and dusty to the ground. One of the onlookers picked up a handful of petals.

As they passed the shattered scene, Natchezians felt sorry

for Frank. Dozens of belligerent Confederates' mansions were untouched, or were to be returned at war's end, after they had been used for hospitals and other purposes. Frank Surget had tried to walk a line between the two sides. There might be a moral in it; or there might not.

Frank had accumulated a fortune across the sea, and in the East. Yet the episode touched his spirit as nothing had ever before. Not yet an old man, he nevertheless grew depressed and aged quickly. One day he announced that he meant to go to France, at the first possible moment, and never return. The Surgets repacked their best pieces and sent them to New Orleans; other objects remained with relatives and friends. When peace arrived, Frank asked passage on the first available vessel.

He never saw France again. Not long before sailing time he sickened and died. Eventually the widow went without him, and for this branch of the family a cycle had concluded; they did not come back to Natchez, then or later.

A second great house of the Surgets began with tragedy but ended more happily. Showing a Surget inclination to the sea, one of Pierre's daughters, Jane, had accepted the proposal of Captain James Hampton White. Not long afterward she became a widow, alone on her lands. The time was 1819. Jane, young and much alive, decided she wanted a mansion on the borders of Natchez, to provide the pleasures of country and town without the discomfits of either.

While relatives speculated, Jane Surget White ordered a home as big as any that Natchez had. She sent to Philadelphia for an architect, scattered orders for materials in New York, France, England and Holland. So that she could watch what went on, she had a temporary cottage set up on the property. For about three years the construction continued.

A red-hued structure, powerfully built, delicate in detail, crowned a slow rise. The widow nodded as she inspected the

EARL M. NORMAN

ARLINGTON
Its Mistress Died on Her First Evening

ARLINGTON
Grandeur in the Natchez Manner

EARL M. NORMAN

ARLINGTON
Its Doorway Is Celebrated

EARL M. NORMAN

templelike projection lifting two stories high at the front, with four shafts of the simple Doric order. Through a fanlighted, paneled doorway, broad and deep, she crossed the threshold to an uninterrupted hallway seventeen and a half feet high; to one side a recess provided space for the curved stairway. At the back she measured another two-storied porch, larger and wider than the front, leading to her gardens. The interior hand-carved woodwork gave a rich, restrained pattern; the feeling was one of precise Georgian, modified to fit the Natchez locale. She chose the name Arlington.

A ball must be held to open Arlington. Delaying her own moving, the widow worked to prepare the last detail, and her cousins came to help. She conducted them about the house of eight rooms, four up, four down. Despite its size, Arlington had only this number; but a lot could be packed in. She paused while they admired the French hand-blocked paper, the sconces dripping crystals. She showed them her nine days' wonder, her "golden drawing room." The whole chamber had a yellow sheen—Aubusson carpet, embellished with floral patterns; lines of gold flowers against the wall paper; satin damask curtains, French mirrors framed in gold leaf; gold-leaf cornices, tie-backs at the windows in the shape of gilt-bronze leaves holding grapes of milk-white glass.

Face flushed in pride, the widow saw that none missed the rosewood furniture, marked by a pierced shell design; and she pointed out the cornices, carrying out the pattern. Over there waited the "chaperone sofa," giving ample space for the couple and stoutest of intermediaries; next to it, the "engaged sofa," allowing an additional closeness, without the watcher. Upstairs, completing the inspection, Jane White showed her prize—the biggest bed in Natchez, four-posted, carved mahogany in acanthus design, surmounted by a canopy. Few could swing themselves high enough to get into this bed. Beside it rested a stair of matching mahogany.

The evening of the ball arrived and Arlington glowed. As guests approached, they heard musicians in the recessed passageway, playing tunes lively and formal by turn. Through the flower-decorated rooms went the excited hostess. Crowds moved back and forth, sampling her champagne and cakes, nougats and ices, from library to porch to imported plantings in the garden. Some time past midnight the last guest left, and Jane closed the doors, to spend her first evening in this echoing house. As the servants snuffed out candles, she ascended the stairs, her fingers passing over a tapestry, pushing back a curtain. With a maid's help she ascended the flight of stairs to what the Negroes already were calling her "steps-bed." She dropped her head against the pillow.

The next morning, a cry went up. Miss Jane, she dead in her bed!

What happened is not certain. A few claimed that Jane White's slim throat bore fingermarks, that a slave strangled her. Others asserted unromantically that she died of acute indigestion, brought on by nerves. The Surgets buried Jane and the house went intact to a sister. After some years it passed to Samuel Stone Boyd, rising lawyer from Cincinnati, and his Natchez bride. Among themselves the servants spoke of the ghost of poor Jane, slipping up the stairway toward her death bed, and claimed they heard her as she threshed about in the grip of her murderer. Paying no heed, the Boyds enjoyed a long stay behind the double-storied portico.

In one respect the new master resembled A. L. Bingaman. Becoming a judge, he carried on the tradition of scholarship, with one of the greatest libraries that Natchez knew—eight thousand volumes in a dozen tongues. He acquired one or two collections of paintings from impoverished British noblemen. To the splendor acquired by the Widow White, the Boyds added signed bronzes, figures in marble, sets of oils that covered many walls. Romanticism was the theme, florid and flower-hung, the work of Italians and Spaniards; Magdalenes in the Desert ran rampant. The Boyds made Arlington's surroundings a wooded park, installing a gazebo or summer house, love seats among the floral patterns, and a rose garden. Here was pre-war Natchez glory on the grand scale.

Years later Arlington was mortgaged, and there came a foreclosure of building and furnishings. Once again, as in the case of Jane White, it lost its owner but stayed intact, to the last terra cotta figure and final crystal pendant. For the bank it was only a big place best classified as an annoyance. Retainers boarded up windows, draped furniture in ghostlike hangings while the rats gnawed the Judge's books and oils cracked in their frames. When two visitors liked it, the bank was glad to get rid of Arlington. The owner died, the widow left, again the building stood empty; and tales rose once more of Jane White's spirit, gliding along the damp floors.

Now the story goes back, to become part of the career of another woman. I know of few who epitomize as does the energetic Annie Barnum that segment of modern Southern women who can stand above misfortune. Several times life knocked her down but she got up again and hit back.

A plantation known as Hanging Moss, in North Louisiana, was the scene of Annie Green's birth. Her father had five holdings, her mother one of her own. I suspect that the daughter inherited a full share of her father's will. They tell a story of the way the father first got a wife. He and the lady had been engaged, but had a tiff and she returned his ring. They were separated by hundreds of miles of wood and swamp. Tom Green, deep in business affairs, paused long enough to set machinery in motion to fix the situation. He wrote a letter, enclosed the ring and re-dispatched it by a Negro horseman. After long travel the servant delivered the message. Supervising the making of cakes, the miss announced airily that she would glance over it at her leisure. The Negro sent word: He was sorry, please, but he couldn't go, no ways, till she read it; Mr. Green gave strict orders. The letter must have been extremely convincing; when the servant came back with a grin and an empty hand, Mr. Green knew he had won.

Hardly the Southern colonel of the novels, Tom Green showed himself a latter-day entrepreneur. In hip boots, he learned the river region as few bothered to do. He understood soil along the Mississippi, every inch of front, every back bayou. He never forgot that a flood could ruin a man but make a farm for the next one; the angry tide of the river left an incomparably rich residue. Tom Green seldom sold, always bought.

From time to time the Greens had their own floods; Annie remembered waking as a child to see water swirling about the house. For days she enjoyed it, until the family found her sitting on the porch, pushing baby chicks into the brown lake. Finally they had to summon a steamboat to pick them off their gallery. Such close contacts with the river, she thinks, took her father's health; he died when she was eighteen, oldest of five children.

The boll weevil attacked cotton; the plantations went one by one. "If we'd only stopped trying to raise more crops at the time," the daughter frowns. "We couldn't realize what was happening." The mother died, and young Annie rolled up her silk shirt-sleeves and went to work. She struggled over accounts, order blanks and bills, mostly bills, but she kept the family going. Things seemed black, but she had most of her clothes, and her trim figure and dark good looks. The latter helped save her. Lucien Gwin of Natchez proposed, and they spent thirteen years together.

Bad crops and bad times came again, and Mr. Gwin was a victim. She had three children, one a year old; a limited life insurance left by her husband, and as before, a pile of bills. Also, she had to keep house for brothers and sisters. She couldn't sit about, wiping her eyes or counting ancestors. "I had no business training," she explains. "I wasn't able to teach or do office work. But I thought of something to try." She would open a dairy. After considerable thought, she made the plunge.

To her one cow she added others, and bought a stable. A

brother-in-law contributed an automobile which, after coaxing, ran. A friend called: "I can let you have a mule." Receiving it, Annie Gwin could hardly believe her eyes. "It looked like a rabbit," she recalled. She converted a children's cart into a wagon and used the little animal. "Everybody helped," she said, smiling. "The Illinois Central gave me a bull, which was real neighborly, wasn't it?"

Hiring helpers, she worked with them, scouring, whitewashing, hosing, sweating. She made her own deliveries, and frequently the children went along. There were some whose noses went up in the air; when an acquaintance tried to glance the other way, she made a point of calling out a greeting. When some still ignored her, she thought to hell with them, and stepped on the accelerator.

Matters began to look up. Passing old Arlington, she set her eye on an adjoining ante-bellum house, Monmouth. Taking a quick look at her account book, she priced it. Before she knew more about it, she had a plantation house to add to her worries. Well, things would hardly be tedious. About this time there came to Natchez an amiable Oklahoman, a holder of oil lands, also a widower. Hubert Barnum poked about Arlington, locked-up and silent, and decided he wanted it. Watching the house next door, he wondered who lived there. Finding out, he paid a call. He liked what he saw and he visited again. Soon he was buying his milk, calling to get it, advising the widow on prices. "I cut a gate in my fence, so he could get through without going all around," she chuckled. "Our Negroes say Mr. Barnum wore a deep path to my door. That's not correct, exactly, but he came." Then one day the widower proposed.

"A man must be a fool to take on a widow *and* children," she told him. He said he'd take the chance. Now Annie Barnum was mistress not only of her Monmouth, but of Arlington as well. The old Jane White place was almost a museum of furnishings; all Annie had to do was sweep away the dust and clear off the mildew. The wall paper must be replaced, but the ancient yellow draperies, five and a half yards long, still hung at the windows. The carpets had not changed, nor had the tie-back metal leaves with their milk-white grapes.

For several years Annie and Hubert Barnum were together, until he died in the big house. Today Annie Barnum, her dark hair turned white, manages Arlington as expertly as she learned to manage her life. Again the title is in a woman's name; during most of its history, Arlington has been a woman's place. The monumental gold mirrors reflect much the same scene that Jane White and her successors saw—the "chaperone" and "engaged" sofas, the paintings of Europa and her Bull, the Roman columns against the dusk. Some things have grown more impressive, among them the camellia bushes, sending clusters to the second story. A serenity has settled about the brick place behind the columns, a calm that it probably did not know during the years of the excitable Surget clan.

One day, after an hour in the quiet garden, I left Arlington to see what had lasted of the other Surget establishments. Here were the grounds of Cherry Grove, Pierre Surget's paternal hearth. The house burned in the '60s, although a trim successor carries the name. Nearby I found the grounds of the Fatherlands, where A. L. Bingaman enjoyed flamboyant days and nights. That building, too, is gone, but there survives a superbly built stable at which Natchez' finest horses were trained. Wasn't that, I asked, appropriate? . . . The sportswoman who was my companion pointed out the expert planning of the stable in its ample stalls and provision for air and light. The stable, I noted, is outlasting most of the Surgets. When I told her that, she shrugged and smiled; and I remembered that her mother had been a Surget.

We walked to a cluster of weatherbeaten huts, hunting the descendants of Surget slaves. To them we talked idly of the old generation, the feuding Jim and Jake, sad Frank the Second and poor Miss Jane. A short distance away, behind an iron fence, rested the bones of the Dutch wife Katrina and of Pierre himself, once "pirate," later patriarch. A thin drizzle began and we started back in the gray afternoon. Like the sheen of ancient, much-used metal, the annals of the golden Surgets have dimmed in the present-day light.

TWIN OAKS

X

"KING DAVID" AND HIS DAUGHTERS

THE Hunts of New Jersey had enjoyed easier times. When the father died, leaving twenty-two-year-old David a small inheritance, the young man decided his sister needed it more than he did, and turned it over to her. David, a medium-sized youth with a face that showed little of his emotions, was known as the quiet sort, with more of a conscience than most.

Taking stock, in this year of 1801, David concluded it was time to move on. Down in Natchez, he knew, Uncle Abijah was doing well as a merchant. The letter of response to David's was cryptic, but it agreed to give him a beginner's place. Within a few months David Hunt was an assistant clerk, dragging barrels around, finding boxes in the storehouse, fitting children's shoes while more experienced hands waited on the plantation owners.

Uncle Abijah turned out to be a gray, stooped, bustling man who had little leisure for the problems of a nephew from far-off. His greeting, though friendly, had a note of restraint; he and his partner clearly were withholding judgment. Still, they fixed an annual salary of three hundred dollars, which wasn't bad, considering. David went about, his small, dark eyes squinting slightly as he applied himself to his business. He spoke little; he said he expressed himself better on paper. Self-conscious that he had not finished his education, he tended to undervalue himself.

David was learning things about his uncle. Abijah, a sutler with the Revolutionary Armies, had used his money to start himself in Natchez. Spreading his capital widely and well, he became the biggest merchant in the region, first Postmaster along the Natchez Trace, and operator of five stores. The nervous, quick-speaking uncle watched the newcomer harder than David realized, asking questions about him. Abijah liked people with more go; but the boy was conducting himself well, he admitted.

Five or six fellow-clerks came and went; but David stayed on. Ending his first year, he became a full-fledged clerk at five hundred. His associates, most of whom liked liquor and were not averse to an inspection or two of the joys beneath the hill, speculated about him. He must have Scotch in his blood, they argued; he saved nearly every dollar he earned, and already he was investing in parcels of land. (On *that* salary, they snickered, in admiration or derision.) What was the fellow trying to be, a monk?

Eventually, however, David branched out. Solemnly he accepted a few invitations to parties, riding in the afternoons along the sunken roadways to the houses in the hills. Fixing his attention on one or two plantation misses, he showed no intention of continuing a monk. In one instance, because of the lateness of the hour, the family asked him to stay overnight. At his bedroom door the father handed David a candle. David shook his head: "I can undress in the dark." What prospective father-in-law should not welcome such frugality? But David lost the girl nonetheless.

By the time the newcomer's second year ended, Abijah and his partner had offered him a further increase and a full partnership. David, his face as usual revealing no sign of feeling, declined; he thought he could do better on his own, sirs. Abijah spoke long and anxiously for he had come to depend a bit on the boy and, damn it, he liked him. He found himself doing all the talking, while David remained calm and expressionless. Finally, a new confidence developing in him, David agreed. He would accept full charge of the stores, if they wished, with a salary of three thousand, and time for handling his outside affairs. Finally they agreed; none could say David wasn't doing well for himself.

Picking out a large country property on Cole's Creek, David carried out other ideas of his own. Like Dr. John Jenkins of Elgin, he agreed with his neighbors that cotton was a fine thing, but he had no intention of turning every inch of ground to it while spending thousands of dollars to import other supplies. He raised everything he could and manufactured most of the rest. All about him men mined their soil; he shifted crops and built back his earth.

To one neighboring house on the creek David made increasing visits. Mary Calvit was a pert girl who liked to sing and dance as much as she enoyed talking. To the wonder of her friends, she accepted a proposal from the uncommunicative David, and a pleasant life began. Mary saw that David became more social, and he brightened up considerably. Then, abruptly, this phase ended: Mary had a child and died almost at once. The mound had only begun to settle before a smaller casket was lowered beside hers.

A third sorrow came. Uncle Abijah was mixing in politics. As a firm Federalist, he cursed Thomas Jefferson with the best, or the wealthiest, of them. Listening, David shook his head; he wished Abijah wouldn't take on so. In 1811 David went on a trip to New Orleans. Standing at his office entrance, Abijah unburdened himself of his views. George Poindexter was Mississippi's rising politician, an individual with a temper that darkened his life. Abijah's lip curled as he expressed his opinion of the man. Remarks were relayed; with an oath, Poindexter challenged.

The older Hunt, a sloping-shouldered man of business, knew nothing of such matters. Poindexter was an expert, his record spotted by many an encounter. Seconds met, and for a time it looked as if explanations might end the sorry affair. Unfortunately for Abijah, one of his representatives had recently had a tavern row with Poindexter, and conciliation collapsed. Officials, making a stiff effort to invoke a new American law against duels, placed Abijah under arrest. Constables chased the fiery politician Poindexter, but he "escaped." When released, Abijah received a note. Poindexter was ready to meet him at 4 a.m. on the Louisiana sandbar.

On a warm June morning, as a breeze swept the flat, the two men stared at one another. A rosy dawn broke, and wisps of fog lifted above the levee. "Gentlemen, are you ready?" A flock of birds made chattering flight from the trees. "One . . . two . . . three. Fire!" Before the smoke cleared, Abijah Hunt had dropped to the ground, his hand to his abdomen. Dying, he told a friend that Poindexter had fired before the signal. For years Mississippi politics rang to the charge and several times the glowering Poindexter fought new duels over it. Yet some have noted that had the violation happened so obviously, there would probably have been other killings on the field because the terms declared that if either principal fired in advance, the other's second was to shoot him on the spot. Whatever the truth, the sordid episode ended without credit to anyone.

Returning from New Orleans, David Hunt found himself heir to a sizeable part of the estate. The other beneficiaries quickly advised that they wanted to put all the property on the market. With the War of 1812 almost upon the country, the moment seemed inexpedient to David. His friends differed, but David, with the courage of his non-conformity, shook his head. Instead he bought out the other heirs, held for a long time and finally sold at a heavy profit. This time he lost not a day with his own plans, investing everything in land. David was finished forever with merchandising; his future lay in planting.

By now he had five properties. With each he held to his first principle, practical self-sufficiency, no matter how achieved. "If I could only make my salt and iron," he said, "I'd be independent of the world." He started a system of slave-training;

his men learned wood-carving, black-smithing, a dozen trades. For years, when a slave sale took place here, word that it was a David Hunt Negro ran the value up. Exercising justice and honesty in his dealings with his blacks, David chose overseers with discernment; at the first word of cruelty, he said, he fired them. Every slave had a right to complain in person of a wrong, and the master acted quickly. It is probable that the Hunt Negroes were as well off as human beings can be under bondage.

Walking one morning along the bluff, he heard the name of a Mrs. Ferguson. Years earlier, soon after he started as a clerk's helper, a fine lady had come in with her daughters. Finishing with the rest, he lifted the last one, Ann, not yet eight, to the counter. As he fitted shoes to her feet, he noticed her soft features, her poised manner. Since then, intermittently, David had caught sight of Ann. Now she was in her late teens, and her beauty and assurance had gained with the years. Today, on impulse, David bowed and spoke with the mother and daughter. For once the young widower did not try to check himself; he flushed when he realized how long he had been watching the play of light over Ann's quiet face, and hurriedly he said goodbye.

Before long he was calling regularly on the Fergusons. There were eighteen years between him and Ann, but that didn't seem to matter; her dignity almost matched his. Early the next year they were married, and Ann went up to Cole's Creek with him. This union was more solemn than the first. When Ann had her first child, they agreed it was a shame to waste the big chamber that had served until now for dances and so it became a play—and school—room. David insisted that the children begin early education, for he never ceased to regret what he had missed.

In all, seven children were born to the couple. David became main patron of a college which he made his pet. Arguing with neighbors, crusading for the institution, he made successive gifts until he had given two hundred thousand dollars, a remarkable sum for the day. Old Oakland, a school with Presbyterian connections, appealed mightily to the rigid David. He brought each of his boys there, and he looked on with a rare display of feeling when his youngest graduated as an honor student. Of all David's triumphs he thought this was his greatest.

Through the years David Hunt expanded. His slaves approached seventeen hundred; he had fifteen, then twenty and finally twenty-five separate plantations—Woodlawn, Fatherland, Homewood, Lansdowne, Arcola, Calviton, Huntley, Georgiana, Wilderness, Waverly, Fatlands, South Side, Brick Quarters, Hole in the Wall, Ashland, Argyle, Belle Ella, Oakwood, Black Creek, Buena Vista, Fairview, Servis Island, Oak Burn, Oakley Grove and Givin Place. Some called him "King David," but not in his hearing.

He could afford a quirk or two. Signing checks, he never made them for the even dollar, always a penny less—$999.99 instead of a thousand, $88,999.99 instead of $89,000. He never explained; there it was. Lending money, he ignored custom, limiting interest to a small, fixed percent. When crops were ruined in floodtime, he scratched across his notes: "No interest charged on acct. overflow." This truly was unorthodox.

Once, stricken by cholera, David thought himself about to die. Recovering, he selected a choice cherry tree and called a servant: "We'll make my coffin out of this, Sam." Practicing self-sufficiency here as in everything else, he had his saw mill cut it, his carpenters fashion it, his ironworkers attach handles. "Not a single outside hand touched it!" he pointed out. Over the family's protests, he had the coffin installed in the attic; "it's there when we want it." But he lived on for years.

Regardless of his means, he told his children he wanted no "display of wealth." Good materials, a becoming cut, yes, but few trimmings, no gee-gaws. For the girls—a simple finger ornament or two, that was all. As might have been anticipated, the plantation maidens did not take easily to such restrictions. They found ways to slip brooches into their pocketbooks, to be pinned on when the carriage rolled away from the house. Preparing to visit friends, they hid extra ribbons into their trunks, and at breakfast they turned their rings so that the father saw only the plain bands.

To be a young Hunt meant a great deal in the 1840s and '50s. As each child married, David gave him or her, as a minimum, a plantation, a hundred slaves, and a set of silver from Baltimore. The daughters married promptly; and in this later day they gave to the Hunt name the tradition that yet trails it.

Charlotte Hunt inherited the dignity of her mother, the quiet purposefulness of her father. When she accepted a husband, David gave her Lansdowne, a six-hundred-acre property a mile or so from town. It was not one of his biggest, and perhaps he felt guilty, because he threw in two additional estates in Louisiana! The couple need hardly have worried. The groom, George Marshall, also inherited considerable means. A banker's son, George was an easy-going individual with light red hair and a casual smile. Together, in 1852, George and Charlotte built their house at Lansdowne.

One-storied, with basement below and a lightly-railed captain's walk above, it was a superior example of balanced construction in stuccoed brick. A portico had four delicately-fluted columns, iron grillwork, and steps curving outward to a front courtyard. The same fineness of detail reflected itself inside and out. An ornamental doorway duplicated the pillars on a smaller scale. Beyond stretched the hall, fifteen feet wide, sixty-five long. Another gallery at the back led to a bricked court, flanked by two-story buildings for office, billiard room, school, and the thing for which Lansdowne acquired rare celebrity—its own gas plant. Most Southern towns had not yet acquired such systems. Open-mouthed visitors poked about its tanks and meters and hoped they would not explode while they were there.

Against a background of gold-and-white French hand-blocked wall paper, white marble mantels and Aubusson carpets, the young Marshalls could preen if they wished. George, of the light hair and light manner, did not concern himself with practicalities, preferring to remain remote from commerce and its problems. He understood the art of living in the setting to which he had been born; and the competent Charlotte was satisfied. She managed most things, making decisions and giving soft orders without impressing upon her husband that he was not doing it. After all, they had overseers and family advisers. Lansdowne, rather too small for the usual cotton operations, was used largely to grow vegetables and family supplies.

George Marshall indulged the habit of travel throughout his life. When he felt the mood, he went to Europe, returning with gifts for Charlotte, oil paintings and trinkets. Too, he passed on recipes. Ever the gourmet, he liked sauces rich, meat dishes flavored with imagination—so much imagination that country relatives sniffed suspiciously. Visiting European horticultural displays, George came back with exotic lilies, peculiarly-hued buddings, a Japanese magnolia. Adopting a French design, he put up a latticed garden house shaped like a pagoda; for a setting, he had his men dig a long pond at an angle best fitted to catch the shadow. He talked always of another project, to which he never got around. The heavy construction of Lansdowne—double walls, oversized chimneys—indicates that he planned to add a second story. Somehow, other interests intervened.

Sampling, acquiring bits here and there, George Marshall added silver-plated doorknobs and bronze chandeliers, beds with prayer-pads built into the sides, armoires so high that ladders were required. But the objects of which George grew proudest were Lansdowne's Du Barry china pieces, scores of them from massive to fragile, bearing a delicate banding of apricot color. The Marshall china . . . women talked of it as much as they did of the Marshall gas-works. As a final note, it may be observed that the elegant George amused himself by teaching his children foreign languages in brisk rhyme, "Dickory, Dickory, Dock," in French!

The aging David Hunt, visiting daughter and son-in-law, might well have speculated as he compared his earlier life with that of the affluent young Marshalls. Presently, however, he had something yet grander to inspect. Another daughter was Catherine. As bright-mannered as Charlotte was firm, Catherine won the highly-endowed William Balfour, planter's son and huntsman extraordinary. David gave the couple Homewood, an estate adjoining Lansdowne. William Balfour, somewhat more business-like than his brother-in-law, kept things going with a deft hand between cotillions and hunt breakfasts. In 1855 his wife Catherine was ready to teach her sister Charlotte a thing or two in this matter of a great house.

High piles of material accumulated at the edge of a clearing. In the swamp, trees were ringed twenty months in advance; to assure mortar of maximum strength, formulae were tested for nearly a year. Walls would be two and a half feet thick; an estimated million bricks were burned on the site. If Charlotte had silver-plated doorknobs, Catherine would have silver ones. Let Charlotte have a gas plant; the sister chose a formidable watering system. In case of fire, the wits said, the Balfours would not only put it out but flood the country for miles around. But before the completed splendor of Homewood they all fell silent.

A thing of soaring extravagances, it had four fluted pillars like those of Lansdowne, but these pushed themselves thirty feet high and were of metal, their elaborate Ionic capitals supporting an overhanging pediment. The columns repeated themselves in the deep doorways above and below. In the shadow of the pillars at the second level perched a small iron-work balcony; at each side of the great building two-storied iron galleries were thrust with metal lace-work of an imperial richness.

Homewood had not one but four halls, forming a Maltese cross and ending in four imposing entrances, each with its outspreading flight of steps. Inside, a grand staircase turned upward three stories toward the observatory, where a smaller

LANSDOWNE — EARL M. NORMAN
Another Daughter Didn't Aim So High

LANSDOWNE — EARL M. NORMAN
Furnishings, Wallpaper, Hangings, Untouched

HOMEWOOD
King David's Daughter Built for the Ages...

EARL M. NORMAN

HOMEWOOD
But It Went in an Hour or Two

EARL M. NORMAN

one twisted out of sight. The rooms had a varied grandeur of fireplaces, pink marble, gray-veined; pink with darker markings, and black and ornamented white. The gay-hearted mistress, Catherine Balfour, pointed to eight bedrooms, each in a different shading. Downstairs, sliding doors connected library and reception halls; when they were opened, a salon stood ready, seventy feet long. The front doorways had panes of soft pink; it was indeed a rose-colored world on which the Balfours looked.

Work lasted so long that the town made bets it would never end. Five years went by, and final details were incomplete when the couple moved in. By this time they had six children. So ended the contest between the two girls who had once turned their rings so that their father would not know they had ornaments. By now old David had grown tired as he eyed the façade of Homewood, and his expression showed resignation. But the young people were enjoying it to the hilt. On the galleries of Homewood, or in the glassed observatory above, the elders watched the red-coated figures on steeds that sped over hill and plain. The children found the upstairs hallways so big they could play tag in them and seldom get caught.

The sands were running low. The year 1860 ended; in all the talk of war "King David" Hunt sat gloomily silent. For him life had lost part of its savor. His boys, of whom he had expected a great deal, had died early. Approaching eighty, David spoke with grimness: "The full ears are taken, but the over-ripe shock is allowed to remain." As men shouted secession, he gritted his teeth. "We'll see one of the bloodiest of wars," his voice trembled. "This country may become uninhabited." The family urged him to get rid of his property outside the South, in Cincinnati. "I won't," he snapped. "Someday it may be our asylum."

"King David" lived to see the secession against which he

voted. Then, at last, they took his home-made cherry tree coffin out of the attic. At the beginning of the war his family did not suffer greatly; David Hunt's program of self-sufficiency kept them supplied. But then the fields lay bare and the quarters silent. The elegant, impractical George Marshall of Lansdowne went off to serve with distinction; his brother-in-law, William Balfour of Homewood, became a major. Their wives, those daughters of David, met war's stresses in different fashions.

The gay Catherine Balfour grew agitated as the Federals approached Natchez, and prepared to leave. Charlotte, always matter-of-fact, argued with her in vain. Catherine set out by carriage with her children, moving restlessly about for a year. The privations of the flight took the lives of four of the young ones. She returned to discover that, despite her fears of what would happen to the house, it had been spared. And her sister, the determined Charlotte of Lansdowne, had a close brush with violence on the homefront, but had stood her ground.

A younger Hunt, riding one day along the road, saw that someone had tossed out pieces of cups and saucers. He looked away, then quickly back. It was Lansdowne's celebrated china, the delicate white with borders of apricot shade. Applying the whip, he raced on. At the house he found the women near hysteria. George Marshall, recovering slowly from injuries at Shiloh, stood speechless. A little earlier, Union raiders had stalked in. Leaving her husband, Charlotte met them. The leader demanded keys to the storage room, and she refused. Perhaps it was a word she added, or her expression; with a curse the soldier slapped her heavily across the face and knocked her to the floor. As if waiting a signal, the men grabbed what came within easy reach and ran off. Cantering along the road, they decided they wanted none of the china trash; so they cast it aside.

To her death-bed Charlotte bore a mark over her lip. In the breaking of the china, however, the vandal had a greater revenge. For years she hated to pass that stretch of highway for she remembered the fragments in the sunlight.

In the post-war years the dead David Hunt once more helped the family. He had annoyed them by refusing to sell his Ohio assets; now these made it possible for some of them to hold on. "We lived off our mortgages, as long as they lasted," a relative recalls. "Then we lived on anything that was left." The careless George Marshall struggled as he had never struggled before, and Charlotte worked at his side. Once they had dismissed the thought of operating Lansdowne as an important enterprise; it was too small. Now they used it for anything they could raise—cotton, sheep, livestock.

Lansdowne saved the George Marshalls. With them labored a number of Negroes who had been David Hunt's slaves, and the justice that David had tried to practice came back to them. When the family could not afford a promised payment, the Negro tenants stayed nevertheless. Dying, two of them willed the Marshalls parcels of land that they had managed to accumulate in their years of unending toil.

Today at Lansdowne lives another George Marshall, the Third; Agnes Marshall Ward, his sister, and James Ward, her husband. With the two Wards I have enjoyed agreeable evenings behind the fluted pillars of that house whose upper story was never added. The graceful tradition has not died; I can testify that Lansdowne's Cuba Libres are Natchez' best. There remain the old hand-blocked wall paper, the original yellow brocade draperies; not least, part of the apricot-banded china that Charlotte Marshall had tried to protect. Walking about the long, resounding hallway, it is not difficult to imagine the gay George Marshall the First in the next room, teaching his children French with "Dickory, Dickory, Dock...."

The later story of Homewood, the sister's house that was built for the centuries, is less easy to record. The family stayed until 1907, when things no longer appeared rosy even through those tinted door-panels. The last Balfour took his family and went away. At the gate, as they turned, the final sight in the early evening was of the four gigantic metal pillars, gleaming white against the red walls, and the glassed doorway behind them, leading to the hallway along which the children had played in those brighter years. Another family came and left, and then a few years ago, a splash of new color arrived, in the form of a lady the town has never forgotten.

An expensive car rolled to a stop and out stepped Mrs. Kingsley Swan, a rarely lovely woman with glowing dark eyes, shining brown hair, and wearing a costume of that sophisticated simplicity that bespeaks New York or Paris. As her high heels tapped over Homewood's portico, she was followed by her chauffeur, a local guide, several enormous German police dogs and her new husband, Mr. Swan. Mrs. Swan, as she said later in her rich, cultivated voice, "fell in love" with Homewood. Returning for a second look, she ordered it for herself. It developed that she was on her honeymoon. Leaving Natchez, she continued her trip, then came back to complete the transaction.

The townsfolk gaped when Mrs. Swan's station wagon passed; they gaped when they saw what she was doing at Homewood in the way of alterations, improvements, repairs. Homewood had a mistress who could appreciate it as much as its first owner, King David's daughter Catherine. Antique shops in New Orleans, New York and the Continent were searched. They yielded bronzes, chaise longues, marbles, Chippendale, Adams and Sheraton pieces; not least, the town observed, a collection of Louis XVI items for one of the bathrooms.

Those whom Mrs. Swan invited enjoyed a sumptuous board and rounds of well-mixed drinks. Their hostess trailed around in dramatic velvet and silks; the handsome Mr. Swan kept quietly in the background, the giant dogs not so quietly. Mrs.

Swan did generous things, gave milk to orphans, made gifts of food. She acquired several warm friends; she joined the garden clubs. Yet she remained always a provocative lady with a luster of the unknown. One night she would be awe-inspiring in sequins, the next appear at a formal affair in slacks.

Slowly she made enemies. She bothered less about pleasing local tastes or prejudices, and she let herself smile over this or that Natchez oddity on two feet. The town, she was known to admit, bored her. It could hardly be claimed that Mrs. Swan bored Natchez. Especially when she appeared at noon in town in Long Island lounging costume, open-toed sandals, big umbrella over her shoulder and German police dogs racing about her. That halted crowds; Natchez, after all a small town, never got used to it. Also it was said that Mrs. Swan was buying rare filet for her dogs, with Beauty-Rest mattresses to ease their sleep. True or not, the stories made good listening. Callers, wanting to look at her Homewood, occasionally found Mrs. Swan annoyed with them, or worse. The local folks thought that eventually there would be some kind of bust-up between Natchez and Mrs. Swan. It came sooner than they expected.

On the night of January 2, 1940, a call arrived from the outskirts—Homewood was on fire, burning like fury! The firemen, delayed, said they arrived to find outer gates tightly closed; they had to argue before they got in, then argue with the furious Mrs. Swan because they had taken so long, then argue again because, she said, they did so bad a job. Some firemen stamped off, and there were more hot words, threatened face-slappings and men ordered out while hundreds looked on. Meanwhile, poor Homewood, built to last forever, glowed all over, as someone later testified, "just like a big plum-cake." When dawn arrived only remnants of walls were standing, with the four great metal pillars and the side galleries of ironwork intact.

Mrs. Swan was only beginning to put Natchez into the papers. Suddenly she sued the insurance companies for sixty thousand dollars, most of it her valuation of Homewood's furnishings. The companies claimed her figures were inflated; they charged she had kept the firemen from putting out the flames. Natchez lifted its ears, and so did newspapers all over the South. Here was one of the region's titillating stories of the year—the lady against Natchez. When court opened, it was thronged with people from three states and a dozen towns in a solid mass. A jaunty new hat on her head, Mrs. Swan walked in, a composed woman of mystery.

The heart of the case, it quickly developed, was high plantation life and how it was lived. The jury, which would pass on matters of marble mantels and continental culture, was made up in good part of gallused, tobacco-chewing farmers who didn't know a Sheraton from a chaperone. The major issue that evolved was: Would a lady call a fireman a sonofabitch?

The imported New Orleans attorney, St. Clair Adams, advised the women in the audience that if they did not "want the blood to rise to your faces," they should leave. Not a woman left. Fireman No. 1 said he had been delayed that night by taking a detour. He had a new engine and didn't want to run it over a freshly-topped road; one truck, using it, had had a $25 cleaning bill. Mrs. Swan cursed him for lateness, but he stayed on for hours, till someone reminded him his fire company was having a banquet; and then he went off. Yes, the lady swore at another fireman. "One phrase, which I will not repeat, was very insulting," said the gentlemanly fire-fighter, crimsoning. "Plenty of people have lost their lives by calling other people that." Pressed, he admitted that in Natchez, folks sometimes used the word among themselves, "but we resent it from strangers."

Fireman No. 2 heard Mrs. Swan ordering other firemen off. "I was in the Army four years, but I wouldn't like to tell what she said, before all these ladies." The ladies looked disappointed. He added: He ran a fire line to a nearby pond, and Mrs. Swan had a little trouble with the owner. Fireman No. 2 saw her "kicking and pushing" the neighbor, but finally she patted him on the back, "with no hard feelings." Fireman No. 3 testified: "She acted like she was nuts, running around, asking, 'When you gonna put water on my house?'" Young Mr. Swan declared it was true he carried a bottle of whiskey at the time, "but only for the firemen," to spur them on.

Mrs. Swan took the stand. Certainly she hadn't interfered with the firemen. "I loved the old place. It was my home." The rich voice broke. The audience leaned forward as she told about herself; she had been an actress and dancer, she had had three previous husbands, then Mr. Swan. For two days, while the jury listened in astonishment, Mrs. Swan listed what she had lost. That Louis XVI set in the bathroom—it had cost $750. (A tiller of the land, with only a privy, swallowed heavily.) Yes, she put candelabra in the bathroom, for $79; a shaving mirror for her husband, yes, it cost $48. That jar of cosmetics, of course it came to $40; it was "a special kind." The shoe horn? Yes, $7.50. Her nightgowns cost $45 each, and she had black ones, yellow, peach, blue and white. For the "Head of Girl," by Greuze—a painting, she explained—she had paid $5000; one of her tablecloths, $1500; lace face towels, $11 each; a marble fireplace, $1000. Why, yes, sets of dinner plates did cost $150 a dozen. "Some are two hundred years old, you know." The farmers stared, real hard.

Attorney Adams interrupted: "You say you lost whole sets of this tableware. Hadn't any been broken at all?" The ladies looked at one another. Mrs. Swan smiled: "No. Because they were cared for. In New York, I had trained servants, French and Swedish. In Natchez, I washed the best plates myself!" The Natchez chatelaines exchanged another kind of glance. So it went. The jurors, after nine bewildering days of life among the quality, took forty-five minutes to bring in a verdict; it was in favor of Mrs. Swan. In the battle of Natchez and the lady, the lady had won. Mrs. Swan, packing up, left Natchez for good.

But Homewood, the house of King David's daughter, was also gone for good.

XI

THREE IN ONE

BEHOLDING Richmond for the first time, strangers have blinked and looked again. I can testify that I have never seen another like it, North or South. It is a trio of houses, as curiously matched as might be imagined, hooked together in one—a three-sectional memorial to a man who never gave up anything, from a sweetheart to a plantation home.

Back in 1770 or earlier, a small, bare building stood there in the forests outside Natchez. Dim tales have pictured it as an outlaws' retreat, a haven for French and Spanish smugglers and river pirates. A deep, disused well-hole has been pointed out, with purple stories of victims dumped in headlong, and of one who wasn't dumped but leaped, to avoid the fate that ladies always try to avoid in such cases. By the time an apprentice bandit was lowered there to bring her up, it was too late. . . .

More dependable is a well-worn document telling of the first known owner, Jean St. Germain, a French linguist who served the Spaniards as interpreter to the Indians. Monsieur St. Germain was a man of parts, owner of land and cattle, dealer in skins. White women being in short supply, he took an Indian squaw and had three children by her. There is nothing to indicate that he treated this wife with less respect than he might have accorded any other mate. On the frontier such unions lasted through lifetimes, as this one did.

In his wooded retreat Jean St. Germain elaborated the older house into a place à la Creole—a raised structure beneath a tall roof, with a good air of comfort. The main floor, the second, rose above a brick-floored basement flush with the ground. For the full width of the house, back and front, there opened a second-story gallery with narrow wooden posts, each resting on a brick shaft below. An iron gallery carried out the Creole flavor, with a wide, iron-railed outer stairway, ending in a formal curve. Inside were heavy wooden fireplaces, timbered walls and doors bolted with thick bars against unwanted visitors. Here, cigar in mouth, St. Germain spent the years with his copper-skinned wife.

Working in the swamp in 1789, he met with an accident. By the time the King's Surgeon reached him he was dead and also, says the record, "wanting one leg." Presently an attorney reported to officials that the property, its Negroes and furniture should be sold at once, because the plantation was "filled with Indians inclined to plunder same"; the Indian woman was "exciting said Indians to claim said property." Creditors come before common-law wives; so she had to leave her home, with her pale children whose eyes and accent were French, but who had no protection of law—French, Spanish or otherwise.

A succession of owners followed until 1823, when a former Baltimorean arrived. Young Levin Marshall got into plantations through a side route, a bank door. A connection of the resplendent Chief Justice Marshall of the Supreme Court, Levin had moved first to Woodville, below Natchez, where he made a quick impression on the planters, and also their daughters. Of slight build, he had a dark, intense face, aquiline nose, thin lips with a slight hauteur that probably became one of his rank. He danced easily, and was deft at paying the proper compliments between the numbers. He could take his choice of the girls. But he must have been more than a mere dandy. Possibly to the surprise of certain Mississippi grand dames, Levin set his eye on a girl whom he met by accident in New Orleans.

Tiny Maria Chotard possessed a twinkling beauty, a charm beyond her years, and practically no money. Her father had been an affluent sugar grower who fled Santo Domingo in the slave uprisings; when Maria's mother and father died, there was only an older sister to look after her. Inheriting her father's Gallic sprightliness, she had something more, a keen brain. At fifteen, she could trounce her elders at chess. At eighteen, she found the boys buzzing about her. At a party the dark Mississippian, Levin Marshall, was about to leave for home when he spied Maria in the corner, and demanded an introduction. He managed his courtship with debonair dispatch; before they parted that season, they were engaged. What followed is a lesson in adroit insistence.

Levin returned temporarily to Mississippi, and the petite Maria Chotard went to Alabama, where her older sister Eliza lived. Before a month passed, Eliza saw that Maria had grown dispirited, especially when she read her fiance's messages. Maria tried to talk about her affairs; for once in such a case, the older girl thought it best not to intrude; as Eliza wrote later in an illuminating memoir, she preferred to let Maria's "good sense be her best guide." That went on until Maria threw herself on her sister's shoulder and wept out her feelings. Eliza still insisted that the decision must be Maria's; that night Maria wrote her refusal, asking Levin to return her letters.

Time passed without response. One day, Maria lay in bed with a headache when a servant knocked. Levin Marshall sent word that he had arrived. He had to go back to Mississippi the next day. He had come to return the letters. (No one asked why he hadn't used the mails.) This threw Maria into a spasm of indecision; she knew the moves in chess, but this new game puzzled her. . . . She was sick, she said; she couldn't see him. This time Sister Eliza asserted herself; Maria would have to get up. The sniffling girl asked if Eliza wouldn't go downstairs with her. Eliza refused and Maria went alone.

After a proper interval, the older sister joined the pair. Meeting Levin for the first time, she was very much pleased with him. But she found that the banker had not achieved a full reconciliation. Fate took a hand; they discovered that the young gentleman had a fever, and they put him to bed. Hours later Levin managed to come out to tea. Meeting other guests, he spread himself, becoming "the admiration of them all."

Well again by the next morning, Levin learned that his carriage needed repairs. That would delay him still more. He went back to the house, and then, sad to tell, his fever suddenly struck once again. As before he spent a time in bed, but rose to charm the visitors. This went on for several days; Maria was warming again, and once more pressing Sister Eliza for an opinion. Eliza thought as little of matchmaking as of match-breaking. She had one bit of advice: Let your heart be your guide; but this time, be sure to follow it. The engagement was renewed, the marriage delayed no longer, and bride and bridegroom left for Mississippi.

The bright young Marshalls cut high figures in the Natchez country. Maria wrote her sister of her "entire devotion" to Levin, and Eliza knew that things had turned out for the best. The sisters met only once again, but Eliza long afterward remembered the girl's face with its look of childlike happiness. Maria and Levin had five children, yet her life had more than its share of dark moments. Only one lived—George Marshall, the gay master of Lansdowne, seen in the previous chapter.

Maria had the consolation of watching her husband's advancement. He represented Nicholas Biddle, then riding high on the American scene as head of the Second Bank of the United States. The Southwest's prosperity had drawn Biddle's appraising attention and for years the New Orleans branch alone did greater business than the main institution in Philadelphia. Biddle decided to create a branch in Natchez itself, and Levin learned that he would run it. Simultaneously came sorrow; Maria died.

Stoically, the lean widower moved to the town with his son. Almost automatically, he made a large role for himself. Because communication with the North was hopelessly slow, branch banks had much leeway, controlling their own loans. In such loans lay power. His easy manner belied the same ingenuity and application that had won him his Maria. In a few years he owned town and plantation property in four directions.

Traveling upriver, he stopped occasionally with the cotton-growing Elliots. He liked the son of the family, a dreamy gallant with a name that rang on the ear—William St. John Elliot. Even more he liked the daughter Sarah, a widow with dash and also a calm competence. In her company he found solace; Sarah, it seems, was much like Levin, easy polish outside, strength within. The marriage seemed pre-ordained and neither partner ever regretted it. They had six children who lived to maturity. For a growing family, and a growing figure in the community, something large in the way of a residence was advisable. Levin and Sarah chose the old St. Germain place, with its low-hung roof and Creole galleries.

After a time, however, the once-ample house appeared inadequate. Some would have put up a new place. Not so Levin, a man who was never inclined to give up a possession. He added a complete new building to the side of the first one, facing at right angles to the Creole structure. A tall, two and a half-storied structure, it had a narrow, high-raised portico bearing four Ionic columns in pairs, elaborately fluted, which rested on a block base. A balustrade was attached at the roofline; from each window extended an individual iron balcony or half-balcony. The net effect was of highly patterned richness—a Greek Revival head with a Creole tail, half-lost at the back. They called it Richmond.

From the new portico opened a forty-foot hallway, much ornamented, with pillars and pilasters, medallions and cornices in heavily classic patterns. Folding doors connected double parlors; beside black Italian marble mantels, gold cornices encompassed the tops of two and three windows. For Sarah, the setting was appropriate; her spirit showed itself in the glistening chambers. In the music room, while callers paused, the handsome matron played by candlelight at her harp and her carved rosewood piano. At the end of the hall stood a pair of dining rooms, the first for Sarah and Levin and their guests, the other for the children, so that they could learn manners under the guidance of servants, without disturbing their elders. On state occasions the two rooms were thrown open to form a banqueting hall, with the smiling Sarah leading guests to the flower-garlanded chamber. Sarah had turned into one of Levin's greatest assets.

The Marshalls and their servants overflowed from one building to the next. Levin weathered vicissitudes. President Andrew Jackson soon reached the climax of his shattering battle with Nicholas Biddle's bank; rampaging democracy struck at the institution, calling it a money power fattening on the people's suffering. The bank went, but Levin made new banking connections.

Levin had irons in other fires. He branched out as an owner of Natchez' biggest hotel, the lustrous Mansion House, famous up the river for duels begun in its halls, for gargantuan meals and no less gargantuan bets. For years the Mansion House mint juleps were part of the river's folklore—drinks of massive proportions, notable for a subtle effulgence. The making of a julep, of course, was a rare art, about which many men had opinions. Some dropped in strawberries, to be soaked in the delectable juices, swallowed as a last celestial touch. At Levin's Mansion House the crowning triumph became a delicate moss rose, flipped in during the final moment of the act of creation.

In 1840 a Natchez paper told of julep-making that would cause a saint's mouth to water. The editor began by describing the best that less-qualified people achieved; for instance, those up at the Louisville Pearl Street House:

Take a large and deep-cut glass tumbler, fill it with sufficient sugar and ice to the brim—half of the ice shaved into snow and the rest in lumps of moderate size. Lay on the top of it three fresh leaves of mint without any part of the stem attached. Pour on just half a glass of fine unimpeachable cognac brandy, then just half a glass of fine old Jamaica rum; then add half a glass of old ripe port wine. Then pour the mass rapidly for some time, back and forth in two tumblers; the longer this action continues, the better. Then plant a small bunch of mint on one side of the tumbler by putting the stems down into the ice, and having the leaves up about as high as the nose of the drinker should come. On the other side of the tumbler, where the mouth should come, rub the edge with half a fresh lemon.

The editor concluded that it "smelled like a bouquet." However, this Louisville julep was merely magnificent; he went on to tell of civilization's transcendent one, from Levin Marshall's hostelry:

On Saturday we were presented with a magnificent julep from the Mansion House that probably excelled anything of the kind made on the continent of Columbus; in fact, it put our late recipe entirely in the shade. It was in a massive cut goblet, with the green forest of mint which crowned it frosted over with sugar snow, and the whole mass underlaid with delicate slices of lemon piled in the pyramid of ice. As for the liquor, it was so skilfully blended that no one could detect its several parts. Ladies drank of it and supposed that some huge grape from the south side of the Island of Madeira had burst open on a sunny day and been crushed in the goblet.

Match that, sir!

Yet another triumph with which the Marshalls of Richmond are connected was the visit of the Scandinavian nightingale,

THREE IN ONE

Jenny Lind, during her American triumph of 1851. The promoter P. T. Barnum was shepherding the possessor of the golden throat. Mr. Barnum had a good thing, and he was working it with the same understanding of audience values as he did with a cigar-smoking midget or a two-headed ox. Jenny's visit had something of the emotional effect of a tornado; the event is Natchez' supreme tribute to visiting art.

La Lind had delighted New Orleans with her appearances there. She also stirred the highminded Orleanians by her charities, and the publicity-wise P. T. spread reports of her generosity far and wide. She was preparing to go upriver to St. Louis, when a group of Natchezians was captured by an inspiration. Couldn't she get off and sing for Natchez, too? Mr. Barnum was willing; for five thousand dollars Mlle. Lind would sing twelve times.

For weeks the Natchez countryside hummed. Who was going to hear her? Who wasn't? The biggest place turned out to be the Methodist church; since they knew Jenny to be a religious little woman, this seemed appropriate. Plantation people from outlying reaches formed parties, arranged to visit town friends so they would be sure to arrive in time. Merchants, lawyers, bartenders argued: Was it true she was a ventriloquist? (This unkind rumor had spread.) Had they heard how a fellow had fallen out of a balcony while he listened, delirious? The lady, it appeared, had better be good.

Tickets went fast, as high as twelve dollars each. All seats in the orchestra—pardon, the main floor pews—were sold. An editor expressed doubt that in any other American city would $6500 be paid for 770 tickets. Suddenly the amateur impresarios discovered there was no piano such as a Lind would require. They pulled their hair, until Levin Marshall came to mind. He had a big one out at Richmond that Sarah was always playing. Would Sarah and Levin lend it? Levin said they would, and made himself a hero.

At New Orleans the steamer was delayed. Some claimed Jenny made things hard by declaring suddenly that, as a good

Christian, she would not ride a steamer on Sunday. Whatever the reason, Natchez' plans had to be put back a night. The delay only added to the titillation. A shouting crowd—in it the excited Levin Marshall, his Sarah and her urbane brother William St. John Elliot—hailed the diva; at Levin's Mansion House men and women dropped back, awed, wet-eyed. The great night arrived, and the seasoned Natchez editor, with a school boy's abashment, drew away from the assignment of appraising a Jenny. He drafted "a lady of our acquaintance," who wrote herself quite a piece about it.

With Jenny's first notes, it had to be reported that faces fell. (Even the Marshalls and their in-laws the Elliots, seated in the front row near their piano, appeared crestfallen.) Why, it sounded only like a woman singing! But as Jenny went on, the lady critic commented, "her soul with her voice appeared to soar higher and higher, seeming as if both must wing their flight to Heaven; and she gave forth such bursts of miraculously great execution, that mingled with other sensations was one of wonder that we had dared to feel disappointed."

Later came Lind's bird song, which transfixed the critic. Fie on those who called her a ventriloquist! "Who would desecrate any one of Lind's peerless, unearthly tones, by ascribing their bringing forth to such power? No! Hearing the original sound and its echo distinctly uttered at the same instant, it is almost impossible to be skeptic to the idea that she possesses some strange faculty, hitherto undiscovered, but certainly as far removed from ventriloquism as from ordinary vocalization." The exultant writer reached her finale: "Lind's bow to the audience is too low; such a one should command and accept such bows, but never give them." After going through all this, the reviewer did not sign her name; a female's place, after all, was not in a newspaper column.

The engagement drew warm notice in journals over the country. P. T. Barnum allowed the word to filter out that his Jenny would give a thousand of her five thousand dollars to Natchez charities, most of it to the town hospital. Now, em-

D'EVEREUX
A Greek Temple in a Deep Southern Setting

EARL M. NORMAN

D'EVEREUX
Ironwork

REBER HENDERSON

D'EVEREUX
Balcony in the Afternoon

EARL M. NORMAN

barrassment. Long ago Natchez had levied a tax for the hospital on "foreign passengers." The steamboat people, listing Lind and company as coastwise travelers, had paid no tax. Controversy broke out and hospital officials sued for their tax. Much hurt, Jenny withdrew the promised thousand. Some charged that the diva was having her great gift and keeping it too, garnering publicity for beneficence without being beneficent. Most critics, however, blamed the circus man. The story ends on a note of anticlimax; one account grew frosty: "Mr. Barnum agreed to come to Natchez for $5000, he came, received the $5000 and left." Levin Marshall sent a cart to pick up Sarah's grand piano, and calm returned to the river.

Some years later, in 1860, the Marshalls completed their Richmond. To the other end of their original Creole house they connected a third building, unlike either of the others, a three-storied red brick structure of a marked austerity. As several said, it might easily have been transported from Beacon Hill in Boston. A single detail relieved the plainness, a series of small iron balconies outside the windows, to match those at the front. Whether so intended or not, the addition gave a new balance. Two tall structures, front and back, enveloped the smaller Creole place of cool, ancient galleries and bricked basement; no longer did it look like a humble appendage, but an integral part of the whole. There it stood, a full forty rooms, three eras of Natchez hooked together in brick, wood and iron—in the words of a native, "a natural sight for the eyes."

Meanwhile a new face had been added to the Marshall circle. Sarah's easy-mannered brother, William St. John Elliot, acquired a wife, the pleasant and highly solvent Anne Conner of

Second Creek. A large-eyed brunette with a good mind, the twenty-three year old Anne already counted herself twice a widow. Yellow fever took her first mate, tuberculosis her second. Each time she acquired another estate. This third marriage would be the luckiest.

The lady found herself the dominant half of the alliance. William St. John Elliot grew more and more dreamy. He interested himself in plantation parties, games and, not least, gardening. She took on sturdier matters, and the arrangement worked out to general satisfaction. William St. John had a final preoccupation—his family and its history. Soon they were building their house in Natchez. He wanted the privilege of naming it, and his wife concurred. It was called D'Evereux, for his mother's side of the family, the side that appealed in particular to him. Together they watched the rise of a structure which has been called a rare example of the pure Greek Revival.

A square, immaculately white, bricked temple, in a gem-like setting of trees and water, it was perfect in its balance. Across all the front rose six fluted columns of rare grace, extending from an elevated porch to a hipped roof, topped by a railed cupola. The widest of entrance stairs covered the space between the four central columns, in what seemed a gesture of easy welcome. No upper gallery interfered with the upthrust pillars; only on close approach did there appear a small upper balcony outlined in ironwork. Emphasizing the classic, the gallery ceiling was paneled and ornamented with medallions.

Six more pillars faced the back, with a full-fledged second story gallery for a family retreat. Oddly, in the original house or later, the rear doorways, above and below, had a greater elaboration than a pair of straight-lined front ones. To the front was unrelieved severity, to the back, wide arches and curved lights in a fleur-de-lis design. Between the entrances stood the hallway, without an interruption; interior stairs appeared in a side recess. Four rooms up, four down went the pattern; everywhere the eye met paneling and cornice decoration. Across a rear court, two side buildings faced one another. The whole of D'Evereux had simplicity and restraint, the beauty of a monument against the sunlight.

The flower-loving William St. John Elliot, much in his element, went to work to provide a background of the kind indicated by such a house. Many of the great trees that had covered the site were left in place to grow more massive, their arms providing a frame for the pale symmetry of that temple-like house. Twelve acres were landscaped, with drives crossing among the oaks. From the back a series of thickly planted terraces sank one by one from the residence, each with its garden of white camellia, of red and pink japonica or pale azalea. At the bottom level rippled a lake on which the careful Mr. Elliot placed swans and boats, with a small mill at the edge. The lake gave more than decoration; William St. John kept it stocked, and a guest could catch his own breakfast.

In the evenings the master gave balls for which the house was illuminated from doorway to cupola. The great white square, alight for hours, shone in the lake like a child's dream of a castle. A swan, floating by, broke the design into fragments; calm would return, and once more the shadow of the house looked back at the beholder.

For fifteen years William St. John and the wise young matron lived in harmony at their D'Evereux. He hoped earnestly for sons to carry on his lineage, but there were none. Enviously he thought of his brother-in-law Levin, who had five children by his first wife, six by his second. D'Evereux still remained empty.

During his later days William St. John Elliot grew more contemplative, more religious and then, in 1855, he died. The will left their estate to his wife, but only for her lifetime. Having wanted a descendant so badly, he provided that the property would then go to his nephew—provided the young man married and took the Elliot name by legislative act, "so as to represent me as my son." If the young man insisted on keeping his own name, D'Evereux would become a male orphanage, and the money would go to care for dozens of children.

Whatever the reason, the nephew did not comply. The widow, reflecting over the matter, was saddened by the thought that D'Evereux would eventually go outside her family. Besides, there must be far better sites and buildings for an orphanage than this eight-roomed establishment in its elaborate gardens on the outskirts. She called upon the Catholic church officials who would have received the place, and they compromised. She gave funds for another structure, and D'Evereux remained hers without hindrance. By this time she had a grand-niece, and she left it to her. And so D'Evereux stayed, after all, in the family, though not with William St. John's side of it.

The next generation saw bad times. The gardens went first. Federal soldiers used the site as a camp, though the house itself was undisturbed. Oaks and magnolias were chopped down to keep the men warm, and horses trampled the delicate terracing and flower bushes. The lake, in which thousands had watched the reflection of the house, went dry. Upkeep proved a problem, and D'Evereux had to be rented. One tenant was a farmer. During his regime horses were tethered on the galleries and hallways, and yams were stored in the rooms of the paneled walls.

With every year D'Evereux approached closer to ruin—a gaunt gray relic that time had left behind. It took a Chicago school teacher to do something about it. Visiting Natchez, Miss Myra Smith walked about the pillared front with the flaking paint and cracked walls; then she bought it and provided the town with a comprehensive restoration. Today D'Evereux glows again in the rich simplicity of the older day. The lake has gone, but the rest is there once more, the trees that hang their moss fringes in a bordering of fertile growth, the ironwork balcony and the fluted columns over which the sun's rays slant in the afternoon.

The Elliots' in-laws, the Marshalls, have never left Richmond, their three houses in one. In later years irony followed the building of that third wing at the back. The banker-father, Levin, put it up primarily for Duncan, the youngest son, who had married about that time. Then Dunc became sickly, and few gave him much time to live. Soon afterward, when Levin knew that his own time had come he made his will, leaving a fortune, but in a way that affected the family in varying fashions for decades. Levin, who never gave up anything, provided that his estate be kept intact through the lifetime of the ailing Dunc. Then, not only did Dunc live; he had eleven children, and survived most of them. Born in 1840, he lasted until he was 87!

The division of the property was held up year after year. The money, kept in trust and invested, brought regular checks which were split among the Marshalls. Finally, in 1927, Dunc went to his grave. It took more than a year to untangle the knots, and then the financial depression poured down upon the nation. The Marshalls could only look on while the fortune, which had been kept aside from them for so long, began to dissolve. For decades they had planned what they would do, what to buy, where to go. But each year brought only a further fall in their stocks and investments.

After some time, matters improved. The present-day Marshalls, living all together at Richmond, form a clan of eight women and a man; they have an easy-going life, each doing things his own way. There are many relatives, many visitors; something always happens in and about the trio of houses. The ornate, balustraded front remains the showplace; the oldest part, the early Creole building in the middle, is the center of family life.

XII

THE APPLECART THAT OVERTURNED

Nobody would have thought, during the greater part of his life, of calling Dr. Stephen Duncan a fanatic about anything. A smiling Brahmin, a "high-toned Whig," this pleasant-faced fellow enjoyed a background of privilege. Born to position, he became a banker, plantation owner and Natchez capitalist. Those who knew him would have called him the safest man on the river, who would go along with his neighbors on practically any subject.

Nor would many have raised any question about the orthodoxy of the lean Dr. John Ker. True, he was a former minister's son, himself a devout Presbyterian. His intellectual mother had conducted one of the earliest Natchez schools. That might have made some people suspicious. But Dr. Ker, a gentle, scholarly cotton grower and medical practitioner, was seldom heard to raise his voice against anybody.

Through most of their years these two friends and associates lived placidly and conventionally. Then suddenly, in their late maturity, a combination of events made them change their roles. Realizing exactly what they were about to do, they plunged into a cause celebre that set most of their friends and acquaintances against them to the furious end. Stephen Duncan and John Ker, it appeared, had peculiarly resolute convictions about rights and justice; and neither liked to be pushed into things. Together they upset a heavy applecart.

Stephen Duncan came from Carlisle, Pennsylvania, and his mother was one of the Postlethwaites, the family which owned Clifton and King's Tavern. Before the boy was ten, his father was killed in a duel in Pennsylvania; the widow saw that Stephen received a good education that ended with a medical degree. Recently I looked over a crumbling "Logic Notebook" of young Stephen Duncan. The handwriting opened earnestly: "Logic is the art of using reason well in our inquiries after truth"; and it went on with long, tightly-argued reflections on duty and God's will. The boy learned his lessons well.

Marrying at eighteen, young Dr. Duncan had two children. He might have remained the rest of his life in Pennsylvania had his wife not died. Wanting to forget his sorrow in a new scene, he moved in 1808 to Natchez, where he made a prompt start. There is no reason to think his connections proved a handicap. Stephen had a way with him, and he did not injure himself when, after a while, he made a second alliance and a high one, with Catherine, sister of the resplendent Adam L. Bingaman. Cotton and finance interested him and he invested, expanded his properties, and gradually gave more attention to his business enterprises than to his doctor's kit.

Yet he still had his love of medicine; or was it a feeling of duty? In any case he continued for years to take a certain number of patients, sharing practice with his close friend, the hard-working Dr. John Ker. Young John, hardly an impractical individual, had been first a surgeon in the Seminole War, then a Natchez doctor and grower. Through it all he had remained a retiring man, kind-mannered and untalkative.

Within seven years of his arrival, Stephen heard of the death of another friend, Lyman Harding. For a long time he had been admiring the Harding house, Auburn. Back in 1812 the architect, Levi Weeks, had erected it, with a comment that it was "the first house in the Mississippi Territory on which was ever attempted any of the orders of Architecture." Whether or not this was strictly correct, Auburn was one of the most elaborate Natchez buildings up to that date. The architect added: "The site is one of those peculiar situations which combines the delights of romance, the pleasure of rurality and the approach of sublimity." Inquiring about it, Stephen Duncan purchased Auburn at once.

The builder exaggerated only slightly in describing the setting—a rolling acreage lined with massive oaks and magnolias, a place of shadowed reaches filled with thousands of birds. On one of the elevations stood an impressive red-brick establishment of unusual width with a majestic portico, a double porch of four Ionic columns and pediment above. Front doorways on both floors were monumental in effect, with white wood carving and side paneling, the whole topped by a broad brick arch. Cross hallways gave entrance to the many rooms, and vaulted walls provided another touch of grace. Casually the architect mentioned a "geometrical staircase," by which he meant a steep spiral, completing a circle between the two floors, so ingeniously balanced that it seemed held up by nothing at all. For years to come, people would be admiring the "geometrical staircase."

Behind the house, a covered passage, brick-floored, led to a two-storied brick structure for kitchen and servants; at the other side rose the dairy with a dark cistern in which were kept milk and other perishables. Vines cascaded over all of the red brick walls, their vivid greens contrasting with the duller hue of the shutters. The profile of the portico, high against the border of trees, proclaimed this a patriarch's house, built for living in the grand style.

The Duncans were prepared for that style. His slaves numbered five hundred. He helped form Mississippi's first bank and then became its president. Expanding his interests beyond the South, he acquired properties in New York and Pennsylvania. A contemporary called him the owner of "an immense fortune . . . a man of rare sagacity and wonderful energy—one of the best business men in the Union." Dr. John Jenkins of Elgin, telling of the deaths of a hundred and thirty Duncan slaves in a yellow fever epidemic, declared: "The loss (about $100,000) is a bagatelle to the doctor, as he has large sugar estates in Louisiana, and in this country has three cotton places and two in Concordia opposite Natchez."

For Stephen Duncan it was a bountiful existence. He joined the Bingamans, Surgets and Minors at Pharsalia race track; on trips overseas he added to his string of prize horses. To his wide house, with its far-flung park, came most of the celebrities who visited Natchez, among them Henry Clay and Edward Everett Hale, to admire the vaulted hall and doorway, to sip wine with the Duncans and Kers at entertainments beneath the lines of magnolias. A man of literary tastes, Stephen sat for hours with the ebullient Adam L. Bingaman, his brother-in-law, exchanging anecdotes, talking over their readings in Greek and French.

For the Duncans and the Kers the decades stretched comfortably ahead. But meanwhile there slowly developed one of the most sharply-charged incidents in the annals of the Mississippi country, the "Ross case."

Captain Isaac Ross always admitted he was a scrapper. The dark-haired, florid old man had been fighting most of his life. He had given an eye in bitter Revolutionary skirmishing, before he moved down to Jefferson county in the Natchez environs. Bringing in heavy crops, he scorned town life and lived contentedly in the rural reaches. An individual of stringent honesty, proud that he had won his own place in the world, he scorned pettifoggers, people who put on airs or tried to cut corners. One thing the neighbors learned early:

What Ike Ross wanted to do, he'd do, and to hell with his detractors.

From the elevation of his house at Prospect Hill, Ike Ross admired the sight of his acres in all directions; he also had a good time entertaining his small circle of intimates. Among them he counted the two doctors, Duncan and Ker. In the evenings with his guests he talked frequently of the way he got on with his slaves. He had put in a training system, under which he rewarded those who advanced themselves. To his friends he explained his progress, laughing over set-backs, asking advice as to ways to make his plans work better.

Between Isaac and his modest wife Jane there was a more than usually intimate bond; she talked over his plantation management with him, helped him in dealings with men and women in the fields.

At Prospect Hill they watched their children marry and move away. His favorites were Ike, Jr., and Margaret, a delicate-featured girl with something of her mother's shyness in her warm blue eyes, and a hint of her father's stubbornness about her mouth.

Margaret and her father were drawn closer by an early tragedy. The girl fell deeply in love with a young attorney; their marriage day was close when a horseman raced to the door, to announce that her fiance was about to fight a duel. Margaret ran to her father, begging him to intervene; before they reached the outside road, they learned that the youth had been killed. The next months dragged by for the girl; some thought she never quite regained her former cheerfulness. A few years later she agreed to marry; very quickly her husband died, and the childless widow went back to her father.

After another interval, Margaret was persuaded to attend a neighbor's party. Her eyes were caught by those of a stranger, Thomas A. Reed of Kentucky, who arranged quickly to be introduced to her. Soon Tom Reed was spending evenings with the Rosses and the mother and father noticed a new light in Margaret's eyes. A second marriage was arranged; the Duncans, the Kers and others attended, and the quiet Mrs. Ross gave thanks that her daughter at last had reached something of the happiness that she herself had known.

The next few years were Margaret's most peaceful. Riding about the country, Tom Reed had noticed a medium-sized house in an appealing location. It dated from the late 1700s; since then it had expanded sidewards, by the addition of new rooms. In 1818 the enthusiastic Reed acquired it, called it Linden and transformed it. Further widening the building, he built a one-story gallery to give a sweep of ninety-eight feet across all the front. He installed ten slim pillars of solid cypress, and added a balustrade above; after that, in the center, came a neat, light second-story portico like a crown to the façade. The doorway, a thing of delicacy, had pairs of pilasters to repeat the gallery lines, with narrow sidelights of woodwork patterning, and a fanlight.

A second long porch was installed at the back, with a rear court as another shaded place for family gatherings. Inside and out, Linden had a feeling of airiness, and of harmony. Oaks and cedars rose close to the house, a curtain of leaves half-revealing, half-cloaking it from the world.

At Linden the circle of friends met again, the Rosses, Duncans, Kers and several more. On the porches in the evenings, they spoke of the crowded plantation life, the word from Virginia watering places, the newest under-the-Hill excitement. As they later recalled, they talked also of slavery and questions that went with it. Ike Ross, his wife Jane nodding at his side, described his methods of encouraging his slaves, his plans for freeing this and that one when he thought it best. He pointed a tobacco-stained finger as he explained: He'd never rest after he passed on if he knew his servants hadn't gotten their reward for all they'd done for him.

He found sympathetic listeners. For years, various men of Natchez had interested themselves in a movement of the American Colonization Society. Dr. Duncan became president of the Mississippi organization; members included Dr. Ker,

"King David" Hunt and dozens more. The purpose was to help emancipated Negroes get to Africa. Motives were complex; in some cases humanitarianism predominated, again a more or less enlightened selfishness, even a hope of strengthening slavery itself. (Many owners believed that the increasing number of free blacks gave slaves examples to make them discontented.) The movement was not that of the abolitionists, who frequently opposed colonization as hostile to their purposes; they insisted that the Negro, by his long labor, had won a stake in the United States.

On a summer night in 1829, a messenger woke Margaret and Tom Reed. Could they come to Prospect Hill? Her mother had died. Hurrying upriver, they found Captain Ross prostrate with grief. He could barely force himself to witness the burial. In the slow procession walked the files of their slaves, who had known of Mrs. Ross' concern for them, her frequent consultations with the Cap'n in their behalf. When many of them stayed behind to take his hand, they cried with him. Margaret remained at his side for a time and persuaded him to travel. He fell ill, returned home, and seemed no better until one day he discovered that an overseer had grown harsh in his absence. Ike Ross jumped out of his chair and went back to work.

Rapidly his spirits improved. When she called again Margaret was delighted. More and more Ike Ross was talking of slavery, and what might be done about it. He went back over conversations with his dead wife, promises he had made to her. Circulating among the slaves, he asked questions. What would they want to do if they got a start as free people? How would they feel about this and that. . . . If things turned out well, one day they'd be their own masters. . . . The Negroes filed away, a flame of hope in their eyes. In the flickering of the cabin lamps, excitement spread. That was Ol' Miss Ross herself, talking through the Cap'n; Ol' Miss and maybe God, too. . . .

That same year the soul of Margaret Ross Reed was tried

again. Her husband had done brilliantly, becoming Attorney General of Mississippi, after that United States Senator. In his early days in Washington Tom gave a notable account of himself until he was suddenly stricken with a hopeless illness. This time, after the last rites, Isaac Ross helped Margaret close up Linden, and he brought his daughter home.

For six years they stayed close together, and Margaret found herself taking part of her dead mother's role. Repeatedly she heard her father's plans for his slaves; sitting with him at his desk, she felt her interest growing. Toward the end, in 1835, Ike Ross called Margaret; he knew that death was near. He was making a number of gifts to relatives, so none would suffer; she knew what else his will provided. . . . He dropped into a final sleep.

Dr. Stephen Duncan, Dr. John Ker and the family gathered for the reading of the testament. A stir ran through the countryside when the terms came out. Ike Ross ordered that most of his hundred and seventy slaves be allowed to vote whether they wanted to go to Africa as free men and women. They would remain as at present until the death of Margaret, who would run the plantation as she knew her father wished, giving them further training. Eventually the plantation would be sold; at that time it had a value of $160,000, with a yearly income of $20,000. The money would be used to transport the people and build a school for them.

Margaret and her brother, Ike, Jr., stood together; they would see that their father's wishes were carried out. Soon, however, whispers reached them. Captain Ross had named five business men as executors; four refused to serve, leaving only the dead man's nephew. The neighbors were growing angry. All those valuable niggers—a crime to let them loose! They'd find a way to stop it. . . . But Margaret and her brother were not really upset until hints were dropped that an effort would be made to break the will.

Unexpectedly, Isaac, Jr., died, and Margaret found herself alone. The Negroes, learning of the situation, came to her.

Was everything all right, Miss? Or was they trying to keep our freedom from us? Margaret's color heightened. Everything would be all right; she'd see to that. As they left, she dropped into her chair. What could she do? A fluttering woman called: As an old friend, she hoped Margaret would drop this whole thing. It was unladylike, all the dissension and trouble. Anyway, didn't Margaret realize what the lawyers said—she couldn't do a thing they couldn't overthrow in court?

When she heard that, Margaret bade goodbye to her guest, fetched her shawl and called her coachman. In Natchez, sitting across from her attorneys, she shuddered at their dubious words. They just didn't know; surely she understood that Mississippi had recently adopted a law saying no owner could free his slaves unless the legislature approved in each case? And the people who didn't like Captain Ross' will were mighty powerful. A chill inside, Margaret had herself driven off.

A little later her vehicle rode through the heavily-grown grounds of Stephen Duncan's Auburn. As she drew toward the thick columns, the trailing moss scratched the sides. Everything was so placid, so comfortable here; would Dr. Duncan, the easy-going, be inclined to help her? For an hour she stayed with the amiable doctor. She explained that she herself was unwell; and she was afraid. His hands folded on his waistcoat, leaning far back in his library chair, he grew slowly less amiable as he listened. Margaret realized that she had never before seen Stephen Duncan really angry. When he spoke, he said only a few words; but his voice had a furious conviction. At once she felt better. Yes, she would do what he suggested, she told him. . . .

Outside Natchez, Margaret stopped at a familiar spot, her old home, Linden. Dr. John Ker had bought it from her when she returned to her family. That long gallery, topped in the center by its wooden portico, welcomed her again. There she had sat with her father and husband and their friends, and spoken of this matter. Now John Ker welcomed her with a happy exclamation, and they spent several hours, debating, considering. At the end John Ker agreed to help, as she had known he would.

Early the next morning Margaret hurried to her desk. As a servant hovered about, she pulled forth papers and began to write, her hand trembling at first, then steadying as the words poured forth. . . . A few months later Margaret fell ill; the doctors, as she had feared, gave her only a short time to live. She called three men, Dr. Ker, Dr. Duncan, and the Rev. Mr. Zebulon Butler of Port Gibson, an old friend and member of the colonization movement. She had left her slaves to the latter two; the three of them must carry out her father's wishes and hers. Her fading eyes fixed upon them: They had to do this, in God's name.

Now the trouble broke into the open. The opposition went into court, to fight both Margaret's will and her father's. These Negroes, they said, couldn't be taken to Africa; it was against Mississippi law to free them. Pressure was applied, slowly at first, them more and more strongly, against the two doctors and the minister, but especially against Stephen Duncan. He had the widest financial connections and in a way he was most vulnerable. Banking associates and fellow planters found ways to bring up the subject as they discussed bank notes, as they sipped punch together. What was the matter with him? Was he their enemy? Didn't he understand what he was doing, interfering, encouraging—

Stephen Duncan tried to explain. This was a dying man's will, his careful determination of what he wanted done with his property. The opposition was hysterical, illogical; from the look that came into their eyes, he understood it was hopeless. Then Stephen Duncan really spoke his mind. If he did nothing else in his life, he'd see that his friend's last wishes were carried out. Let them just remember that! With him, likewise defiant, stood his associate, Dr. Ker.

A year passed, and another. The matter hung on, delayed, argued, reargued. Ike Ross, it was charged, had been mentally unbalanced; this was a hasty, death-bed document, made in fear of the grave, under the influence of "priests and fanatics." Calmly Duncan and Ker went into court, citing all evidence to the contrary. Ike Ross had been lucid to the end. These plans had been in his head for years, discussed on successive occasions. They offered testimony that, far from being minister-ridden, Ike Ross had had a good natured tolerance toward all faiths. More years passed, and the delays went on, through court after court.

Finally, after every possible technicality had been brought up, the Mississippi Supreme Court ruled in favor of the Rosses. True, it said, the state had provided a rigid control over emancipations; but this could not prevent a man from disposing of his slaves beyond the limits of Mississippi. The law had been passed to prevent an increase of free Negroes in the state; that could hardly prevent the removal of slaves *from* Mississippi in order to free them. The decision was very clear. In Auburn's library, Stephen Duncan and John Ker conferred on ways to carry it out. At last the fight was over.

But it wasn't. Suddenly new barriers were thrown up. Having lost in the courts, their opponents went to the legislature, and here they would have won in a moment, except for one fact. The earnest Dr. Ker happened to be a member of the Senate that year. Arriving one morning, he was startled to learn that the other legislative body, the House, had adopted a resolution declaring it a "dangerous example" to let the Ross slaves leave, an example to which the House members "would not consent."

John Ker jumped up. This scheme would legislate away the rights of American citizens! It was not for them to decide whether Ike Ross had acted wisely or unwisely; his clear wishes must be followed. Shouts arose, and men exchanged blows in the halls. Dr. Ker realized that a bitter battle was in prospect; he saw individuals moving about the halls, conferring with the legislators, introducing others connected with the litigation. A shower of pamphlets descended; long articles were

AUBURN EARL M. NORMAN
He Defied the Neighbors, and the Slaves Went Free

AUBURN REBER HENDERSON
Its "Geometric Staircase" Is a Masterwork

AUBURN EARL M. NORMAN
The Doorway Saw Triumph and Disaster

placed in newspapers attacking him, Dr. Duncan and Isaac Ross.

In the midst of the tension John Ker rose again. He spoke in a low voice, marshaling every fact at his command. He told the history of the case, all he knew of it. As the oppositionists glared, the hall quieted. John Ker appealed to the fellow Senators. How could they, as fair men, give approval to a resolution such as this? A hoot sounded at the back; the presiding officer beat his gavel for order. The two sides faced each other as a vote began. To the end, the count remained neck to neck; then, by a single ballot, John Ker carried the issue.

Even now, the opponents had not finished. In the lower house, the rules were unexpectedly dispensed with and, without a roll call, another measure passed. No person, it declared, had a right to remove the slaves of a dead man in order to free them; such slaves must be distributed among the last relatives just as if there had been no will! John Ker's face darkened. He looked closer; the bill lacked the usual provision saying it did not apply to cases already risen. This seemed to be legislation for a purpose, and with a vengeance. He made an appeal; wouldn't they at least be willing to provide that it would not be retroactive? The lower house refused.

For hours John Ker struggled, beating his hands on the table as he argued. Once more the room fell silent; again by a close margin he made his point. The measure was "laid on the table" until the session's end, thus killing it—or so he thought. Leaving the room shortly afterward, Dr. Ker met another legislator, a life-long friend. The man shook his fist. If those damned Ross wills weren't stopped here, they'd do it another way. Didn't Ker understand what would happen? Every man in the Ross neighborhood was opposed to him; five hundred were ready to take guns to keep those niggers from being removed!

Returning to the meeting place, John Ker stopped short. The bill he had defeated, that last one, had been brought back in his absence. Running forward, the doctor cried out. This was illegal; they couldn't get away with a thing like this. He demanded that the record be consulted. The officers hunted it up, and John Ker saw that it had been doctored, to misrepresent the proceedings, so that the whole affair was reopened!

The galleries rumbled; men shouted threats. John Ker felt as if an avalanche were about to descend on him. It had been all arranged, then, to smother the opposition, by any means that came to hand. Never in his life had the gentle doctor known such an emotion. Slowly he looked about the crowded room, half the faces showing either bitter hostility or calm indifference. He paused, then thundered: What kind of men were they to do a thing like that? So they were proposing to browbeat the courts, violate the basis of their government. His voice deepened with his feeling; he pointed a trembling finger at them. If they did this, they could do anything, anything. He warned: "The poisoned chalice may soon be returned to your own lips. We may be the next victims. Has it come to this, that the laws of our land are to be annulled because one man, or even five hundred, do not like the way a will is made?"

Lines shifted and new cries arose, but Dr. John Ker carried his point. Ultimately a law was passed which, though it forbade any freeing of slaves by a will, declared that in matters pending, bondsmen could be removed during the following twelve months. John Ker and Stephen Duncan let out deep breaths of relief; at least they had won the fight in their case. Yet still again, if the two men thought their enemies had given up, they were wrong. The twelve-month provision made the next strategy clear—delay. Fighting rear-guard action, the other side presented one excuse after another. Duncan and Ker went about with set lips as former friends passed them, unfriendly looks on their faces.

Bitterness bred bitterness. Captain Ross' old house, Prospect Hill, burned down during the night, and a child was lost. Relatives charged that the slaves, infuriated at what was happening, had done it. On the spot, without trial, seven or eight of them were hanged or burned.

And still delay. The two doctors went into court to force the will into operation. Despite open threats, they found a close neighbor of considerable bravery who was willing to act as receiver for the Negroes, giving bond of a hundred thousand dollars for faithful performance. The higher courts ordered the sheriff to place the estate in the receiver's hands. And now the sheriff set himself up against the higher courts. This was a matter involving wills, he said, and only a probate court had authority. The making of such legal distinctions seemed hardly part of a sheriff's duties, and the courts snapped out an order to that effect. After thinking it over, the sheriff agreed to obey, and told the receiver to appear at a certain hour to get the slaves.

The sun rose on a grim morning. There was talk that armed neighbors were assembling, planning ambushes, the mass killings of all the blacks. The receiver gathered his own friends, also with guns. Hours passed, and the sheriff never appeared. As he started out, the county coroner rode up and put him in jail, for trying to "violate the authority of the probate court"!

How long? Nearly twelve years had gone by. The slaves had increased from one hundred seventy to more than two hundred fifty, meaning that the cost of transporting them would be considerably higher. In all the conflict, the plantation suffered. Earning much less than before, its sales value had dropped. The costs of the court disputes, and the expense of administering the drawn-out estate, ate deeply into funds intended for the slaves. Now it was found that the estate, once large enough to provide several times the needed amount, had become inadequate. The colonization society had to appeal for public help, which, at the end, was forthcoming.

John Ker died, still fighting; yet the hardest part was over. It fell to Dr. Stephen Duncan, Brahmin of Brahmins, to solve the problem. He sent word to the slaves who came under his authority. He wanted them to "escape" on a certain evening. When they came to the river bank, a vessel would take them to freedom. Other slaves of the estate went in different fashion, but at last they were on their way. The troubles did not end even then, for some of them died of disease, and it was claimed that carelessness in handling was responsible. But at long last most of them had freedom.

In the following years Stephen Duncan, though a slaveholder, made no secret of his Unionism, of his opposition to the Confederates. Many of his former friends refused to forgive him; when war began he stayed on for a time, until he went North in the middle of the fighting, and died there within a few years. I searched among Natchez papers of the day; the passing of this man, once one of the most celebrated of their citizens, drew a scant sentence or two.

A son returned only intermittently, spending much of his time in Europe. He had few decisions to make in matters of right and justice. And after a time the Duncans remained away for longer and longer periods. Auburn, their great house, fell into disrepair, a place of boarded windows, its tall portico unkempt. In 1911 the heirs gave the house and adjoining properties to the town; now it is maintained as a park and memorial building to Stephen Duncan. The pendulum has swung and the nonconformist is again an honored name. (Some guides get the story slightly mixed; one said the doctor left Natchez "because he couldn't stand the Yankee horrors"!)

Auburn of today serves a greater number than it did at its earlier height. Children run about swings and merry-go-rounds; tennis courts and a superior golf course are crowded. A group of Natchez women, "adopting" the house, collect furnishings to replace scattered items—chandeliers, tables, four-poster beds to go with the vaulted ceilings. One of the great oaks under which Stephen Duncan sat has gone; the other flourishes, casting a perpetual shade over the lawn. And heels again tap up and down that full-circle staircase, the "geometrical" one that the architect mentioned in 1812, hardly thinking it would be in use in the 1940s.

A few miles away, Dr. John Ker's Linden seems yet more fortunate. It continued to grow with the decades; wings at the back now provide a three-sided, shady court with the same easy atmosphere of earlier days. The long, ninety-eight foot sweep of front gallery is unimpaired. When I was last there the summer wind came lightly through the close-hanging trees with a hint of sweet olive; it was good to sip and talk in the comfortable rockers, and then to walk the grounds with Mrs. Frank Fauntleroy, the present mistress. The place has kept its pleasant comfort, its dignity that is airy and unpretending. I remember it best as the house in which Margaret Ross Reed knew her least difficult years, after her early troubles and before her last ones.

Both Auburn and Linden are, I think, monuments to two men and a woman of good will and good conscience.

OAKLAND

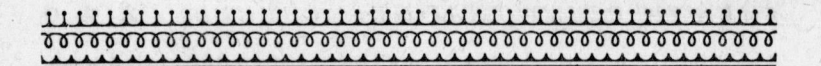

XIII

VIVA LA REVOLUCION!

On a raw December night of 1821, as the wind whipped about the bluff, a heavy-set individual of twenty-three climbed off a keelboat. Practically penniless, an inarticulate young man inclined to gloominess, John A. Quitman had reason to ponder his situation. A Lutheran minister's son, John had been born among German settlers along the Hudson, had tried teaching and disliked it, then law and hadn't done very well at that. Words twisted in his mouth when he grew excited and many found him well-meaning but generally dull. Yet the big fellow, with his long straight nose, flowing moustache and head of thick dark hair, could not be called unprepossessing. John had a pair of fists of tremendous power. A friend said he "never struck a man without knocking him down, except on one occasion and that, he claimed, was a glancing stroke." In truth, Quitman was a man of mixed characteristics.

Up in Ohio, where he settled for a time, the Griffith family described Natchez to him as "an excellent place to make money." The Griffiths added: "Men of talents are much wanted, and the general profligacy and idleness render young men of talents, morality and application to business, objects of public confidence and esteem." The stalwart Quitman was ready to chance climate and alluring lechery as well. "My ambition is of a more exalted nature," he wrote with a nice touch of priggishness; he sought "fame and fortune, not empty and evanescent pleasures." Settling in the town, he learned quickly that, whatever his morals or financial status, in Natchez he must "appear as a gentleman, or I cannot be treated as such." The would-be lawyer invested his last dollars in a handsome costume, and sallied forth.

William B. Griffith, of the family he had already known, was willing to let John use his law office and books. The new arrival, as the older attorney had suspected, turned out to be less than brilliant but dependable and hard-working. Within a month he became Griffith's assistant for routine affairs. Meanwhile the youth's delighted eye observed the general situation: Plenty of money, plenty of arguments, "court in session twenty-eight days without disposing of the criminal business." A lawyers' paradise!

Under the hill swam a hell's broth; above he observed "a genteel and well-regulated society." The planters "live profusely, drink costly port, Madeira and sherry, after the English fashion." There was good reason for this profusion, he discovered; some planters netted fifty thousand dollars for a single crop. The young men dressed in clothes made to order in Philadelphia, of extravagant cut and cost. Suits came to $100 each, three or four for winter, double that number for summer; shoes were brought from the North or from Paris, at $10 to $14 the pair. It was indeed a new atmosphere for the minister's son.

Almost at once John Quitman was absorbing the plantation spirit. Staying in the outskirts during a fever epidemic, he exclaimed: "Your coffee in the morning before sunrise; little stews and sudorifics at night, and warm foot baths if you have a cold; bouquets of fresh flowers and mint-juleps sent to your apartment; a horse and saddle at your disposal; everything free and easy, and cheerful and cordial. It is really fascinating. . . ." Often juleps began the day, and then breakfast on the gallery. After that, hunting, riding, fishing, morning visits, or chess and reading and lounging until two o'clock dinner. That meant dishes "in the Creole style—very rich." Within two more hours the household was asleep, the ladies enjoying the siesta in their apartments, the men on sofas, benches, hammocks or under the oaks. Before sunset, a tea-table was set in the garden, and there until bedtime, they strolled, sang, played croquet or whist. "It is an indolent yet charming life, and one quits thinking and takes to dreaming."

The Natchezians found more to John than his outward manner indicated. His superior took a trip East. Returning, Mr. Griffith discovered that the youth had won the favor of plantation men, commission dealers and financiers. From then on John was a partner. Meanwhile the new arrival stirred attention in another fashion by forming a volunteer military company. Spruce, high-stepping, the Natchez Fencibles were a young girl's dream. Uniformed in French blue, braided all over, with silver buttons and silver lace, they lined up, chins high, hands in salute as the band blared. At their head, his heavy face flushed, stood the moustachioed Captain Quitman.

It was as chief Fencible that John met Eliza, pert and independent only daughter of the elegant Judge Turner, social arbiter of the town. Eliza's bright green eyes twinkled behind her fan; she had had fifty proposals but she wasn't one to object to a fifty-first. More and more often, the chaperones noticed, Eliza was dancing with that Quitman man. Always self-willed, Eliza had the reputation of getting anything she liked. Abruptly she made up her mind; this time it was John Quitman.

When the engagement was announced, the gossips twitched —the young man a mere newcomer, hardly comfortably off. Not even an Eliza could ignore the talk. The couple had a long talk; who took the initiative we can only guess, but the two of them walked unexpectedly to a lawyer's office and made out a marriage contract. If she died without children, John waived all claim to her property. Furthermore, Eliza retained the right to manage her estate.

But it wasn't long before the town knew who was wearing the trousers in this marriage. As a well-pleased housewife,

Eliza grew less pert, less independent with every month. The children came quickly; and John revealed himself as an expert manager of his wife's property as well as his own. Shortly afterward, in 1826, John picked a mansion that he liked despite the tragic story about it. Monmouth had been built a few years earlier for John Hankinson. Riding with his wife, Hankinson spied a man leaning against a fence. The poor fellow was ill, and they took him in. That night the man's condition became worse; only then did they realize it was yellow fever. He died, and so did both Hankinsons.

Now the Quitmans started their life at Monmouth. A man's house, many have called it. Built solidly against the elements, it had little delicacy, no fluted or filigree detail. From the straight bricked front rose a portico with heavier pediment than usual. Out of the ground came four square pillars, almost gaunt in their power, of no particular order of architecture. The effect of strength was carried throughout; another thick building was attached as a separate wing at the back. To the other side a third unit, with an arcade, had a line of deep arches. Inside, halls and rooms reflected the same masculine purposefulness. Monmouth matched Quitman as if built as a frame for him.

Here, with Eliza beside him, John planned his next step. He would run for the legislature against the high-placed A. L. Bingaman. To most Natchezians it seemed a ridiculous competition; poor Quitman was certainly storing up grief for himself. To the end of the campaign, it appeared that Quitman would fail; his hot, jumbled words were no match for the fluid eloquence of the gifted Bingaman. But out in the country, where numerous small farmers lived, it might be different. A combination rally and county fair decided the issue. John rode up, and used his muscles to show the folks he was one of them. Stripping off coat and vest, he wrestled the crossroads champion, boxed, ran a foot race, and lifted weights. He won the election.

In his new political interest, John followed a course notable for its erratic quality. Properly or improperly, he won something of the reputation of a trimmer. Slowly, however, he was developing two lines of thought that would become rigid with the years. Once a Northerner, he looked on Yankees with repugnance and scorn; he was also cultivating an extreme State rights attitude.

After a trip East, he wrote: "Wherever I have traveled in the free states, I have found preachers holding three, four, six and eight days' meetings, provoking revivals and begging contributions for the Indians, the Negroes, the Sunday schools, foreign missions, home missions, the Colonization society, temperance societies, societies for the education of pious young men, distressed sisters, superannuated ministers, reclaimed penitents, church edifices, church debts, religious libraries, etc. . . . I am heartily tired of the North." The preacher's son had rebelled with a vengeance. He was a spiritual father of the Southerners who were sure any one of them could lick a half dozen Yankees, except that Quitman thought the figure should be a full dozen. The hotheads of the period just before the Civil War, were, by comparison, Johnnies-come-lately.

At twenty-eight, he was named to the high office of Mississippi's chancellor. Some called him distinguished in the post; opponents pointed to his many reversals in the courts. For years to come, there would be constant controversy about John Quitman. Old John, friends generally agreed, was hardly a genius, but he worked energetically and people liked him. Having a few vehement thoughts, he cherished them to the exclusion of practically all else. Before his term as chancellor ended, he resigned, but the voters sent him to the state Senate. There he hacked away at his opposition and others whom he disliked, including the democratic Andrew Jackson. Always a conservative, he despised any who "flattered and tickled" the electorate.

He had been watching developments in Texas. On the issue of Mexican territory, Quitman had a single conviction—take it! He dreamed of himself storming the ramparts. In 1836, trouble rumbled to the Southwest. He talked of little else. He had a family and a growing one, but he had to go anyway. Gathering a crowd of shouting followers, he financed his own organization and led it to the frontier. Applause ringing in his ears, he returned to Eliza and Monmouth, trailing his glory behind him. He had time again for easy evenings about the heavy rectangular columns, for hours with his children in the court at the back.

But quickly he left them again. Chosen to fill a vacancy as Governor, he saw a rich opportunity to push home his favorite themes. As Charles S. Sydnor has noted, until this time few Mississippi executives had come forth with a full justification of slavery. Many conceded, as had other earlier Southerners, that their people would be well rid of it at some future date. In 1828 Governor Brandon had described Negro bondage as "an evil at best," making rich richer, poor poorer and keeping the state backward. Here, however, came Quitman, bristling defiance: Slavery was Mississippi's own affair, whose morality it would not permit others to judge; it would not "degrade its character," "prostrate its dignity," even by discussing such matters with "foreign powers," that is, other states.

There was significance in Quitman's rather early appearance with such sentiments, and he created a stir. But he was in office only a short time, and then he had to give his attention to pressing personal problems. He had overspent himself, and must work hard at his law business. "With a revenue of $45,000," he groaned, "I cannot build a greenhouse for my wife or buy a new piano." He added in a letter to a friend, "When I meet ———, the trader, or ———, the Christian Shylock, I am compelled to acknowledge the superiority which the look of 'You owe me, and can't pay' gives them." More than that was disturbing him, for he itched with an ambition that had never been fully realized: "I know I have arrived at the period when the effort for fame should be made, if made at all. It soon will be too late." These were gloomy days at

Monmouth; two of his children died, and he and his Eliza saw the world through saddened eyes.

War saved him. Trouble broke out in Mexico, and with a frankness that surprised officials, he demanded he be named to command the Mississippi volunteers. Facing down those who favored regular Army men, he got what he asked. Feverish to go, he bade Eliza a long adieu and marched off. From the beginning he fretted that General Taylor, the commanding officer, moved too slowly; however, certain of John's associates thought that the war could be well managed without a Quitman to advise the professionals. But when he received assignment to brigade command, he demonstrated a swift courage, a vast skill in inspiring his men. When his horses were shot beneath him, he leaped onto others and dashed ahead. Taking a great deal upon himself, he won successive points, then turned about to argue with his superiors over what he had done.

Monterey, Vera Cruz, Buena Vista . . . over hot sands, through thirsty nights, John Quitman led his soldiers. Then came the onslaught against the City of Mexico. No matter what the grand strategy, Quitman broke through in triumph; before him lay a brooding panorama—all his. Flag in hand, he took a victorious place in the hall of Montezuma, as commander of the city, the only United States citizen ever to hold such a rank. He went home to receive a warrior's acclaim.

In her place beneath the square pillars of Monmouth, there waited the smiling Eliza. She had married him to the scandal of his detractors; now the walls held proof of his greatness —oil paintings of the hero on his battle steeds, drawings of him in action. In 1848 the Democrats gave him strong consideration for Vice-Presidential candidate; but largely because of his position as an ultra of Southern ultras, he lost. He had a consolation in that Mississippi rushed to make him Governor. On inauguration day cannons boomed, while women in white flung flowers, singing "Hail to the Chief." Quitman, wearing one of his Mexican uniforms, rode forward on a great white horse.

At last he had full opportunity to advance his views. He roared out his anti-Federal attitude, going farther than any Mississippian who preceded him. His stand on slavery had remained unchanged; as much as anything else, he cried, it had been responsible for the country's growth and prosperity. Doing more than talk, he joined South Carolina's Governor in urging immediate secession. In 1850, impassioned men at Charleston toasted him as the coming President of "our Southern republic." But Henry Clay was offering his famous compromise, urging peaceful settlement. This was exactly what John didn't want; in an effort to head it off, he slammed down a legislative summons. A constitutional convention was called, with authority to order secession. At the same time he ran again for Governor.

To John Quitman's chagrin, quick opposition developed. This was eleven years before the Civil War, and many Mississippians could not believe the time had come for a break-up of the union. In secession lay disaster, they argued. A strong candidate was brought forward against him, and the issue crystallized. Quitman strained every energy; here was the thing for which he had hoped and fought so long. He had to win! The campaign grew so stormy that he and his opponent once exchanged punches on the platform. Then, overnight, he received not victory, but the most galling disappointment of his life. His constitutional convention lined up against him, and by an almost unanimous vote. Sadly, Quitman withdrew from the race to succeed himself as Governor.

Yet wherever this man went there would be violence. His term was not over, and quickly he was involving himself in a heated collision with the Federal government. For a time it appeared that, in a bloody defiance of Washington, he would lead a mass-scaled filibustering expedition against the island of Cuba. The venture was no idle one for it precipitated a series of crises in international affairs—crises which the master of Monmouth helped provoke.

General Narciso Lopez, a handsome military man with a head of shining white hair, had fled Cuba with a fiery story. To certain Southerners he presented a dour picture of conditions, proposing a Cuban uprising with their help. The liberty he sought would apply only to the whites; he and his followers favored slavery for the rest. What was needed, Lopez felt, was a military figure to draw North American youths to the banners. He and his friends approached Jefferson Davis and Robert E. Lee, offering a hundred thousand dollars or more in cash, plus sugar plantations and similar inducements. Each man declined. High on Lopez' list stood John Quitman. The Cuban talked persuasively, his eyes ever on the Mississippi Governor's, picturing a new empire to the South. The beguiling prospect fitted Quitman's ambitions. As a friend wrote: "The battlefield and its glory, the clangor and the charge rose up like a gorgeous pageant to dazzle his imagination."

Quitman gave his earnest advice, the use of his name in several connections, and his money. Whether he would emerge as military leader, he would have to decide later. For years he was to maintain his warm concern with the enterprise and similar ones; through all the tangled incidents, hints were made that at the propitious moment, Quitman would spring forth with sword in hand.

For decades New Orleans had been a base for the recruiting of filibustering parties. Agents walked the narrow French Quarter streets; bankers, merchants and other chance-takers sipped coffee and spun schemes. At this time Lopez opened quarters in a downtown arcade. Ships were bought, supplies accumulated. Up in Natchez mass meetings brought burning resolutions and recruits; all over the South and in parts of the North, young men marched forward. Some saw the Spaniards as tyrants and Cuba a battleground of human freedom. Others, sympathetic to slavery, believed that the United States' destiny lay ever to the South; the land should be theirs. Many hotheads simply wanted a fight. Lead them to it! The enterprise, none could deny, had its risks. Growing disturbed, the Federal government called it an "adventure for plunder and robbery." If they won, they would be heroes; if losers, pirates.

Opinion exploded in New Orleans as recruiting spread. On a bright May day three vessels, bearing several hundred men, slipped away. The Lopez forces landed in Cuba but suffered heavy losses. Out of the blue a Spanish warship came into sight; hastily the invaders scrambled back, and a furious chase began across the sea to Florida. The Spaniards gained; for a while it seemed certain that the Lopez expeditioners would be caught. Then they tried a last extra effort; a green shore loomed, and the vessel made Key West by the narrowest of margins.

Yet neither Lopez' nor Quitman's enthusiasm flagged. Plans sped for a new invasion; many were sure that Quitman would now come out and assume full command. (A close Quitman associate later explained that Quitman had such plans but insisted that Lopez' men must first win some measure of Cuban control and declare their independence. Quitman, joining them, would then be able to say he was not violating neutrality. In 1853, two years later, Quitman signed a contract with the Cuban Junta agreeing to lead a revolution when financial support came through. If he won, he would get a million dollars. The program collapsed.) Then the United States took action; a Federal grand jury in New Orleans suddenly indicted Quitman for violation of American neutrality. The incident spawned a seething new controversy. Friends urged Quitman to surround himself with armed forces and tell the United States to go to hell. Quitman said he would refuse, while Governor, to appear voluntarily and make bond for a later hearing; to do that, he cried, would be to admit that the Federal government had authority to act against a Governor.

Mississippi was a sovereign government, he protested; one of the states couldn't arrest the President, therefore the Federal government couldn't arrest a Governor!

An awkward pause followed, with talk of battles between the two sides. It looked as if the Federal government would insist he must make bond like any one else, or face arrest. Quitman didn't give it a chance to take the next step. He resigned office and agreed to submit to the court's jurisdiction, as a "private citizen," to save Mississippi the humiliation it would suffer if invaded by the United States, a "foreign power." To another ultra, he suggested a movement to abolish Federal courts in the states! Once again Quitman found himself a hero. In New Orleans men and women marched on the streets to serenade him. At Natchez citizens gathered in a torch-light ceremonial. Fifteen guns were fired for Quitman, fifteen for the Southern states; for good measure, several rounds for mankind in general. It was impossible to get juries to convict him and his associates, and this part of the matter ended.

Meanwhile l'affaire Lopez was moving toward a savage climax, and in it Natchez shared, not only through Quitman but also George Metcalfe of the Cherokee-house Metcalfes. George could hardly be termed an important man, but George the rambler, the all-too-human George, who always did exactly what occurred to him, seems to me as engaging a cuss as ever lived in Natchez.

His scholarly doctor-father was eminent and straight-laced. George must have been a happy throw-back. In his early teens he was plastering down his hair, practicing spitting out of the corner of his mouth, and eyeing the girls. Further paining the family, he disclosed no inclination for polite learning, including even spelling. Turning sixteen, he slipped away from Natchez. From New Orleans, he broke the news; he "hated very much leaving you all, but I wanted to do something for my self." Would they pay his debts at home?

MONMOUTH
A Man-Sized House for a Bravo of Bravos

REBER HENDERSON

CHEROKEE
Viva La Revolucion!

EARL M. NORMAN

(Clearly George had gotten around.) He ended: "Don't let anyone see this for it is ritten so bad."

A month later he was scribbling home again. For the past week his health had suffered, his weight falling from 105 to 97 pounds. If he stayed in New Orleans he would "certainly die of the consumption"; and so George found a more healthful occupation—that of a soldier! War with Mexico was breaking out and he had volunteered, being "sure it will make another boy of me." He promised to fill his pockets with "dimonds from the minds of Mexico." George was to fill his pockets with a great assortment of things, but never diamonds.

The Mexican venture ended, and George sandwiched in some fighting against the Indians—also for his health, probably. Then the family stepped in; at eighteen he showed up in an odd place for him, a school. The going was slow; he wrote 'Dear Farther' about it: "I believe I can be honourable and quit lying and not sweare but a little now and then; I believe that is enough for a young man of my line." He was having trouble with his studies, and he admitted that to him "all gals look like Sugar candy." He had thought he "never could like no other than C. Boyd, but as the Irishman says, the last cheese is always the best."

It wasn't long before George, with sugar candy and other outside interests on his mind, left school. In New Orleans he met new excitement, in the enrollments for Lopez' second Cuban expedition. He took his young brother Henry with him into the mixed crew, high and low, river rat and dandy, that was in the final stage of assembly. On a hot August morning, their vessel swung down the Mississippi. They received cheering reports—later proved to be fakes—that the Cubans were rising in rebellion. The way lay clear ahead. *Viva la revolucion!*

Landing at Bahía Honda, Lopez and his men, including the Metcalfes, struck inland. After a few small successes, everything went wrong. Lopez' forces proved too scant, badly placed, badly handled. Under heated fire, they had to fall back. Trapped and separated, they were hunted down with gun, bayonet and bloodhound. The natives greeted them, not with the shouts of joy they had expected, but with spit and slaps as they were dragged through the towns: Dirty North American invaders, pirates—kill them!

Captured, Lopez was found guilty of treason to Spain and strangled to death by the garrote. On that same day of September 1, 1851, George Metcalfe, lying in chains in a stinking Havana cell, wrote his friend A. K. Farrar: "We are all in prison in irons. Advise all of your friends and my friends not to come here for there is no patriots here. Col. Crittenden and all of his men are shot. I don't know what they will do with us." George and his brother Henry looked for death at any moment. Two and three at a time the prisoners were being taken off. Hourly they asked each other if they would be next.

But weeks before, in enlisting, George had shown untypical foresight. For nationality he had put down Irish and now he could claim protection of the British flag. The British consul scurried around; at the last moment, George and Henry were saved. Soldiers let them out, still in chains, and thrust them into a ship that took them to Spain. After further delays, their captors released them.

Young Henry hurried back to Natchez. For George, it seemed as good a time as any to do some sight-seeing; so he spent six weeks wandering about the various towns. Arriving in New York, unshaven and in frayed costume, he was greeted by relatives, kissed and given a gold-topped walking stick proclaiming him a hero. For a few hours George speculated what he could do with the stick. Then he sold it for a jug of wine and, thus equipped, went home, but only for a while.

It might have been expected that he would now eschew war and its hazards. Those who thought this did not know George. Going to California after gold, and not finding it, he returned to New Orleans and learned that William Walker, most famous of the American filibusters, was launching an excursion under auspices similar to Lopez' fatal one. He walked right in to sign up. The officials raised quibbling points, and only that kept him from going. When adventure called the next time, he stepped promptly forward, to serve three years with the Confederacy.

After that George performed one of the most curious acts of a lifetime of curious acts. The boy who had such trouble with his spelling became a school teacher. Understandably, that bored him; next he turned up as manager or assistant manager of the upriver Hurricane plantation, owned by Jefferson Davis' family. A letter from there shows George drooping in spirit, at least temporarily. He had been married, and a child had been born, dead. He didn't know what he would do next. "I would like to live anywhere if it could be some place where I am not known or know anybody. I am worth no more today than I was when I landed in New Orleans six years ago."

A last message remains, written when George was seventy-one; his hand-writing wavers as he tells of his "rhumatism." His good wife has died, and he stays on with one of his children. "I live one quarter of a mile from . . ." Wearily he does not complete the sentence. "I work a little in my garden." Life has finally grown tranquil for the restless George. He ends: "Think of it, my first enlistment in New Orleans," and he describes his other wars. It hadn't been too bad a life.

Within the present town limits stands a steeply elevated house dating from the 1790s. Here, at Cherokee, live George Metcalfe's great-grand-daughter, Myrtie Cavin Byrne, and her husband, Charles J. Byrne. The location formed part of the hillside on which Quaker Ellicott's troops camped. Under the Spanish regime one Jesse Greenfield laid out a long, narrow wooden house, shaped to fit the curve of the ground. During the first quarter of the last century a new owner added a section several times larger than the original, with a delicate front rare for Natchez—a recessed gallery, two columned in the center, a room extending at each side to the outer line of the house.

In the 1850s Duncan Metcalfe owned Cherokee; after that it had a procession of other masters and mistresses until a few years ago Mrs. Byrne, a young and energetic descendant of the adventuresome George, took hold of it as it lay in drab disrepair. The Byrnes have managed skilfully. Cherokee's white stuccoed walls shine in ancient pride, with the rich green of the many shutters and the dozens of panes of glass for a contrast. Over one of the high brick retaining walls that protect the soil, vines hang carelessly, and shrubs and trees give further mellowing touches. Inside, in the wide drawing room, George is remembered today while most of the more eminent Metcalfes have been forgotten. Wherever he is, he may enjoy a triumph if he wishes.

For John Quitman, the last years went more quietly. His chances at national office were gone, but he could win elections to Congress, and he did. As a warm expansionist, he wanted the United States to take hold of the lands all about it—Cuba, Mexico, whole sections of Central and South America; and frequently he went before Washington with his proposals. Slowly, however, his health weakened. In his late fifties, he was one of the many who suffered the effects of the famous banquet for President Buchanan, in 1857, when a bad water supply poisoned the participants. He was brought home and put to bed in one of the wide chambers of his Monmouth, with his paintings of military glory on the walls.

He got up for an important event, the marriage of a daughter; and he and Eliza together recalled the events of their life in this house. Feeling tired, he retired and never rose again. On a warm July morning, wearing his favorite uniform, with the equipage and trophies of the warrior on his coffin, he was buried beside several of his children in a grave on the Monmouth estate. It was 1858. Had he survived a little longer, he would have seen the struggle for which he had so long worked.

John Quitman's man-sized Monmouth is now the property of Mrs. Hubert Barnum, who, as mentioned in an earlier chapter, took it for her dairy venture. The severe square columns still present their heavy outlines, and inside are a few last relics of the General. The years have left tracings on the exterior, but they have been unable to remove the impression of power. The façade has the same strength that may be sensed in the grizzled face of an aged man, unwilling to submit to time's tyranny. John Quitman's house has, I think, something of the quality of the stubborn warrior himself.

Scattered over the river country hang dimming pictures of Quitman, copies of engravings once to be found by the hundreds, and pamphlets telling of days such as those when the women in Grecian white threw flowers as he rode by on his charger. In the halls of Monmouth may be seen a monumental walnut sideboard, pier tables and mirrors, some of it brought back, they say, from the Palace at Mexico City, where John Quitman ruled for that climactic occasion. There are no Quitmans left in Natchez; the hero's house outlasted everything else.

⸙XIV⸙

VARINA OF THE CAMELLIAS

A TALL girl with a red flower in her hair paused at the brink of a cliff from which the earth sank sharply to the river. Her eyes moved from the drifting of the clouds to the steep drop of the red-brown soil, and then to the vines, the oaks and magnolias and pines that tangled the scene about her.

At seventeen, Varina Howell stood slim and dark, the possessor of a warm, almost sensual loveliness. There was a maturity in her figure and a poise in her round face that seemed beyond her years. Varina, as many Natchezians knew, had been brought up rather differently from most of the plantation girls—a long education, her own way in various matters, a freedom of expression that traditionalists disapproved. Those Howells were certainly spoiling the girl. Early as well as late, some did not like Varina, calling her haughty, quick-tongued, inclined to be dominating.

About Varina, during most of her life, there would be contention—attack, defense, disapproval, eulogy. Yet even her greatest detractors did not call her a fool; none denied her a burning spirit that she would keep through her extended career. Others would remember her with a feeling of pity, as a woman who enjoyed triumph beyond that of almost any in the South, and then an almost unending progression of sorrows. For a few years every hope she ever had, appeared to be realized; after that, every fear. For she was to be the wife of the President of the Confederate States.

On this day of 1843, as Varina watched along the bluff, her mother fingered a message. It was hardly an ordinary invitation; it came from Joseph E. Davis, an older friend of the Howells, an intimate who had helped Varina's father on numerous occasions. The girl knew the bustling individual as Uncle Joe. For a long time Joe Davis had wished Varina to pay his family a visit at Hurricane plantation, up the Mississippi near Vicksburg. Last year she had been working hard to complete her studies; also, the Howells had thought Varina not quite old enough to get about in society. But this time the mother would agree. Stepping to the arched doorway of the house behind the bluff, she sent a servant for the girl, and she began to plan.

Varina's father, William Burr Howell, had arrived in Natchez from the North, after fighting in the War of 1812. Her grandfather had been eight times Governor of New Jersey; her grandmother could claim kinship to Aaron Burr. Moving downriver, young William had acquired a bride with a strong Southern background, the gentle Margaret Louisa Kempe of the Virginia Kempes, who had moved to Natchez. Nobody pretended that the strapping blond William Burr Howell matched his military exploits with his peacetime accomplishments. A likeable fellow with a broad smile, he ambled easily along. The Kempes reached out an occasional, discreetly helping hand, and William's charm carried him through.

Their place, The Briers, came as a present from William's father-in-law. Of white frame, an ample elaboration of an earlier planter's cottage, it had even then an old-fashioned look, a serene simplicity in its dense greenery. It was built some time before 1818, in a location isolated from the town: the name arose from the matted vines and wild plants along the deep bayous of its grounds. The house was a well-constructed establishment of symmetrical beauty, with grace of line and finished detail. Two and a half stories high, including basement, it had rooms in the upper flight, despite the sloping of the roof, that were wide and deep. The Briers was a bigger building than it looked. Across the front stretched a porch, seventy feet long, with a series of slim posts.

The gallery had three arched fanlighted doorways, one at the center, the others near the sides. From the long roof thrust four dormers whose outlines repeated the delicate arches of the doors. A pair of brick buildings, steep-roofed and high walled, provided at the back for schoolrooms, kitchen and other purposes. Everything at The Briers was spacious; the many windows were arranged to admit the winds that swept in all directions across the bluff. Surrounding the white rectangle of the house, in contrast with the wildness of the woods toward the bluff, rose thick bushes of red and pink camellias, always Varina's choice among the flowers.

In this setting Varina spent a bright childhood with her brothers and sisters. Sent to a school in Natchez, she showed signs of a sharpening intelligence. On the advice of teachers, the Howells sent her to Madame Greenland's institute in Philadelphia for several terms and, as Mrs. Eron Rowland tells it, the girl acquired an additional ease of manner.

Meanwhile another family friend, the bearded Judge George Winchester, was watching the girl's progress. He asked permission to tutor her; under his direction, year after year, Varina drilled herself in languages, literature, history, arts. The Judge was, she declared, one of the great influences of her life, "my childish ideal of 'Great-heart,' eminent, incorruptible, his charity wide as the horizon." At sixteen she was pushing herself to "finish my course of English and Latin classics" and she spoke and wrote with a precision that frequently amused newcomers to the household.

More than most girls of her age, Varina was spending her time in the company of her elders. From the Judge, as from others about her, she imbibed attitude as well as facts. To them and to her, the high Whigs ruled by natural right; the name of Democrat was anathema. Wild men, she well understood them to be—dangerous in their ideas, and also the commoner class. Like the adults, Varina read her *National Intelligencer,* following the stern views of Editors Gales and Seaton. Proudly she wore a "Sub-Treasury brooch," a shell cameo pin showing a strong-box in relief, a Whig ornament supposed to convey reproach to Democrats. Despite all this, few could have described Varina as a forbidding miss, or a blue-stocking. Her skin had a creamy quality, her lips a redness that people remembered, her handsome face a vivacity that sparkled when her interest was aroused.

Now and then Varina curtseyed before their older guest, Joseph Davis. When her father first arrived in Natchez, Joe Davis had taken him about, helping him select lands and stocks. But the Davises, as the sharply perceptive Varina gathered, were "new people," not of the Natchez country elite. They were Baptists, not Episcopalians. The father had been a smaller farmer, generally unprosperous, who had moved from one state to another before coming to Mississippi. When his older children married, he was able to give each a single slave, a fact that would hardly have impressed a Whig.

In recent years, however, the ambitious Joseph Davis had taken his dead father's place as head of the family, growing rich with the place and times. A lawyer-planter, he was pointed out as the coming man of his locality above Natchez. Still, however much he might wish to identify himself with his section, Joe Davis did not seek an alignment with the Whigs, remaining a firm Democrat like many voters about him. In this stage of Southern development the Democrats could still claim to represent primarily the less wealthy man, the farmer on the rise. In Mississippi the rough-and-ready Andrew Jackson and his Democrats had ardent followers, but few in Natchez. Now and then Varina asked herself questions about the Davises, but thus far she had not greatly concerned herself over the matter.

Now it was decided that her teacher, the respected Judge Winchester, would take Varina to the Davises. It was December; the invitation called for a Christmas holiday visit. The pair went on the packet *Magnolia*. Years later Varina remembered it as an object of floating majesty, much bigger than later steamboats, "an ideal mode of travel." She gazed on while the captain bowed to the planters at the landings and sent gifts of ice and fresh fruit to the growers' wives. Almost before she knew it, the time had come to get off at her first stop, Diamond Place, home of Joe Davis' married daughter, and a house filled with presents and Christmas cheer.

A few days later Varina glanced out of the window in surprise, to behold an individual of striking appearance, who "rode with more grace than any man I have ever seen, and gave one the impression of being incapable either of being unseated or fatigued . . . erect, well-proportioned, and active as a boy." Brought before her, he bowed gravely, and she learned he was Jefferson Davis. That night she wrote her mother:

"Today Uncle Joe sent, by his younger brother (did you know he had one?) an urgent invitation for me to go at once to 'The Hurricane.' I do not know whether this Mr. Jefferson is young or old. He looks both at times; but I believe he is old, for from what I hear he is only two years younger than you are. He impresses me as a remarkable kind of man, but of uncertain temper, and has a way of taking for granted that everyone agrees with him when he expresses an opinion, which offends me; yet is most agreeable and has a peculiarly sweet voice and a winning manner of asserting himself. The fact is, he is the kind of person I should expect to rescue one from a mad dog at any risk, but to insist upon a stoical indifference to the fright afterward. I do not think that I shall ever like him as I do his older brother Joe. Would you believe it, he is refined and cultivated, and yet he is a Democrat!"

As has several times been remarked, few people in so short a space have so well analyzed the character of Jefferson Davis. This man,—he was then 36, twenty years her senior—irritated Varina, yet he drew her. Caught between liking and vague resentment, she showed above all a keen interest. Jefferson had an impressive yet somewhat puzzling air, for others as well as Varina. A long straight nose, square jaw, cheekbones that stood high below his eyes, a high forehead, these she observed; but it was the eyes that dominated—gray eyes that looked forth beneath heavy eyebrows, eyes sensitive, intent and yet remote. They were the eyes of a man of high intelligence and rigid views. For Jefferson Davis life would be a matter of principle and inflexibility.

Varina patched together scraps of stories concerning him. He had seen only a little of his family's less comfortable days for they sent him off to several superior schools, brother Joe making certain that Jefferson received the advantages. At West Point Jeff acquired a consuming interest, the military. Going to the Northwest frontier, he saw hot Indian fighting under Zachary Taylor. Finding himself in love with Taylor's daughter, Sarah Knox, he clashed with the father, who had developed a personal dislike for the Mississippian. Finally the girl told her father she intended to marry Jefferson, and went away to join him in a ceremony at a relative's house. Joe Davis provided the couple with a plantation next to his Hurricane; here they stayed for barely two months before the "chill and fever" season struck.

Hurriedly Jefferson and his bride went to nearby Bayou Sara in Louisiana. There, promptly, he caught the fever; after him his bride fell victim. He heard her singing deliriously in the next room and struggled to her side, to find her dying. For a month Jefferson seemed on the point of death. Slowly he recovered, but the shock turned him into almost a recluse. On his river place he lived for nearly seven years in a closed world of working and studying. As they talked together in the evenings, the tie between the two brothers grew yet stronger. Only lately Jefferson had begun to go out again. Politics had become an absorbing concern, and the far-sighted Joe was encouraging him. Jefferson had been bound for a public meeting, in fact, the day he stopped off to see Varina.

Now others came to take her to The Hurricane. A fine mount was provided her; an old-fashioned high-swung carriage and pair held her bonnets and petticoats; "and 'all in the blue unclouded weather' we rode over the rustling leaves through the thick trees to The Hurricane." Varina, delighted, inspected the big place. Her alert mind missed little, and she learned a great deal regarding the two Davises. When not riding about the plantations, the brothers sat together, talking of "books, law, agricultural experiments . . . made and perfected theories about everything." During this Christmas season, the women joining them in the evenings, Jefferson read Congressional debates to his brothers. His eyes tiring, one of the women took up for him. Varina accepted her turn, and talked about what she read. The intellectual Jefferson showed his surprise. The girl knew Latin, history, even politics, though he hardly agreed with her Whiggery.

Quickly it became clear that Jefferson was observing more than Varina's mind. The family noticed that the pair walked more and more often together. With Jefferson Varina spent hours on horseback, admiring the thirty stalls of the Davis animals, racers, brood horses, colts, all of them superb specimens. They rode to adjoining country properties; they sat together on the porch. One day the couple had a long talk; the next morning her "sub-Treasury brooch" was gone. Love had elbowed politics aside.

Back in Natchez at The Briers, Varina found that, Whiggery notwithstanding, the Howells thought well of the tall Jefferson as a prospective son-in-law. Within a few days he followed her, and the neighbors were told there would be a marriage. A mild stir resulted; there were those who felt Davis was not quite up to the Howell rank. The amiable William Howell ignored the veiled hints; when they reached Varina she went quickly to Jefferson's defense and her own. Suddenly the once-sturdy Whig discovered herself arguing for the Democrats! Sometimes, however, she felt qualms; would she have to mix, she asked primly, among grubby, unpleasant people?

Yet a change was coming over Southern affairs. The Whigs faded, the Democrats forged ahead, and they too were modifying. Jeffersonian liberalism slipped away, and with it Jackson's preachings of equality among men. The Democrats were evolving into the Southern party of property; no longer did men say, as had the earlier Virginians and other Southerners, that slavery was a bad thing which eventually must end. Quitman and men like him defended it as a blessing approved by God Himself. In this historic shift, Jefferson Davis was to play a growing role, with Varina at his side.

Often in these days the sunken road to The Briers, hemmed in by trees and creepers, sounded to the hoofbeat of Jefferson's steeds as he called on the Howells. The couple climbed the peak of the bluff to survey the Mississippi's slow curves and the greens and golds of the Louisiana flatlands. Interrupting his campaigning, Jefferson sometimes spent most of a night riding across country lanes to be at her side for an hour or two, then raced back to keep a speaking engagement. Varina found that her man was not as physically vigorous as she had imagined. Several times he sickened; but, as she observed, "his mind dominated his body in so great a degree that he was able to endure nearly what he pleased." Through the rest of her life she was to see him struggle with pain, aggravated by overtaut nerves.

The engagement was to last a year. Suddenly Varina herself, intent on Jefferson's career, fell ill. She lost weight; in her pale face her big, dark eyes looked bigger than ever. The wedding had to be postponed, but a little later Jefferson came back, to find her face alight; and the family agreed to have the ceremony at once. Whatever Natchez thought, The

Briers became the scene of a quiet affair, unlike the usual plantation wedding, only the immediate families attending.

Varina's trousseau was not ready; her cousin, Margaret Sprague, had her own wedding gown prepared, for the ceremony at which Varina was to be her chief bridesmaid, and she suggested that Varina use it. And so Varina, though she hadn't planned it, wore something borrowed. Already, in February, the year had a touch of spring's warmth as the camellias bloomed scarlet on the bushes about the white Briers. Varina was able to wear the flowers in her hair and at her bosom. The couple stood before the Episcopal minister in a room facing the gallery, and the world ahead looked very promising.

The marriage began with a "tour of visits." They stopped first at Jefferson's sister's Locust Grove on Bayou Sara, the plantation to which he had gone with his first bride, to watch her die and bury her in the Davis cemetery. One wonders how some women might have felt. The grave Varina accepted the situation and frequently spoke, tactfully and in good spirit, of the woman who had preceded her. The second marriage was a profoundly happy one for both partners. Eagerly Varina identified herself with the man and his career, warm in her pride over his successes, sharp in her resentment of his reverses.

But meanwhile the "tour of visits" went on. At Woodville, she met Jefferson's mother, still a handsome woman at eighty-four, though confined to her chair. Then came New Orleans and the St. Charles Hotel where, admitting her naivete, Varina saw "the first poet I had ever encounted," a relative of Oscar Wilde. She sat listening, "expecting his flow of conversation to become rythmical," when Jefferson brought up the celebrated General Edmund Pendleton Gaines of the American Army.

Varina beamed when the old General called Jefferson a fearless young man; to him she confided "in a foolish little way what I thought of Mr. Davis, and how much my husband thought of and loved him; and we found each other mutually agreeable." Here is a happy, unpretending self-portrait. Then

Varina was introduced to the General's wife, the petite redhead, Myra Clark Gaines, who at that time was only knee-deep in her cause celebre—seeking to prove her father had left her about a third of New Orleans. Each woman had married an older man, and each was accustomed to scrutiny by others. They looked closely at each other, but Varina disapproved of Myra; in her memoir she called her "lawless." Even a new Democrat did not have to like a daring female!

Six weeks later Varina took up her life at Brierfield, Jefferson's upriver place that adjoined Joe Davis', to enjoy the last hours of truly private quiet that she would know for years. Jefferson had designed the cool "cat-and-clayed" house, less elegant than many she visited, but she was delighted with it. They raced each other on their horses; they read aloud what interested them in the newspapers. In this comparatively unsettled locale, game was more abundant than chickens. Wild geese, fattened by waste corn in the fields, swept by in heavy flights. She passed white and blue cranes in wet places, "standing on one leg among the immense lily pads . . . with lemon-colored flowers as large as coffee cups." Every once in a while Jefferson went off with a gun, to track down an alligator that stalked their calves.

Regularly she and Jefferson rode to Natchez to see the Howells at The Briers, and again they wandered to the border of that high bluff. The family glanced after them as they stood there. It had turned out well, no matter what the prophets had said.

Gradually public affairs were taking Jefferson from her. At the beginning Varina hated it: "Then I began to know the bitterness of being a politician's wife, that it meant long absences, pecuniary depletion and ruinous absenteeism, illness from exposure, misconceptions, defamation of character, everything which darkens the sunlight and contracts the happy sphere of home." But in her pride for her husband she learned to swallow such feelings. Varina was absorbed in his career. They talked over his speeches and she went to his meetings and made her comment afterward. She suffered with him when he memorized a speech and delivered it haltingly; she exulted when, discarding this method, he made the roof ring with easy declamation.

In these days she grew accustomed to riding for hours in stiff-backed railroad cars, to spending evenings in miserable taverns; and she has recorded one of her observations of the "frankness of the uneducated classes." She and Jefferson made a long northern trip by water; a pilot's wife, a fellow-passenger, resented the cool reticence of Jefferson. When he did not answer some of her questions about himself and his destination, the forthright lady flushed: "My name is McGruggy, and I ain't ashamed of it, and I'm going to Cincinnati, and I don't see but what I am good enough for that man to tell me whar he is going!" (Jefferson, alas, seldom felt at home with plainer white folk.) But Varina could unbend, and did. Their mutual discomfits brought her and Mrs. McGruggy closer. The trip ended with the older woman praising Varina profusely and giving her, in token of her changed feeling, some apricot seeds. Varina planted them at home and never forgot the tree that sprung up; she called it "The Pilot's Wife."

When Jefferson was elected to Congress, Varina went with him to a city where social activities counted for a great deal. At first, she admitted, she suffered as she realized her gaucheries, because for all her learning, Varina had seen little of the world. She looked on, entranced, sometimes breathless, at the procession of Presidents and Senators, diplomats, great names of which she had heard; Webster, Clay, Supreme Court Justice Woodbury, one Appolonia Jagello, "a Polish heroine with a heavy moustache and a voice to match" and several Presidents' wives, who smiled on the bright young matron and liked her. Like Jefferson himself on those first occasions, men of affairs drew up short to hear the lovely woman talking with such a knowledge of affairs, and such good sense.

Gradually Varina became a well-known hostess, a considerable help to her husband. With growing self-possession came

EARL M. NORMAN

THE BRIERS
Jeff Davis Married the Girl of the Camellias

RICHMOND
Three Houses Latched Together

EARL M. NORMAN

VARINA OF THE CAMELLIAS

a gain in beauty; in these days Varina was making a mark for Jefferson and for herself as well. From time to time a man or woman disliked her; social reminiscences describe her occasionally barbed wit. For the most part, however, Varina did well. Her shining eyes drew others to her; she felt at her best, her most engaging.

Then suddenly war broke with Mexico, and Jefferson, seizing the chance to indulge his inclination for the military, went off as Colonel of the First Mississippi Regiment. Back in Mississippi Varina spent wretched months, moving from Brierfield to Joe Davis' Hurricane to The Briers in Natchez, where she could at least have a few restful hours with the family. Then at last hostilities ended, and Varina stood with hundreds of others at the foot of the Natchez hill to await her husband. Whistles blew, and the crowd screamed. A barouche, almost hidden beneath its flowers, stood ready for the conqueror. At last, she told herself, Natchez had granted Jefferson his full due, though it took a war to bring it about! They had triumphed in a new way, the two of them. She trembled as she saw him, hobbling on crutches; then the throng swallowed them.

Once again she left Mississippi, when Jefferson became Senator; and then he went on to the Cabinet as Secretary of War. None in Mississippi's history had risen higher. After years of waiting, their children came, and they knew a heightened happiness. But tension was increasing meanwhile between North and South, and Jefferson Davis had an enlarging part to act. After a time few regarded him as a hot-head; certain Mississippians protested that he lagged behind Quitman in forays against the Yankees. It was about this period that Varina walked in one evening to find her husband with an eloquent foreigner—Lopez of Cuba, asking Davis to head his expedition. She was terrified at the thought, and grateful when Jefferson declined. Not long afterward they received the news that Lopez, strapped in a chair, had been garroted.

The fury of the sections grew louder; Jefferson returned to

the Senate, and with him Varina witnessed American destiny in the shaping—successive crises, compromises, the beginnings of secession. She was there for that strained scene when her husband, ill and gravely troubled, rose to make his last speech in the Senate. They traveled home to Brierfield for a short period of ominous quiet. For Davis, ambition lay in the military sphere. He was anticipating a call to service. The Confederate leaders, meeting to set up their provisional government, clashed over their major candidates. One afternoon Varina and Jefferson were working in their garden, making cuttings of their roses, when a horseman pounded up. Jefferson stared at the telegram; suddenly he looked "so grieved that I feared some evil had befallen our family." After a hurtful silence, he told her. He had been chosen President of the South.

The ensuing years took her from Mississippi, to Montgomery and Richmond, capitals of the Confederacy. At the beginning, she exulted in good news from the fronts; then she found herself shuddering at the reports of disasters. She stood constantly beside her husband, who suffered physically and emotionally in a position that many have thought no man could hold with success. As First Lady of the Confederacy, she received guests and interviewed petitioners. Before them she smiled, but more and more often, alone, she asked herself how it would end. Two of her children died. The second one, young Joe, fell from a window to the pavement; and the father walked up and down the floor, his face twisted, his grief deep inside him. Varina herself lay gravely stricken for a time.

Jefferson Davis was attacked furiously by his subordinates, and by the newspapers. He quarreled frequently with the generals, and many blamed him for the Confederate losses. Varina, too, sustained violent criticism from her own side. She was haughty, some felt, and thoughtless and unfriendly to

VARINA OF THE CAMELLIAS

boot. Certain Virginians looked down on her, despite her Kempe blood, as practically an upstart from the West. And it was claimed that she "interfered" in military and civilian affairs, trying to "run things."

On a final day of black tidings, as the capital was about to fall, she was told she must take her four young children and leave Richmond. She and Jefferson managed to join on the road. Then, in a gray dawn, Union forces surrounded them. She tried to help her husband escape; he was about to make a dash for it, when Varina suddenly realized that he would be killed in the attempt. In desperation, she threw her arms about him and held him as the enemy closed in. With the leader of the defeated South she bowed to her captors.

Jefferson remained in prison for months, and she feared he would die. With desperate energy she fought for his release, and ultimately she succeeded. Before them lay the Mississippi river country and their own declining years. The Natchezians saw her again, her face marked with her experiences, yet serene and still a little proud. She wanted to help her aging husband find a place for himself; Jefferson tried one or two businesses that failed. She comforted and guided, letting herself be led when she thought that best. The love that had been born on that Christmas party of 1843 had never faltered through the years.

He went before she did; all but one of her six children died ahead of her. She lived on, a stout, tightly-corseted old woman. Her finances fluctuated; for a time they were so pinched that she went nowhere, as she told a friend, unless the entertainment was free, "for I feel hourly the necessity of pinching at every turn." She spoke of herself as "floating uprooted." Later, conditions improved. Before his death, she had helped her husband write his version of the war; now she prepared her own recollections, terming them, in reverent style, "Jefferson Davis: A Memoir by His Wife." When she died in 1906, it was in New York, far from The Briers and its bluff, its dry, vine-grown bayous and its camellias. But for Varina Davis the memory of the camellias had never faded.

Her family had lived at Natchez until the 1850s, then gone to New Orleans. Walter Irvine took the house and the Irvines stayed for decades. The last of that family ran a dairy in the old building, and it wore badly. Shrubbery died away; roses and camellias went to ruin. The floors rotted and one of the back buildings burned down. In 1927 Mr. and Mrs. William Winans Wall acquired The Briers and restored it.

A cool, deep roadway leads through the jagged earth of the bluff. Overhead arms of trees meet, and creepers hang low, to brush the top of the head. Through an iron gateway in a brick wall, a driveway opens, and a winding passage leads toward the house behind a row of tall pines. A crimson circle of Louis Philippe roses blooms against the outline of the long white gallery and the framework of many greens. To the side the ground lifts in an irregular progression toward the edge of the cliff, with its cedars and beeches and twisted vines. At the peak there is a well-worn spot, the same, perhaps, where Varina Howell stood as a child to inspect the wide vista of the world before her.

GLENFIELD

XV

THE LOVES OF THREE LADIES

DUNLEITH and Green Leaves—each has been a "social" house, of festive events and entertainments, and many handsome women have presided or been celebrated guests within the walls. Of them all, three have outlasted the years, to become almost legendary figures. The ones who have been forgotten were, I suppose, largely content with what fate and the Natchez country brought them. Those three unconventional ones went forth, seeking the kind of life they desired, and though they had varying fortunes in the pursuit, they at least struck out in their own behalf. They were, in the order of their appearances, Sarah Ann, the pepper-pot; Miss Percy, the lady ghost, and Consuelo, the girl who won herself a duke and the goodwill of a king. Love had something to do with all of them.

Sarah Ann Ellis was a spry little girl who might not have won the attention that came to her had her mother remained a widow. Mrs. Ellis appreciated Sarah Ann, but after all, she had her other children to look after. It took the stepfather to spot Sarah, and he made her the Galatea to his Pygmalion.

Sarah Ann's stepfather had made his own stir around Natchez. Charles G. Dahlgren was a tempestuous son of a tempestuous family, child of the first Swedish consul to the United

States, descendant of King Gustavus Adolphus. A hot-blooded youth, Charles entered the American Navy and enjoyed several uninhibited years. For his limited age he accumulated a fantastic record of successful duels and dead rivals.

Returning to land, he quieted hardly at all. Odd as it may appear, young Charles turned to banking. He moved South, where the thin-edged rules of honor seemed made for a man of his temper. Banker Dahlgren was alternately joyous and furious, throwing his big arms in jovial greeting about a friend, or stalking past him with a hard frown. Frequently his hot moods would vanish and he would sigh and bow his head in apology; but meanwhile, likely as not, he had run a sword through his companion. He went from New Orleans to Vicksburg to Natchez, prospering and also accumulating dueling marks as he went. Eventually he grew a beard to cover a few of his scars.

One day Charles Dahlgren made a proud inventory of his major wounds: a deep scar on both sides of his left hand, where he caught the edge of an opponent's Bowie knife to keep it out of his intestines, and held so tightly that the blade severed the little finger; two pistol balls inside his body, one against the ribs, the other he wasn't sure where; a scar on the top of the head, made by another knife; a little lower, beneath the scalp, the broken tip of yet another, grown into the skull bone. He didn't count mere cuts on cheek, forehead and throat underneath his beard.

In Natchez he was drawn to the young Widow Ellis, who had been one of the Routh clan. Routh holdings stretched for nearly fifteen miles along the river. The widow found the great big fellow appealing and amusing. Half the town feared this warm-tempered Dahlgren; she calmed him with the lift of a finger. Against the advice of her brothers and sisters, she became Mrs. Dahlgren. The marriage proved eminently successful, though she didn't break him of his dueling habit.

Once, it is said, she cited to him the story of the way another Natchezian, unquestionably brave, quelled a troublemaker.

The opponent, with much arm-waving and cheek-puffing, approached the first man on a narrow sidewalk, and rumbled: "I never step aside for a dog!" The composed one looked the roarer up and down: "I do, sir," and skirted him. Hearing this, Charles Dahlgren promised he would follow the example. The next week, with superhuman effort, he calmed himself and walked away from an enemy. A few steps on, however, his fury got the better of him and he ran back to redeem himself. The two then shot it out.

The thoroughly male Dahlgren was delighted when he became the father of a boy, and then another and another. After that, with a pensive air, he asked the Lord for one girl, anyway. They continued to have their children—seven of them, all boys. With the four by Mrs. Dahlgren's first marriage, that gave them a houseful of eleven children. Of them all, his stepdaughter Sarah Ann—a slim, sharp-eyed child of a quick and logical mind—interested him most. Soon after he discovered Sarah Ann had an intellect, Charles Dahlgren went to work to develop it.

He retained a parade of tutors. Sarah Ann studied history, languages, literature; strangely for the time, law and even bookkeeping. For balance, the stepfather added the harp and ballroom dancing. In her early teens Sarah Ann went abroad, and overseas connections of the Dahlgrens saw that she did the right things and met the right people.

For Sarah Ann, learning was no dull vegetable process, no placid imbibing of pre-digested stuff. Into everything she did, she threw all of her energy and curiosity. What she didn't know, she asked; when the answers failed to satisfy her, she asked again. Though her mind apparently never became a highly organized one, she developed a sprightly interest in a variety of subjects. Her stepfather admitted that she showed a will no more flabby than his own. "She was impulsive," he declared, "and it took not only a strong arm but a steady one to hold her. Once she started in pursuit of an object, it was like trying to rein in a whirlwind." For the time being, anyway, Charles Dahlgren was keeping a stiff hand.

In the meanwhile Mrs. Dahlgren decided that their first home—a big brick place acquired from her family, the Rouths—needed a fashionable new touch of terra cotta chimneys. Afterwards, returning from a trip, they found that lightning had struck, burning the house to field level. Charles Dahlgren blamed those damned chimneys; then he cooled down and put up a more resplendent substitute. On the same spot, about 1849, Sarah Ann and her brothers watched the rising of Dunleith, a baronial establishment with a colonnade on four sides.

A Greek Revival temple on a grand scale, Dunleith reflected something of the influence of Louisiana's bayou and river region, where Creole sugar planters wanted their mansions entirely bordered by pillars. It was a high house, on a well-terraced rise. Each column was thick but graceful in proportions and stood on a separate pedestal. Wide double galleries followed all of the house, with lines of precise ironwork between the columns above and below. A brisk walk twice around the house, and Sarah and the other children had their constitutional for the day.

From the roof protruded dormer windows topped with small pediments, and highly ornamented wooden designs at the sides. Symmetry was the rule inside and out, with a central hall and square rooms to each side. A two-storied kitchen wing stood at the back, attached to the residence; and some distance away, separated by a sloping lawn, remained the earlier stables and other side buildings in brick. The grounds spread in several directions and a deep bayou slashed the earth a little to the side, its course traced from afar by a heavy growth of greenery. Seen from the outer roadway, Dunleith would ever be a showplace, remote in the distance, arresting in its march of the columns, the sun slanting along them in changing lines of yellow light.

Here little Sarah Ann added polish to her early training; and here she and her companions met the woman who came as a temporary resident—the woman who remained, even past the grave, at Dunleith. This was the wistful Miss Percy, a relative of Mrs. Dahlgren's first husband, a lady who chose Dunleith when her former life seemed too much to bear.

Even Sarah Ann's mind, at work on the mystery of Miss Percy, brought up only a few facts; for neither Miss Percy nor the elder Dahlgrens wanted to say much. Many years earlier Louis Philippe of France had visited Natchez in his princeling days. One of his party met the bright young Percy girl and won her complete affection. In a tearsome departure, she promised to join him when he was able to call her.

She waited, rejecting a number of marriage proposals, or so the story goes. After an upheaval in France, her summons came and she answered it. For years she dwelt about the court of the Citizen King, an alien figure, often gossiped about, not always happy. She lost the bloom of youth, her fresh charm of manner, but she was still willing to remain there near the man who had chosen her. After some years, the break occurred. Drying her tears, putting her last hopes behind her, Miss Percy sailed for home. Arriving at Dunleith, she caught the hands of her old friend, Mrs. Dahlgren, and they were closeted together for hours. After that it was understood she would live at Dunleith indefinitely. With her she brought a single trunk, the same that she had taken with her to France. She had left behind her court costumes *de rigueur*, her jewels, anything that might have reminded her of those other days.

In spite of all that the Dahlgrens tried to do for her, Miss Percy stayed alone, reading a much-thumbed book of French poetry, walking about the bayou near the house, playing the harp in the drawing room. She coached the sprightly Sarah Ann in French, and occasionally she told little stories to the younger children; but it seemed a great effort, and Miss Percy was very tired. The children were cautioned not to disturb her. Music became more and more her solace; daily at dusk the muted harp notes would sound through the hallway. Until almost the end, she played to herself. Or was it only to herself? From a remark that she let drop, she appeared to feel that the man across the sea could hear her. In other years they had sat together at this hour.

One day she did not come down; a servant tiptoed to the harp and slipped a cover over it. Thereafter, on certain afternoons as dark came, the family at Dunleith thought it could hear the passing of fingers over the strings. Silence would fall, a faint breath of air would be felt; the lady was going back to her room. She would return, if not tomorrow, perhaps next week or next month. The spirit of Miss Percy would never leave this retreat from the world.

Growing up, Sarah Ann thought often of Miss Percy. Her quick brain was developing a markedly romantic bent. By the time she had reached her early twenties, Sarah Ann was following her own impulses, more often and more directly than her stepfather approved. Galatea grew less docile, while Pygmalion could only fume. To stop her when her mind was set, was, as he had written, like trying to "rein in a whirlwind." But thus far he had only an indication of what Sarah Ann's will could be like. In the early 1850s, for the first time, Sarah Ann fell in love. The man was Judge Samuel W. Dorsey, who was considerably older than the girl.

The bearded stepfather, beating his fist, announced that this was the last straw; he just didn't propose to allow the marriage. Sarah observed, quietly, that it was really unfortunate he thought that way; and at once she married her judge. For nearly a quarter century daughter and stepfather avoided each other, the bond forever broken between them.

For Sarah Ann these were crowded years. Marriage alone appeared hardly enough for one of her quick energies. She began by teaching her husband's slaves to read and write, no matter how the neighboring slave owners protested such dangerous goings-on. She wrote a book of religious reflections;

she tossed out magazine articles, scholarly essays, poems, philosophic reflections, and general observations of the scene about her. After that, feeling she had only hit her stride, she turned to fiction. There Sarah Ann could really let go, and she did, with a series of lushly embroidered fancies, full of mad maidens, dastards and thwarted lovers. One was withdrawn when a Natchez family found resemblances rather more than coincidental; several horrified lady (and some men) readers called them "morbid" and "sensational." It was a day when authoresses had to watch their literary step.

But this was only one part of Sarah Ann's career. During the Civil War her house burned down, and Sarah Ann went on to Texas to become a Confederate nurse, her warm Southern spirit involving her in a dozen other enterprises. For the rest of her life she would fight for the Confederacy and its name. Out of her observations came her best book, war recollections of Henry W. Allen, the Louisiana Confederate Governor. It gives an excellent indication of what Sarah's talents, differently directed, might have produced.

Meanwhile, her no less active stepfather fought in the war, winning high honors as a general. (On this subject, anyway, Sarah Ann and her former mentor could agree.) Eventually, however, as in so many other cases, the bearded Charles Dahlgren was engaged in a howling dispute, this time with Jefferson Davis over conduct of the war. For the rest of his life he never forgave Davis. Returning to Natchez with a few additional scars, the General looked around unhappily, then went North. And in his later years he clashed once more, spectacularly, with his forthright Galatea.

Sarah, by this time a widow, lived at Beauvoir, an estate along the verdant Mississippi Gulf Coast. She invited the aging Jefferson Davis, with his family, to be her guest at a cottage on the establishment. There he wrote his version of the war. Davis made payments toward the purchase of Beauvoir. Dying a few years later, Sarah left Beauvoir and other properties of high value to the Confederate President, "my most honored and esteemed friend." In her will she explained: "I do not intend to share in the ingratitude of my country toward the man who is, in my eyes, the highest and noblest in existence."

Once again, the girl whom Charles Dahlgren had molded made him quiver in anger. She had benefited the man whom the much-hating General hated most in life. Learning of what she had done, the General issued burning communiques, telling all he had done for Sarah, threatening to break her will, and also tossing a few bolts in Jefferson Davis' direction. But the document remained in effect, and Jefferson and Varina spent tranquil years on their Gulf estate. Sarah Ann, as usual, had done what she wanted.

The stately Dunleith of the columns had a procession of new owners. For a time it belonged to Alfred Vidal Davis, a flavorsome combination of Spanish and Quaker heritages, who is remembered for his devotion to champagne. He felt hurt when his guests did not keep up with him in their quaffing. Consulting an artisan, he evolved a glass shaped like a hunting horn. Once wine was poured, it couldn't be put down until empty, else the tablecloth would be spoiled. And as soon as it was empty, the well-trained servants filled it up. Then, after the Davises came the good-humored Hiram Baldwins, and with them a woman in satin who is the river country's major contribution to international society. Like poor Miss Percy, Consuelo Yznaga del Valle of Ravenswood plantation rubbed shoulders with nobility, but far from pathetically. As one of the first young, and also rich, American beauties to marry into the ranks of the titled British, Consuelo deserves a place among American girl pioneers.

Her story unites two Natchez houses, Dunleith and nearby Green Leaves. Appropriately named, the latter sat half-lost beneath the twisted arms of trees older than itself. One vast oak, some three hundred years old, has been described as a former council tree of the Natchez Indians. Part of the house had been there since the early 1800s; some time before 1845, George Washington Koontz elaborated it into a well spread-out one-story place, part brick, part wood, with a Corinthian columned portico at the front. To the rear, long, three-sided galleries faced a court with a sunken garden, canopied by the black boughs of its oaks. Here was a home with an air of luxury in informal setting—one of the most restful spots in the river country. G. W. Koontz, banker and close friend of Jefferson Davis, was commissioned during the war to seek Confederate loans in Europe. Peace returning, Green Leaves and Dunleith shone with something of their old-time entertaining; and now Natchez' bright light was the fair Consuelo of Ravenswood, a connection of the Surgets.

Her mother was a Louisianian, an Anglo-Saxon, her father an owner of sugar plantations in Cuba and the Creole state. They gave the world three beauties, Consuelo, Natica and a son, Fernando. A few Natchezians recall the Consuelo of this day—a tall girl with light brown hair, creamy complexion, a certain assurance. Side-saddle, in dark riding habit with white gloves, she made them all turn as she swept by, like something out of a romance. As a guest at Green Leaves and Dunleith, Consuelo frequently shocked the conventionalists. She laughed when young maidens were supposed to be demure; she played a guitar, danced Spanish dances, sang plain people's songs—the equivalent of today's blues, perhaps—and also Negro tunes, in a day when none attempted such feats in the drawing room. Over in the corner, smiling broadly, sat Señora Yznaga, another free spirit, "full of fine scorn and humor," says a Natchezian who is herself full of fine scorn and humor. The Señora eventually jolted them when she dug down into her purse, took out a cigarette and lit it!

Consuelo's brother Fernando went East, connected himself financially with the Vanderbilts and married the sister of Mrs. W. K. Vanderbilt. Consuelo danced her way between Natchez, New York and London. The Natchezians tell a story, perhaps apocryphal, that the mother of young George Victor Drogo Montagu, who would become Eighth Duke of Manchester, wrote Mrs. Yznaga that her boy was planning to spend some time in the American South. Would Mrs. Yznaga see that he kept free of entangling connections with American persons, female? A few months later the young lord had met Consuelo, and the field was hers. In May of 1876, they were married in New York.

As Lady Mandeville, Consuelo took over her English life with a firm hand. To her salon she drew statesmen, diplomats, people of letters; the *London Times* once paid tribute to her "witty and sparkling talk, framed in an accent all her own." (Ah, those Americans.) Ever herself, Consuelo is supposed to have entertained occasional poets and dowagers with Negro songs from Natchez. There is nothing to indicate how they accepted these strange selections. But it was the approval of the then Prince of Wales, later Edward VII, that meant most to Consuelo. Edward was the first among the British royalty to find a circle of handsome, well-placed American women more amusing than his proper English intimates. While the dowager Queen Victoria continued to hold the throne far beyond the expected span, her party-minded son amused himself with gay pranks, such as taking the role of a "corpse" in a scene in which a favorite Parisian actress played.

Edward became a frequent guest at Consuelo's home in London and her place at Biarritz. Another Natchez story, unverified, tells how the King, sitting at her table, swallowed a fish bone and began to choke. The company sat frozen; what did one do in such a case? Only Consuelo thought of jumping up and pounding him on the back. "Now, Edward, cough hard!" To some the incident proved what peculiar things American females would do.

Consuelo did not forget Natchez, or her in-laws the Vanderbilts. For the Vanderbilts she managed what few others could have done; she got them into the innermost circle of New York society. The Vanderbilts, yearning after social position, were still classified as nouveaux riches; the Astors said No. The William K. Vanderbilts put up a three million dollar town house at Fifth Avenue and Fifty-second Street, filled with sections of castles from Europe, Moorish billiard rooms, Japanese parlors and cathedral windows. But architecture wouldn't pull the trick. Coming over for a short visit of a year, Consuelo had a suggestion—a great masked entertainment, described at the time in a simple superlative, "the grandest ever given on this continent." By accounts of the day, the experienced Lady Mandeville managed the show with the skill of a P. T. Barnum with a Lind.

For months rumors thickened about the recherché affair—twelve hundred guests, orchids for a "tropical forest," roses by the thousands, glittering costumes for Borgias, Louis XIVs, Pompadours, King Arthurs. Everybody would be something royal or near-royal. Caroline, daughter of Mrs. Astor, presumed she would be invited and went to work on a "Star Quadrille." Then, striking at the last, delicate moment, Mrs. Vanderbilt let it be spread around that she could hardly have Miss Astor; Mrs. Astor had never paid the Vanderbilts a call. Thus it was that the Queen of Society, after reflection, stepped into the Astor carriage, drew up at the Vanderbilts' and left her card. The Vanderbilts were in! The ceremonial evening turned into a victory ball. And Consuelo reigned happily.

Her sister, Natica, also won a nobleman husband, becoming Lady Lister-Kaye. Consuelo's mother shifted between England and Natchez, and appeared to prefer the latter. She often quoted the comment of Debby, her dark Mississippi maid, who didn't think much of royalty's "plantations." When Debby saw the historic Tiber she sniffed: "We got better back bayous in Louisiana!" One of Consuelo's children, like his father, went to America and was drawn to a well-to-do commoner—Helena Zimmerman of Cincinnati, whom he married. Afterward a cablegram arrived in the Natchez country; attorneys were commissioned to dip a jug in the Mississippi. The contents, sealed and certified before a justice of the peace, were to be sent to Consuelo, now dowager Duchess, for a christening.

—◈—

Since Consuelo's early days the colonnade of Dunleith has offered a changeless façade—a cool, far-off place above the surrounding terrain, its unending pillars a sharp white against their shadows. Four generations of Carpenters have lived here —the first Joseph Carpenter, a man who could make the cotton market sink or rise with a word or two, and his descendants. For a time the Carpenters left, but recently young Leslie Carpenter returned from war duties with Mrs. Carpenter and the children. They share Dunleith with that permanent guest, Miss Percy, who outlasted Sarah Ann, Consuelo and everyone else. She still plays that harp.

—◈—

The other house, Green Leaves, is presided over by a present-day chatelaine who has broken a few rules in her own way, Ruth Audley Beltzhoover, a gentle-faced, blue-eyed young matron with soft blonde hair. Her deep-shaded Green Leaves has been in the possession of a single family and its connections since George Washington Koontz acquired it a century and more ago. Her marriage to Melchior Beltzhoover united branches of the banker's family that were already allied through the decades. She enjoyed casual years, entertaining as the financier's wife, receiving friends from New York, managing a crowded household that centered about the terraced court with its live oak of the Indian legend.

Then with the crash of the 1920s bad times fell. Her husband became ill; the Beltzhoover fortunes shrunk. Green Leaves itself was threatened. One of the few remaining assets happened to be an interest in a department store, until then regarded as a distinctly minor possession. The store was not doing altogether well at the moment. Ruth Audley Beltz-

GREEN LEAVES
Its Ladies Have Made Legends

EARL M. NORMAN

DUNLEITH
A Lady Ghost Outlasted Them All

REBER HENDERSON

STANTON HALL
An Irishman's Dream Come True

EARL M. NORMAN

hoover walked downtown, looked it over and decided that she would cease being merely a handsome Natchez ornament. She took over the management, listening to all advice but making up her own mind. She went to New York, and dealt with clothing wholesalers, learning prices and values. Those New Yorkers, too, learned something. Ruth Audley, as Natchez could have informed them, was one of those charming, amenable Southerners with a will of iron.

She took over her family; she put the store on its feet, and she watched staff and business volume more than double. It wasn't easy; she had to wean friends away from their habit of going to the cities for their clothing. She had tact, but she had to grow yet more adept in exercising it when country brides asked advice about hats and shoe-buckles. . . . By the time her husband died, Ruth Audley Beltzhoover knew she had won the fight. Today she goes on much as before, alternating between the wide white residence and the store some squares away, training her children to take over in her stead.

Once more there is easy assurance at Green Leaves, where the fair Consuelo once sang and ruled. The garden, dominated by its oaks, remains the house's heart. Its tiered walks are bordered by the pinks and reds of camellias and azaleas and the lavender clusters of wisteria. Nearby waits a swimming pool; in contrast, the servants move in and out of a bricked kitchen, connected to the main house, that has never been out of use.

⸺❦XVI❦⸺

ELIZA, THE EARLY BRIDE

The youthful Lows were good people, fervent and hardworking. Few plantation families knew them, because the Lows lived and worked in the seething section under the Hill. Jacob Low, a short man with a kindly face, marked with lines of worry, had had a difficult few years when he first floated down to Natchez during the Spanish regime. He worked at odd jobs—a helper in stores, a middle man for the sale of pelts. What came to him, he saved; he was cautious in what he did and said, keeping out of trouble despite flying bullets, chest-thumping bullies and other hazards of life along the turbulent waterfront.

As time went on, Jacob Low had his own shop. Then a stroke of bad luck befell a friend, but indirectly it brought better times for Mr. Low. The man in question, who operated the ferry between Natchez and the Louisiana bank, was inclined to temper tantrums. One day, as a party of swaggering louts stepped aboard, he lost his control. Five of them jumped him, slashing off an ear, leaving him a cripple. Able to move about again, the first thing the ferryman did was look about for a successor. Would Jake Low want the ferry?

Jake Low did. He gathered all his cash, made appeals for loans and, after much arranging, he had the concession. The new operator, a little frown wrinkling his forehead as he worked, had no trouble keeping himself intact. With a calm voice and one or two well-muscled assistants he enforced order and filled his treasury box nicely. In a row of four or five notably clean houses, he found living quarters for himself, and arranged for a Negro to look after it daily. He married a slim, light-haired girl with a quick smile, daughter of a merchant friend, and together they continued in the small place under the Hill.

On slack days the Lows found time to stroll up the narrow road to the top and watch the planters in their broadcloth suits and wide-brimmed hats riding into town with a flourish. Some day, they told each other, they would move up here. Things would be different, all right. The wife, sometimes afraid that she had said too much, assured her husband that she was satisfied with matters as they were; but now and then he caught her glance as she inspected one of the ladies with tall bonnets and flowing ribbons, riding by in a carriage. Well, some day . . .

The Lows had only one child. Eliza had her mother's slim stature and her smile, with a sprinkling of freckles and soft reddish hair. The little girl played on her narrow porch with one or two children from next door, gazing curiously at the carmined women who strolled by Silver Street. When any of the under-Hill denizens tried to speak to Eliza, she couldn't understand why her mother pulled her in, or came forward with a look that sent the people scattering. The children next door were seldom there for long. Families moved a great deal down here, and Eliza had long spells of loneliness.

Whenever she could, Eliza's mother walked up the hill with her, to sit on a bench along the cool esplanade, and walk slowly past the big white houses. Frequently they went to the edge of the bluff, to a spot dominating the river's curve, where a disintegrating huddle of timbers marked the site of old Fort Rosalie. It was an historic point, where France had first maintained her outpost in the wilderness on the site of the bloody Natchez uprising. In recent years it had been abandoned, and now the battered walls were falling away in a bird-filled thicket.

The freckle-faced Eliza liked the spot as well as any she knew. She enjoyed the air above the bluff, the golden light that seemed all about them here, not like the dark and smelly streets where she lived. From this border was an unparalleled view—the fine streets atop the hill, the settlement below and the well-worn road that led to it, and in the distance the dimmed green flats of Louisiana.

The Lows were surprised to learn that the land on the hilltop, about the old fort, belonged to one of their friends, busy Peter Little. Like the Lows, Peter was working to elevate himself, and like them he made his living below the Hill. He was a gaunt-framed, narrow-faced fellow with sandy hair and a tanned skin, as easy-humored as any they knew. People assured one another that Peter would make a name for himself no matter what happened; and they told the story of the way he started out as the first lumberman along the river.

Having only a few dollars, Peter had needed a windfall to get started. A well-loaded boat sank one night at the waterfront. After a day or so of probing, the owner gave up and went back to Georgia; the river was too deep for salvage. Peter Little used his last dollars to hire a crew and ropes. For nearly a week he sweated with them on the spot, and brought up the contents. Selling them for a remarkable profit, he was able to open a lumber mill. He invested nearly everything that came to him in a store, in fixtures for his mill and eventually in that land on the bluff that nobody else seemed to want.

When the red-haired Eliza was twelve, the Lows heard about Lorenzo Dow, the minister who was storming the Southwest. When Lorenzo gained permission to preach in Natchez, the Lows took Eliza with them to the crowded hall. On their way they passed the lank figure of Peter Little. Didn't he want to go along? Peter thanked them and grinned. Religion was all right for those that wanted it; he could take it or leave it. His friends entered the hall, and for weeks afterward they talked of the way Lorenzo impressed them. For Eliza it was an evening never forgotten.

The emaciated Lorenzo stormed across the platform, his shadow enormously elongated in the lamplight. Eliza had never heard such words, such overpowering evocations of the life beyond. She trembled until her mother drew her close and tried to persuade the child not to listen. But no, Eliza wanted to hear; she kept her small green eyes on the vehement evangelist. The next day she still spoke of the powerful things he said.

It was the beginning of the hot season and one day that same month Eliza's father ran home, the lines of care suddenly deeper about his eyes. One of the flatboatmen had just dropped to the floor of the ferry; it was the black vomit! When a thing like this happened, yellow fever was upon them. The boatmen, unacclimated, died by the dozen under the Hill, and the scourge spread everywhere.

Where could they go? The young wife looked wildly about her. They knew few people up on the hill. And would one place be any safer than another? They could only stay home and take the remedies that doctors recommended—garlic, sulphur and mixtures of odorous oils, and keep away from crowds. For days the mother, with the nervous Eliza at her side, remained indoors, hoping, praying. Men and women died on the wet, garbage-laden streets; at the waterside, boatmen were falling to the bottom of their skiffs, to rot there because none would go near them.

Nervous officials burned tar in the hope of "purifying" the atmosphere, and the carts rumbled toward the cemeteries, corpses hanging over the side. Crews dug long trenches and dumped in the bodies; there was no time for anything else. Bars and bawdy-houses shut tight. Boats came and went as rapidly as possible, and farmers who had to visit the town eyed the rest with suspicion and fear. Still the toll increased; in the next house to the Lows a family of six were dead.

One evening Jake Low walked slowly home, a look of puzzlement on his face. A little headache, he started to say, then slumped to the floor. His wife screamed to Eliza: "Get the doctor, quick!" The doctor's servant said she'd ask him to call whenever he could. The desperate Eliza found their friend Mr. Little, and they raced together through the half-deserted streets. By the time they shoved open the door, they found the father unconscious on his bed, Mrs. Low red-eyed and trembling as she sat beside him. Her voice hoarse, she whispered that she had it too. Pushing the frantic Eliza behind him, Peter Little went to work to do what he could.

Jake Low died quickly, but his wife lingered for days, delirious, her words rasping in her throat. At the end she quieted, and she motioned to Peter. It wouldn't be long for her, she knew; wearily she shook her head when he tried to stop her. She wanted him to make a promise. When Peter Little, his head bowed, agreed, she went on: No matter what happened, would he look after Eliza? They'd hoped to make things better for the girl, take her somewhere else. But now . . . she pleaded: Would he swear he'd watch over her?

A little later, Peter drew the sobbing Eliza to his side. That night Peter Little took Eliza to his house, and asked his housekeeper to do what she could to make the child rest. Within the month the attorneys read the will. Peter had been made administrator; they had expected that, but all looked up sharply when the lawyers estimated the property's value. The hard-struggling Lows had accumulated a sizeable little fortune; financially, Eliza need never worry.

Peter Little contemplated the situation. The child was pretty, despite those freckles—an appealing little thing, though her manner was highly restrained, almost timid. Thus far she had received only a rudimentary education; she needed considerable training to prepare her for her new place in the world. All things taken into account, it would hardly be wise to attempt that here, would it? He called Eliza. How would she like to go away for a few years to a school for young ladies? Eliza, her eyes staring at the floor, agreed. That would be nice, thank you.

A few months later, as the time approached for Eliza's departure, it was the housekeeper's turn to be amazed. Although Mr. Little and Eliza had talked things over frequently, and the girl seemed to be regaining some of her old spirit, the housekeeper was unprepared for Peter's announcement: He and Eliza were going to be married. For reasons of property, and to protect Eliza in her dealings, they had thought it best. ... Eliza smiled nervously, Peter Little looked grave, and the housekeeper kept her questions to herself.

On the day of Eliza's leaving, the oddly-mated couple took their vows before a minister. Immediately the bridegroom gave Eliza a fatherly kiss, bundled her up and escorted her to the vessel. There, waving goodbye to his bride, Peter assured her she must not worry about anything; he would be waiting for her when she returned.

Encouraging letters arrived from Maryland. Yes, Eliza was progressing rapidly, attending to her lessons, English, history, singing, dancing. Oh, yes, her behavior was fine; sometimes a bit too subdued. (Peter had reason to be amused at that, from a pedagogue.) She was an extremely religious child, the most devout in the school, the teacher continued; she talked frequently of a certain minister and his powerful preachings, a Mr. Dow. Peter frowned to himself. He had been a little worried about Eliza's excessive piety. Well, they could attend to that when she returned.

Several years later, as one of the steamboats slipped into the landing, a brightly dressed girl with red hair stood at the rail. Peter Little stepped forward in astonishment. Eliza had grown much taller, filled out admirably, emerging with the kind of loveliness for which he had hoped. The sweep of her bell-like skirts, the feather in her hat, the fit of her pelisse—everything was as he wished. The green eyes had a composed look, but a line of freckles still crossed cheeks and nose, seeming only to add to her charm.

This time the kisses would not be fatherly. The couple went to New Orleans for a long visit. The smiling husband escorted Eliza to the opera, to the places of refreshment on stilts over the lake; they met Creole friends of Peter's and spent long hours in the arched courtyards, with the tinkle of fountains in their ears. Peter Little told himself he was indeed fortunate. Back in Natchez, he introduced Eliza to the families with which he had aligned himself in recent years; and again the girl met the test. Peter, Eliza discovered, had reached out in several directions, as landowner and speculator, cotton grower and fair-sized capitalist.

There was only one matter that disturbed him. Eliza had gained, rather than lost in religious fervor. For a time Peter tried to reason, telling her that such zest was—well, out of place for one of her new rank. The plantation people with whom they were coming increasingly in contact—didn't she see that they took these subjects without so much seriousness? Eliza listened, but still he found her talking of religion.

To her own annoyance, it appears, Eliza had her light moments. She enjoyed visits to the theater, concerts by musicians who stepped off the steamboats, dances on the plantations. Peter was particularly pleased with a local amateur theatrical group, to which he belonged, and Eliza went regularly, smiling over the antics—some of it behavior which her conscience told her was not entirely worthy. But Peter liked it all, and she must be an obedient wife.

During an interval in Eliza's struggle between her soul and the theatrical fleshpots, Peter brought her news. Did she remember that land he owned on the bluff? That's where their new house would be. Eliza's eyes brightened as she recalled those mornings, long ago, when she and her aproned mother had sat there and surveyed all Natchez from the heights.

She smiled contentedly as their great place took shape on the most commanding site in town. A little to the side of the site of the fort, the workmen built high red-brick walls in a square, and raised a stately, two-storied portico with four brick stuccoed columns of the simplest Doric pattern. They supported a narrow dentil-bordered pediment with a many-paned oval light in the center. The wall along the portico was stuccoed to match the pillars, setting it off from the rest of the building. The front galleries had recessed doorways above and below, columned, with arched fanlights in a classic pattern. It was Southern plantation architecture, but the delicate detail had more than a touch of the Georgian. Peter had achieved a building combining warmth and restraint.

The bricks had a special fineness; windows showed simplicity and perfection of detail, their green shutters against white woodwork and red brick. Wide, out-curving steps led from the gallery to the front garden, with an iron railing ending in a swirl. Over the grounds Eliza worked with the gardeners, setting out parterres of roses, boxwood and azaleas, fringing circular walks that followed the shape of the bluff. A latticed summer-house, poised near the end, seemed from below to be hanging over the elevation. The rear of the house had a six-columned porch, opening upon a bricked court that led to two tall brick utility buildings. The whole was topped by a white-paneled cupola, the highest point for miles, a many-windowed room from which Peter and Eliza could survey their world. For them this point of proud vantage might offer a symbol of a rise to eminence that neither had quite anticipated. The date was about 1820, and the house took the name of the fort, Rosalie.

The couple hoped for children, but it became evident that there would be none. Otherwise for the easy-mannered Peter Little the days passed in contentment. He found himself occasionally disturbed over Eliza's religious bent. Yet a friend who wrote of Eliza and her spiritual life observed that at this stage the young matron was "far from being weaned from the world"; she continued to "love gay dressing and to some extent gay company."

The friend explains: In her meetings with the Methodist

ministers, Eliza's face grew earnest as they touched on the comparative sinfulness of silken plantation life. The harsh words of the divines might have made less devout individuals resentful; but, this informant goes on, "it was a most redeeming trait in her character that the more plainly the preachers dealt with her, the more she seemed to esteem them." However, he almost sighs, Eliza went intermittently to "places of amusement not favorable to Christian piety," until she made one last essay in this field.

The famous musician, Ole Bull, was in Natchez for a performance with which few found exception, except that it *was* a performance. Peter Little, coming back to town from a business tour especially for the purpose, was enthralled. Not without a few misgivings, Eliza accompanied him; the first person she met was a grave elder of another church. At first, we are told, Eliza felt gratification that such a one would sample beguiling amusements as she did. Then, as she mused, a new, sterner light entered her green eyes. "She was never again seen on such doubtful grounds; nor does it appear that she ever again had the slightest longing for these fleshpots of Egypt." Peter could go alone.

From then on, Eliza concerned herself increasingly with the church. Peter groaned, but she left off her richly-woven mitts and bright hats, wearing only clothes of brown and black, unjeweled. More and more she talked of religious abstractions. When no services were being held at the Methodist church, she had herself taken to the Presbyterian. She became a Sunday school teacher, diligently instructing pupils until she emerged as an accomplished lay theologian, and instructed teachers. She helped establish an orphan asylum and acted as one of its managers. Into her home she took three orphans, one the niece of her husband. Peter liked the children; having them almost made up for the religion. . . .

Yet Eliza had more surprises in store. Now the palatial Rosalie, with its rich draperies and its air of lavish pride, was turning into a minister's way-house. Circuit riders, passing through Natchez in a stream, were breakfasting, dining, staying overnight. Eliza Little was giving them the same hospitality that any plantation woman offered her less pious guests —warm baths in the evening, hot chocolate and rolls at the bedside.

The ministers were dazzled by such treatment. Eliza met them at the landing with her footmen and carriages, sent them with outriders about the countryside, kept her kitchen staff in readiness for arrivals at all hours. Every time he came home from a trip, Peter told a friend, he found a new reverent face at the table. Most of the guests were extremely polite, though a few could not conceal faint disapproval of this man's lack of concern with matters of the spirit.

The most amiable of husbands will finally turn. Peter Little scratched at his sandy hair. Where would it all end? With all those preachers around, his evenings had the same flavor as a ministers' Sunday chicken dinner. One day, as Eliza sat at her dressing table, he drew up his lean form and made a pronouncement. He had no objection to feeding and housing the devout, but he'd do it in another house. He'd build one for them!

Hurriedly Peter called in workmen and drove them to their tasks. He arrived ahead of them in the morning, and was the last to leave at dusk. With incredible speed a neat and handsome galleried place went up across the way from Rosalie. He named it, not without a wry look, "The Parsonage." He made good his promise to Eliza that the ministers would receive care just as elaborate as that to which she had accustomed them. He set up a full staff of servants and he charged a housekeeper with the duty of keeping it ever prepared for the arrival of the circuit riders—coffee, chocolate, hot baths and all. When Eliza wanted to see her ministers, she had only to call her maid, put up her parasol and walk across the path.

It was the solution, and Peter's salvation. Eliza followed her religious duties out of his earshot; at other times she entertained *his* friends in the way he liked. He did not get her back to gay dresses and flowered hats, but he probably never expected a miracle. A procession of smiling preachers moved in and out of The Parsonage. Eliza looked happy, and Peter showed himself the happiest of all. To prove it, he let himself be taken over there to meet the devout—once a year.

Curiously, it was Peter who made preparation for death sooner than Eliza. In 1837 he wrote a will: "I know I have not a moment that I can call mine. I am upward of fifty-five years old, and have often wondered how I have been spared so long." Then he lived for nearly twenty more years; and Eliza preceded him in death. In the words of her religious associate, she had slowly "ripened for heaven." In 1853, surrounded by her adopted children, she died on one of her country estates, rejoicing that "my pilgrimage is ended." Three years later, Peter followed her.

Only two families and their connections have occupied Rosalie. Friends of the Littles, the Andrew L. Wilsons, purchased it. They too were a couple without children and again the chatelaine became a foster mother. The Wilsons had both planting and commercial connections; one of their guests was often Jefferson Davis, a few years before his time of destiny as the Confederacy's President.

When war came, the Federals surveyed the fine location of Rosalie. It was an ideal spot for occupation, and one that could not be permitted in the hands of suspect pro-Confederates. The Union forces took it for their main headquarters. Rather oddly, however, they permitted the Wilsons to stay. Mr. Wilson had gone to Texas with his slaves, in the hope of saving them from the Yankees. Mrs. Wilson remained behind with the children. The lawns about the house, including the site of the ancient fort, were covered with tents. As the natives sat tight, none other than General Ulysses S. Grant arrived in Natchez and chose Rosalie for a short stay. With him he brought his wife and two children.

In an upstairs room, the Grants occupied a tall, family-sized four-poster bed; not many owners of Deep Southern mansions could claim they had a piece of furniture in which Grant slept. And Grant ate at the same table at which Jefferson Davis had dined. To Rosalie came General Walter Q. Gresham, with his observant wife, whom we encountered earlier. The house had two mistresses, and, incredibly, Mrs. Gresham got on famously with Mrs. Wilson. Mrs. Wilson shared the upper floor with the guest-mistress; the officers had the lower one, and all went merrily. "I never let her forget that I recognized it was her house," wrote Mrs. Gresham. Everybody was polite; at one time the Federal children were told not to sing Union songs to avoid hurting the feelings of the Wilsons!

The Wilsons' rosewood furniture and brocade curtains remained in place, until General Gresham himself suggested they be stored for safety. (A woman who traveled with another Federal officer had suggested that Mrs. Gresham "crush" the curtains—pack them up and send them home.) Before the war, however, the Wilsons had been worrying about their great gold mirrors. These had been left on the walls during a shelling of the town, but as the Federal occupation forces arrived, the mirrors were taken down, packed in wooden containers and buried close to the site of the fort. The family could only hope nothing happened to them there.

At Rosalie Mrs. Gresham watched the planters, "neutrals" or Unionists, and she went to many a dinner with the owners of Natchez houses. She saw the fraternizing of Natchez Confederate girls and Union officers. She and her husband cautioned a few younger officers that one evening they would be surprised and captured while out calling; but the officers still called. A Natchez family of women on the outskirts received a favor—a guard of two Federal soldiers, one old, one young. Men being needed elsewhere, the soldiers were to be moved. The ladies protested. They were told they could keep a single guard, the elder. Again they objected; they wanted the young one! All the time, however, the General's wife understood that a Confederate secret service was in operation at Natchez, and among the operatives were some of the smiling women whom she met.

The friendly General and his wife left, and then their agreeable hostess, Mrs. Wilson, herself turned out to be a member of the secret brigade at which the General's lady had hinted. Mrs. Wilson got into a dispute over ammunition in her possession. After two days and nights in the guard house, she was "banished" for the rest of hostilities to distant localities. She became a Confederate nurse and worked so hard that magazine stories were written of her efforts. After the war, Gresham returned to Natchez once or twice, with Mrs. Gresham—as house guests of the Wilsons. At Rosalie the guests noticed the curtains and rosewood furniture back in place, and also the big mirrors. Dug up in the yard, the glasses were found as bright and untarnished as ever.

In the years since then, Rosalie has seen everything about it alter. Its acreage was reduced by business thoroughfares; mills and factories moved ever closer, and traffic hummed a few yards away. The two "Rumble girls," Rebecca and Annie, later Mrs. James Marsh, stayed here and watched over their treasures. In 1938 the Mississippi Society of Daughters of the American Revolution acquired Rosalie and restored it. An adjoining warehouse has been taken down, the old walks and gardens are being brought back; and the Rumble sisters have stayed to greet callers.

Mrs. Marsh points out the family pieces. This is a double set of solid-back Belter rosewood furniture, twenty-four pieces, the red damask upholstery the same that was first used in 1858. These are the pieces removed during the war at the suggestion of the friendly Federal general. On the walls hang the mirrors once buried in the garden. The floors have Aubusson carpets from the same days; in a china closet stands a set of Sevres china of the Rose Pompadour pattern. Originally the family counted five hundred pieces; a few were lost, they divided the rest, and two hundred and twenty-five remain. Each piece is different, with decorations ranging in size from a small orange to a heavy artichoke. And here is another object, unconnected with the others, a baby's plate with a moral lesson: "Dost Thou Love Life, Then Do Not Squander Time. There Will be Sleeping Enough in the Grave." It is a firm lesson, much in the spirit of Eliza the religious.

Outside, the cupola has been time's major victim. The 1840 hurricane ripped it off and scattered it so thoroughly that the fragments were never found. A railed observatory, giving a view of all the surrounding terrain, is still symbolic of the story of Peter and Eliza Little. Below, beyond the line of the bluff, stands what is left of Natchez Under the Hill, and to the other side, the present town. In the mornings, when the red circle of the sun rises over the irregular hills, the first lights catch at the windows, as they have done for nearly a hundred years. At dusk, as the sun drops behind the misty Louisiana flats, its last rays illuminate the glass panes of Rosalie.

Across the way, also fronting on the heart of an earlier Natchez, stands The Parsonage, the house that Peter Little put up for his wife's religious friends. Today it is the property of the Orrick Metcalfes, who maintain it as a private residence. A few years after Peter died, his heirs permitted the church to sell the building and buy one at another point. The ministers could well remember their days across from Rosalie; none ever had a finer parsons' house.

THE PARSONAGE

XVII

"I DREAMT I DWELT IN MARBLE HALLS..."

To HAVE the "biggest house of them all" was the aim of one Natchezian after another. Out of many, three succeeded best. Each could say for a time that he had outdone his predecessors. But before long each knew the penalty of trying too hard and reaching too high. They received their houses, and also other things for which they had not bargained.

General John Quitman, that New Yorker-turned-Natchezian, who regarded Yankees as he did snakes, picked a surprising individual for a legal assistant. John McMurren liked practically everybody, even Northerners. Like Quitman, McMurren was born in the East, had read law in the West and then had chosen Natchez' greener fields. There the resemblance ended. While Quitman fought and fumed, McMurren took matters differently. A stout, highly logical fellow, he never turned dogmatic. Chuckling his way through a case, he won it and then walked out with his hand about the shoulder of his defeated rival.

Launching himself in Mississippi, John McMurren made the older lawyers take notice. When his partner died, hero Quitman was glad enough to take McMurren on as his associate.

MELROSE
Solid Monument to a Dream of Grandeur

REBER HENDERSON

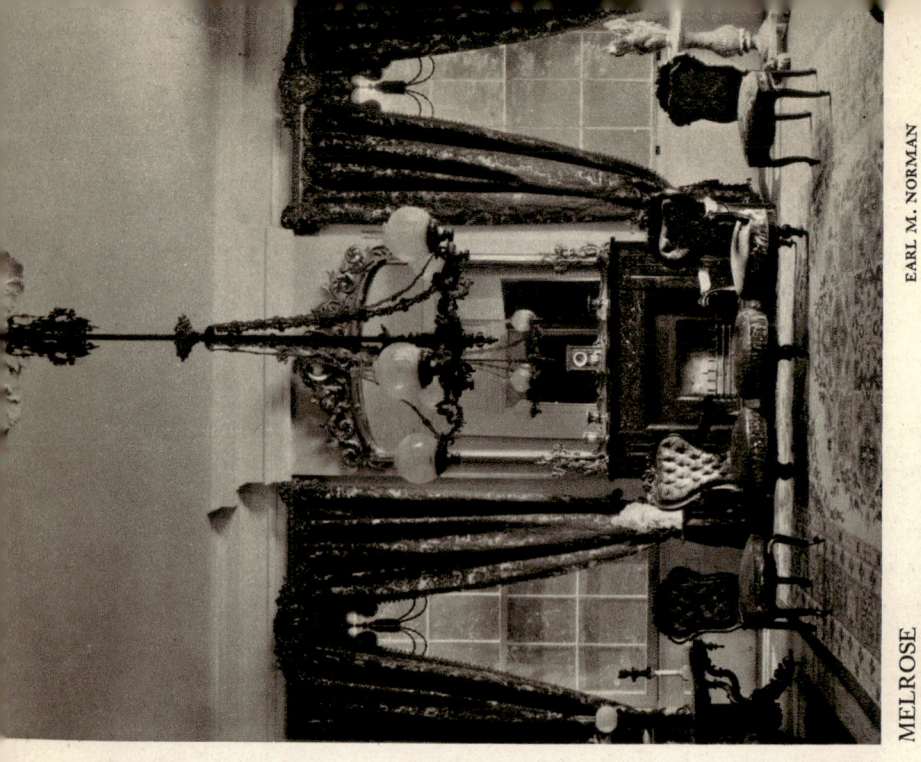

MELROSE   EARL M. NORMAN
Parlor with Chaperone's Stool

MELROSE   EARL M. NORMAN
The Interior Also Has Majesty

After a time some thought McMurren at least as good a lawyer as his explosive colleague. Yet Quitman, with his forays into Mexico and his shouts about Cuba and the Yankees, was winning higher places. Still, John McMurren didn't mind. He was managing quite well, he thought, accumulating a steady balance at the bank, investing in plantations and stocks.

As the years passed, the two men's connection strengthened. They married double first cousins. John McMurren took the almost regal Mary Louise Turner. It would appear that Mary Louise, a girl with ideas, thought her husband needed a touch of extra ambition to push him ahead; and she set out to give it to him. Ever one to oblige, John squared his shoulders and went through busy motions. Inevitably, however, his good nature got the best of him, and he eased along as before. Mary Louise could only look annoyed. The man might make himself famous, but he didn't seem interested.

If she couldn't win fame, vicarious or otherwise, Mrs. McMurren would take a substitute—a house to make Natchez remember. She didn't, of course, suggest anything so bald as that; she merely described a few things she had in mind, which would cinch the matter. At first, John hesitated; such a home would require an outlay of a kind he had never contemplated. It would eat deep into their capital. He continued to express his doubts, but Mary Louise went on visualizing refinements of her project. She knew she would get it. After a while John McMurren grew so enthusiastic that he considered the whole scheme his; and Mary Louise, a wise wife, let it go at that.

Together the couple drove to the outskirts and saw their Melrose take shape. Probably nothing in Natchez was ever put up more sturdily. Thick red-brick walls, two-storied, ended in outer cornice work of striking size and elaboration. The portico, a mass of brick and stucco almost as broad as the building itself, had two pairs of powerful Doric columns upholding a pediment. Ironwork bordered the galleries, above and below; a balustraded captain's walk on the roof seemed to extend over half the elevation. Melrose had a sophistication and a worldly look about it. The date was the middle 1840s.

Through a glass-framed doorway opened an outer hall, leading to a central passage of grand proportions, setting the tone of the interior with its elaboration of paneling, cornice and frieze work. Over the inside doorways perched rows of candles, to be lighted for special occasions. To one side, an opening bordered by fluted Ionic pilasters with a glassed, canopied fanlight, led to a recessed stairway. Near it, in a dining room twenty-two feet square, hung Natchez' most celebrated punkah, a much-carved mahogany display item built for the house.

Double drawing rooms were connected with folding doors, bordered by pilasters. One was in green and gold, the other rose and gold. Near a marble fireplace nestled a set of two horse-hair seats, between them a stationary stool—the whole supposedly a "courting set," with a place in the middle for the unsleeping chaperone. (Some have maintained that the device was used, instead, for games; but Natchez won't accept so unromantic a contention.) Behind the drawing rooms was the library, bordered by walnut bookcases eleven feet high. For a party, all the folding doors were thrown open, connecting the three rooms with a sweep of space as long as the house.

Conducting a tour of inspection of Melrose, John McMurren always ended it before a circular table, inlaid with a pattern of birds in mosaic, with small diamonds to represent the eyes. Of all his splendors, he liked best this "jeweled table." He had only a few flush years in which to admire it. The Civil War came. John Quitman lay in his grave, but he would probably have turned in it had he known that his former partner, ever good natured and adjustable, was entertaining the Federals at Melrose.

Even this congeniality, however, did not help the McMurrens when hostilities ended. The enormous house had become even more of a burden than he had originally feared. The McMurrens borrowed and begged for extensions, and finally realized the inevitable. In 1865, they had to give it up.

For Mary Louise McMurren the blow came harder than for her husband, but the days seemed lack-luster to both of them. Then the following year involved John in an episode which gave him his major, if posthumous connection with fame.

Having observed Christmas with his family, John McMurren boarded the steamboat *Fashion* for New Orleans. He found it packed amidships with nearly 2600 bales of cotton; there was an excited holiday spirit among the three hundred passengers in the cabins and on deck. It was a busy down-river trip, the vessel pulling to and from the shore at regular intervals. A few miles above Baton Rouge, chimney sparks cascaded suddenly to the deck, and a woman's cry went up. The cotton was aflame! People ran in both directions, toward bow and stern. Deck hands struggled over the smoking bales, and sought to calm the passengers. They'd land in a minute, things would be all right. Rounding a bend, the pilot knew that to one side loomed a steep bank, to the other a fairly flat shore; with luck he could beach it. Down in the vessel the engineer worked with desperate haste. Both engines racing, the *Fashion* sped toward land.

Yet the fire quickened and spread. Nearly everything above deck was burning—wagons, produce, supplies. With maddened whinnies horses leaped into the water; others sank under the smoke and burned to death. Women screamed as the billowing fumes blotted out the shore. In his perch, the pilot clung while flames licked all about him, the wheel beginning to blister under his fingers. But the point of greatest peril was the engineer's; the machinery might explode about him in a minute.

The unexpected happened. The vessel rounded to the windward; changing winds drove the flame through all the tiers of cotton. The captain saw what was happening, yet he could not risk a change in orders for the whole thing might burn apart before they reached safety. They approached shore and the pilot ran her in—high and dry at the forward end, in deep water aft. The people at the front leaped over and crawled to safety; those at the other end were trapped. The fire was eating quickly toward them as the deck grew heated beneath their feet. Men and women stood there, half-dazed, children in their arms. Through the smoke others yelled to them: "Jump!" Men on shore saw their families marooned, and ran crazily about, appealing for help. Some tried to paddle to them and drowned.

The crew managed to get two lifeboats into the water. One capsized and the other went adrift. Two Negroes, clothing aflame, slipped down; a brief hiss, and that was all. The pilot, groping about, called to a friend: "I can't swim!" For a minute or two he was in a circle of flame, and then he was gone. Fifty or sixty people were in the water, crying in fright, battling those who tried to save them. Finally no more figures moved. Men and women knelt in the mud, weeping over those they had lost. The engineer was not found until much later; he had stayed at his post and died. Among those who lay half-conscious was John McMurren. Jumping to shore from a cotton bale, he broke his hip. As the new year began, John McMurren died in a New Orleans hospital, Natchez' major victim of this major river disaster. . . Long afterward the engineer's son told the story to John Hay. The poet changed the tale, giving the engineer, "Jim," a couple of wives, one in Natchez Under the Hill. He ended with lines famous for years with those who wanted sentiment straight and thick:

> "He weren't no saint,—but at jedgment
> I'd run my chance with Jim . . .
> He seen his duty, a dead-sure thing,—
> And went for it thar and then;
>
> And Christ ain't a-going to be too hard
> On a man that died for men."

McMurren's Melrose went to a friend and fellow-attorney, George Malin Davis. All the house, and most of its magnificent furnishings, remained intact; the only alteration was the addition of still more pieces. Mr. Davis' daughter married Dr. Stephen Kelly, and Melrose passed to their son George. For twenty years the family lived in New York, leaving Melrose empty, its splendors covered, its furnishings shrouded. The dark "Aunt Jane" looked after it, seeing that no one touched anything, including the towering camellia bushes.

Then in 1909 George Kelly and his young wife returned. She caught her breath when she walked the echoing hallways. The walls dripped water by the bucketful; a few of the carpets had rotted, and several draperies had been eaten by moths. Wooden doors warped so badly that some could not be opened; dead birds and small animals had fallen down the chimney. Yet all the furniture, the paintings, the fluted columns were there. Melrose had waited.

"Aunt Jane" took the couple in hand, to educate them out of their New York ways. Acquiring an early automobile, the Kellys wanted to bring a horse to a friend; they prepared to drive in, the animal trotting behind. Aunt Jane came running: "Don' you dare do that! We got niggers that takes horses!" Again, she found Mr. Kelly chopping wood for exercise and charged at him: "Don' you never let me see you doin' such an ungentlemanly thing. You gotta learn better, you hear!". . . In 1945 George Kelly died, and when I was last at Melrose Mrs. Kelly told me that Aunt Jane lay very ill. They cautioned her visitors: She must not know he was gone; it would upset her too much.

In this big house whose interior is Natchez' best preserved, some of the heavy curtains are the originals, having survived dampness, the moths and the years. Last is that "jeweled table" with the bird design. Its tiny eyes have been plucked out; the story is that a Federal soldier did it with his saber.

Melrose has one of Natchez' great pictures. John James Audubon spent many months in and about Natchez, trying to attract pupils by teaching them drawing and vocalizing. The erratic genius trudged the woods, picturing the wild birds of this moss-hung paradise. Some of his best productions date from this period in his mixed life. Yet the Natchez people, who frequently rewarded the smoother, less gifted flatterers among itinerant artists, gave him little recognition.

A town matron asked Audubon to do a large oil of Natchez. He completed a panoramic view, showing houses, courthouse, stores and church towers. The matron died and apparently the family did not accept the picture. Audubon sought desperately to sell it, cutting the price several times, but none wanted it. Audubon left the picture with Emile Profilet, who displayed it at his store, without success. It happened that Mr. Profilet's shop showed in the painting, and he thought relatives in France would be interested. He sent it to them and forgot it for years, until he visited there shortly before the Civil War. Then he brought it back to America, where no one indicated any interest, until finally the Kellys of Melrose acquired it. Today it is safe.

Then there was the house of the Irish Stantons, always a white elephant. From Belfast came the twenty-one-year-old, moustachioed Frederick Stanton, brother of those other Stantons of Windy Hill Manor. With a good eye for trade, Frederick concluded that a commission merchant's route was a quicker way to wealth, and less risky, than a cotton grower's. He had a debonair manner, a bright outlook, a fine fund of stories. He would get on. Within little more than a decade he was able to move to a place we have already seen, Cherokee. He enjoyed an expansive touch; his quiet wife, Hulda, and his children had carte blanche in their finances. Once a year, on January 12th, Frederick summoned them all for a solemn lecture on economy. This duty over, he never mentioned the subject until the next January 12th.

With the panic of the 1830s, Frederick Stanton learned

that a handler of cotton could go broke as quickly as a plantation man. He had to give up Cherokee and move to a country place, where he raised poultry and cursed politicians. As their finances improved, the Stantons went back to Cherokee. With the '50s, however, the house looked too small for the Stantons. The smiling Frederick remembered his home in Ireland, "White House," but intended to do even better than that. Picking a vacant hillside in town, he began a construction project that lasted several years. Finding matters well launched, he made a European trip to pick the furnishings. He left the patient Hulda behind for she might have put a damper on his mood for big things—marbles, crystals, rugs, draperies. Gaily he chartered a ship to bring the treasure home. It wasn't big enough, so the rest had to come in separate lots.

Returning early in 1858, the master took time to bestow kisses on his wife and children, then had himself driven to the nearly completed place. Hm, he tugged at his moustache. That part was nice, but he'd like the doorway bigger, and how about more ironwork? Still, the general effect pleased him. For this place, immense was a better word than massive. Bricked, heavily stuccoed, it stood higher than usual; two outer flights of brick steps, separated by a stretch of lawn, were needed to reach it. The double-decked, iron-railed portico had four columns, fluted with the heaviest of Corinthian capitals, its floor of marble marked in checkerboard pattern. Portico ceilings showed paneling. The upper gallery floor was shaped in curves to fit between the pillars. Along one side of the house lifted a two-storied ironwork gallery; at the other, a pillared porte-cochere. Outside and in, the decorations had a motif of grapes, roses, fruits, in ironwork, wood or anything else that came to hand.

Through a recessed foyer opened the central hallway, sixteen feet wide, to be used as a banquet hall when other rooms did not seem big enough. "To break the monotony," the hallway's long lines were interrupted by arches, much carved, and the eye caught gilded cornices, medallions and other decoration. In a recess curved a stairway, circle upon circle, three stories high to a retunda. Despite the vastness, the first floor had only four rooms. The "long parlor" or music chamber at the front measured forty-eight feet by twenty-two; folding doors connected it with the second one, to be opened into a ballroom seventy feet long. A series of marble mantels of white Carrara offered full-sized replicas of roses, pears, persimmons, pomegranates, with surfaces heavily realistic, smooth or rough or pocked. Gigantic inset mirrors at each end reflected and re-reflected the fabulous scene. From the walls hung black-bronze chandeliers, with cupids, seraphs, tambourines in patterns described, with understatement, as "profuse."

The library had a show-piece chandelier, depicting the first French soldiers at Natchez, with their armor, shields and weapons. Beyond it in the dining room hung another that was in some ways the house's most celebrated object, an ornament planned to summarize in lyric style the earlier history of the town—Indian warriors on horseback, fighting with bows and arrows, and swirling oak leaves, growing maize, wild buffalo and flying eagles. But everything did not work out as planned. Despite all of Frederick Stanton's purchases, the family found empty walls here and there. A New Orleans furniture maker who had helped arrange the purchases came up with extra pieces to save the day. Finally Hulda Stanton lined up the seventeen house servants needed for the place, and they moved in. Frederick christened it Belfast after his town in Ireland.

Here stood the ultimate exhibit of the cotton era. Overblown, almost over-ornate, Belfast was like the ripe red rose that bears within itself the seeds of decay. The days of simplicity had ended; Belfast appeared to sum up the last tense days of the Deep South, when planters, as if in defiance of an impending doom, were piling elaboration upon elaboration. Frederick Stanton had his wish, but he received little joy out of it. Within less than a year he died, and Hulda and the relatives soon groaned over the cost of maintenance. It seemed too big to keep warm, too grand to be entirely comfortable.

When war came, parts of the building were commandeered by the Union forces. Two Stanton girls took their best silver upstairs and hid it under their bed. Word trickled out; as they slept one night, a marauder "slightly chloroformed them," and the silver went.

After the war, the relatives kept it as long as they could. As an example of the deflated conditions of 1870, the property was valued at $550,000, but a scant $7000 was all that could be raised on it. It became the Stanton College for Young Ladies, then went to a bank; eventually it changed hands for less than the original cost of the iron fence that surrounded it. Today, as Stanton Hall, Frederick's place has had a revival. Still unwieldy for private use, it was acquired in 1940 by the Pilgrimage Garden Club. An extensive restoration has made progress in that typical furnishings are being assembled. At the windows hang silk draperies in a golden pattern, and crowds throng to see the bronze chandeliers, the iron and marble for which the Irish merchant drew upon the world. In one respect the scene improves on the original. The oaks that the Stantons planted have grown in a way they never visualized, to provide a framework that magnifies the building's magnificence.

Yet of all the Natchezians who wanted to build something different, Haller Nutt succeeded best, and for all time. He gave his region one of its greatest of sights, its peculiarity of peculiarities—Nutt's Folly.

These Nutts were exceptional people, no mistake about it. Haller's father, Dr. Rush Nutt, had been a Tidewater Virginian of oddly speculative mind. Bored with fox hunting, he set out in 1805 on a year's horseback jaunt about the continent, staying with Indians, poking around deserted mounds, asking about people, customs and diseases. Home again, he decided the Natchez region was the place for him; packing up slaves and other property, he moved down near the settlement of

Rodney. Putting science to work, he improved the cotton gin with a model that was used for decades to follow; he perfected a compress. With the cotton plant itself, he performed his greatest service. The growth was currently suffering from an infestation that wiped out whole fields at a time. After long struggle Dr. Rush Nutt came forth with a new variety, "Petit Gulf"; from it cotton was grown all over the South. There has been a mystery about this Nutt seed as the doctor never said where it came from or how he developed it.

Some thought he gathered the strains while abroad, on two world tours. J. L. Stephens in his book of early travels to Greece and Turkey gave considerable space to the unconventional doctor. To him Rush Nutt explained that he had been speculating about the world's origin. After watching the unending deposits of the Mississippi, he wanted to see and study the Nile's banks. He rambled over the pyramids, dug into Egyptian temples and decided he had been right all along—the world was far older than six thousand years. Despite his global interest, Dr. Nutt demonstrated a "thorough contempt for the usages of society." Knowing only English, he "despised all foreigners and detested their 'jabber.'" In Constantinople he found himself at a boarding house with a friendly, cosmopolitan crowd, French, British, German, Russian. The clatter of tongues disgusted Dr. Nutt. Reminded that, after all, there was an Englishman among them, he grew only angrier. He abhorred the British even more than he did the rest; and he stalked out of the establishment.

Meanwhile, in quieter moments, Rush Nutt had taken a wife, sister of Dr. John Ker of the Ross slave case. Their son, Haller, joined the father in his inventive bents and also in successful planting, but he was apparently of a more romantic disposition. He set his heart on a brisk, rose-pink blonde, Julia Williams. The girl was suffering from a sad love affair, and the family took her to the country. Haller, working hard, caught her on the rebound.

Haller's marriage went well, except that Julia liked the town of Natchez, and talked often of a favorite plantation near it, Longwood. Inquiring, Haller learned it was not for sale, but he left instructions with his attorneys to keep their eyes on the place. After several years he received a note that pleased him mightily. After a while he suggested a trip to Natchez. Julia saw nothing unusual in the bustle about the slave quarters, or the fact that she and Haller took passage on a rather leisurely steamboat. Soon after their arrival, Haller proposed a little jaunt out to Longwood. As they drew up, her mouth dropped. On the gallery stood her grinning house servants. She ran inside; the house had been hurriedly filled with all her possessions, brought on a faster packet. Longwood was hers.

Here the junior Nutts enjoyed many good seasons. Julia liked the location as much as she had expected, but after a while the house palled. It was old and rather nondescript. Again Haller aimed to please. Many times he had heard his father talk of Oriental buildings, arabesques and Moorish palaces; at home he had drawings of them. About the same time America was being subjected to a minor mania for octagonal houses. On the Hudson, in the West, all over the country men were finding strange virtues in buildings with eight sides. Haller Nutt fell victim to both the Oriental and octagonal delusions.

Going to Philadelphia, he called upon the highly-regarded architect, Samuel Sloan, and Mr. Sloan obliged. Back in Natchez he used his slaves for the rougher part of the work, then imported Pennsylvania artisans. Gradually the new Longwood was rising like no other residence ever seen here—sixty feet, then eighty, finally one hundred. It would have at least five stories. Fluted wooden columns, hollow-centered, were fashioned in the North and brought here for assembly. Work went on for two years; 1860 sped by, and war was perilously close. But Haller Nutt, one of Natchez' many Unionists, shook his head. He wasn't sure there'd be any war; anyway, he'd finish in time.

He almost did. Natchez could now make out what the

house would be like. A great base had been dug for concrete foundations; upon that were placed several stories, all octagonal. Around the two lower floors stretched fantastic galleries with pairs of narrow pillars, each topped by jig-saw-like ornamentation. Higher up began a tower several stories high, also bracketed and ornamented, ending in an onion-shaped red dome climaxed by a thin steeple. From the walls scores of narrow-arched windows looked out in sets like tiny eyes; eventually to be glassed, thus far they were only dark sockets.

Inside, the new Longwood looked more puzzling still. On every floor there was to be a central eight-sided room, with eight doors leading to eight outer sections. Each room had eight panels; downstairs the first object of furniture would be an eight-sided settee. Not a hallway could be found; whether this was something Moorish or arabesque, or merely Nutt, is not clear. As the family explained, you would be able to walk about all the house from any direction "without opening the same door twice." Everywhere were niches, in which statuary was to be placed. Soon the townspeople discovered more. The inventive Haller was planning, in 1860, a system of indirect lighting, with mirrors. He installed large ones in the dome and arranged glassed-over openings on each floor. On bright days every one of the thirty rooms would have sunlight!

An artificial lake was dug, and gardeners set out growths imported from abroad; avenues of trees were planted, leading to spots in which his children were to put up their own homes. Most of the exterior had been finished. In Ireland linens and laces were being woven; at Italian ports, marbles were collected. On the ground floor the Pennsylvania artisans plastered walls and installed marble mantels. On the floors above they labored on scaffolding, nailing brackets and attaching strips.

Early one morning in 1861, a horseman raced up to Longwood. War had started! The Pennsylvanians looked at one another, shucked off their overalls and filed down. They wanted to go home right away, Mister. Wearily, Haller Nutt paid them off.

Natchez had a new name for the new Longwood—Nutt's Folly. Orders for costly supplies were countermanded; silver, laces and tapestries remained in far-off warehouses. Some furnishings arrived and were sent back, or fell into Federal hands to be confiscated. Several cancellations were too late. A marble stairway arrived from Italy, with several statues; years later, they ended up in Northern museums. Meanwhile, Haller Nutt called his slaves to board over the upper windows and other openings. The outside was practically complete, and he knew it would last. Inside, the lowest floor was ready; above stood the empty interior, skeleton-like, only the framework of the upper stories extending to the dome.

Haller Nutt sighed. Better times would come, and they would finish. He assembled a handful of furnishings and moved into the lowest floor. It had been intended for a basement, with billiard room, wine cellar, playroom for the children. The dim, damp place now became the family residence. It must have been like living in the tomb of one's hopes. Friends said that every time he went to the upper section, Haller saddened; eventually he went there no more. Birds and bats found their way through crevices in the towers, and frequently they heard noises, the settling of timbers, chirpings of sparrows, the moaning of the winds. The growing children took friends to point to the niches for statuary that had not been installed. That room would have been finished in blue satin, the other in green.... After a time they, too, stayed away.

During the war, Haller entertained the Federals on a number of occasions, but gradually he remained more and more alone. Sir Arthur Fremantle, visiting during the war, made a definitive comment: "Mr. Nutt's place reminded me very much of an English gentleman's country seat, except that the house itself is rather like a pagoda..." Before the war ended, Haller Nutt had died. His wife took over the care of their family; for years she lived between Natchez and Washington, fighting claims for war damages. The artificial lake dried up and the gardens, begun so grandly, went to waste. Nothing was done to complete the unfinished wonders of Nutt's Folly.

The Nutts have never surrendered their marvel, declining all offers for purchase. The years have added an eerie look, a pervasive sadness. To go there on a gloomy day, as I once did, is to know it at its most spectral. The approach is by a twisting passage through the woods, along the last remnants of foreign plantings that Haller introduced. The house cannot be seen until the last moment, when the road shifts. It stands there, suddenly, like a forlorn creature of another era, alone and forgotten. The trees press upon the gloomy pile, pushing against it draperies of motionless moss. It has faded; the rains and sun of eighty years have worn and warped it, and nothing has been repainted or retouched.

A wind swept by. On this early winter day, a few black branches of the trees thrust out like stiff, dead fingers. No birds could be heard; for a few minutes nothing moved in the hazy light. It took a little while to circle the eight-sided building. Everywhere the eye met the same gray combination, over-embellishment and drabness, the rococo and the desolate. How different from the scene Haller Nutt planned—the voices of his grandchildren echoing, the movements of servants, lights in the tower and windows. At the back, a great oak grows from a mound, sinking serpentine roots into the soil. Successive rains have washed away much of the soil, and the mottled bark is exposed like leprous hands upon the earth. At this point Haller Nutt planned a summer house; now there is only the rustling of dry leaves.

As I knocked at the rear basement door, the rap had a hollow echo. A half-seen animal stirred, then crept around the corner. Suddenly a little man, grayed and with the expression of a leprechaun, looked out. He opened the door with a grin. The basement breathed dampness; under the circumstances it has been impossible to keep ceiling plaster from falling in spots. Here in a cracked frame, hung an oil of Haller Nutt, white-vested and dignified; another of his blonde wife, the lady who had to be pleased, and a last one of two Nutt daughters. Like so much else here, the last portrait was incomplete, the background roughly sketched in.

Above, we stared into the framework of those higher stories, a mass of raw timber and scaffolding. Over the planking at the sides, we followed a precarious path, past empty niches, along boards that led to the balconies outside. It was chilly; a wind swept from below, and through chinks in the boards pattered a few drops of rain. Parts of the ornate designs had fallen away; several brackets clutter the path. We thrust our heads out of a window; the steeple which formerly surmounted the bulbous dome was riddled by woodpeckers and dropped off many years ago. Where the front marble stairway would have been there was a wide gap. The family had no chance to put in a substitute; and was there any need for one—stairs that ended in blank space?

To the rear, stands a two-and-a-half story brick house, in which the family waited while Nutt's Folly went up. It is as simple as the master house is ornate. Resuming our climb inside, I felt a sense of loss and desolation. The interior seems like a back-stage scene of unpainted boarding. In the dimming light, we came to a room that made us halt, a chamber that sums up all the frustration of this establishment. At this point the artisans were laboring when word of war arrived. Here, beneath the scaffolding, is a brush, dropped to the floor, and the last smear of paint made by it; and a pot, another brush thrust into it and left in the congealed liquid, which has since then cracked into fragments. Cobwebs drop in long strands, and over a carpenter's wooden horse hangs a discarded pair of overalls. In the nearly ninety years that have gone by, the garment has begun to ravel apart and rot, but it yet bears marks of green paint that the wearer rubbed into it on that day of nervous departure.

Here, in one quick moment, is the story of what happened when the cannons pounded at Fort Sumter. Afterward, things were never quite the same. It was dark as I bade goodby to the descendant of the Nutts who serves also as Longwood's caretaker. He joked about the ghosts that hang over the place, "little things that climb in the trees like monkeys." If ghosts climb anywhere like monkeys, it must be at Nutt's Folly. In a slow drizzle, stumbling over the snaky roots of the trees, I beat a retreat. From the road, I glanced back; no light was visible, only the ornate black bulk of the Folly, faintly ominous, in a wind that whined of what might have been.

COTTAGE GARDENS

{XVIII}

THE *NATCHEZ* AND THE ROBERT E. LEE

THE crew and officers of one of the tinseled river steamers had been noticing something they could not explain. In one of the best cabins, nearly two months earlier, an elderly, jovial-mannered individual had taken passage at Natchez. Arriving at New Orleans, he announced that he would not get off, but remain until they reached St. Louis. At St. Louis he gave notice that he would stay on until they arrived back in New Orleans; and so it went.

The old fellow wasn't a gambler; that they knew, because they could spot the brotherhood a vessel's length away. He wasn't a thief or a murderer; he smiled along, talking, offering cigars, buying toddies, sitting around with the rest of the passengers. Still, they were disturbed by this phenomenon. Finally the captain had to do something. With several mumbled apologies, he brought up the subject.

His guest's answer became historic. "Of course, sir, I'll tell you. It's the finest way to pleasure myself that I know. No hotel in America can equal this. The finest food—your wild game, your glazed fish, your roasts, sauces and pastry!" The gourmet purred. "My cabin—it's as finely equipped, as well decorated, as any room I've enjoyed in my life. The bar, the cabin, the promenade—nothing to match 'em, I tell you. And the company! I meet all my friends, the best people in the world. Why should I want to leave?"

The captain, pink with pride, bought the man a drink. The incident went the rounds, but the explanation brought little surprise. Everybody agreed the man was right.

Steamboat days, steamboat people, glory on the river . . . there never were such days, such glories, before or after. To the Natchezians they brought an aura, a drama that nothing could approach. What could be more magnificent than a white packet, slipping up the river as gracefully as some pale bird in the darkness? Men's eyes misted, their throats caught—and their fingers itched to make a bet. Any kind of bet would do, about any kind of steamboat—speed, capacity, number of firemen below, age of the pilot. A foreigner, or a Yankee, could be killed for implying that a river packet was anything less than the peak of man's constructive arts; and most river-border dwellers would agree that, by damn, he deserved it.

The first steamboat slipped into Natchez in 1811—Nicholas J. Roosevelt's *New Orleans*. (Mrs. Roosevelt made the trip, shocking the conventionalists.) By the '30s they were approaching their true splendor. Year by year they grew more richly bedecked, faster, more glorious in gilt and velvet, plush and ornamented spittoons. They survived the Civil War and seemed for a time on their way to yet greater heights. The railroads were making deep inroads; but for several decades enough traffic remained to permit the steamboat owners to elaborate, placing wonder atop wonder.

A swimming volcano they called the river steamboat; Babylon's daughter, a bride decked out for her wedding, said the yet more flowery. Like some women, Babylonian or otherwise, they were as dangerous as they were alluring. A steamboat's life was brief—a few years and it was worn out, burned up, or otherwise useless. It stuck on sandbars, it collided with other vessels, it sank or, in all too many cases, it simply exploded. Repeatedly, these explosions occurred in races with rivals.

The outer design had little variation—always the two tall smoke stacks, ending in feathery trimming at the top; the big wheel-houses, holding the paddle-wheels which might be three to four stories high; wide decks for heavy produce from cotton bales to mules, and for deck passengers who rode in the open; and the great name painted in black letters, with a vividly hued scene, or a castle, a setting sun, a giant face. When you used the word steamboat you implied cotton; a few could carry as many as six thousand bales, piled tier on tier up to the hurricane deck, hiding practically everything else. In such cases a steamboat looked like one vast pile of cotton, and it sank so low in the water that some were afraid to go on.

The cabin was a sight to make the unsophisticated halt—long vistas of white walls, plush curtains, thick carpets, rows of chandeliers tinkling in the light motion of the vessel. Oil paintings hung on the walls, statues rested on pedestals, and mirrors reflected flattering images of men and women amid these luxuries. In the vast dining rooms, tables stretched so far that those at one end barely made out friends at the other; and between them rose mountains of food, garlands of flowers, bright-colored ices and desserts in patterns that the lady passengers tried to imitate at home.

There were saloons, barrooms, barber shops, women's cabins, private suites, private rooms for card games—practically anything a hotel could claim, except a garden—and the potted ferns made up for that. State-room doors had floral patterns, hand-painted. A number of steamboat captains offered bridal suites as their specialties, all pink and blue with painted cupids chasing across the walls. The planters talked crops over their gin fizzes; children ran up and down the white stairways under the eyes of governesses; matrons folded their hands and kept a hawk's view over the behavior of all who passed before them, while their sons and daughters strolled arm in arm about the decks.

On some vessels twenty to thirty stewards remained on regular duty. Bands played in the big rooms, and also blared out serenades to Natchez, Vicksburg and other towns at which stops were made. But one thing above all a steamboat had, and that was white filigree trimming, outside, in, wherever the designer found a spot to stick it on.

To service a big steamboat for a trip took the produce of a dairy, the supplies of a farm; the best grades of meat to be found in four or five market places, a fair portion of the output of ice plants, coal yards and wood yards. The best of everything, sir; nothing inferior for a river packet. Part of it was the captain's vanity, the other part a matter of showmanship. The trade tended to go where it received a good show and a full stomach.

On the larger packets the chef and his assistants had to be adept; frequent passengers became connoisseurs. They expected perfection, prepared with imagination, executed with a flourish. Let quality suffer, and they would be talking about it up and down the river. At the table there was no restriction on the amount a man was allowed; he might eat all day long without a stop provided his stomach held up. If he wanted five helpings of smothered robins or teal ducks, he could have them; if he indicated a liking for three dishes of blanc mange with jellied peaches on the side, they were his. Service had a fillip. Waiters glistened and bent low; chambermaids, usually mulatto, were trained in all the delicate arts of assistance to the ladies.

At the important landings, a wise captain took steps to maintain a boat's repute. In each case, one or two waiters slipped ashore, head high, with trays so heavily laden that they could hardly be carried. These held polished fruit, frozen creams, rare confections for the ladies, all to be handed about with a flourish, "courtesy of the Captain." For the planters the captain sent out a neatly folded newspaper from a town in which they were interested, and an invitation to step on board and have one with him. The vessel might be behind schedule; sticklers might fret at the delay, but the captain and his associates must exchange full compliments, sip and sample cigars. And the captain was ready to do favors for any customer. He would take orders for ice, cakes or cocoanut, have them filled at a store in town and drop them off on the next trip. (If the captain maintained his own discount arrangements with the stores, that was his own business.)

On and on the system went, showing little decline even in the years that immediately followed the war. The boats grew more superb, and the races more heated. Perhaps surprisingly to some, it was not until 1870 that the river saw the greatest steamboat competition of all time, and the most exciting, the contest of giants—the *Natchez* against the *Robert E. Lee*. That race in turn meant, above all other things, the man Tom Leathers, Captain Tom of the *Natchez*.

Hardly anything that walked the earth could compete for dramatic importance with the steamboat captain. He was lord, tyrant, temperamental monarch, a man of gracious favor for those he liked, of thundering contempt for those he disliked. It was no wonder that he was pointed out on the street, that children gaped and matrons thrilled at this symbol of male power rampant; that nearly everyone else looked on him as God's right hand helper. He had largesse at his command, a carpet of wonders; he strode about with the assurance of a banker, the temperament of an opera star.

Tom Leathers was probably the steamboat captain of all steamboat captains. He adopted Natchez as his own, loving her with all the fervor of his explosive soul; after her he named a succession of seven majestic barks. Tom Leathers was a man of height, with girth and bulk to match. He stood nearly six feet four in his big bare feet, and he weighed two hundred and seventy pounds. His locks and curling, flowing white moustache stayed in place to the last hair; his costume, sheer flawless whites with white hat or dark, expensive black with black hat, was practically a uniform. He carried a cigar almost as if it were a baton, and his blue eyes changed from smiling agreement to raging command. A man of extremes, he ranged between overflowing generosity and Jovian fury. It is only fair to add that the river people varied similarly in their attitude toward him; they either admired him extravagantly or they wouldn't set foot on one of his boats.

Captain Tom had a manner with ladies and his big planter friends that was so heavy and courtly it seemed almost a caricature. Among roustabouts and crew members, he was hailed as the "best curser on the Mississippi." His mastery of invective had a phenomenal breadth and versatility. In five minutes, it was said, he could shrivel any man, without repeating a single oath. Once he is supposed to have asked a friend, in all seriousness, "What's the use of being a steamboat captain if you can't tell the world to go to hell?"

And did the Captain pick a great house to match his size and inclination? He selected, instead, a small gem in the town of Natchez itself, almost a baby-scaled version of the plantation type. Situated at Pearl and High Streets, Myrtle Terrace had the charm of the diminutive and the restrained—everything that the Captain was not. Slightly raised, it stood a story high with half floor above, and three dormers projecting through the sloping roof. Six slim colonnettes stretched across the front gallery, with wooden railings between, and a wide outer stairway led to a rectangular doorway with side- and over-head lights. At the front an ornate little iron fence topped a brick base. A skilful architect had built it, and it had exactly what the Captain demanded.

When Myrtle Terrace was built none knows, but it was standing in 1844 when the Carpenter family of Dunleith acquired it. Ten years later Tom Leathers took it. In the transaction he showed a practical touch that the river people well recognized. His agreement, as Mrs. Edith Wyatt Moore noted, declared that the house must be placed in the best of condition, and he set specifications to the ultimate detail—a carriage house, spic and span; a stable to be put up for him, blinds on all windows except dormers, latches, cellar-door fastenings and even hinges.

The Captain was a Kentuckian of Kenton County, born in 1816. He had an elder brother, Jim, who lacked Tom's gusto, being merely a colorful individual. As a schoolboy Tom yearned after a life on the river; at twenty he was on it, riding between New Orleans and Natchez, shifting from one vessel to the next, learning to know the Mississippi as he did the palm of his hand. To be Captain of a big boat, one had to be a business man, a shrewd and efficient one; the Captain was "making his contacts," acquiring connections and capital. By the 1840s he was erecting the first of his series of boats called *Natchez*; with his first wife he was beginning to build up his family. She died, and the widower went to the Natchez country for a second bride, one of the high-placed Claibornes, the same family that gave Mississippi its early territorial governor.

Again, Tom Leathers chose something small. In her teens or just out of them, the girl was as short as he was tall; her weight sometimes reached one hundred pounds, but not often. She was as gentle as he was imperious, and she had rare tact. Tom Leathers presided at home in the same grand style, almost as grand anyway, as he showed on the water. He wished everyone at home at a certain hour, to the dot. (He was that way with his steamboat departures.) The children were expected to eat every item of food, or tell the Captain why. (On his boats, sometimes, the Captain grew miffed if his guests did not show the proper delight over his delicacies.) He saw that the cuisine at home matched that on his vessels, in quality and bulk. And every day that strawberries were in season, the Captain liked them before him in heaping bowls. Before he signaled to the butler to pass them, he went through a rite. Over each bowl he sliced and squeezed the biggest lemon that he could get; and not once did he omit his remark: "This brings out the flavor, you know." A guest who did not enjoy a lemon taste did not eat Leathers strawberries. Every once in a while the Captain began to roar at home; only then did the serene little wife intervene. She said only two words: "Now, Tom," but they had more decision in them than even the Captain's flow. He became silent immediately.

The Captain could unbend, and the Natchezians tell dozens of stories of his generosity. A widow in difficulty found him ready to help, with hardly a question in advance. Let a sick child or an injured man appear, and he would drop everything to assist. One case among many tells how a woman approached him at the Natchez landing. Her husband was very ill in a little Ohio town; she had only a dollar or two. The captain bowed and removed a male passenger from a room to make space for her; when they arrived upriver, he paid her transportation from Cincinnati to the inland point and back to the river, where he picked her up with the husband and saw that they arrived home. More than that, the Captain was known to be, if properly approached, the softest of touches.

He built so many vessels called Natchez that, half affectionately, half derisively, the river experts nicknamed him Pushmataha, after the Indian chief who was a friend of Andy Jackson. (People still remembered Natchez' Indian origin.) On the wheelhouse of his vessels he painted a figure of a mighty Indian in war-paint and feathers. Whenever he was in a race, it is claimed, the Captain would have an artist do a little extra work, so that Pushmataha-on-the-wheelhouse had his tomahawk lifted!

The Captain seemed always in a fight, trying to cut a rival's time, dropping rates, or bankrupting his opposition. Part of it was sheer bravado, or truculence; the rest, horse-sense. The public wanted steamboat captains that way; it wanted fireworks, and Tom Leathers could provide them. He liked to crowd other boats, using a trick to take an advantage—the sudden dropping of a tub of lard into the boilers for an unexpected spurt, the crossing of another's path by a sharp maneuver at a river bend. He was known to fire his cannon across the bow of another, for no reason except to irk a competitor and put on a show for the gallery. There was little, then, in the way of established rules of courtesy, safety or fair trade practices. Tom Leathers enjoyed delaying his departure, deliberately, to let another leave ahead of him. Then he would catch up, pass it and hear the crowd cry its appreciation. The trade went to the man who made the big splash.

On went the line of Leathers' *Natchezes*, each more richly embellished than its predecessor. No. 3 was in commission less than six weeks when it burned at New Orleans in a fire that took a dozen vessels; Tom Leathers' brother Jim, asleep in his room, was killed. The fourth *Natchez* came a few years later, then in 1859 arrived the fifth, perhaps the most heavily ornate of all. His vessels always pictured Indian life but this one went to unusual lengths for its effects. In rich reds, yellows and blues, the cabin skylights showed a series of panoramas, "The War Dance," "Smoking the Pipe of Peace," "The Hunter Returns to His Family" and many more. Wall panelings, draperies, even some of the gilt work was supposed to look Indian. It all had a sad fate. Ever a rigid Confederate, Tom Leathers was in New Orleans as the city was about to fall to the Unionists. To save his *Natchez* from capture, he took her upriver near Yazoo City and tied her up, then helped the Confederates take her expensive machinery and use it for war purposes. The Federals learned of his attitude, and ultimately they were accused of smashing his proud boat almost to nothing. For years after the war, the Captain waged a warm legal fight with the government; now and then he received a favorable verdict, but collected little. The situation hardly improved his feeling for the North.

During the war, when matters quieted a bit, Mrs. Leathers decided that she wished to live in New Orleans. The great captain, ever devoted to Natchez and his Myrtle Terrace, said No. He would never move; he was settled there for all time!

And so the quiet Mrs. Leathers soon had him packing his things, and he sold Myrtle Terrace in favor of a more extensive establishment in the Creole city. But the Captain returned to Natchez at every chance, to survey the field and swap yarns with his friends.

War's end brought a temporary upsurge for the steamboats. Tom Leathers stepped forward as before, inspecting the trade from beneath his shaggy brows. Somewhat older, he grew hardly more mellow. It was the Leathers of this day who drew the description: "the Eagle of his Tribe, with war paint in his words if not on his face, and a tomahawk in his logic." For years he had been proclaiming himself cock of the run between New Orleans and Natchez. In 1855 he had made the distance upriver in seventeen hours and thirty minutes. At his Natchez wharfboat he nailed up a great pair of buckhorns, painted the time below them, and challenged the world: "Take Them if You can."

Now, suddenly, there was tension. Captain John W. Cannon, like Tom Leathers, was a Kentuckian. Several times he had been the victim of Leathers' contemptuous tactics. His boat, the *Robert E. Lee*, was launched in 1866. Three years later the newest *Natchez* came along and everybody said the two were rather evenly matched. Most people felt that the *Lee*, though slightly smaller, was not a delicate, graceful boat; she appeared to thrust her bow deep in the water, struggling and straining, with a great swell. The *Natchez* cut through the river like a sharp finger, with hardly a ripple. But now here was the *Lee*, making new, ever-quicker runs. Tom Leathers made several disparaging gestures toward John Cannon. The newspapers, scenting excitement, carried tales back and forth, touching the captains' pride by provocative items. Then the die was cast. There'd be a race. By God, said each man, he'd show 'im! On June 30, 1870, the two vessels were scheduled to leave New Orleans for St. Louis. That would be it.

The nation pricked up its ears; so did part of Europe. Word

spread with fantastic rapidity; no such event in history ever had such an audience. Men were betting, punching, now and then stabbing one another in arguments over the matter. The *Lee* didn't have a chance! No, the *Natchez* was the goner! At the exclusive clubs, on the Natchez plantation porches, gentlemen swapped opinions over brandies. In the drawing rooms their wives stopped sewing to debate. At the Mansion House in Natchez, in New Orleans' French Quarter, the subject was talked among longshoremen, schoolteachers and stable-attendants. In New York, Philadelphia, Boston, St. Louis, Memphis, the money piled high; millions began to change hands. In London and Paris purses accumulated. Great newspapers arranged for telegraphic coverage; several did the unusual feat of sending correspondents to New Orleans for the start.

The day neared. Opinions changed, odds fluctuated. Men claimed that the *Natchez* was faster on a clear run; but her heaviness meant she lost time whenever she stopped. Others were sure that, no matter what the differences, Tom Leathers wouldn't lose. He just couldn't. Captain Cannon had little to say, but shortly before the big day he performed drastic operations on his boat. His men stripped her of every excess foot, even inch, of timber. Off came the boxing of her wheels, her chains and anchors, windows, doors, spars, cattle dunnage, beds, tables, chairs, chandeliers, even heavy curtains and oil paintings! Anything went that might hinder the *Lee's* swift passage through water and along the winds. The air would race through what now looked like a broken crate, kept afloat by a prayer. The Captain, it was said, took along only one extra pair of drawers; anything more might help slow them up.

Further, Captain Cannon rejected freight and passengers. He wanted no extra pound of any kind; he wanted no stops that the bare necessities did not require. At the end, he had to take on a few who were to get off at Cairo; that was all. Tom Leathers, learning of it all, gave a laugh, and waved a hand. He'd haul up any freight, anybody who wanted to ride;

and he wouldn't rip away his boat that way. In spite of it, he'd win! As a taunt in the direction of his opponent, he even announced he would accept all the freight and passengers the *Lee* passed up. He added to his revenues and annexed some of the *Lee's* regular customers. But meanwhile both captains took on heavy assortments of pine, resin, candles, tubs of lard, pitch and even discarded bacon fat; and they arranged, as was customary in races, to have coal barges ready along the river. Both were deadly earnest.

The morning arrived. Though the event was not scheduled to start until 5 P.M., a mass of spectators appeared at dawn, pushing and pulling for favored positions at the harbor. As the pale sunlight hit the filigree work at the top of the pairs of smokestacks, still more people crowded the bars and coffee-houses near the waterfront. Canal Street was packed tight. The mass thickened, darkening the decks of other steamers, crowding the ledges of every building within range of the harbor.

On board the *Lee* and the *Natchez*, the two captains stepped quickly about, Cannon in cold-eyed seriousness, Leathers bluff and self-sure. At five, a boom rang out. Catching his rival by surprise for once, Cannon shot his *Lee* out on the exact stroke. A stream of heavy black smoke lifted into the air, then trailed behind as the *Lee* backed out, rounded to and tore away. Shouts and screams rose. A little less than five minutes later, the *Natchez* slipped off, and thousands of onlookers yelled as she chugged after the other. Along the harbor thousands of pairs of eyes followed them for miles. Twenty-four miles upriver the *Lee* still led, by four minutes and 40 seconds. Crowds made out both vessels, shining like animated boxes, showers of sparks flying in their trail as they forged ahead. At regular points on the levee watchers stood nervously, instruments in hand, then ran to the telegraph stations. At Baton Rouge, nearly 140 miles upriver, a message ticked out. The *Lee*, 1:28 A.M.; the *Natchez*, 1:38. The *Lee* was gaining!

Below decks Tom Leathers stalked around, raging. What was the matter with them all? More of that fat pine; faster, nigger! The firemen, naked to the waist, their bodies almost scorched in the heat, wiped the sweat away and jumped into action. Bells rang, the engines beat relentlessly. The wash of the paddles rose in their ears, as the big vessel seemed to pant with the exertion. Outside, sparks were falling into the water with a hiss. Paint cracked on the deck, and now and then flames licked out of the red-hot stacks. Still Tom Leathers fretted. A whiskey bucket was slapped down, with a tin cup, for everybody knew that made a crew work faster. In spite of it, the *Lee* gained more and more.

A barrel of resin was tossed in, and a new roar shook the boat. But Tom Leathers, despite his anger, was mumbling that he wasn't going to wreck his ship, run it so hard that the boilers would blow up, or have a black man sit on the safety valve the way some did. He would win, but alive, and with his boat intact. And he was carrying out practically his normal schedule, stopping to drop men and freight. Yet it wasn't quite the usual scene. The roustabouts scurried on and off with unprecedented speed, using hardly a waste motion, leaping back with wild excitement. Anybody who didn't run right on again would be left behind.

The observers' pulses quickened. Slowly, the *Natchez* was gaining! The imponderables, certain small points of supremacy, were beginning to tell. With every few miles she was cutting down the margin, to three quarters of an hour, a half hour, twenty minutes. If only this kept up. . . . Just ahead, Captain Cannon was tearing at his nails. He wanted the *Natchez*, far, far behind him. Still, he had a few surprises for the old buzzard Leathers; they'd find out. . . . Natchezians rose the next morning and packed the land below the hill, the roadway along the cliff, the edges of the bluff. This was Tom Leathers' town, and it waited to acclaim him. At some time before ten A.M., a man with a spyglass cried: Smoke down there, around the furthest bend! Excitement lifted. There was the first vessel, then the other, just a little behind! A sad cry rose. The *Lee*, not the *Natchez*, was leading.

An old man, at that time a boy, tells the story: "It was a bad time for us. We were running behind. I stood on shore, watching with the rest, and some people looked like they were crying. But it was such a grand sight, the two boats so close together, and straining with every inch, that we couldn't stay downcast. As the enemy boat came up, we had to shout." But they soon lost their delight. Captain Cannon was ready for one of the triumphs of his life. Standing on the hurricane deck, he ordered the *Lee* to steam in toward Leathers' wharf, where the buck antlers, symbol of Leathers' mastery of the run, stood out in the sunlight. "Take down those horns!" his hoarse cry cut through a sudden silence. He had beaten Leathers' old time record to Natchez, making it in 17 hours and 11 minutes, against Leathers' previous 17 and 30. One of the Lee's officers snatched the horns, and the vessel puffed out. The *Lee* lost minutes by the stop; the *Natchez* berthed there only six minutes later. The race was tightening.

But North of Natchez, the river current had a stronger surge, and experts felt that the lighter, ripped-down *Lee* would make greater headway. They were right. On the course to Vicksburg, the *Lee* gained, coming in sixteen minutes ahead. Just above Vicksburg, Cannon provided his greatest surprise—a controversial stunt. The steamer *Frank Pargaud*, heavily powered, every foot of space packed with pine, resin and other supplies, waited in midstream. The *Lee* let out a blast; the *Pargaud* slipped into a direct line with the racer; the *Lee* slackened while the roustabouts tied the vessels together, then it pulled full speed ahead. The *Pargaud* kept her own engines working, to help the *Lee*, giving it extra engine power during the loading. The Negroes worked at raging speed, then the ropes were slashed, and the *Lee* ripped ahead. It had gained many minutes by the maneuver.

At Memphis the day of July 2 became a holiday. As evening approached, hundreds of fires were lighted. A newspaper reported that "Even the women are out in force, infants in arms—to bet off, probably, since horses, houses and clothes already have been staked." Shortly before 11 P.M. the *Lee* steamed close; an hour passed before the *Natchez* puffed in. On they sped toward Cairo, to be hailed by men standing and waving flags, blowing horns, waving bottles. The *Picayune* correspondent described this part of the race: "As we steamed along . . . the whole country on both sides of the river seemed alive with a strange excitement, expressed in the waving of handkerchiefs and hats, and running along the shore as if to encourage the panting steamer; and now and then far-off shouts came cheeringly over the water, and were plainly heard above the roaring of the fires, the clattering of the machinery, the splashing of the water, and the escape of steam."

But at Cairo Cannon and his *Lee* came suddenly close to rasping failure. He slowed up, to unload the few passengers he had taken along. Exultant, the Captain ordered drinks for everybody; jigs were danced, kisses and handshakes exchanged. He could afford a breather; the *Natchez* was way behind. All at once something ground below them, and the whole vessel trembled. They were stuck tight on a sandbar! Cannon ran out to direct operations; everyone on deck caught his breath, and some said prayers. Three minutes passed, five, six, as the pilot maneuvered, running wheels in reverse, trying every method of shaking loose. Then, with a slow groan, the *Lee* succeeded, and Cannon let out a breath of relief. A little later, as they went on again, a startling signal reached them. The *Natchez* had been sighted; old Leathers had gained amazingly on them!

Once more the two vessels were within sight of one another, and tempers ran high. On they pushed; every time he looked back, Cannon made out the smoke that told him how close Leathers was keeping after him. Then Cannon's eyes contracted. Just ahead in the late evening there floated a puff of gray, that grew wider as they watched. Fog. Wetting their lips, he and the pilot stared up the river. It got worse, swirling before them, behind, to both sides, until they had only a little margin. Midnight had passed. The men exchanged apprehensive looks. Wouldn't they have to stop? They were courting disaster to run through this soup. . . . Behind them Tom Leathers bit at the ends of his white moustaches, and thought hard. Then he turned: "Tie 'er up! I'm not crazy."

But John Cannon shook his head. They'd keep right on. Leadsmen were stationed to sound the river as they slipped ahead. For long, tense minutes they felt their way. Once or twice, in this gray mystery of fog, they appeared about to strike something, escaping disaster by inches. They couldn't keep this up forever; the men's nerves would crack. Suddenly, after an hour, the pilot shouted the good word. Fog going up! Quickly it dissipated, and the night stretched dark and beautiful ahead. Behind them, the *Natchez* lay idle at the bank, for six hours.

After that, none doubted who would come first. At St. Louis on the Fourth of July, and along the river below, the people stirred in the stages of final exultation. Railroad locomotives tooted, guns boomed, church bells rang. "The whole of St. Louis had turned out to welcome the champion of all champions in the greatest race that had ever been run on the Father of Waters," wrote John Coleman. It was 11:25 A.M. The *Lee* had made it—three days, 18 hours and 14 minutes. So many pushed onto her decks that she nearly overturned.

At 6 P.M. Tom Leathers and the *Natchez* pulled in, to receive almost as warm a reception, and that night the captains were thumped and toasted for all they were worth. But even now, Tom Leathers insisted he had not lost. Deducting the hours he had laid up in the fog and other delays, he figured that his time was better than Cannon's. Generally in America the bets were paid in Cannon's favor; but thousands asserted that the victory could not be termed a clear-cut one. In Europe most wagers were called off on the grounds that the stripping of the *Lee* and the use of the *Pargaud* in loading vio-

LONGWOOD
Oriental Delusion, with Eight Sides

EARL M. NORMAN

STEAMBOAT GLORY SHOWED ON THE INSIDE, TOO
J. M. WHITE

ON TOWARD NATCHEZ-ON-THE-MISSISSIPPI

lated the normal standards. Today, among a dwindling few in Natchez, you can still get up a strong argument on the score. Tom Leathers has never lost his supporters.

The Captain carried on, building more vessels with the name of Natchez, enjoying a lion's life, drawing bows and cheers whenever he stepped ashore in his favorite town. There were more races, and these he won, but none ever took the attention of the one in which, for once, he dropped behind. On his eightieth birthday Tom Leathers died at New Orleans in an ironic accident; a hit-and-run bicyclist struck him, leaving the Captain lying on the street. In modern Natchez tokens of him are to be found—decorations from his steamers, mementos of trips made under the eye of the white-haired tyrant. A rural church is proud of a chandelier from one of his wrecked boats. His Myrtle Terrace, for which he cared as earnestly as he did his steamers, looks prim and proper behind its iron fence in its neat landsman's setting. Mr. and Mrs. McVey Butler own it, and there appear scant hints of the booming Tom Leathers. But wherever there are older Natchezians and memories, the Captain remains.

THE ELMS

XIX

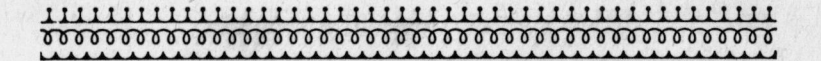

GOAT CASTLE

For four young people of the town, the future had a golden cast, in those days of the 1880s and '90s—an easy security, the probability of marriage, perhaps the fame that follows a high talent. As the four rode about, light-mannered, in casual survey of their scene, the less well-to-do watched them in approval or in envy. What they did mattered because of what they were, and what they counted for.

Forty years later, one couple stood against the other, a corroding hate and bitterness between them, for the rest of of the world only a cold contempt. Somewhere they had lost their path, wandering away from the life and the ways of most others, to move in twilight existences of their own. Their careers crossed at intervals; when they met, they turned aside, lips compressed in fury. Each couple knew that they were being pointed out, giggled over, as peep shows for the irreverent. Their former friends exchanged glances, unspoken questions in their faces. How had it happened?

Then, early on a sultry August evening, along the path of the ancient Natchez Trace that had witnessed innumerable acts of violence, a series of shots rang across a shadowed gallery, and there was a woman's cry of terror. After that, in an explosive fashion that drew the notice of the nation, the story came out, or most of it. There are parts that have never been clarified, that probably never will be.

Jane Surget Merrill was born to the rank of Natchez princess. She was the granddaughter of Frank Surget the First, great-granddaughter of "Sir William" Dunbar. Her mother was a Surget, her father Ayers P. Merrill II, a bland and easy-going son of a well-to-do doctor. With Ayers' bride, some years before the Civil War, came a sumptuous present, Elmscourt, a firmly-built house erected in 1810. The Merrills gave the building a considerable elaboration, to make it different in appearance from any in Natchez. The railings and gallery posts were replaced by an imported framework of iron, in a heavy pattern of grapes, with arches instead of pillars, fretwork at the roof line. It was a house of great width, the central section two storied, with double galleries above and below, and single-level wings at each side. Thick vines climbed along the ironwork patterns; from this cool retreat the Merrill children looked upon a society that bowed before them.

Jane, or Jennie, was a small, dark girl who dominated her playmates. They did what Jennie wanted; she chose the games, she called the turn. Across the back of Elmscourt, another long iron-ornamented gallery led to a terraced sunken garden, tier on tier extending to a many-hued rose garden, bordered by lattice-work. Near the steps the family put up a doll house that became Jennie's "favorite place." About this doll home, with miniature lantern and shelves for her toys, the child spent her early days.

Ayers Merrill II fitted the part of a plantation master. Suave, cultivated, he was a handsome man with small features, narrow moustache, heavy shoulders which he held with careful erectness. His quiet wife showed her affection in every glance. At his best with a houseful of guests, Ayers gave soirees that made Elmscourt a gay-spirited spot. From the thickly-planted rose gardens the servants brought blossoms to be twined about the ironwork; over doorways and windows lines of candles were lighted, and every room glowed for Elmscourt's "balls of a thousand candles."

Jennie and her six brothers and sisters grew up with the recollections of scores of such fetes, the rustle of satins, the lift and fall of feathered fans, all glimpsed from posts of vantage at the head of the stairs. They traveled, making long calls on relatives; they learned the graces from one tutor after another. They had a shining example in their urbane father, "dancing through life," as a descendant puts it.

Yet sometimes the dance had off-key notes. Ayers Merrill counted himself a Union man during the war, to the anger of several neighbors. At one time, shortly after the war's end, threats of barn-burning were made. Ayers was a friend of U. S. Grant; in 1876 the President made him Minister to Belgium, a post obviously to his taste. By now Mrs. Merrill had died; the widower shepherded his well-mannered seven to Brussels. The girls, Jennie in particular, never forgot the scenes of regal life, the King's receptions, champagne and flowers. About this time young Jennie, in her teens, was presented at the Court of St. James. She had developed into a girl of unquestioned loveliness—tiny, weighing little over a hundred pounds, with olive skin and dark hair in ringlets about her lively face. She saw one of her sisters marry happily on the Continent; the years stretched ahead, with high promise for Jennie, the small queen of the Merrills.

Minister Merrill, falling ill, had to resign; before long the family returned to Elmscourt. There the house stood, little changed behind its highly decorated facade; there, unhurt in the court behind the house, waited Jennie's doll house, and she cried to see it again. The old life started once more, and for a time the younger set clustered about Elmscourt. To the drawing room came a couple who appeared unusually sympathetic, Dick Dana and Octavia Dockery. The idealistic son of the Episcopal rector, Charles Bachus Dana, Dick descended from the same family as Editor Charles S. Dana of New York and the artist Charles Dana Gibson. Before arriving in Natchez, his father, a highly-regarded minister, had been for years in charge of Christ Church in Alexandria, Virginia.

Some of the girls thought young Richard over-solemn, though many felt this quality went well with his long, high-arched nose and his sensitive lips. The ascetic type, he was much to the liking of those brought up on Sir Walter Scott. He went to Vanderbilt, where he won high honors; he had studied music, and played the piano so well it was understood he would eventually go on the concert stage. In the Natchez drawing rooms Dick played for the company, bowing happily at the applause, flushing at the predictions of a grand career.

The girl who sat near him, the beautiful Miss Dockery, seemed like Dick in several ways. Her father was the Confederate General, Thomas Payne Dockery of Arkansas; she had studied in New York, and graduated. She was a girl of contemplative manner, slim and fine-featured, red-haired, with eyes that could burn with poetic feeling. Before me I have a picture of Octavia at twenty-three, a belle if ever one posed for a cameraman. The hourglass figure shows firm arms and white throat; a furred cape is draped carelessly over one shoulder. (The gown came from Worth of Paris.)

Octavia Dockery liked to "do things," often surprising things. She wore her titian hair in unconventional styles, almost a boyish manner close to her head, or hanging loose at her back. She became one of the first Natchez women to ride astride a horse, scorning the side saddle; and there she went, the flame of her hair streaming behind her. Gifted, she wrote poems and articles, and editors sent highly encouraging comment—freshly written, a brilliant career ahead.

Octavia did articles on unfinished Longwood, "Nutt's Folly," its dome seen through a "tangled forest," and Gloucester, "standing grim in the shade of handsome trees and past recollections, a veritable Bleak House with its air of mystery and secrets." Again, the New Orleans *Picayune* ran one of her poems, "Ignus Fatuus," telling of a "beauteous maiden" "dancing on the stream of life," and asking if she sought a far-away light, "always luring, called happiness." It ended with a warning against this beguiling light, this "vanity of wishes deathless." Certainly Octavia, moving from ball to ball, could think of herself as dancing on life's stream. Between parties, she sat often with her friend Dick Dana, talking of poetry and things romantic and distant, and of their ambitions. He would be the celebrated musician, touring the continents, she the poetess, her words quoted, her complete works in embossed volumes in all the libraries.

In the gardens of Elmscourt, where Jennie Merrill saw Dick and Octavia, there were still champagne and roses; and now, for the dominant little Jennie, there was love. More and more often there stood beside her a well-appointed youth, strong-faced, with high cheek bones that some thought a family trait—Duncan Minor, great-grandson of Stephen Minor, heir-potential to many acres, and a gallant of the hour. Jennie and "Dunc" had known each other from childhood and the first days of the doll house behind Elmscourt.... For this couple, as for Dick and Octavia, these were moments of impending fulfillment; all seemed bright in the best of all possible worlds.

And then the bubble burst. All four fell victim to economics, to family pride and misunderstanding. Their futures died before them, not in searing explosion, but in the slow rust of the years. Conditions were tightening; the wide cotton acres lay idle, or grew less and less productive. At Elmscourt the flow of the wine ended and the roses began to droop, as one terrace, then the other, was neglected. The family was dividing; Ayers Merrill III, succeeding the dead father, tried one thing, then another, but the situation developed against him. A mortgage in the hands of one of the Surgets fell due on handsome Elmscourt. A Surget daughter was to be married, and the Surgets took the house.

Between the Merrills and the Minors a feud broke out. Jennie and Dunc were cousins; an obvious fact known all along, but now, all at once, there were objections to their marrying; it would not be allowed. Both were of age, but estates were involved. Though financial conditions were bad, each should eventually fall heir to considerable land; and the threat of disinheritance was made.

Jennie, having left the house she had known best, lived alone, restlessly, unhappily. First she went to Glenwood, a big white house, to which Frederick Stanton of Stanton Hall had moved in his temporary bad times. Then she transferred to locked-up Gloucester, the old Winthrop Sargent place, the brooding Gloucester of which Octavia Dockery had written —the house of "mystery and secrets." Jennie occupied only part of it, shifting from room to room when leaks developed in the antique roof. Jennie Merrill, once presented to the Queen of England, now saw only the walls of a half-empty house that the neighboring children called haunted. With her it became a spot of new mystery, new secrets.

Gradually Miss Jennie was changing. At what precise point she turned her small feet in the direction of eccentricity, it is impossible to say. But she was seeing fewer of her friends; she accepted no invitations and paid scant heed to happenings about her. At times in the past, in her sharp, head-strong way, she had snapped at those who approached her, and her contemporaries had quavered at her temper. Now her face set in harsh lines; her manner sharpened. After a while whispers went that her door was shut to all except Duncan Minor. Eventually the nation's newspapers would carry the fact that Natchez understood: Every evening about dark, Duncan Minor got on his horse and rode to Miss Jennie, to be with her until dawn. Then he rode home, and rose a little later, to have breakfast with his mother—the mother who had forbidden his marriage to Jennie.

Certain Natchezians swear the couple married secretly in another state; they talk of a document regarding an inheritance, which she signed as Mrs. Duncan Minor. But she is supposed to have made Duncan promise that, no matter what happened, he would never reveal the wedding. They hadn't wanted them married, had they? Well . . . Duncan, too, was developing quirks. He changed from the gallant youth to a quiet, phlegmatic man, who lived much to himself, remote from anything that happened about him. Miss Jennie dominated him, as she had dominated nearly everyone else; if "Dunc" ever rebelled, none knew it. As far as Natchez could tell, the graying man with the high cheek-bones seemed content with life as it had shaped up for him.

And now Miss Jennie had made her last restless change of residence, to Glenburnie, a galleried establishment across the highway from Elmscourt, that iron-bordered place in which she had once lived so happily. Whenever she passed the entrance, where the roadway curved into the woods, Miss Jennie felt a surge of bitterness. She grew furious when people came up to her house, to ask where Elmscourt was. She put up a sign at Glenburnie, "No Admittance." To make her meaning clearer, she added: "MERRILL. Inquire Elsewhere for Persons of Other Names."

Now Miss Jennie had neighbors whom she had known in earlier days. Adjoining Glenburnie was Glenwood, where she had lived for a time; the two houses were separated by about three hundred yards, with a thicket between them. It became vacant and Dick Dana moved there. His father, the Episcopal rector, died and Dick received a fair estate. The house was a good one for the bookish son of the bookish father—mahogany and rosewood pieces, excellent library, busts of Dickens and Shakespeare, oil paintings of the rector on the wall. More and more Dick talked of his musical future, but he did nothing about it. As he lowered a window one day, the sash crashed down on his hand, ruining his fingers. Dick continued to play the piano, skipping notes or missing them; yet his hope of a career was over, and slowly Dick came to realize it.

His contemporaries began to notice funny things about Dick; the kindlier put them down to excitability. He stayed alone for days, agitated, or dreaming. He imagined that people were holding things against him. Sometimes he grew confused, forgetting where he walked, calling one friend by another's name. The young townsmen, after joshing Dick about his Galahad-like courtliness toward the girls, played a cruel joke. Gathering together, they stormed the house, swearing they represented a neighborhood maiden that Dick had wronged and must marry. Teeth chattering, Dick bolted up the stairs to the attic and through a trapdoor to the roof. There he stayed for two days, staring wildly in all directions. After that he seemed stranger than ever.

About this time someone else came to his house. On his friend Octavia Dockery, the quick-minded and independent Octavia, trouble had also fallen. Her father, the General, kept up appearances as long as he could, but his last years were dimmed. A sister helped for a time, but her husband died, and she could do little more. As for Octavia, the predictions of a glowing future had never been realized. Her clippings turned yellow, and finally she put them aside. The last of her Worth frocks fell away. Dick Dana visited frequently and even he saw their plight; he offered his hospitality to the last of the Dockerys. Townspeople called it a funny household at Glenwood; for his guests it provided a haven. After a time death left Octavia alone with Dick. Long years later, her eyes dulled, she explained that she had nowhere else to go, and so she stayed. The last flower had faded for the poetess. There was, she shrugged, "nothing between us, nothing at all."

Dick needed her guiding hand as much as she needed the security of his roof. He shied away from people; now he was taking to wandering for days in the woods. Sinking into a long "spell," he hid behind trees. Accustomed as she was to all this, Octavia gasped one day when she beheld him. Dick had dressed himself in potato sacking, punching holes in a bag and slipping it over his head for a suit. His matted hair falling in his eyes, he refused to change costume; he liked it that way, and so he moved in and out of the old plantation house. He stopped shaving, and a gray-brown beard hung over his scrawny chest. The face, once proud and remote, had a blurred expression, a blinking uncertainty. At Glenwood, Octavia sat alone, reading her books of poetry, trying to forget her cares. Neighborhood youths organized bands to hunt down the "wild man"; Dick would be caught in a tree, his bloodshot eyes staring in terror. Running to the scene, Octavia would chase the boys away and try to persuade him to come down.

She was aging, her red hair fading, her slim hands dark and twisted. By this time she had to do the housework. Hard days were catching up, too, with Dick Dana; no money came in, and they had used up what Rector Dana left. She must clean the large rooms, look after chickens and hogs, supervise the few Negro tenants who lived precariously in the worn quarters. All at once Dick was bringing cats and dogs and ducks to the house. When she protested, she got nowhere. A friend told him he had a lot of cats. Dick stared: "Only nineteen!"

In these days it was a question whether he would admit his identity. For weeks he walked, glassy-eyed, past his oldest friends. Pressed, he had an unvarying answer: "Sorry, I'm not Dick Dana; I'm R. S. Ament. Dick's up in New York, singing in Christ Church choir." Politely he would conclude: "Any message I can give? He'll be sorry he missed you." Frequently he took scant boxes of peaches to former companions. In one mood he was Dick Dana; in another he called himself R. S. Ament: "Dick asked me to take these to you."

The years crept by. The plantation house stood paintless, unrepaired. A pillar of the upper gallery fell, to lie untouched on the flooring; another followed it. The pair acquired a herd of goats for milk; after a while the goats were moving about the house, with the chickens, cats and ducks. Octavia grew yet more listless; or was she only more tired? In gingham dress and straw hat she looked like any sharecropper's wife. She couldn't do farm work and housework as well; they needed the farm income, and so the housework went. Hardly anything was touched—four poster beds, piano, sofas. Dick and Octavia, the pair who had once exchanged high thoughts in the candle-lit drawing rooms, sat across from each other, mute, the fragments of their lives about them.

Foolish people, or merely curious, harassed them, calling needlessly, to pry. Dick and Octavia resented that and showed it. After a time few dared approach the gullied grounds with their wild, forsaken look; it was whispered that Octavia had a gun and would shoot. Eventually the couple quarreled with Duncan Minor and Jennie Merrill. Dick Dana's shattered house sold for taxes, and Dunc bought it, or thought he did. By now, however, Dick was acting altogether too peculiarly; Octavia had him declared legally irresponsible, with herself as guardian. Dick and Octavia were able to cite a technicality, and they got their house back.

Now the strong-tempered Jennie Merrill was having spats with them—or perhaps a stronger word might be used. The Dana goats foraged about, crawling through Miss Jennie's prim hedges, damaging her gardens. She sent fierce notes; a new feud burned. Miss Jennie gave warning; one day she took her gun and with fine accuracy shot down one or two of the animals. The matter went into court. Once these four had exchanged smiles and compliments; in these later gray years, they faced one another in hard bitterness.

The vinegar in Miss Jennie had grown more concentrated, and also the individuality. Acquiring an automobile, she drove it through Natchez, ignoring every stop-light. The police never objected; "you just don't disturb Miss Jennie." Other people got out of their cars to enter the stores; Miss Jennie drove to the curb, honked, and the clerks brought things to her to pick from—bolts of cloth, shoes, stockings. Walking into the courthouse, she ignored the waiting lines, to rap on the counter: "Miss Merrill's taxes, please!" Newcomers, stopping her politely, would ask a direction. She would survey them with a baleful eye: "I do not know you," and stamp off.

Her clothes never varied from the style of the nineties, puff-sleeved shirtwaist, skirt, little hat. When she reached home she drove her car beneath the porte-cochere and, calling her servant, wrapped it carefully in cloth until it was protected from top to bottom. She always wrapped her car.

Duncan Minor followed his own fashion in behavior. He hated to spend money, he hated change of any kind. At his house, Oakland, the roof leaked badly; he bought shingles, but thought the cost of fixing it was too high. So the shingles lay there for years. He purchased new posts, to replace those about to fall; they also turned moldy in the grass. Once he bought a great pile of cotton and stored it. It remained there for years, storage charges mounting, bale covering wearing off. Cotton went up to the phenomenal figure of nearly forty cents; still he would not sell. It dropped and he held till it sagged to five cents, when he got rid of it. In the meantime he lost a fortune. Yet he was kind to many people, never charging interest on loans, never foreclosing. Kind—but peculiar, almost an automaton in his behavior. He went about on his horse on a schedule that never varied by a few minutes. The horse moved always at a slow walk, Duncan sitting there, staring stolidly ahead, with an umbrella over him.

The 1920s passed; the year was 1932. To one side stood the squalor of Dick and Octavia's Glenwood, to the other Miss Jennie's Glenburnie. For Jennie, economic conditions had again changed. She had held her land, hoarding, investing shrewdly; she and Dunc were well-off again. She continued to dominate her gaunt friend, yet their lives remained a mystery. Dunc's mother, who had opposed their marriage, died, but no change was made by either of the two. The rest wondered: Did Dunc sometimes wince, like nearly everyone else, under the lash of Miss Jennie's anger? For all his originalities, many pitied him. Dunc, succeeding to wide family holdings, had a considerable, though quiet, importance in the town. People asked what his life would have been like had things developed differently between him and Miss Jennie. Would he behave otherwise if something happened to her? As for Miss Jennie, few admitted kindly feelings. And she knew she was exciting another kind of emotion. Prowlers, floaters speculated about her money; several times she saw dim figures in the bushes. For them, or for almost anyone else, she had her gun handy.

August 4 of 1932 was a stifling day. About fifteen minutes after 7 p.m., before total darkness had fallen, a shot split the somnolence at Miss Jennie's Glenburnie. A scream broke out, then more shots; and then stillness. Two or three Negro tenants, some distance off, stood rigid, not sure what they heard. Was Miss Jennie killing more of them goats, and maybe fighting going on? One went toward the gallery: "Miss Jennie!" He saw nothing. Fooling in white people's affairs could mean trouble; nervously he walked around. Where was Mister Dunc? It was near time for him to be coming on his slow horse. Dunc finally appeared, to listen in silence to the story, then walk inside.

There he found blood everywhere. A frenzied struggle had taken place; in a corner a man's overcoat, covered with blood, had fallen. Miss Jennie was gone. For an hour or so Dunc and the Negro hunted about the house and grounds; they came upon her broken lamp, also covered with blood, in the grass, but nothing more. Then Dunc Minor went to the sheriff, to tell him about it. Posses searched through the night; not until dawn, however, did someone push into the clump of woods a short distance from the house. There lay Miss Jennie, shoeless in a cotton dress, her small face upward to the rising sun. She had been shot through the head and chest.

Hours earlier, after consultation with Duncan Minor, the sheriff's men made several quick arrests, and among those taken were Octavia and Dick. Deputies discovered both of them at home, Dick washing a shirt. (The sight of Dick washing anything, they observed, was remarkable.) The Sheriff said Dick made a number of strange remarks about the killing; but most Natchezians did not think that peculiar. When didn't Dick say strange things? Growing confused, he told stories that did not quite match. No, he hadn't gone next door at all that night; "last time I paid Miss Jennie a visitation was in 1915, about a red, white and blue pig. She resented it, so I didn't go back." Yes, he had heard the noise but didn't investigate. "I thought it was just a nigger chastising his wife," he said, smiling. Octavia sat there, a mask of humiliation and fear on her face, her worn hands knotted in the lap of her apron.

In the first hysterical excitement, every finger pointed at Dick and Octavia; they found themselves in jeopardy. But even then a few raised questions. There were peculiar circumstances here, that certainly didn't indicate them. Would Miss Jennie, always suspicious, with a gun handy, have let them get so close to her? It was too easy a solution. When officials tested the shirt that Dick had been washing, they found no sign of blood. But their house had been left open and, while everyone concluded that Dick and Octavia were guilty, they were subjected to the world's examination. That night, for the first time in years, outsiders walked through the Dana-Dockery residence, and what they saw went into practically every American newspaper.

Dust lay a quarter inch thick in the wide hallway and parlors. Chickens roosted on the sagging cornices of four-poster beds; hens sat on nests of eggs in rosewood furniture that once belonged to the Lees of Virginia. Goats climbed the stairs, nibbling the stuffing of sofas whose upholstery they had chewed away; as far as they could reach, they pulled off strips of curtains. The marble fireplaces were stained with the smoke of cooking fires; in the tall book-cases, on embossed first editions, sat dishes with the remains of dried food.

Droppings of birds and goats were everywhere; the floors

were strewn with remnants of feather beds that had fallen apart, to lie untouched for years. A pig squealed from its place beneath a dining room table. Strands of cobwebs, yards long, hung from the ceilings. Window panes, broken years ago, had never been repaired. Through a window, whose shutters hung crazily, grew vines, twining along a wall to the chandelier. A piece of Chippendale furniture had been chopped up for firewood. In the middle hung a proud oil of the dead Rector Dana, in vestments. The mottled highboy held a sheaf of faded notes, the minister's, for a sermon in the 1870s. Next to a broken statue lay the faded tunic of General Dockery of the Confederate Army.... The place received a garish name that it would never lose, "Goat Castle." Octavia became the Goat Woman, Dick the Wild Man of Natchez.

Octavia tried to explain the terrible appearance of things. Her voice was so low that she could barely be heard: "I couldn't help it. It was drudgery, morning to night. I had no time; I had to earn our living." Everything was hers to do, yard and crops and animals. Half the time Dick was out in the woods. She lifted her head: "Do you know I had to walk nearly three miles just to get our drinking water?" The cracked nails of the once delicate hands buried themselves in her lap, and repeatedly she denied knowing anything of the killing.

Yet the outlook darkened, and the sheriff's office made formal charges of murder against Dick and Octavia. Duncan Minor worked with the officials as a parade of frightened Negroes passed before him. Yes, he knew that one; he didn't know the other. Blurred fingerprints, taken at the scene, showed a deformed hand; an official declared that they very much resembled Dick Dana's. A tenant said he had seen a white man passing the scene soon after the shooting; the Negro had asked him to go to the scene with him, but the fellow refused. A couple had caught sight of a man wearing an overcoat and walking on the grounds about the same time; who he was, nobody could be sure.

Now "Skunks' Nest," an odorous little road house of other

days, entered the story. The rickety building stood on the Dana property. A white logger had lived there temporarily, but Octavia and Dick had evicted him a few days earlier for non-payment of rent. The bloody overcoat in Miss Jennie's house was identified as the logger's, but the man said that he had left most of his clothes, including the coat, in the shack. Dick Dana confirmed this; he had had one of the Negroes bring the stuff up to Goat Castle—all except the overcoat, which was left in the shack. Curiously, it developed that the logger also had a mutilated finger, but efforts to connect him with the killing quickly failed.

A new fact came out. Miss Jennie's German police dog had been locked up in the back that night, a thing that had never been done before. An inside job, said the knowing; would the dog have permitted a stranger to do that? (Certainly not Dick or Octavia.) More arrests were made, Negroes, white operators of stills. Hints were made of a mysterious "big Negro," a Chicago or Detroit man who had been hanging around Natchez. Duncan Minor told of meeting such an individual near the property a day or so earlier, and being asked, "insolently," for work. But the officials were swearing to themselves. Some folks around here knew more than they were telling. . . . Dunc Minor added to the excitement by a quick change of attitude. Annoyed at officials and reporters, he shut up tight; he took up residence at Miss Jennie's Glenburnie, and said nothing to anyone.

Dick Dana's movements of the late afternoon were elaborated. The next property was Auburn, where Dr. Stephen Duncan once lived; it had become a city park. An hour or so before the killing, Dick had gone there, to sit at the piano. He played dreamily, without sign of any agitation, said one who had listened; and he had no overcoat at the time. The police made computations. By making exceptional speed, he might have gone to Skunks' Nest, picked up the coat and gotten to Miss Jennie's in time. But he would have had to do it on the run, and certainly that would have attracted notice.

GOAT CASTLE

Peep Show for the Nation — EARL M. NORMAN

Mildewed and Faded Glory — EARL M. NORMAN

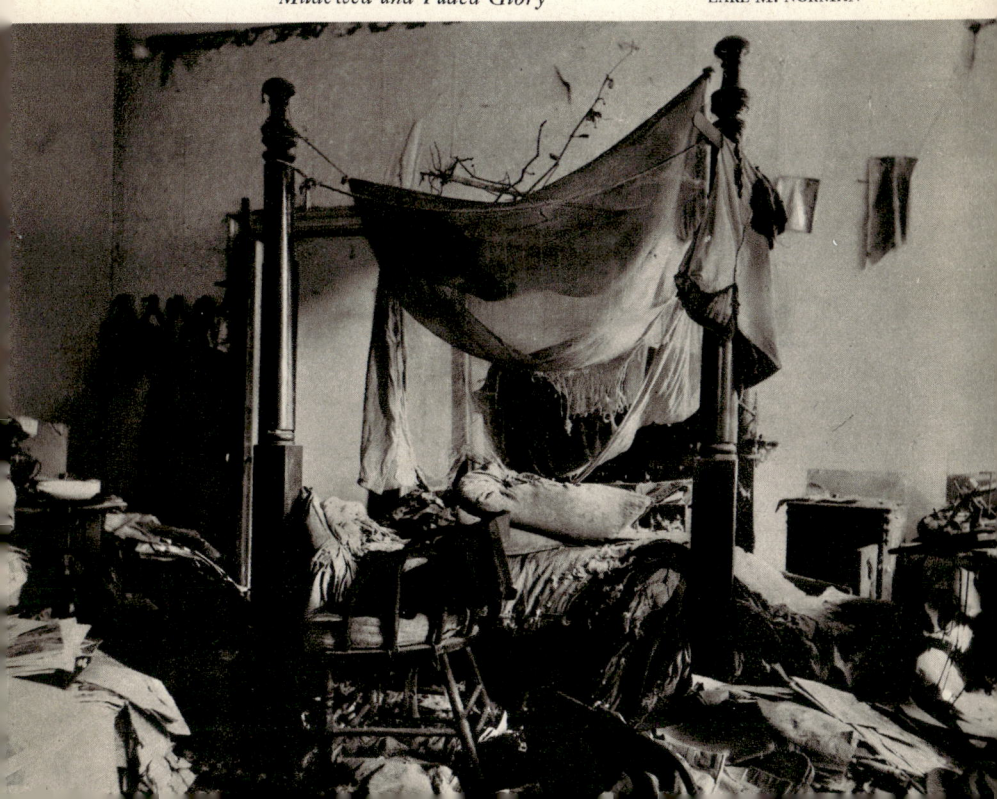

EARL M. NORMAN

ROSALIE
A Palace for the Child Bride

Duncan Minor came back into the news. Scratching among papers at her house, he and officials found Miss Jennie's will. The police gave it to him, but day after day went by, and he did not file it. The Sheriff insisted that he do so; Dunc refused. Only when the sheriff threatened to go into court about it did Duncan Minor comply. There was a new flurry; Miss Jennie had passed over all her relatives, leaving everything to Duncan, "who knows my wishes and will execute them accordingly." Yet the family showed no concern; they had expected such a provision, they said. Outsiders grew more puzzled than ever.

Meanwhile the Goat Castle story became an American sensation. Hundreds of columns of newspapers were filled; correspondents swarmed on Natchez with photographers, staff artists, girl authorities on love and murder. For the moment the Goat Woman and Wild Man found themselves as well known as Daddy Browning. Town opinion shifted, and some thought that certain people, for reasons of their own, were trying to pin things on the bedraggled couple. Natchezians sent flowers and compliments, though Dick and Octavia were held incommunicado; a plantation lady called at the jail: "Is Miss Dockery receiving today?" The attendant spat out his tobacco: "Nope, Ma'am, she sure ain't."

Oddity bred oddity in the case. The police officials turned mysterious in their own way. A second set of fingerprints was found at the scene, and a third. But the first "identification" of Dick Dana's prints grew less positive as the days passed, and then officials were no longer talking of fingerprints. Duncan Minor was called back for questioning. The police authorities were no less exasperated.

Suddenly, in Pine Bluff, Arkansas, a Negro was halted by police. They said he pulled a gun, and they shot him dead on the spot. The man, George Pearls, had a deformed finger, and officials declared that a bullet from his gun matched those used in the killing. He had been in Natchez at the time, and now it was announced that his fingerprints matched one of the sets the police had. A complete solution, cried the impressed. But there seemed to be more to the matter than this; there were too many loose ends. It looked like more than the simple effort at robbery, and then murder, that the police story indicated. If Pearls did the actual shooting, others were behind it.

Yet now Dick and Octavia could demand their freedom. The charge of murder remained against them, but they were released on bond. They found themselves famous, and thought it wonderful. The South's "greatest murder story of the century," its boosters called it. Miss Jennie and Dunc became, in the ripe words of the tabloids, the "aged Romeo and Juliet," separated by Natchez' Montagues and Capulets. But Dick and Octavia elbowed them aside for attention. From all over the South and part of the North, curiosity-seekers were coming by automobile, train and bus, to look at them and their Goat Castle.

If people wanted to see, why not? Dick and Octavia cleaned up things a little, but not too much, and charged two bits a head. They posed with the goats; Miss Octavia was pleased to oblige by holding one of the kids in her arms, and "Old Ball," leader of the flock, rose on his hind legs for his admirers. To give guests their money's worth, Dick sat at his broken piano and played. Then, pushing aside chickens and goats, he took them on a lecture tour of the house. Miss Octavia added a bookish little talk of her own, the theme of which was "The Old South."

Plans were made for special weekend excursion trains to the spot, and a "Mississippi Day" was proclaimed at the Castle. Dick spruced up some; he appeared with two belts and two pairs of suspenders. "Gotta be safe," he grinned. Why he wore two cravats, one below the other, he failed to explain. Women wrote to tell him they would like to marry him. Dick was delighted: "I'm no stick with the ladies!" After a bit he decided he would be a stick if he didn't get new store teeth. "It embarrasses me to show my gums to the other sex," he smiled. He got his teeth, and also basked in a new title, "Colonel Dana." Growing expansive, Dick arranged a tour during which he played the piano on the stage of theatres or movie houses, and Octavia made a talk, all "to present our side of the case." Dick had the concerts he had always dreamed of, and crowds heard Octavia's poetic words, but hardly as either had once planned it.

For Duncan Minor, the man of gaunt cheeks and gray-white hair, the happenings of that hot August night brought even greater change. He became practically a new Dunc. Giving up the walking horse, he bought an automobile and began to spend money. He went to parties, he took trips about the country, to watering places and races. Those who had asked how things would have been for Dunc, under changed circumstances, now had their answer.

Unexpectedly came another development. Officials arrested Emily Burns, a Negro, who ran a boarding house. After concentrated grilling she cried out a hysterical story. Yes, the man Pearls, who was killed up in Arkansas, had stayed at her place. Yes, she had gone to Miss Jennie's with Pearls, to rob her; Pearls did the shooting. But the next day she made another confession, materially different, then changed it again and implicated Dick and Octavia. They had been behind the whole thing, she sobbed. But still many were sure that Emily Burns was not telling all she knew; or they were uncertain what she did know.

Dick, hearing the news, frowned. "That Emily Burns is crazy," he said. Coming from him, this might have been taken as authoritative. (As a matter of fact, a doctor eventually testified that she was a mental case.) The Grand July failed to indict Dick or Octavia, but charged Emily Burns and also a Negro undertaker. Despite the testimony about her mental condition, and though her fingerprints were never found at the scene, Emily Burns was declared guilty as an accessory to murder. The jury could not agree on a penalty, and she was sent up for life. The undertaker was acquitted.

Now Dick and Octavia took a surprising step of their own,

filing suit for $32,000 damages against the sheriff for false arrest, cruel treatment and public humiliation. Almost instantly the sheriff struck back; they were indicted for part in the murder. "I'm tired of those people making money and getting all this publicity at my expense," he fumed. "My motto is, 'When somebody throws you a ball of fire, throw it right back!'" The balls were tossed back and forth. When their damage case came up against the sheriff, Dick and Octavia did not press it. But now they had to face trial, and all at once they sensed their danger. "They can't do anything to us, can they?" asked Octavia. "Can they?"

Natchez never knew a day like the one that followed. Everybody packed into court. The judge cried that it was a "big circus"; others nodded in agreement, but none left. After more than three hundred persons were disqualified for the jury, the judge declared a mistrial. The courtroom broke into applause, and some emotional folk wept to themselves. Octavia and Dick went home, picking up a can of sardines and a bunch of bananas on the way. Their Sunday matinee crowds were unprecedented. A new sign went up: "Visit the Nationally Famous Goat Castle. Save the Old Folks' Home."

Still, few thought the real story told. Many became convinced that Emily Burns, the only person convicted, had received a raw deal, and petitioned state officers for her release. But county officials, having gotten somebody into prison, were quite satisfied. For eight years Emily Burns was confined at hard labor, until the Governor, convinced of her innocence, released her. A newspaper expressed a common opinion by declaring that though the man Pearls had seemingly been the actual killer, "the identity of the person who inspired the murder will never be officially known, or proved."

A little before then, death had come for Duncan Minor. Ever procrastinating, he had made no will, but his family gave back to the Merrills the money that had come to him from Miss Jennie. With him ended any hope that he might have explained some of the things that only he and Miss Jennie could have told of their lives together.

Along the road out of Natchez, Miss Jennie's Glenburnie sits white and remote. Across the highway, a winding passage leads to Elmscourt, where the McKittrick family has stayed since the Merrills went away. Inside is dim grandeur. On the walls hang prints of prize Surget horses; a Negro servant, with an air of tired pride, identifies himself as a descendant of Surget jockeys who rode at old Pharsalia track. Elmscourt has had its ups and downs; a patina of age gives a pale green coloring to the balcony ironwork with its grape motif. In the spring, the careless clusters of wisteria hang close to the house, their delicate shadings softening and brightening the old walls. On one of my last visits, in the garden behind the house, I found that doll house with its shelves for toys, where Jennie Merrill had enjoyed her happier days. There are few young children at Elmscourt today; Jennie's doll house has become a doghouse.

A short distance away, Dick and Octavia stay on. They and Goat Castle have never lost their bizarre fame; a fairly steady current of visitors has continued, though the return is little more than enough to keep the pair going. They have hired a Negro assistant to help people about, and also to watch that their guests do not steal the belongings behind their backs. For some years they have had no legal claim to the place. A New Orleans man acquired it, and several times the courts have upheld his title. Eviction notices have been issued, but nothing has happened. "We won't go," says Dick. "It's ours." The owner once lamented the situation. Friends, hearing that he wanted his property, stopped speaking to him on the street. "What can I do?" he asked. "I'm no Simon Legree."

A few months ago I revisited Goat Castle. The approach is over the wildest terrain in the countryside. Crossing a rickety bridge, my car found a place between one from California, another from Connecticut. Dick Dana, hair awry, beard mussed, bowed with a flourish and his voice tumbled out in a flood of sentences, none bearing much relation to another: "This fine religious painting—the basis for challenging comparative religion." He pointed to a broken chair: "This condition is due to a storm. Now take the Commodore Perry expedition. Do you know my father went to Virginia in 1836? This house, now, it's in a sympathetic situation. This is a historic bed, used by General Lee. Note the steel engraving, representing the marriage of Pocahontas. Some day I intend to catalogue my periodicals." (These pile six feet high; Dick seldom throws a paper or magazine away.) "Somehow, in my busy life, I have never had the time."

He seemed in a race with himself; his voice grew strident, as if he were afraid he was not receiving full attention. He got little enough; the tourists, unable to follow the farrago of words, were looking hard at the conglomeration of furniture, rickety tables and torn curtains, and some were grinning. If he noted his guests' behavior, Dick gave no heed.

"Would you like to hear me play?" he asked suddenly. Almost apologetically he looked at the Californians: "I know your time is limited." As he went to the piano with its discolored keys, a chicken ran by. A goat nuzzled him, and a picture frame, empty, fell from a disordered mantle. Octavia Dockery crept by on crutches, to sit on the corner of a sofa. She had spilled hot soup on her foot, she said. Her tired voice trailed away, and Dick's notes rolled out—a sugary waltz, full of trills, runs and crossing of hands. Catching my eye, he murmured, apropos of nothing: "I'm a confirmed invalid, but not a menace to society." Then he resumed, his tongue thrust out a bit, his eyes fixed ahead of him, and he forgot his audience. It was hard to listen without a catch in the throat, and I walked away.

The past pokes a bony finger, cackling wildly to itself at Goat Castle. It is a vast joke, but on whom, or what? For fifty cents, now, you may get in and peer and feel superior, if you can.

AIRLIE

XX

PAGEANT OF THE HOOPSKIRTS

For years most people conceded that Natchez was drying away, sinking into a state close to torpor—a place that time had passed by. The river remained, but the old-time traffic had left; what boats there were, seldom stopped at the old port. Under the one-crop plantation economy, soil had been overused; the boll weevil ate its way through much of the cotton that was produced. Some have estimated that production in the vicinity fell off by eighty-five percent.

All that Natchez had left was its past. That past lay like a thin, palpable film over all the town and its environs—the deep-walled roads that looked little different than they had in the era of the Natchez Trace; the stories of the ancient days, from those of Andy Jackson to Varina Howell, and memories of Natchez under the Hill, the fiery John Quitman and Lorenzo Dow; and also the houses, especially the houses. In architecture, at least, Natchez stayed rich.

In these drowsing years, when few newcomers came and few old people left except on that last ride to the cemetery, Natchez lived in and with and, some observed, for its past. Behind the graceful, peeling columns the families thought not of today and tomorrow, but the day before yesterday—what Henry Clay told Grandpa, how those twenty-three pieces of furniture came by ship from England, the way a marauder shot that hole in the fanlight window at Green Leaves. . . .

For some the times were desperate. They had only the house, a place they could not afford to heat in winter, in which they must live through the summer without ice because their budget would hardly permit that extra expenditure. That famous description of a Southern class—"too poor to paint, too proud to whitewash"—hardly gave an adequate assessment of the situation. Whitewash would have cost too much, too. A garden went to ruin as several elderly cousins tried to keep the vast interior as clean as possible and worried about the next mortgage payment.

At whatever the cost, they usually managed to stay, losing everything except the house and their pride. The new generation might go away to New Orleans or Chicago or New York; the elders remained. Or they took little jobs, half or quarter time, in stores, garages, offices; every dollar helped keep things going. Granddaughters of mansion builders walked a mile or so into town from the big house to save a nickel. Descendants of men who had owned twelve plantations wondered whether their employers could meet a payroll that included twelve dollars a week for them.

For the most part the town business men thought little of the dim hulks of houses, not worth the cost of tearing them down and moving the timbers. Bankers groaned when they looked at entries opposite the once-shining names, but frequently they preferred to allow people to stay on; at least they would prevent the place from burning down. The creditors were glad to take a little in the way of payment, yearly, because a little seemed better than nothing.

Not always was it this way. By means of a timely inheritance, a certain furious energy, or plain luck, a few fortunate ones kept affairs going. Newcomers took over various places. By and large, however, the connections of the original families continued in more or less uncertain possession. A few were the eccentrics, the ones that all Mississippi and Louisiana told you about. Natchez was *like* that, yessir. That was only part of it, of course. But in this respect Natchez differed little, essentially, from other small Southern towns, except that in Natchez it all appeared more so.

It remained a fine place to visit, if you knew the right people. Through the years friends liked to go there, to enjoy the quiet, sloping streets, the sight of those columned establishments, the yarns about the dead. Only it hardly seemed that they were dead. In Natchez the past looked alive, sitting on the next chair and sharing highballs with you, laughing about what Great-Uncle Ab said in 1830, and the manner in which Jenny Lind took a remark, and the time Henry Clay came in late, as a guest at D'Evereux, and a servant mistook him for a lurking river rat and set the dogs on the high one. . . . And whether or not they knew furniture or period objects, the visitors stood silent before the panorama of relics that Natchezians had retained.

Along the highways that sank and rose with the sloping of the bluff land, there sounded, as ever, the clop-clop of horses drawing cotton wagons from the ginger-colored soil on the outskirts. In the shade of the sycamores and pines, in town and out, the galleries waited invitingly, the ironwork darkened, the wooden railings worn but serviceable, the whole retaining a certain part of its former grandeur.

The 1920s, the early '30s saw more of the same—again, only more so. When the nation-wide depression hit in '29, everything tightened, even in places in which it appeared that the last bit of tightening had already occurred. Where it would end, none was sure. And then there occurred the event that changed the lives of the plantation house owners, and the houses themselves.

The garden movement was spreading over the country; for the spring of 1931 the Mississippi State Federation of Garden Clubs arranged its annual meeting in Natchez. The exact order of the next occurrences is what may be termed, by way of understatement in Natchez, controversy. According to one side, Natchez suffered a blighting freeze on the eve of the meeting; there were no gardens to show, and suddenly they thought of the houses. By the other version, one or two farsighted women realized that, in the bad times that had come, the plantation gardens were gone; the only things to show were the homes. In any case, it was a matter of houses, not plantings.

After some argument, owners of many big houses were persuaded to show them to the federation delegates. That year for the first time hundreds walked in groups through the echoing rooms, pausing in astonishment before the profusion, the expanses of drawing room and hallway, paneled ceilings and gold-bordered pier glasses. Polite eyes passed over a cracked wall, a slightly damaged sofa that had kept its lines. The meeting was a success; the delegates talked for months afterward, and so, too, did the town folks. Now enters a woman whose story is much the story of these later days—Katherine Grafton Miller, a dark-eyed, brunette young matron with something of the pent-up energy of a buzz-bomb.

Mrs. Miller, as thousands have since come to know, is a combination of Miss Nelly of N'Orleans and Tallulah Bankhead, with a slight dash of P. T. Barnum. She has the deceptively easy charm of the old time Southern belle, together with a rigid determination to get what she wants. She was, and is, a dramatic lady, who deals in large things, frets over trifles, hates routine and drives everybody, including herself, close to a breakdown. She talks faster than anyone I ever met, including Tallulah; once I counted that, in a five minute period, she took up and settled the United Nations, ways to prepare shrimp gumbo, the French Quarter of New Orleans, women who smoke too much (including herself), the Long Island set and what Mrs. Roosevelt said to a Louisianian who tried to be insulting.

Katherine Miller is a visionary with a steel-vise mind for certain practicalities. She has a gift of magnificent irrelevance; half of what she says may be beside the point, but when it's over, you find that she has made, with neat precision, the exact point she wished. She says darling to everybody or nearly everybody, with some notable exceptions; she is convivial, a liker of people of varied kinds, and as Mississippi as baked sweet potato. You will get ten opinions about her in Natchez, none the same, ranging from unlimited enthusiasm to spluttering resentment. The Katherine Miller of today is a woman made by her own ideas, by one in particular. Katherine, says an approximately impartial Natchezian, is more full of ideas than of anything else, fifteen to a minute, "thirteen of them ridiculous, two brilliant or something close to it." The problem is how to tell the last two from the rest; doing that has taken a great part of her life.

She comes of an older Natchez family; her grandfather was a Presbyterian minister, her father editor of the town paper. She grew up in Natchez' slack-water days, going to dances, enjoying visits to Memphis and New Orleans, "dressing up" and liking it. "I was always doing something, full of hobbies, collecting, dabbling around," she says. Her contemporaries probably regarded her as a flibberty-gibbet; there went Katherine, talking like mad again, nobody knew about what. She tried a lot of ventures. "I wanted money, to do things with," she observes with a touch of the honesty that disarms. "The things I did . . . I collected rent for a cousin; I think I got about ten dollars a month, maybe. Then I had a dancing school. I didn't charge much; they wouldn't have paid. They either stopped coming, or I got tired of it, either one."

She pauses for breath, but not for long: "After a while I took shorthand, the Pernin system, you know. You don't? Well, it's very good." And here she takes time to describe it in some detail. That, it turns out, got her a job at sixty a month, as stenographer for a Yankee who docked his girl employes whenever he went out of town. "I walked up to him, right off, and said you're not going to dock me. Well, he didn't, for five months. He went away a week; while he was gone I got sick, *one* day. And he docked me, and I quit. But I lasted longer on the job than anybody, and I'm proud of that. Next, I thought I'd sell automobiles." She made a kind of arrangement with a friend, who found a buyer and, unaccountably, wouldn't give Katherine the commission. "She didn't understand business very well," Katherine sighs. Anyway, she went on, "getting interested in one thing after another, but violently, you understand." Between other interests, she suddenly remembers, "I got married and got sick for a year." As the wife of Balfour Miller, one of the town's business men, she eventually found herself president of the Natchez Garden Club.

She also acquired a house, a striking antiquity, Hope Farm, part of it dating back to 1775. Her husband didn't quite agree with her judgment about it; "I told him he could get all the hunting dogs he wanted if he'd let me get this," she explains; and they agreed. Governor Carlos de Grand-Pre, a Frenchman who served the Spaniards and involved himself in many of the early Natchez disputes, liked the pert Creole place that he found here, with its deep roof, small gallery across the simple front and terraced earth. About 1789 he added more rooms, a new structure at the back and connected them, forming an L, with a quiet Spanish courtyard at the rear, green-grown and shaded through most of the day.

Under Katherine Miller's direction, a sympathetic restoration kept the mellow quality of Hope Farm, with its back galleries and low-ceilinged rooms. The front wall was stuccoed in a lemon-yellow shade, the softened green of the shutters providing a note of harmony. Inside were examples of ancient construction, cypress beams held together by the tongue-and-groove method, and furnishings of the earlier day. The whole was re-terraced and planted in old-fashioned flowers, bulbs and small shrubs, iris and japonica, and rose.

Meanwhile there came that garden federation tour. Katherine, says her faction, birthed the project, but others deny her the credit. She volunteers the information that many chortled at the thought of her as president of the garden club, or anything. But now it was the houses that had become Katherine Miller's new hobby; and though some may not have sensed it,

Woman had met Career. With others, she was quickly pushing a scheme for a broader plan, a "pilgrimage of houses" the following spring, with an invitation to the whole country to come to Natchez. Why not charge admission, arrange a week or so of visits, and let the money be used to restore the houses themselves?

There was hesitation when she and her co-workers called on the home owners. Protests were tentative or firm. Complete strangers would be tracking in and out; and would they be interested, anyway? The advocates of the idea went about town, talking to everybody, business men, city officials, Negro congregations, urging them all to join the plan, grow flowers, help along. They worked the way white people aren't supposed to work in the South. Some of the hardest arguments were with those in the big houses. They tried many presentations: Natchez had a story to tell the world, something to show that the nation would want to look at. It would assist the town, assist everybody; it was patriotic, wasn't it? They would only be doing what others did. American towns offered the country electric power, lake sites, facilities for paper making. Natchez had one asset, one natural resource—its past.

They won out, but then they began to worry. Suppose, after all, nobody did come? They organized the town, drafted volunteers, buttonholed bankers, doctors, storekeepers; they "borrowed" stenographers to type letters, they found the Natchez *Democrat* a strong ally. They circularized newspapers, addressed women's clubs and men's organizations. The business men proved dubious; how could a thing like this work? After appealing to these merchants in every way except by tears, the garden club obtained a concession of a few dollars, and worked away with that.

Toward the end, as April approached, they grew jittery. They had received many letters, but how could they tell what would happen? Finally they added a parade; that would at least draw the country people, and assure some crowd. The night before, they sat around trying to joke but listening to their knees shake. Early the next morning they went downtown, with a handful who had agreed to serve as guides, if necessary, and took places at the empty registration tables. Knees still quivered.

Suddenly it happened. From all directions, by car, bus, and train, people were pouring in—women alone, women in parties, women with husbands and children, young men with cameras, teachers with pupils, aged travelers with chauffeurs and laprobes, honeymooners, professors, architects; and more were coming every few minutes. Nobody had expected it to be quite this way; for a while everything went awry. Then hurried calls went out for help. Hopefully, they had arranged to have six or so automobiles for the first arrivals; now automobiles were appealed for, begged, almost commandeered. More guides were pressed into service, given a quick briefing, and sent forth.

Stores sent stenographers and clerks to help. Hotels stretched their space; owners of homes agreed to take in guests. Restaurants added extra waitresses, called in cooks to throw together sandwiches, pots of shrimp and rice, more coffee, more everything. Garage attendants scurried to take care of lines of cars such as they had never seen; piles of picture post-cards ran out in an hour. More long-distance calls were made from Natchez in two or three days than it had ever known. It was terrible, and wonderful too, said those who took aspirins and rubbed their feet and throats after full days of walking and talking. "We'd never had anything like this since the Federals took the town in the war."

Practically everybody shared in the prosperity—jobs, money at the drugstore, money at hastily improvised "tea-shops." The business men were either exultant or sheepish. "I'll be damned," said one, summing it up for his confreres. "I'll be *good* and damned." (Many, against it from the start, now discovered that they had expected this to happen, all along.) A matron, who ran a tea shop, told about her Negro girl helper, who stood there puzzled as she cleared a table. By a plate she found a fifty-cent piece. "Lawdy, somebody lef' 'is money!" She had to be persuaded that this was her tip. Few incidents better illustrate the effect of the pilgrimage.

When Natchez subsided limply, it was found that each home owner would receive some hundreds of dollars. To outsiders the amount might look small; but for some it meant a house saved, enough to live on, with care, for a year. "Now we can have two pints of milk this summer, instead of one," said an elderly woman, her hand trembling. Oddly, it was discovered that some of the last hold-outs, who had been sure they had not wanted outsiders prying about their houses, had had the best time of all. Several stood there talking so long about their families that they had to be prodded into letting the tour continue.

After that the matter was settled. The town wanted the pilgrimage and more of it; so, it would seem, did people from everywhere else. By word of mouth, the name of Natchez spread. Depression or no depression, new routes to Natchez were blazed. More were arriving by automobile than had ever visited in the steamboat days. The prosperity overflowed through following months, and people still kept coming. It became Natchez' event of the year, socially, financially, and in other ways. People talked about it, planned for it, thought about it. The men, forgetting any questions they had raised, presented Katherine Miller with a loving cup.

The events expanded by the year, in scope and scale. A Confederate ball was started, with tableaux ending always with the flying of the Stars and Bars, in rousing climaxes that found the No'th'ners, too, standing while the band played Dixie. Now and then it was noted that every Confederate man in the tableaux had the rank of General, but that didn't matter. Wasn't every girl a belle? More and more balls were held, with kings and queens. Why should New Orleans' Mardi Gras have a monopoly on make-believe royalty? Afterward came candle-light dances, a "ball of a thousand candles," barbecued chicken picnics. Even the Negroes, hardly to be counted among Natchez' privileged, were given a part—a pageant, "Heaven Bound," performed in a church, with Good Man, Sinner and Undecided acting out a morality play in the aisles and at the front. Everybody was getting into the act.

The ladies had started by dressing in hoopskirt style, in bright prints. As the affair took on more color, more dash, these were replaced by satins and taffetas. Women went up to their attics, to pull out ancient costumes, donned mitts and carried lace umbrellas that their ancestors had sported. They persuaded their Negro helpers to wear bandannas or livery and escort the "pilgrims" in and out. Some Negroes may have wondered at the quality's bowing this way to Northerners, who had freed their slaves back in reb-time; but they could enjoy it like anybody else.

This was only the beginning. The word Natchez became a kind of talismanic one. "Southern perfumes," sometimes manufactured in the Mid-West, were named for the place, and then wallpapers, wall draperies and other patterns. Natchez houses, doorways and galleries were copied in homes all over the country. Those who came to Natchez during the pilgrimage after some years of absence, were startled at the way it was sprucing up. Out of the spreading interest, plans crystallized for restoring and beautifying parts of the town, the bluffs, old roadways, old public buildings. The pilgrimage had much to do with crystallizing the movement for the recreation of the Natchez Trace, between the town and Nashville.

Beyond this, the pilgrimage did much to revitalize the town, perk up its drooping spirits. The spring show had become one of the town's major industries, perhaps its most dependable. Natchez had tapped the American desire to travel and the country's nostalgia for the past. It is easy, of course, to snicker at much of this—the vapid tourist, the ever-smiling hostess. For a time everything became "ante-bellum." When a woman from Pennsylvania asked a Natchez child what kind of dog that was, she replied: "Oh, nothing special. Just a little old ante-bellum dog."

Yet by and large, both sides have held up well. A few have been of the supposedly standard type of uncomprehending gapers; some complaints arose that sightseers were indulging their American habit of filching ash trays and baby spoons for souvenirs. A little skill in arranging, and that was eliminated. On the other hand, a number of Natchezians spread Old South so thickly that it brought a bilious reaction in the listeners. For the most part, the Natchezians extended an easy, good-mannered welcome; the callers behaved with no less tact.

This also I know. The Natchezians met more new people and learned more about the rest of the world than most of them had ever done in their lives. That, along with the spread of a little more purchasing power among blacks as well as whites, didn't hurt anyone in Natchez. Town horizons lifted in more than one way. If it made the people, plantation or not plantation, want a little more—an indoor toilet, another store-bought dress—that wasn't to the bad.

As for the houses, pilgrimage money made it possible to paint some for the first time in decades. Sagging pillars were shored up, roofs put back; now and then it meant the saving of a doomed home. Others, that had been empty in decay, had new owners, or old ones back again, to rescue them from oblivion. So things went, higher, higher. Then, 1935, and high-pitched hell broke over Natchez, in what the town has ever afterward called "the split." It developed over personalities, individual rivalries, principles if you will, and also money—specifically, the take. Yearly the pilgrimage organization had expanded. But now various home owners were complaining that they were being outvoted by folks who didn't have even a flower pot. Also, they thought they should get more than two-thirds of the money that came in. The other side denied the charges about the voting and argued that this other third should go to pretty up the town.

The first thing you knew everybody was pink in the face. Doors slammed in heat; there were battles of proxies, talk of unladylike knifings, "misrepresentation" and so on. Katherine

Miller went up the river for a time, to organize the "Descendants of the Participants in the Campaign, Battle and Siege of Vicksburg," with tableaux to match. Then, all at once Natchez had not one but two pilgrimages, Natchez Garden Club and Pilgrimage Garden Club. (The Millerites were the latter.) More houses were shown, and there were two Confederate balls, two kings, two queens, and so on down the line. At first matters didn't work out too badly. The events were stretched out twice as long; hotel, restaurant and other business men were not unpleased. Everything was so polite between the rival groups that it hurt the teeth to listen. Somebody called it "honey time"; all the ladies were telling their guests: "Glad to see you, come again, honey." As one wit put it, the slogan was: "Come see my house, not her house," but everything was genteel.

For a time Natchez had even a third pilgrimage. The Merrill murder case had broken, and Dick Dana was inviting the world to Come to Goat Castle, where another part of the New South lived. Slowly, however, the snakes were crawling about the pilgrimage gardens. Like everything else, hot feeling was doubling. Life-long friendships broke up; cousins on different sides stopped speaking. Families united by generations of friendship went in different directions. To be seen drinking coffee with the opposition was to invite ostracism; or you might come home and find your wife giving you the silent treatment. When one organization had its show, practically every house in the other group slammed shut, with "No Admittance" signs on the door. Only one or two people managed, or tried, to keep out of the depths of the fight. One salty Natchezian penned a famous ditty:

"I'm wild and woolly, and I'm full of fleas,
"But I'll show my house when I God-damned please."

Gradually the situation tightened. In this petticoat battle, this War of the Camellias, there could be no neutrals. You had to be one or the other, see? The whole town was drawn in. The amused Ernie Pyle came to Natchez, had such a fine time that he said he didn't know whether he was Jeff Davis or himself, but admitted that the hostilities had him whipped: "It's the AFL and CIO all over again." The ladies jockeyed for position, preferred time, use of the auditorium and so on.

The year 1941 brought the blow-off. Without attempting to give the details, it may be observed that the two pilgrimage dates overlapped. "Pilgrims" arrived one day to find both going full tilt. Rival headquarters operated a block or so apart. Negro musicians played loud and long, and old battle hymns and sweet Southern songs rent the air. A campaign of banners, placards and circulars ensued, "making the town look like a carnival show." as an official put it. Somehow Negro employes got mixed in the thing, handing out cards for the white folks. Inevitably bewildered tourists found themselves pulled in two directions. A few announced that this was altogether too much Dixie hospitality and stalked off. A florid Westerner stood as much as he could, and slumped over with a heart attack.

A contingent of Yankee soldiers from a nearby military camp unloaded on Natchez, to find two sets of hoopskirted ladies smiling at them, determination in their eyes. "Such popularity . . ." murmured a captain from Brooklyn. "Was the Civil War like this, ma'am?" A tactful officer hit on a solution. He split the soldier-tourists in half. You guys go to this one, you guys to that one. At ease! In the middle of it someone thought of the law. Into court went the Natchez Garden club, demanding an injunction against the Pilgrimage Garden club. Two judges had their thumbs mashed in the mix-up. The first one gave the injunction, then took it back almost at once, saying he'd made a mistake. The ladies picked a judge in another town, and he agreed with them. Stern orders were handed down, forbidding the second club to keep up its performance.

Thick-fingered deputies started out, nailing notices to Georgian doors. One chatelaine, not knowing what was happening, saw the law coming up her walk and mistook it for a tourist. She dropped him a deep bow, "and then he handed me an injunction!" That, sir, was hardly the act of a gentleman. Certain ladies scurried about town, fleeing justice; one rode to the Devil's Punchbowl, where bandits of the Natchez Trace used to hide out when the law was tailing them. Town officials, pressed to "do something," stared at the ground. The mayor found he had business in New York and left for a week; many husbands wished they could follow him.

Two can play at the game of justice. The Pilgrimage Garden club turned around and sued the Natchez Garden club. Both sides asked damages, charging humiliation and many more things. The judge listened patiently, looked over their voluminous books, and cleared his throat to utter a few truths. The pilgrimages, he pointed out, were supposed to show the world "how the old South lived." This was hardly it, now was it? The success of the pilgrimage had been a Godsend, he observed, but he expressed his suspicion that this wrangling might be killing the goose that laid the golden eggs. He dismissed the whole matter and sent all the ladies packing, hoopskirts and all.

In one respect, the judge wasn't quite right. The fight, despite the snickerings, brought Natchez more attention than anything that had happened there. Thousands of Americans made up their mind to go there, to see the houses that all the fuss was about. They're still doing it.

World War II forced a suspension of pilgrimages, though thousands continued to visit the town. The year 1947 brought peace. The ladies sat around a council table and worked out a formula; the clubs remained separate but joined for a full month of pilgrimage, and all the houses were open. There was one Confederate ball, with King and Queen to be divided among the two groups. Things went as merrily as an old time candle-light dance. Mrs. Melchior Beltzhoover, president of the Pilgrimage Club, bowed on the stage to Mrs. Homer Whittington, president of the Garden Club, who bowed back in a swirl of skirts. They shook hands, and the audience broke into shouts of joy. It was, said a sniffling matron, a little like the fine climactic scene in which the Blue and the Gray clasped hands. A philosopher observed that since the ladies had shown they could do it, he had become more hopeful that the United Nations would work.

The recent years have brought other bounties for the town by the bluff. New mills have arrived, a tire plant, a shirt factory, a mill for the manufacture of insulating board. Then, overnight, came another change that shook Natchez to its roots. Oil was discovered on the outskirts, in this and neighboring counties. Oil companies raced to get here; thousands of newcomers moved into town—oil roughnecks, drillers, lawyers, geologists, contact people. Men and women plantation owners found strangers handing them contracts and pens and holding out checks for forty and fifty thousand dollars at a time.

For the worn land of the Natchez country has been found to contain a source of gold such as the first cotton planters never dreamed of. Thousands of acres that nobody wanted, that descendants had held while friends urged them to unload, suddenly became the most sought-after property for hundreds of miles. The oil boom may end, but for years ahead Natchez and its houses will show the effect.

Yet basically Natchez remains Natchez. The long lines of small shops look hardly changed; the ring of horses' hooves sounds as ever on the street, and buggies creak in from the country. The tree-lined streets drowse on, the mist of the past as thick as ever upon them. Seen across the river, the town sits on the high elevation, a cluster of squatters' huts below, the roofs against the sky. On the shadowed, deep-cut roads, the continuing somnolence is broken only by the approach of a wagon pulled by mules, with a dark-faced man holding the reins. As ever, the side-roads open off the main ones, and the passages curve beneath the hanging vines and gray moss, with the drone of the insects loud in the afternoon stillness. Then, around the turns, there wait the houses.

RAVENNA

THE END

NATCHEZ
on the Mississippi

ALONG THE WAY

IN AND about Natchez are many houses, great and small, in addition to those treated in the preceding chapters. A stroll along any of the streets in the town will reveal dozens of residences of rare architectural appeal, sharing the general feeling and atmosphere of the others already discussed. For visitors who wish to explore the town this quick guide has been prepared.

MONTEIGNE, on Liberty Road, is a skilfully remodeled house dating from about 1850, originally built by the salty Confederate General William T. Martin, a man of warm theories and warmer tempers. Once, in a rage or perhaps merely in an effort to prove a Spartan streak, he slashed off the top of an ailing toe. Natchezians tell a detailed story of the way the Federals turned the drawing room into a stable, using a grand piano as feed box. The present owners, Mrs. Mary W. Kendall and Mr. and Mrs. J. W. Kendall, preside over the pink stuccoed establishment of Georgian design, with terraced greens, sunken gardens and flagged passageways.

RAVENNA, 601 South Union street, is set in magnificent plantings. Two-storied, with double galleries at front and back, it has a notable interior featuring a hallway whose stairs have often been copied. Built about 1835, it was the home of Zuleika Metcalfe, who smuggled supplies to the Confederates along a nearby bayou. Arresting her, the Federals ousted her from home and bayou edge, but she took up residence a short distance off and continued, figuratively, to snipe at the Yankees. Mrs.

Louise Metcalfe, a member of the Learned family of Magnolia Vale, now occupies it.

OAKLAND, on Liberty road across from Monteigne, belongs to Mrs. Jeanne Minor McDowell, descendant of Esteban Minor, who, though American-born, served as Spanish governor of Natchez. Considerably larger than it first appears, it is a massively built structure dating from about 1838, of an unornamented elegance, with ancient wall paper, interior furnishings of rich style, marble mantles of pink and black, and trophies of the racing days of the Minors, Bingamans, Chotards and Surgets.

THE ELMS, Washington and Pine streets, reflects much of the feeling of Natchez' Spanish period, and is said to have been built about 1785. Irregularly shaped, with many long galleries, it has low walls, constricted windows, an iron stairway, an "eagle house" in the garden, and an old set of slave bells—each with a different ring for a different slave. It is owned by Mr. and Mrs. Joseph Kellogg.

TWIN OAKS, a short distance off, on Homochitto street, is an old white house of considerable grace, built in several sections. It dates from about 1815, an early land grant from the British crown. Lewis Evans, first territorial sheriff of Mississippi, built it; now, Dr. and Mrs. Homer A. Whittington own it.

AIRLIE, at the North end of Myrtle avenue, is a wide, rambling, galleried structure, with rare interior furnishings, heavy mahogany, Du Barry china and other objects. It goes back to about 1790. An early owner was A. H. Buckner, who figures in the story of a duel over his bride. Eventually the Ayers Merrill family moved here from Elmscourt, and the house is filled with portraits of Merrill connections; Frank Surget of Clifton, Sir William Dunbar of The Forest, and others. The Merrill sisters are owners.

COTTAGE GARDEN, 816 Myrtle avenue, is a story-and-a-half frame house with a pediment over a wide gallery. It occupies part of a grant to Jose Vidal, one-time Spanish official of Natchez. Don Jose, living for a time across the river in Vidalia, buried his young bride high on the Natchez bluff, so that the sun's rays outlined the grave for him every day. The house is now owned by the Foster family.

MELMONT, North Rankin between B and Oak Streets, is a brick house with a double-galleried portico, dating from about 1850. Mrs. John Ayres and Miss Corinne Henderson, owners, are descendants of John Henderson, merchant prince of Natchez. A mahogany bureau provides special chests for storing wigs.

THE BURN, on Union near Oak Street, is impressive in its balance and simplicity. It has fluted columns for its one-storied portico, and a doorway of unusual grace. It was built about 1835 by John P. Walworth. It has a striking unsupported stairway. The owners are Mr. and Mrs. Sol B. Laub.

GLENFIELD, on Canal Street near its meeting with Providence Road, is a red brick house of odd construction, its original heavy plainness ornamented with Gothic details. Said to date from a Spanish grant, with an original building about 1814, it shows successive phases, some rooms low-ceilinged, others high. Mrs. Lee Field is the owner.

CHOCTAW, Wall and High streets, is a towering structure with high front stairs, Ionic columns and massive pediment, built about 1835. It was long occupied by a merchant-philanthropist-library enthusiast, Alvarez Fisk. Gallery woodwork has an unusual motif of Indian weapons. The American Legion, the owners, recently restored it.

BELVIDERE, on Homochitto near Dunleith, is a doll-house version of a plantation residence. Built about 1830, it was once surrounded by many acres of land. Mrs. Florence Henderson Kelly is the owner.

MT. REPOSE, on the Pine Ridge road beyond Lansdowne, is a many-roomed, several-sectioned house with a double gallery and six square columns in the center. The original unit, built in the early 1800s, was part of the property of a Scotch settler, the bluff John Bisland. Expecting Henry Clay to be President, one of the Bislands announced he would not open his new driveway until after the election. Clay lost; the entrance remained on the side! Descendants, Mr. and Mrs. J. D. Shields, occupy it.

EDGEWOOD, nearby, was another part of the old Bisland estate. Built about 1850, the pink brick house has strong lines and good construction, but with its Corinthian columns and bracketing, it shows the beginning of over-elaboration. The interior has some of Natchez' best period pieces, and also portraits by James R. Lambdin, artist-ancestor of the family. Mr. and Mrs. Jeff Lambdin are the owners.

MISTLETOE, on the old Selsertown Road near Edgewood, is also part of the old Bisland property, built about 1807 for one of the Bisland sons. Small and simple, it shows its heavy early beams, wooden pegs and sturdy construction. Notable is a painting of a lady, part of whose charms have been painted over by a Puritan who believed in high necklines. Property of Mr. and Mrs. Jeff Lambdin.

BONTURA, 107 South Broadway, is strikingly reminiscent of house in New Orleans' Vieux Carre. L-shaped, two-storied, it has rich ironwork balconies facing the street, a long rear section, courtyard with old cistern, and a driveway through part of the house. The oldest section is said to date from Spanish days; later construction was in the 1830s. It is owned by Mr. and Mrs. Hugh H. Evans.

MAGNOLIA HALL, Pearl and Washington streets, is a stately, double-galleried place with imposing Ionic columns and high pediment. It was built in 1858 by Thomas Henderson and reflects the flush days. Later it was owned by Audley C. Britton, whose family is connected with the story of Green Leaves. Owned by Mr. and Mrs. George W. Armstrong, and operated as a hotel.

PLEASANT HILL, a square away on Pearl street, dates from about 1803 and represents the early American era of Natchez. A tiny portico gives entry to a long house filled with relics of Postlethwaite and Henderson families. The residence was moved from its original location some distance away. The occupants are Mr. and Mrs. Lathrop Postlethwaite and their family.

WEYMOUTH HALL, on Cemetery Road, is a heavily-built, three-storied structure with elaborate outer stairway, long galleries and captain's walk giving a view of the river country. An earlier house, dating from 1820, it was remodeled about 1850. It is owned by the Zurhellen and Morton families, descendants of the builders.

The NATCHEZ CEMETERY is an ancient burying ground in which rest many of the individuals mentioned in

ALONG THE WAY 355

this book, with epitaphs pathetic or tragic or puzzling. Ironwork and statuary are often worthy of attention.

LAWYERS' ROW, at South Wall and State Streets, is a half block or so of small quarters in which some of the most famous of old Southern attorneys had their offices. The Spaniards first put them up in the 1790s, apparently for a military commissary or for a similar purpose. With the American regime, a paradise of lawsuits drew young attorneys from many sections of the country. Unmarried, most of them boarded here and practiced in the same structure. Nearby are the ADAMS COUNTY COURTHOUSE on Market Street; the PARISH HOUSE OF SAN SALVADOR, built in 1786; the MERCER HOUSE, at South Wall and State Streets, a delicate Georgian style of house built about 1815; the CONTI HOUSE, 207 South Wall Street, about 1785, in early Spanish style; "OLD SPANISH HOUSE," South Wall and Washington, brick and stuccoed and dating from 1796; the FIRST PRESBYTERIAN CHURCH, South Pearl and State Streets, its heavy columns dating from 1829; MEMORIAL HALL, built in 1852; OLD COMMERCIAL BANK BUILDING, 206 Main Street, about 1810; the "BANKER'S HOUSE," 107 South Canal Street, the same date.

From ROSALIE and THE PARSONAGE extends the ancient ESPLANADE, laid out by the Spanish rulers, and below is old NATCHEZ-UNDER-THE-HILL, with the remains of wicked Silver Street.

MARSCHALK'S PRINTING OFFICE, North Wall and Franklin Streets, once housed Andrew Marschalk, pioneer printer of Mississippi. ST. MARY'S CATHEDRAL, South Union and Main Streets, of Gothic style, was built between 1840 and 1850. ST. JOSEPH'S ACADEMY, State and South Commerce Streets, was put up in the 1860s. TRINITY EPISCOPAL CHURCH, South Commerce and Washington Streets, goes back to 1822, and has a tiny slave gallery.

WINDY HILL MANOR, which figures in the text of the book, is reached via Liberty Road at a point some four and a half miles beyond Oakland; from the side road a winding passage leads through irregular terrain, difficult of passage in bad weather.

ELGIN, which also figures in the text, is reached along Highway 61 South of Natchez, some five miles farther than GLENBURNIE and GOAT CASTLE.

Ruins of WINDSOR, a remarkable sight, are found on Highway 61 North of Natchez toward Vicksburg, about 70 miles beyond Natchez. The complete line of massive plantation pillars remains intact, with flowers growing from the capitals. Continuing on South to Natchez is BRUINSBURY LANDING, on Bayou Pierre, where Andrew Jackson conducted a business. Forty miles to the South is old GREENVILLE, where "Little Harpe" died. Two miles to the South stands SPRINGFIELD, where Andrew Jackson married Rachel Robards. About 15 miles Southward is PROPINQUITY, a two-storied frame house with a long history. In 1797 a committee met here for one of the earliest political assemblies in the lower valley. PROPINQUITY was built about 1810 by Brigadier General Leonard Covington. It is notable for original wall paper and furnishings, an old melodeon and antique hand-painted window shades. Owned by Mrs. M. E. Fauntleroy.

JEFFERSON COLLEGE, a pioneer Deep Southern school, founded in 1802, stands a mile or so to the South. On this spot Andrew Jackson set his camp on the way to and from the Battle of New Orleans; here stand the AARON BURR OAKS, marking the point at which Burr faced trial.

ACKNOWLEDGMENTS

PRIMARILY, to Mrs. Edith Wyatt Moore and Mrs. Katherine Balfour Miller, for their sympathetic assistance over a period of many months, and others in many places, in and about Natchez and elsewhere, who aided in research—sometimes in more ways than they knew.

To Dr. William McCain, director of the Mississippi Department of Archives and History; to Miss Charlotte Capers, his assistant, and Mrs. Laura Harrell of the staff; and to Mrs. Dunbar Rowland for her generous interest.

To Dr. Garland Taylor, librarian of the Howard-Tilton Memorial Library of Tulane University, and to Miss Marguerite D. Renshaw, Mrs. Margaret Hughes, Mrs. Mary Bell Herndon, Miss Nell Russell, Mrs. Elizabeth Shannon and Miss Muriel Richardson of the staff. To John Hall Jacobs, librarian of the New Orleans Public Library; George King Logan, assistant librarian; Miss Margaret Ruckert, Miss Gladys Peyronnin and others of the staff. To Stanley C. Arthur, executive director of the Louisiana State Museum, and Miss Josie Cerf, librarian; Miss Essae M. Culver, executive secretary of the Louisiana Library Commission; Miss Katrina Perrault of the Fisk Public Library of Natchez, and Miss Lily Carson of the staff.

To John M. Dawson, assistant librarian of the Howard-Tilton Library.

To Paul North Rice, chief of the reference department of the New York Public Library; Miss Martha L. Ellison, McClung Historical Room, Lawson McGhee Library, Knoxville, Tennessee; F. H. Price, librarian of the Free Library of Philadelphia; William D. Hoyt, Jr., assistant director of the Maryland Historical Society of Baltimore; A. F. Kulhman, director of libraries,

Joint University Libraries, Nashville; Miss Winifred Ver Nooy, reference librarian of the University of Chicago; Jesse Cunningham, librarian of the Cossitt Library, Memphis.

To Luther Evans, librarian of the Library of Congress; to G. R. Lyle, director of libraries of Louisiana State University; Miss Ruth Campbell, curator of the Louisiana Room, Hill Memorial Library, Louisiana State University; to Dr. William R. Hogan, formerly associate archivist of Louisiana State University.

To Dr. Wendell H. Stephenson, chairman of the history department and professor of Southern history, Tulane university, and Dr. Fred Cole, professor of history at the university.

To these, in particular, among the many Natchezians who helped: Mrs. Jeanne Minor McDowell, Mr. Tom K. Green, Mrs. Charles J. Byrne, Mrs. Earle Rowe Glenn, Mrs. F. D. Brown, Sr., Mr. and Mrs. Lathrop Postlethwaite, Mrs. Ferriday Byrnes, Mrs Agnes Marshall Ward, Miss Theodora (Pedodie) Marshall, Mrs. John R. Ayres, Miss Corinne Henderson, Mr. R. P. Stewart, Mrs. Eliza Conner Martin, Mrs. Francis Dixon, Mrs. James Ogden, Mrs. George M. D. Kelly, Mrs. Richard Metcalfe, Mr. A. B. Learned, Mr. Howard B. Peabody, Jr., Mrs. Alice Walworth Graham, Mrs. W. W. Worthington, Mrs. Hubert Barnum, Mr. John Martin, Miss Margaret Martin, Sheriff Audley Conner, Mary Postlethwaite.

Mr. Gerard Brandon, Miss Amanda Phipps, Mr. and Mrs. Leslie Carpenter, Mrs. Lenox Stanton, Miss Maude Stanton, Mrs. Ruth Audley Beltzhoover, Dr. Pierce Butler, Mrs. Annis Dunbar, Captain William Harper, Mrs. James Marsh, Miss Kate Baldwin, Miss Inez Montgomery, Miss Courtney Winchester, Mrs. Richard Murrell, Mrs. Jonas Lehmann, Mr. Charles Perrault, Mrs. Doris L. Sanguenette, Mrs. A. B. Foules, Mrs. W. S. R. Beane, Mrs. Frank Fauntleroy, Mr. David McKittrick, Mrs. Grace McKittrick MacNeil, Mr. Tom Ketchings, Miss Margaret Merrill, Mrs. John B. Dix, Mrs. W. W. Wall, Mrs. Jeff Lambdin, Rabbi Mordecai Thurman, Mrs. Joseph Dixon.

To Mrs. Vidal Davis, Miss Myra Smith, Mr. and Mrs. J. D. Shields, Mr. Henry Carson, Miss Zaida M. Wells, Mrs. A. C. Register, Mrs. Orrick Metcalfe, Mr. Hobson Alexander.

Mr. Motte A. Hamilton, Birmingham; Mrs. Charles Hazlitt Parsons, Crystal Springs, Mississippi; the late Judge Everett Truly of

ACKNOWLEDGMENTS

Fayette; Miss Joan Balfour Payne, Churchill, Mississippi; Mrs. Frederick Kratz, Bethesda, Maryland; Mrs. Clara W. Forrest, Jackson; Mrs. L. K. Pollard, Madison, Wisconsin; Mrs. Evon G. Till, Hammond; Mrs. W. S. Myrick, Memphis; Mrs. Merrill Parish Hudson, Memphis; Mrs. Walter Sellers, Sr., Rosedale, Mississippi; Mrs. Lucille May Grace, Baton Rouge, Louisiana; Mr. Dawson A. Phelps, Tupelo, Mississippi.

Mr. J. H. Percy, Baton Rouge; Mrs. Julia Arnold, Vicksburg, Miss.; Mr. V. Blane Russell, Vicksburg; Mr. W. H. Watkins, Jackson; Mr. Jean Selby, Vicksburg; Mrs. R. G. Robinson, New Orleans; Mrs. Carroll Sandefur, Vicksburg; Mr. John Stofer, Mt. Sterling, Kentucky; Mr. Harry Sanders, Jr., of San Francisco; Mr. Cecil Morgan, Baton Rouge; Mr. Howell Morgan, Shreveport; Mrs. Ernest Bennett, Alexandria, Louisiana; Mrs. Will Whitaker, Baton Rouge.

Miss Pauline Bowie, Philadelphia; Mr. Thomas Shields, Jackson; Mrs. Leonard Snedecker, Brooklyn, New York; Mrs. J. F. Lentz of Marshall, Texas; Mrs. Fay Profilet, St. Louis; Mrs. Andrew Payne of New Orleans; Mr. H. R. Gaither, Jr., of Piedmont, California; Miss Zoe Posey of New Orleans, and Mr. Irwin Shannon of New Orleans.

To Clair A. Brown and T. E. Landry of Baton Rouge, for their assistance in connection with data on plantation gardens; to James W. Lambert of the Natchez *Democrat* for uniformly generous help, and to Tom Reed of the Natchez Chamber of Commerce, who responded on many occasions; to Mrs. W. J. Kane, Anna Marie Kane, Florence Kane Reynolds; to Mrs. Burdette Waldo Higgins; to Wilbur Goubeaud, who first suggested the book.

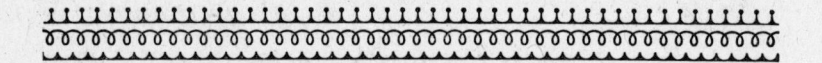

BIBLIOGRAPHY

Aaron Burr Conspiracy. W. F. McCaleb. New York, 1903.
Adventures in the Wilds of the United States. Charles Lanman. Philadelphia, 1856.
"Agricultural Reformers of the Ante-Bellum South." A. O. Craven. *American Historical Review,* XXXIII, 1928.
Albert Gallatin Brown. James B. Ranck. New York, 1937.
American Colonization Society. E. L. Fox. Baltimore, 1919.
American Negro Slavery. Ulrich Bonnell Phillips. New York, 1918.
Andrew Ellicott, His Life and Letters. Catherine Van C. Mathews. New York, 1908.
Andrew Jackson, The Border Captain. Marquis James. Indianapolis, 1933.
"Articles on Jackson-Robards Marriage." S. C. Heiskell. *Knoxville Sentinel,* November 19, November 26, December 3, 1922.
Autobiography of a Pioneer. Jacob Young. Cincinnati, 1859.
Bench and Bar of Mississippi. James D. Lynch. New York, 1881.
Bench and Bar of the South and Southwest. Henry S. Foote. St. Louis, 1876.
Bernardo de Galvez in Louisiana, 1776-83. John Caughey. Berkeley, 1934.
Biographical and Historical Memoirs of Mississippi. Chicago, 1891.
"Brief History of the Mississippi Territory." James Hall. *Mississippi Historical Society Publications,* IX, 1906.
Brief History of the Ross Slaves. New York Colonization Society, New York, 1848.
Bright Side of Life. George L. Prentiss. Asbury Park, N. J., 1901.
British West Florida, 1763-1783. Cecil Johnson. London, 1943.
Casket of Reminiscences. Henry S. Foote. Washington, 1874.

Catholic Church in Louisiana. Roger Baudier. New Orleans, 1939.
"Colonial Natchez: The Early British Period." C. N. Howard. *Journal of Mississippi History,* VII, 1945.
Complete History of Methodism as Connected with the Mississippi Conference. John G. Jones. Nashville, 1808.
Cotton Kingdom. William E. Dodd. New Haven, 1919.
Cradle Days of St. Mary's at Natchez. Bishop Richard Oliver Gerow. Natchez, 1941.
Dealings of God, Man and the Devil. Lorenzo Dow. New York, 1856.
Delineation of American Scenery and Character. John James Audubon. New York, 1926.
Domestic Manners of the Americans. Mrs. Francis M. Trollope. London, 1832.
Down the Great River. Willard Glazier. Philadelphia, 1883.
Early Days in Mississippi. H. S. Fulkerson. Vicksburg, 1885.
Early Life of George Poindexter: A Story of the First Southwest. Mack Swearingen. New Orleans, 1934.
Early Romances of Historic Natchez. Elizabeth Dunbar Murray. Natchez, 1938.
Famous American Horse Races. Philadelphia, 1877.
Fifty Years on the Mississippi. E. W. Gould. St. Louis, 1889.
Filibusters and Financiers. William O. Scroggs. New York, 1916.
Flush Times of Alabama and Mississippi. Joseph G. Baldwin. San Francisco, 1883.
Forty Years a Gambler on the Mississippi. George H. Devol. Cincinnati, 1887.
Gentleman of the Old Natchez Region—Benjamin L. C. Wailes. Charles S. Sydnor. Durham, N.C., 1938.
"Glimpses of the Past." Helen D. Bell. *Mississippi Historical Society Publications,* II, 1899.
Glory Seekers. W. H. Brown. Chicago, 1906.
Greek Revival Architecture in America. Talbot Faulkner Hamlin. New York, 1944.
Hawkers and Walkers. Richardson Wright. Philadelphia, 1927.
"Historic Adams Country." Gerard Brandon. *Mississippi Historical Society Publications,* II, 1899.
Historical Narrative and Topographical Description of Louisiana and Western Florida. Thomas Hutchins. Philadelphia, 1784.
"History of Banking in Mississippi." Charles H. Brough. *Mississippi Historical Society Publications,* III, 1900.

History of Mississippi, The Heart of the South. Dunbar Rowland. Chicago, Jackson, 1925.
History of Transportation in the United States before 1860. B. H. Meyer. Washington, 1917.
History of Travel in America. Seymour Dunbar. Indianapolis, 1915.
History of Virgil A. Stewart. H. R. Howard, New York, 1939.
Human Geography of the South. Rupert B. Vance. Chapel Hill, 1932.
Humor of the Old Deep South. Arthur Palmer Hudson, editor. New York, 1936.
Impressions of America. Tyrone Power. London, 1836.
Isaac Franklin, Slave Trader and Planter of the Old South. Wenell H. Stephenson. Baton Rouge, 1938.
Jefferson Davis, Ex-President of the Confederacy: A Memoir. (Mrs. Jefferson Davis.) New York, 1890.
Jefferson Davis. William E. Dodd. Philadelphia, 1907.
Jefferson Davis, President of the South. H. J. Eckenrode. New York, 1923.
Jefferson Davis: The Unreal and the Real. Robert McElroy. New York, 1937.
Jefferson Davis, His Rise and Fall. Allen Tate. New York, 1929.
John Archibald Campbell. H. G. Connor. Boston, 1920.
"John Carmichael Jenkins, Scientific Planter of the Natchez District." Albert G. Seal. *Journal of Mississippi History,* I, 1939.
Jottings of a Year's Sojourn in the South. A. De Puy Van Buren. Battle Creek, 1859.
Journal of Andrew Ellicott. Andrew Ellicott. Philadelphia, 1803.
Journal of a Tour. Francis Baily. London, 1856.
Journey in the Back Country. Frederick Law Olmsted. New York, 1860.
Judicial Cases Concerning American Slavery. Helen T. Catterall, editor. Washington, 1926-37.
Life, Adventures and Opinions of David Theo. Hines. David Hines. New York, 1840.
Life and Correspondence of John A. Quitman. J. F. H. Claiborne. New York, 1860.
Life and Labor in the Old South. Ulrich Bonnell Phillips. Boston, 1929.
Life and Times of General Sam Dale. J. F. H. Claiborne. New York, 1860.

Life and Times of Seargent Smith Prentiss. Joseph D. Shields. Philadelphia, 1884.
Life, Letters and Papers of William Dunbar. Eron Rowland. Jackson, 1930.
Life of Andrew Jackson. John Spencer Bassett. New York, 1911.
Life of Andrew Jackson. James Parton. New York, 1860.
Life of Andrew Jackson. Alexander Walker. New York, 1858.
Life of Walter Quintin Gresham. Matilda Gresham. Chicago, 1919.
"Life of General John A. Quitman." Mrs. Rosalie Q. Duncan. *Mississippi Historical Society Publications,* IV, 1901.
Lopez's Expedition to Cuba, 1850-51. Anderson C. Quisenberry. Louisville, 1906.
"Lorenzo Dow in Mississippi." C. B. Galloway. *Mississippi Historical Society Publications,* IV, 1901.
Lorenzo Dow, the Bearer of the Word. C. C. Sellers. New York, 1928.
Loyalists of America and Their Times. Egerton Ryerson. Toronto, 1880.
"Luxury at Natchez in 1801." Mack Swearingen. *Journal of Southern History,* III, 1937.
Main Currents in American Thought. Vernon Parrington. New York, 1930.
Memento: Old and New Natchez. Stephen Power. Louisville, 1897.
Memoir of S. S. Prentiss. George L. Prentiss. New York, 1856.
Memories of Fifty Years. William H. Sparks. Philadelphia, 1870.
Methodist Saint. Herbert Asbury. New York, 1927.
Mississippi: A Guide to the Magnolia State. American Guide Series. New York, 1938.
Mississippi as a Province, Territory and State. J. F. H. Claiborne. Jackson, 1880.
Mississippi: Comprising Sketches of Counties, Towns. Dunbar Rowland, editor. Atlanta, 1907.
Mississippi Question. Arthur P. Whitaker. New York, 1934.
Mississippi Scenes. Joseph E. Cobb. Philadelphia, 1851.
Mississippi Steamboatin'. Herbert and Edward Quick. New York, 1926.
Mississippi—Storm Center of Secession. P. L. Rainwater. Baton Rouge, 1938.
Mississippi Territorial Archives, 1798-1803, Dunbar Rowland. Nashville, 1905.

BIBLIOGRAPHY

Mississippi Valley Beginnings. Henry E. Chambers. New York, 1922.
Natchez Country. Richard F. Reed. Natchez, n.d.
Natchez, Its Early History. Joseph D. Shields. Louisville, 1930.
Natchez: Symbol of the Old South. Nola Nance Oliver. New York, 1940.
Official Letter Books of W. C. C. Claiborne. Dunbar Rowland. Jackson, 1917.
Old Times in Tennessee. Josephus C. Guild. Nashville, 1878.
Oliver Pollock. James A. James. New York, 1937.
One Hundred Years with "Old Trinity Church," Natchez, Mississippi. Charles Steitenroth. Natchez, 1922.
Outlaws of Cave-in-Rock. Otto A. Rothert. Cleveland, 1924.
Outlaw Years. Robert M. Coates. New York, 1930.
Pageant of the Packets. Garnett Eskew. New York, 1929.
"Philip Nolan and His Companions." J. A. Quintero. *Texas Almanac*, 1868.
Pictures of Southern Life. William Russell. New York, 1861.
Proud Old Natchez. Thomas Reber. Natchez, 1909.
Rampaging Frontier. Thomas D. Clark, Indianapolis, 1939.
"Real Philip Nolan." Edward Everett Hale. *Mississippi Historical Society Publications*, IV, 1901.
"Real Philip Nolan." Grace King. *Louisiana Historical Quarterly*, X, 1917.
Recollections of Mississippi and the Mississippians. Reuben Davis. Boston, 1889.
Recollections of the Last Ten Years. Timothy Flint. Boston, 1826.
Reminiscences of a Mississippian. F. A. Montgomery. Cincinnati, 1901.
Retrospect of Western Travel. Harriet Martineau. London, 1838.
"Running Mississippi's South Line." Peter J. Hamilton. *Mississippi Historical Society Publications*, II, 1899.
Scientific Interests in the Old South. Thomas Carey Johnson, Jr. New York, 1936.
Seargent S. Prentiss, Whig Orator of the Old South. Dallas C. Dickey. Baton Rouge, 1945.
Second Visit to the United States of North America. Sir Charles Lyell. New York, 1849.
Seventy Years in Dixie. F. D. Srygley. Nashville, 1891.
"Sir William Dunbar—The Pioneer Scientist of Mississippi." Franklin L. Riley. *Mississippi Historical Society Publications*, II, 1899.

Sketches, Historical and Descriptive, of Louisiana. Amos Stoddard. Philadelphia, 1812.
Sketches of Western Adventure. John A. McClung. Dayton, 1854.
Slavery in Mississippi. Charles S. Sydnor. New York, 1933.
Slave States of America. James S. Buckingham. London, 1842.
Southern Plantation. Francis Pendleton Gaines. New York, 1925.
Southwest, by a Yankee. (J. H. Ingraham.) New York, 1835.
Steamboat Days. Fred E. Dayton. New York, 1939.
Sucker's Progress. Herbert Asbury. New York, 1938.
Sunny South. J. H. Ingraham, editor. Philadelphia, 1860.
"Theatre in Natchez." William Bryan Gates. *Journal of Mississippi History,* III, 1941.
They Found It in Natchez. Theodora Britton Marshall and Gladys Crail Evans. New Orleans, 1939.
Three Months in the Southern States. Sir Arthur Fremantle. Edinburgh, 1863.
Traffic History of the Mississippi River. Frank H. Dixon. Washington, 1909.
"Transition from Spanish to American Control in Mississippi." Franklin L. Riley. *Mississippi Historical Society Publications,* III, 1900.
Travels in America. Thomas Ashe. London, 1808.
Travels on an Inland Journey. Christian Schultz, Jr. New York, 1810.
Varina Howell. Eron Rowland. New York, 1927-31.
View of the Mississippi. Robert Baird. Philadelphia, 1834.
Vue de la Colonie Espagnole du Mississippi. Berquin Duvallon. Paris, 1803.
Westward Movement, Justin Winsor. New York, 1897.
Whig Party of the South. Arthur C. Cole. Washington, 1914.
White Pillars. J. Frazer Smith. New York, 1941.
Wilderness Road. Thomas Speed. Louisville, 1886.
"Willing's Expedition down the Mississippi, 1778." *Louisiana Historical Quarterly,* XV, 1932.

Also consulted were bound files of newspapers of New Orleans, Natchez, and Jackson, Mississippi, and other newspapers, as well as *DeBow's Review* of New Orleans, and other journals.

INDEX

The names of HOUSES are in capital letters

Adams, St. Clair, 188, 189
Adams County Courthouse, 355
AIRLIE, 333, 352
Allen, Henry W., 257
ARCOLA, 179
ARGYLE, 179
ARLINGTON, 166-169, 171-172
Armstrong, George W., 354
ASHLAND, 179
Astor, Caroline, 261
AUBURN, 206, 212, 218-219, 326
Audley, Ruth, see Beltzhoover, Ruth Audley
Audubon, John James, 283-284
"Aunt Jane," 283
Ayres, Mrs. John, 353

Baker, Colonel Joshua, 69
Baldwin, Hiram, 258
Balfour, William, 182, 184
Balfour, Mrs. William (Catherine Hunt), 182, 184
Bandits, 6, 63-73
"Banker's House," 355
Barnum, Hubert, 171-172
Barnum, Mrs. Hubert (Annie Green Gwin), 169-172, 235
Barnum, P. T., 197-199
Beane, Mrs. W. S. R., 59
BEAUVOIR, 257-258
BELFAST, 285-287
BELLE ELLA, 179
Beltzhoover, Melchior, 262
Beltzhoover, Ruth Audley, 262-263, 347
BELVIDERE, 353
Biddle, Nicholas, 192, 195

Bingaman, Adam Louis, 150-158, 172, 207, 223
Bingaman, Mrs. Adam Louis (Julia Maria Murray), 151-153, 156-157
Bingaman, Catherine, see Duncan, Mrs. Stephen
Bingaman, Christian, 150
Bisland, John, 353
BLACK CREEK, 179
Boatmen, 128
BONTURA, 124, 354
Boyd, Samuel Stone, 168
Bradbury, John, 125
Brandon, Governor, 225
BRIERFIELD, 245, 247
BRIERS, THE, 237-238, 243, 244, 245, 247, 249, 250
Britton, Audley C., 354
Brown, Andrew, 133-137, 139, 140
Brown, Andrew, Jr., 137
Brown, Elizabeth, 137, 138-139
BROWN'S GARDENS, see also MAGNOLIA VALE, 135-137, 139, 142
Bruinsbury Landing, 356
Buchanan, James, 234
Buckner, A. H., 352
BUENA VISTA, 179
BURN, THE, 96, 353
Burns, Emily, 329, 330
Burr, Aaron, 6, 28, 34, 37-38, 40, 41, 237
Butler, McVey, 311
Butler, Rev. Mr. Zebulon, 213
Byrne, Charles J., 233-234
Byrne, Myrtie Cavin, 233-234

Calvit, Mary, see Hunt, Mrs. David

INDEX

Calviton, 179
Cannon, John W., 304, 305-310
Carmichael, Dr. John A., 52
Carondelet, Governor-General, 88, 89, 91, 92, 101
Carpenter, Joseph, 262
Carpenter, Leslie, 262
Cave-in-Rock, 65
Chapline, Jane, 34
Cherokee, 233-234, 284, 285
Cherry Grove, 147, 149-150, 172
Choctaw, 353
Cholera, 57-58
Chotard, Eliza, 192-193
Chotard, Henry, 16
Chotard, Maria, *see* Marshall, Mrs. Levin
Claiborne, William C. C., 17, 69
Clark, Daniel, 103, 105
Clark, Dinah, *see* Dunbar, Mrs. William
Clay, Henry, 207, 227, 246, 334, 336, 353
Clifton, 160-161, 164-166, 205
Coates, Robert, 66
Coleman, John, 310
Concord, 85-86, 95-96, 104, 110
Confederate ball, 342, 345, 347
Connelly, Patrick, 90, 110
Connelly's Tavern, 90, 95, 110-111
Conner, Anne, *see* Elliot, Mrs. William St. John
Conti House, 355
Cottage Garden, *294*, 352
Cotton, 4-5, 13-14, 18, 35, 46-47, 52, 53, 56, 122
Covington, Leonard, 356
Cuba, 228-230
Culture, 14-16

Dahlgren, Charles G., 251-253, 257, 258
Dana, Charles Bachus, 315
Dana, Charles S., 315
Dana, Dick, 314-315, 316, 318-321, 322, 325-333, 345
Daughters of the American Revolution, 276
Davis, Alfred Vidal, 258
Davis, George Malin, 283

Davis, Jefferson, 228, 240-250, 257-258, 259, 274
Davis, Mrs. Jefferson (Sarah Knox), 241
Davis, Mrs. Jefferson (Varina Howell), 236-250, 258, 334
Davis, Joseph E., 237, 239, 241, 242
Davis, Samuel, 153
Depression of 1837, 18
D'Évereux, 200-203, 336
"Devil's Punchbowl," 68, 347
Dives, 128
Dockery, Octavia, 314, 315-316, 319-321, 322, 325-333
Dockery, Thomas Payne, 315
Dorsey, Samuel W., 256
Dorsey, Mrs. Samuel W. (Sarah Ann Ellis), 251, 253, 254-255, 256
Dow, Lorenzo, 73-76, 266-267, 334
Dunbar, Annis, *see* Jenkins, Mrs. John C.
Dunbar, William, 43-52, 81, 82, 102, 108, 116, 313, 352
Dunbar, Mrs. William (Dinah Clark), 47-48
Duncan, Dr. Stephen, 204-207, 209, 211, 212-214, 216-218, 326
Duncan, Mrs. Stephen (Catherine Bingaman), 205
Dufour, Marie, 129-130
Dunleith, 251, 254, 258, 259, 262

Eagle Bottom, 56
Edgewood, *78*, 353-354
Edward VII, 260
Elgin, 54-59, 356
Ellicott, Andrew, 87-95, 102, 110, 233
Elliot, Sarah, *see* Marshall, Mrs. Levin
Elliot, William St. John, 194, 198, 199, 200, 201-202
Elliot, Mrs. William St. John (Anne Conner), 199-200, 201
Ellis, Martha, 82
Ellis, Sarah Ann, *see* Dorsey, Mrs. Samuel W.
Elms, The, 311, 352
Elmscourt, 313, 314, 316, 331
England, 3-4
Esplanade, 355
Evans, Hugh H., 354

INDEX

Evans, Lewis, 352
Everett, Edward, 153

FAIRVIEW, 179
Farrar, A. K., 232
FATHERLAND, 179
Fauntleroy, Mrs. Frank, 219
Fauntleroy, Mrs. M. E., 356
Ferguson, Ann, see Hunt, Mrs. David
Field, Mrs. Lee, 353
First Presbyterian Church, 355
Fisk, Alvarez, 353
FOREST, THE, 46-52, 53-54, 59-60
Fort Rosalie, 265-266
France, 2-3
Frank Pargaud, 308, 310
Fremantle, Sir Arthur, 291
Fruit, 55-56, 59

Gaines, General Edmund Pendleton, 244-245
Gaines, Myra Clark, 245
Galloway, Charles B., 74-75
Galvez, Bernardo de, 80, 81
Gambling, 127, 128, 130-133
Gayoso de Lemos, Don Manuel see Lemos, Don Manuel Gayoso de
GEORGIANA, 179
Ghost towns, 19
Gibson, Charles Dana, 315
Girty, Jim, 129-130
GIVIN PLACE, 179
Glass, Anthony, 67
GLENBURNIE, 318, 322, 331, 356
GLENFIELD, 250, 353
GLENWOOD, see also "Goat Castle," 317, 318-321, 322, 324-325
GLOUCESTER, 120-121, 122
"Goat Castle," see also GLENWOOD, 325, 327, 328, 330, 331-333, 345, 356
Goat Woman, 325, 327
Gold, 138
Grand-Pre, Governor Carlos de, 339
Grant, Ulysses S., 274-275, 314
Great Revival, 73
Green, Thomas Marston, 23, 26, 169-170
GREEN LEAVES, 251, 258-259, 262-263, 334

Greenfield, Jesse, 233
Greenville, 356
Gresham, Walter Q., 275, 276
Gresham, Mrs. Walter Q., 162, 275, 276
Griffith, William B., 221, 222
Gwin, Annie, see Barnum, Mrs. Hubert
Gwin, Lucien, 170

Hale, Edward Everett, 109, 207
HALFWAY HILL, see also WINDY HILL MANOR, 30-31
Hamilton, Alexander, 29
Hankinson, John, 223
HANGING MOSS, 169
Hanna, Mr., 92-93
Harding, Lyman, 205
Harpe, Big (Micajah), 64-66
Harpe, Little (Wiley), 64-65, 67, 68, 69-70
Hay, John, 282
Henderson, Miss Corinne, 353
Henderson, John, 353
Henderson, Thomas, 354
History, 2-21
HOMEWOOD, 179, 182-183, 186-189
HOPE FARM, 339
Horse racing, 154-155, 207
Howard, Colonel, 80
Howell, Varina, see Davis, Mrs. Jefferson
Howell, William Burr, 237, 242
Howell, Mrs. William Burr (Margaret Louisa Kempe), 237
Hubbard, Katrina, see Surget, Mrs. Pierre
Hunt, Abijah, 174-177
Hunt, Catherine, see Balfour, Mrs. William
Hunt, Charlotte, see Marshall, Mrs. George
Hunt, David, 174-180, 181, 183-184, 210
Hunt, Mrs. David (Mary Calvit), 176
Hunt, Mrs. David (Ann Ferguson), 178
HUNTLEY, 179
HURRICANE, 240, 241, 242, 247
Hurricanes, 142, 277

INDEX

Indians, 50, 62, 64, 100, 116, 147
   liquor and, 91, 115, 118
   Mexican, 99, 101

Irvine, Walter, 250

Jackson, Andrew, 6, 22-28, 30, 195, 239, 243, 334, 356
Jackson, Mrs. Andrew (Rachel Donelson Robards), 23-28, 356
Jagello, Appolonia, 246
Jefferson, Thomas, 17, 49, 243
   Nolan, Philip, and, 102-103
Jefferson College, 356
Jenkins, John C., 52-59, 176, 207
Jenkins, Mrs. John C., 53-54, 55, 56, 57, 58
Juleps, 195-196, 221

Kellogg, Joseph, 352
Kelly, Mrs. Florence Henderson, 353
Kelly, George, 283
Kelly, George M. D., 110
Kelly, Dr. Stephen, 283
Kempe, Margaret Louisa, *see* Howell, Mrs. William Burr
Kendall, J. W., 351
Kendall, Mrs. Mary W., 351
Ker, Dr. John, 204-205, 209, 211, 212-217, 219
King, Ricardo, 63
King's Tavern, 61, 63-64, 77, 78, 205
Knox, Sarah, *see* Davis, Mrs. Jefferson
Koontz, George Washington, 259, 262

Lambdin, James R., 354
Lambdin, Jeff, 354
LANSDOWNE, 179, 180-181, 185
Laub, Sol B., 353
Lawyer's Row, 355
Learned, Andrew Brown, 141
Learned, Rufus, 137-141
Learned, Mrs. Rufus (Elizabeth Brown), 137, 138-139, 140
Leathers, Tom, 299-311
Lee, Robert E., 228
Lemos, Don Manuel Gayoso de, 85-87, 114
   Ellicott, Andrew, and, 87-95
   Minor, Stephen, and, 87-95
   Nolan, Philip, and, 102, 105, 106
Lewis, Meriwether, 63
Lind, Jenny, 197, 199
LINDEN, 209, 211, 212, 219
Linton, Charlotte, *see* Surget, Mrs. Frank, II
Lintot, Bernard, 94, 104, 108
Lintot, Fannie, *see* Nolan, Mrs. Philip
Lintot, Katherine, 83-85, 95-96, 97-98
Liquor, 126, 128-129
   Indians and, 91, 115, 118
Lister-Kaye, Lady, 261
Little, Peter, 134, 266, 268-274
Little, Mrs. Peter (Eliza Low), 265-274
LOCUST GROVE, 244
London Times, 260
LONGWOOD, 289, 315, *see* NUTT'S FOLLY
Lopez, General Narciso, 228-230, 231-232
Louisiana Purchase, 49
Low, Eliza, *see* Little, Mrs. Peter
Low, Jacob, 264-265, 267-268

McDowell, Mrs. Jeanne Minor, 352
McMurren, John, 278-282, 352
McMurren, Mrs. John (Mary Louise Turner), 279, 281
MAGNOLIA HALL, 354
MAGNOLIA VALE, *see also* BROWN'S GARDENS, 140, 141-142
"Man Without A Country, The," 109
Mandeville, Lady, *see* Montagu, Mrs. George Victor Drogo
MANSION HOUSE, 195, 198
Marschalk's Printing Office, 355
Marsh, Mrs. James, 276
Marshall, Duncan, 203
Marshall, George, 180-181, 184, 185
Marshall, George, III, 185
Marshall, Mrs. George (Charlotte Hunt), 180-181, 184-185
Marshall, Levin, 191-199
Marshall, Mrs. Levin (Maria Chotard), 192-194

INDEX

Marshall, Mrs. Levin (Sarah Elliot), 194, 195
Martin, William T., 351
Mason, Sam, 67-70
MELMONT, 353
MELROSE, 279-280, 283-284
Memorial Hall, 355
Mercer House, 355
Merrill, Ayers P., II, 313-314
Merrill, Ayers P., III, 316
Merrill, Jane Surget, 313, 316, 317-318, 321-322, 323
Metcalfe, Duncan, 234
Metcalfe, George, 230-233
Metcalfe, Henry, 231, 232
Metcalfe, Mrs. Louise, 352
Metcalfe, Orrick, 277
Metcalfe, Zuleika, 351
Mexico,
    Davis, Jefferson, and, 247
    Metcalfe, George, and, 231
    Nolan, Philip, and, 99, 101, 102, 103, 105-108
    Quitman, John A., and, 224-225, 226
Miller, Balfour, 339
Miller, Katherine Grafton, 337-342, 344-345
Minor, Duncan, 316, 317-318, 322-324, 325, 326, 327, 329, 330-331
Minor, John, 102
Minor, Stephen, 8, 79-87, 89, 91-92, 93-96, 102, 352
    wives of, 82-85, 95-96
Mint juleps, 195-196, 221
Mississippi River,
    changing course of, 141, 142
    railroads and, 18
Mississippi Society of Daughters of the American Revolution, 276
Mississippi State Federation of Garden Clubs, 336
MISTLETOE, 354
Modisett, Mrs. Jean Register, 77
MONMOUTH, 171, 223, 235
Montagu, George Victor Drogo, 260
Montagu, Mrs. George Victor Drogo (Consuelo Yznaga del Valle), 258, 259
MONTEIGNE, 42, 351
Moore, Mrs. Edith Wyatt, 63, 301

MT. REPOSE, 353
Murder, 126, 129, 131
Murray, Julia Maria, see Bingaman, Mrs. Adam Louis
Murrell, John, 70-73
MYRTLE TERRACE, 300-301, 304, 311

Natchez, 299, 301, 303, 304-311
Natchez Cemetery, 354-355
Natchez *Democrat*, 340
Natchez Fencibles, 222
Natchez Garden Club, 339, 345, 346, 347
Natchez Trace, 5-6, 61-64, 77-78, 334, 343
Natchez-Under-The-Hill, 355
National Intelligencer, 239
New Orleans, 296
Nolan, Philip, 97-109
Nolan, Mrs. Philip (Fannie Lintot), 97-101, 102, 103-106, 108
Nutt, Haller, 287, 288-291, 292
Nutt, Mrs. Haller (Julia Williams), 288-289, 291
Nutt, Dr. Rush, 287-288
NUTT'S FOLLY, 287, 289-294, 315 see LONGWOOD

OAK BURN, 179
OAKLAND, 219, 352
OAKLEY GROVE, 179
OAKWOOD, 179
Ochre, 46
Oil, 348
Old Commercial Bank Building, 355
"Old Spanish House," 355
Ole Bull, 272
Olmsted, Frederick, 15
Osmun, Colonel Benijah, 30, 33, 34

Panic of 1830, 284-285
Parish House of San Salvador, 355
PARSONAGE, THE, 273, 277, 355
Peabody, Howard, 141-142
Pearls, George, 327-328, 330
"Peculiar Peggy," 75-76
Percy, Miss, 251, 255-256
Pharsalia race track, 155, 207
Picayune, 309, 316
Pilgrimage Garden Club, 287, 345, 346, 347

Pilgrimages, 340-348
PLEASANT HILL, 354
Poindexter, George, 176-177
Politics, 17, 223-224, 226-227
Population, 4, 6, 7-8, 9, 10-11
  idiosyncrasies of, 20-21
Postlethwaite, Henry, 77
Postlethwaite, Lathrop, 354
Postlethwaite, Sam, 77, 160
Power, Tyrone, 14-15, 131, 153-154
Prentiss, S. S., 10
Price, Madeline, 31-34, 37-38, 41
Profilet, Emile, 284
PROPINQUITY, 356
PROSPECT HILL, 208, 216-217
Prostitution, 126, 127
Pyle, Ernie, 346

Quitman, John A., 220-230, 234-235, 278, 334
  Cuba and, 228-230
  Mexico and, 224-225, 226
  politics and, 223-224, 226-227
  slavery and, 225, 227
Quitman, Mrs. John A. (Eliza Turner), 222-223, 226, 234

RAVENNA, 349, 351-352
RAVENSWOOD, 258, 259
Reed, Thomas A., 208-209, 210, 211
Reed, Mrs. Thomas A. (Margaret Ross), 208-209, 210-213, 219
Register, Mrs. A. C., 77, 78
Religion, 73-76, 270-272
Restoration, 340-348
RICHMOND, 190, 194-195, 199, 203
RIVER PLACE, 56
Robards, Rachel Donelson, see Jackson, Mrs. Andrew
Robert E. Lee, 299, 304-311
Roosevelt, Nicholas J., 296
ROSALIE, 270-271, 272-273, 274-277, 355
Ross, Ike, Jr., 208, 211
Ross, Captain Isaac, 207-208, 209-211, 213, 214, 215
Ross, John, 44
Ross, Margaret, see Reed, Mrs. Thomas A.
"Ross case," 207-219
Rowland, Mrs. Eron, 238

"Rumble girls," 276
Russell, Captain John, 132-133

St. Germain, Jean, 190-191
St. Joseph's Academy, 355
St. Mary's Cathedral, 355
Sargent, George Washington, 123
Sargent, Julia, 124
Sargent, William, 112-124, 317
Sargent, Mrs. William (Maria McIntosh Williams), 117-118, 119, 123
Sawmills, 134-135, 139
SERVIS ISLAND, 179
Shields, J. D., 353
Shields, Joseph Dunbar, 4, 67
"Skunk's Nest," 325-326
Slavery, 71, 161-166
  Quitman, John A., and, 225, 227
  "Ross case" and, 207-219
Sloan, Samuel, 289
Smith, Myra, 202
Soil erosion, 18
Spain, 4, 127
  Dunbar, William, and, 46
  Ellicott, Andrew, and, 87-95
  Mexico and, 105-108
  Minor, Stephen, and, 80, 81
  Nolan, Philip, and, 101, 105-108
Sparks, W. H., 28
Sprague, Margaret, 244
Springfield, 356
Stanton, Bea, 36, 40, 41
Stanton, Elizabeth, 36-38, 39, 40, 41
Stanton, Frederick, 284-286, 317
Stanton, Dr. Frederick, 34-36
Stanton, Hulda, 284, 286
Stanton, Mrs. Lennox, 124
Stanton, Maude, 36, 38, 41-42
Stanton, General Robert, 34
Stanton College for Young Ladies, 287
STANTON HALL, 287, 317
Steamboats, 16, 130-133, 295-311
Steer, James, 8
Steer, Mrs. Samuel, 108
Stephens, J. L., 288
STOCK FARM, 56
Surget, Frank, 148, 159, 313, 352
Surget, Frank, II, 159-166
Surget, Mrs. Frank, 148-149, 159

INDEX

Surget, Mrs. Frank, II (Charlotte Linton), 160, 163, 164-165
Surget, Jake, 148, 149-150
Surget, Mrs. Jake, 149, 150
Surget, Mrs. James, 123
Surget, Jane, see White, Mrs. James Hampton
Surget, Jim, 148, 149-150, 152
Surget, Pierre, 145-148, 158, 172
Surget, Mrs. Pierre (Katrina Hubbard), 146, 148
Swan, Mrs. Kingsley, 186-189
Sydnor, Charles S., 225

Taylor, General Zachary, 226, 241
Tornado, 18
Trinity Episcopal Church, 355
Turner, Eliza, see Quitman, Mrs. John A.
Turner, Mary Louise, see McMurren, Mrs. John
TWIN OAKS, 173, 352

Valle, Consuelo Yznaga del, see Montagu, Mrs. George Victor Drogo
Vanderbilt, Mrs. W. K., 259, 261
Vidal, Captain José, 106, 352

Wales, Prince of, 260
Walker, William, 232
Wall, William Winans, 250
Walworth, John P., 353
Ward, Agnes Marshall, 185

Ward, James, 185
Washington, George, 64, 113
WAVERLY, 179
Webster, Daniel, 246
Weeks, Levi, 206
WEYMOUTH HALL, 354
White, Captain James Hampton, 166
White, Mrs. James Hampton (Jane Surget), 166-168
Whittington, Dr. Homer, 352
Whittington, Mrs. Homer, 347
Wild Man of Natchez, 325, 327
WILDERNESS, 179
Wilkinson, General James, 29, 30, 100, 103, 109
Williams, Julia, see Nutt, Mrs. Haller
Williams, Maria McIntosh, see Sargent, Mrs. William
Willing, Captain James, 45-46
Wilson, Andrew L., 274-275
Wilson, Mrs. Andrew L., 274-276
Winchester, George, 238, 240
WINDSOR, 356
WINDY HILL MANOR, see also HALFWAY HILL, 34-42, 355
Woodbury, Supreme Court Justice, 246
WOODLAWN, 179

Yellow fever, 57-58, 207, 223, 267-268

Zimmerman, Helena, 261

ABOUT THE AUTHOR

HARNETT THOMAS KANE, born in 1910, is a native New Orleanian and lifelong resident of the South. He was graduated in 1931 from Tulane University, where he was editor of the school paper and won the Dorothy Dix feature story award. He began newspaper work, full time, while a sophomore at Tulane, and continued on the New Orleans *Item* for sixteen years, during which he covered everything from murders to the business run, and served for a time on the city desk and copy desk. When the famous Louisiana scandals broke, young Mr. Kane was assigned to cover them; from that assignment, which his newspaper called one of its greatest examples of reporting, came his first book, *Louisiana Hayride: The American Rehearsal for Dictatorship*. The success of the book settled his future: since then he has been writing full time.

His second book, *Bayous of Louisiana*, opened a wide new field for Harnett Kane. In it he presented the strange life on the waterways and bayous of Louisiana in a way never before attempted. In quick succession came *Deep Delta Country* in the American Folkways Series, the saga of the land about the Mississippi River mouth, where people live in houses like matchboxes on stilts; *Plantation Parade*, giving the panorama of the sugar barons of Louisiana; and *New Orleans Woman, a Biographical Novel of Myra Clark Gaines*, an instant success.

Harnett T. Kane is recognized as one of the most popular writers and leading authorities on the South. He is a prophet with honor in his own country, where each of his books has drawn a wider audience, and *Natchez on the Mississippi* bids fair to enhance that reputation.